KANSAI INTERNATIONAL AIRPORT PASSENGER TERMINAL BUILDING

関西国際空港旅客ターミナルビル

国際設計競技優勝案／レンゾ・ピアノ・ビルディング・ワークショップ・パリ＋オーヴ・アラップ＆パートナーズ
基本設計・実施設計作成共同体／レンゾ・ピアノ・ビルディング・ワークショップ・ジャパン＋オーヴ・アラップ＆パートナーズ，日建設計，パリ空港公団，日本空港コンサルタンツ

CONTENTS

PROCESS: Architecture

4	Introduction by Noriaki Okabe

Articles

8	Interview to Renzo Piano (Interviewer: Hiroyuki Suzuki)
14	Trees, Wind, Light and Sound of Piano by Hiroyuki Suzuki
20	The Glamour of Complexity by John Thackara
24	Gateway to a Different World by Teiji Matsumasa
30	The New Atlantis by Thomas Fisher

33	**I Down to the Sea**

43	**II Technological Island**

53	**III Passenger Terminal Building—The Skin**
54	Geometry
66	Roof Cladding
90	Airside Glazing
100	Endwall

109	**IV Passenger Terminal Building—The Space**
120	Circulation
124	Main Terminal Building, Roof Structure
136	Open Air Duct, Air conditioning and illumination membranes
146	Wing
164	Anti-Subsidence Measures
170	Fire Prevention
174	Canyon

	V Appendicles
190	Winning Design of the Competition
192	New Departures—Background to the PTB
196	PTB Designers' Credits
198	Afterword by Noriaki Okabe
200	Authors' Profiles
201	Credits

Cover photo by Kazuaki Hosokawa

カバー撮影：細川和昭

4	序文　岡部憲明

論文

8	レンゾ・ピアノ　インタビュー（聞き手：鈴木博之）
14	樹木・風・光そしてピアノの響き　鈴木博之
20	複合の魅力　ジョン・サッカラ
24	異界への開口　松政貞治
30	ニュー・アトランティス　トーマス・フィッシャー

33	**I　海へ**

43	**II　島——テクノロジーの地形**

53	**III　旅客ターミナルビル——被覆**
54	ジオメトリー
66	ルーフ・クラディング
90	エアサイド・グレージング
100	エンドウォール

109	**IV　旅客ターミナルビル——大空間**
120	動線計画
124	メインターミナルビル
136	オープンエアダクト：空調と照明の白い膜
146	ウイング
164	不同沈下対策
170	防災計画
174	キャニオン

	V　付記
190	設計競技優勝案
192	新たなる試み——設計共同体
196	設計共同体クレジット
198	あとがき　岡部憲明
200	執筆者経歴
201	クレジット

No.122
Publisher: Murotani Bunji
Editor-in-Charge:
Renzo Piano Building Workshop Japan,
Noriaki Okabe
Co-editor: Taichi Tomuro
Photographer: Kazuaki Hosokawa
Editorial staff:
Miwako Ito, Yumiko Fujimaki
Chiho Minamiguchi, Midori Yano
Editorial Assistants:
Kyoko Shibazaki, Keiko Kanasashi
Junko Hashimoto
Translator:
DHC Corporation (p.4-188), W.R.Tingey (p.190-201),
Masako Akamatsu (English-Japanese)
Cover Design:
Takahisa Kamijyo (Kamijyo Studio)
Published by
Process Architecture Co.,Ltd., Tokyo, Japan
Reproduction by
TOPPAN PRINTING CO., (S) PTE.,LTD.
Isozaki Printing Co.,Ltd., Tokyo, Japan
Printed by
Isozaki Printing Co.,Ltd., Tokyo, Japan
Executive and Editorial Office
1-47-1-418 Sasazuka Shibuya-ku Tokyo 151 Japan
Phone (03)3468-0131, Fax(03)3468-0133
Copyright © December 1994 by
Process Architecture Co.,Ltd.
All right reserved.
ISBN 4-89331-122-0

第122号
発行日：1994年12月1日
発行人：室谷文治
責任編集者：
レンゾ・ピアノ・ビルディング・ワークショップ・ジャパン
岡部憲明
編集協力：戸室太一
プロセスアーキテクチュア編集部：
伊藤美和子, 藤巻由美子
南口千穂, 矢野みどり
撮影(航空写真を除く)：
細川和昭
編集アシスタント：
芝崎恭子, 金指恵子, 橋本純子
和英訳：
㈱DHC(p.4-188), ビル・ティンギー(p.190-201)
英和訳：赤松正子
表紙デザイン：上條スタジオ(上條喬久)
制作・写植：
㈱協和クリエイト, ㈲ユニット, 大西写植
印刷：磯崎印刷㈱
発行所：
株式会社プロセスアーキテクチュア
〒151東京都渋谷区笹塚1-47-2-418
電話 03-3468-0131 FAX 03-3468-0133
振替 東京6-57446
取次店：
トーハン, 日販, 大阪屋, 栗田出版販売, 誠光堂
禁無断転載

INTRODUCTION
序章

Bird in Space

The dream of flying, which human beings have cherished since ancient times and finally made a reality with the beginning of air transport in the early twentieth century, was early on depicted in visual form by the futurists and by the members of the Russian avant garde; it also inspired the science fiction writers of the era. After World War I, the combatants' fighters and reconnaissance planes were remodeled and put to use as commercial air transports and passenger aircraft. The 1920s would become a memorable age for the airplane, lifted aloft by boom times in the world economy.

From the beginning of the 1920s and for many years thereafter, the gifted modern-art sculptor Constantin Brancusi used the energy directed by living creatures toward the sky as a major abstract motif in his work. His "Bird in Space," a masterful crystallization of the human urge to fly, demonstrates the dynamic beauty of curved shapes in abstract form. This sculpture seems to evoke in very sharp contour the vast potential of the dream and thrill of flying that challenged the people of the twentieth century, a dream that today is sinking into oblivion.

After the rapid strides made in aircraft technology during the Second World War, air transport developed worldwide, as the advent of the jet doubled not only the speed of air travel but passenger and cargo capacities as well. The airplane ushered in an unprecedented revolution in long-distance travel. For the generation who were young adults in the 1960s and 70s, nothing seemed more exciting and romantic than a career as a pilot or airline stewardess.

It was not so long ago that the experience of flying was limited to only a few. The TWA New York Terminal building, begun in 1956 and completed in 1962 by Eero Saarinen, was designed for those well-off and fortunate few. It was a time when the cultural capital of the Western world was gradually shifting from Paris to New York, where air travel was developing more rapidly than in Europe. The creative potential inherent in a city then brimming with vigor and vitality was fully visualized and projected outward by the highly sculptured design of the TWA terminal building.

But when the age of the jumbo jet arrived, a boom in overseas travel pushed annual travel by airline passengers in Japan alone over the two million mark by 1973, and existing airports in world-class cities rapidly became too small to deal with this much expanded air service. Even Saarinen's TWA masterpiece, which had so confidently taken up the challenge of transcending international modern architecture and which was built upon what was originally a very generous site, could not cope with the rapid expansion of airport facilities and business. The airport's ingenious structure, featuring an organic structure of interior and exterior space that seems to have

序　空間の中の鳥

空を飛ぶという人類の夢と情熱は，今世紀初頭の航空輸送のあけぼのの時代に，未来派やロシア・アバンギャルドたちによってさまざまな形でビジュアル化され，空想宇宙時代のＳＦ小説を誕生させた．第一次大戦に出現した初期の戦闘機や偵察機は，戦後に商業輸送機に改造実用化され，1920年代には上昇気流にのった世界経済を背景とした輝かしき飛行機の時代となった．

モダンアートの巨匠のひとりルーマニアの彫刻家コンスタンチン・ブランクーシが，ダイナミックで美しい流線型の抽象形態に実現した『空間の中の鳥』の彫刻は，空への飛翔という憧れをみごとに結晶化した作品である．ブランクーシは空へと向かう生物のエネルギーを1920年代初頭から長年にわたって抽象的モチーフとした．この彫刻は20世紀が抱き続けた飛行の夢と情熱，今私たちが忘れつつあるその肥沃な原野をシャープに描きだしているように思える．

第２次世界大戦によって航空輸送技術が躍進的な発展を遂げた後，航空事業が各国で発展し，ジェット旅客機の登場によって，スピードや輸送量が一挙に２倍になり，飛行機が花形となる遠距離交通の革命が訪れた．パイロットやスチュワーデスが空のエリートとして憧れの象徴だったのは現在40代から30代後半の世代の青春時代，1960年末から70年代の中頃のことである．

飛行体験はかつてはほんの少数の限られた人たちのものだった．1956年に開始して62年に完成したエーロ・サーリネンのＴＷＡニューヨークのターミナルビルは，こうした当時の旅客エリートたちのために建設されたものである．アメリカが西欧に比較して航空事情が飛躍的に発展し，文化の都はパリからニューヨークへとあきらかに移行しつつあった．そうした当時の躍動的で生き生きとしたニューヨークという都市に内在した創造のポテンシャリティをＴＷＡの高度に造形化されたデザインは，外部に発光するイメージとしてあますところなく視覚化していたように思える．

だが，大型ジャンボジェット機が誕生し，日本でも200万人を突破する海外旅行ブームが開始する1973年頃から，これまでの空港は年々手狭になりはじめる．インターナショナルな近代建築を超える表現と空間の豊かさに挑んだサーリネンのＴＷＡも，こうした空港と空務の拡大の風潮には逆らえなかった．外部と内部を有機的に構造化した昆虫の細胞のようなみごとな空間構成も，つぎつぎと詰めこまれていく新たな装置や機械，さら

Interview to Renzo Piano 8
(Interviewer: Hiroyuki Suzuki)

Trees, Wind, Light and Sound of Piano 14
by Hiroyuki Suzuki

The Glamour of Complexity 20
by John Thackara

Gateway to a Different World 24
by Teiji Matsumasa

The New Atlantis 30
by Thomas Fisher

レンゾ・ピアノ　インタビュー　8
（聞き手：鈴木博之）

樹木・風・光　そしてピアノの響き　14
鈴木博之

複合の魅力　20
ジョン・サッカラ

異界への開口　24
松政貞治

ニュー・アトランティス　30
トーマス・フィッシャー

---

been designed on the motif of an insect's cells, has gradually been filled with new furnishings and equipment, and today is hard-pressed to handle the massive flood of travelers. As airports everywhere are handling agreatly increased numbers of international flights, many have had to expand to accommodate vastly increased and more complicated functions, forcing them to repeatedly expand their terminal complexes and other facilities. In the process, the pathways designed to guide passengers from one place to another grow more and more labyrinthine.

Most airport terminals, forced to hastily expand their functions in the face of the onslaught of rapid technological innovation, have become in actuality no more than clusters of boxes — the easiest solution to the need for more space. In terms of volume and frequency of use, airports in the age of the jumbo jet are as different from those of the past as a bird from a butterfly. Unfortunately, no matter how many times a butterfly might metamorphosize, it can never become a bird. The international air terminals of today's consumer society are no longer finely crafted, costly chapels of elite travel but massive cathedrals whose ample portals serve the age of mass transpiration.

The railway stations of old Europe, which were the land transportation centers of old, were built on the grand and ponderous scale of cathedrals. But airports, from which human beings take off to fly in the skies and into which they alight, have to be built from spatial concepts based on lightness and dynamism. The design concept for the New Kansai International Airport Terminal is inspired by the dynamic perfection of the stream lined forms epitomized in Brancusi's "Bird in Space" and by the image of a glider lifted and carried by the air currents.

— *Noriaki Okabe*

に大量の旅客の集中のために，現在では無残な状況になっている．国際間の乗り入れの活発化に伴い，空港は機能の複合化と複雑化に対応しなくてはならなくなり，パンクした内部空間を抱えて，多くの空港が拡張工事につぐ拡張工事を余儀なくさせられることになった．そして旅客の動線はますます迷路のように複雑化する．

実際のところ空港ターミナルビルの多くは，急速な技術革新の波をまともに受けた機能拡大に追われながら，ただ安易にスペースを増強していくだけのボックス群になり下がってしまったような気がする．輸送量や使用頻度などの点で，ジャンボ時代の空港は，かつての空港に比較して，昆虫と鳥を相手にするほどのスケールの差が出てきたのだが，脱皮と細胞増殖をいくら重ねても昆虫が鳥に進化することは難しい．消費社会の国際ターミナルとなった現在の空港は，TWAのような精緻で高貴なチャペルの時代に終止符を打ち，大衆の移動を支え，ジャンボに乳をふくませることのできる大規模なカテドラルが必要になったのだ．

地表の交通を司どる拠点となった昔のヨーロッパの駅には，崇高で偉大な大聖堂の重厚さをもったものがある．しかし空を飛び，空から舞い降りる人間の発着地点としての空港は，スケールがどんなに巨大になっても，かろやかに飛翔する軽快さとムーブメントのダイナミズムが空間表現のコンセプトにならねばならない．関西国際空港旅客ターミナルビルのデザイン・コンセプトには，ブランクーシの『空間の中の鳥』の開いた完結性としての流線形と，空気の流れにそって飛行するグライダーのイメージが隠喩として発想源となった．

（岡部憲明）

Interview •

Of Monuments, Machines and Temporality

レンゾ・ピアノへのインタビュー
鈴木博之

Renzo Piano kindly granted us an interview on a recent visit to Japan. The interview was held at Piano's Japan Office, on the 26th June, 1994, and was hosted by Noriaki Okabe. The interviewer was Hiroyuki Suzuki.

Suzuki: First of all, I would like to ask you what I am sure you must have been asked many times before. What do you think is the significance of the airport in the contemporary age, not only from a functional point of view but also from a psychological one?
Piano: The airport is almost an icon, a monument of the modern era. Just as cathedrals and railways stations were in their own age, so the airport is a contemporary icon, which did not exist a century ago. Consequently, it occupies a most significant position in the history of construction. Unfortunately, as I have said many times before, I believe that the airport has been quite badly treated up to now. If you look at the railway stations which were built at the beginning of the century you realize that those buildings were icon-like and were important to the city. They were meeting places, a reference point, a place where people congregated, and a place of adventure, too. So the railways stations were very important monuments. This is true of all the big stations which were built at the turn of the century. Take the stations in Paris, for example — the Gare du Nord, the Gare de l'Est, the Gare de Lyon — each one is a monument. In Milano it is the Stazione Centrale, in Torino again there is a central station; London, too, has it's main termini — it is the same wherever you go. They were all powerful monuments and a significant part of the city. And today, if you look at these stations, you realize that they were monuments located right in the center of the city.
Suzuki: The German critic, Walter Benjamin, said that the station was a cathedral of its times.
Piano: Exactly. The stations were built in two parts. One part actually facing the city and the other to house the lines, belonging to the trains. So it was really like a cathedral — monumental, strong. The station building itself was built of stone and the train shed of steel. The building was "mass" and the shed was "lightness". So the station building was almost the link, the connecting element between the train and the city. The building was an expression of the sense of pride of the city, and an expression of the capacity to produce a building which was beautiful and strong. So it is inevitable to begin any conversation about airports today, by talking about railway stations. But the situation is totally different. Airports by necessity and by definition are far from the city. However, if we look at the history of the construction of airports we find that there is something quite interesting. Although, for instance, the TWA building at Kennedy Airport by Eero Saarine and the one he did at Washington, too, are good, airports (airport buildings) are usually conceived as shoe boxes. They are usually seen as something functional only, as a functional machine without any of the sense of pride, or sense of celebration that is typical of an important building. So I was surprised and very happy to find that Japan had set up a competition with the intention of creating something special. The idea of making an island was already special and the idea of having a major, international design competition was also special. The intentions were very strong and I appreciated that.

It has to be said that the difference in cost to produce a bad building and a good one is not immense. It is actually very little. Investment in constructing runways and in equipment generally when an airport is built is, however, immense and so the cost of the architecture is little by comparison. The cost of the building is not that much. The money mainly goes into construction work, creating an infrastructure —

レンゾ・ピアノへのインタビューは，同氏が日本を訪れた1994年6月，レンゾ・ピアノ・ビルディング・ワークショップの岡部憲明氏のアレンジで実現した．聞き手は東京大学教授の鈴木博之氏．

鈴木 まず，ピアノさんにとってはこれまで何度も繰り返し質問されたことでしょうが，基本的な質問をさせていただきます．現代における空港とはどういう意味をもつとお考えですか．機能的な面だけでなく，社会的あるいは心理的な側面も含めてお伺いします．
ピアノ 空港はいわばイコン，近代社会のモニュメントです．カテドラルや鉄道駅がそれぞれの時代にそうであったように，空港は現代的なイコンです．1世紀前までは存在していません．したがって，空港は建設の歴史に重要な意味をもちます．残念ながら私がこれまでも何度かいってきたように，空港は今日にいたるまで決して正しく扱われてこなかったと思います．今世紀初め頃に建てられた鉄道駅を見れば，それらがイコンとしてふさわしく存在し，街の重要な施設となっていることがわかります．そこは人々が集まっておしゃべりしたり打ち合わせたりする場所であると同時に人々にとっての冒険の場でもあります．だから鉄道駅は重要なモニュメントたり得ているのです．これは19世紀末から20世紀初めにかけて建てられたすべての大きな鉄道駅にいえることです．たとえばパリの北駅，東駅，リヨン駅のどれを取り上げてもすべてモニュメントです．ミラノやトリノ，ロンドンの中央駅もすべてそうです．メインのターミナルがあり，どこに行っても同じです．それらは力強いモニュメントであり，街の重要な部分を構成しています．今日どの街に行っても，その中心にこれらの鉄道駅が位置し，モニュメントとなっていることがわかるでしょう．
鈴木 ドイツの批評家であるウォルター・ベンヤミンは「駅はその時代のカテドラルだ」といっていますね．
ピアノ そうです．駅舎は2つの顔があります．1つは街に向けた顔であり，もう1つは線路側の列車，あるいは鉄道そのものに付属する部分です．だからモニュメンタルで強くて，本当にカテドラルのようです．

駅舎そのものは石造で，ホーム上屋は鉄骨造です．いいかえれば駅舎はマッスでホーム上屋は軽快さを表わしています．したがって，駅舎は列車と街を結びつけるまさに絆なのです．建物はある意味で，その街の自慢の表われであり，美しく強い建物を生み出す可能性の表示でもあります．

今日の空港について云々するに際し，鉄道駅についての言及は避けて通れないことですが，状況は全く異なっています．必要からいっても，その定義からも空港は都市や街とはかけ離れた存在である．しかし，空港建設の歴史を振り返ってみると非常に興味深いものがあります．例えばニューヨークのケネディ空港のエーロ・サーリネン設計のTWAビルやワシントン・ダレス空港ターミナルはすばらしい建築です．それまで空港施設は単なる箱でした．ただ機能的なだけの，効率のよい機械のようなものが多く，そこには重要な建物がもつプライドも祝福されるべき価値も存在していなかったと思います．日本が新しいなにかを創造するという意図をもった空港施設のコンペを開催すると聞いて，私は驚くと同時に大喜びしました．人工島を造成するというだけでもすでに非常に革新的です．そこに主要施設のデザインを国際コンペで決定するというのもまたすばらしいことでした．この意志は明快だったし，私も大いに評価しました．建物や施設の善し悪しと予算の多寡はあまり関係ない，とはよくいわれていることです．実際，その差は大した金額ではありません．滑走路の整備や空港特有の設備のための費用の膨大さに比較すれば，建築費用はわずかな金額です．建物の建設費は本当に安い．建設費の大半は，鉄道の航空支線，橋梁，滑走路，ハンガーなどのインフラ整備や，エレベーター，電気設備，シャッター，手荷物輸送設備などに充てられます．それは実に巨大な金額になります．

この意味で，私は関西国際空港に思いきった気前のいい提案をしました．しかし，それは決してレトリックで誇張しているわけではありません．最近はようやく，空港施設に本来与えられるべき価値づけをし，重要性をもたせることは当然のことになりつつあります．しかしまだ，かつて鉄道駅が都市の中で果たしてきたような役割を空港は充分に果たしてはいません．空港の役割は地球規模レベルです．空港の特性は，鉄道駅とほぼ同じですが，駅が都市やその周辺への対応であるとすれば，空港はもっと大きくグローバルなスケールに対応するという点が異なります．もちろん空港

feeder trains, bridges, runways, hangers, service equipment such as elevators, electrical equipment, shutters, luggage handling systems — the cost of this is so immense that the cost to produce a good building in comparison is really not very much. So, my intention with the Kansai Airport scheme was to be generous in some way, but I didn't want to become too rhetoric, because that is certainly not good.

It would certainly seem that there is a new tendency to give the airport due attention, to give it the sense of importance it demands. But it doesn't play the role the railway station did in the city. It's role is more at a global level. The airport is the same thing the station was to the land around the city, except that it is on a much larger scale — a global scale. The airport has a relationship with a much larger area. But that is not the only thing. Although an airport "belongs" to a particular country, at the same time it is just one airport of a network of airports. So this makes the airport a bit more universal. It is not just a building, like a big school or a house — it is not something which totally depends on its location. It is part of the world. If we look at the station once more — the shed was for the trains and the building was part of the city. But at the same time the station as a whole was part of the city and part of a network, too. And the airport is the same but the scale is quite different. The (international) airport is the link between the plane, the flying machine and the country, so in this sense, the airport is both local and universal. It belongs to the place but at the same time it belongs to the earth. So the scale is totally different.

Once we begin thinking in this way, therefore, there are certain implications. You must be careful to reflect this. In the case of the new Kansai airport, the building has Japanese aspects. Not because it looks like a Japanese building. We have not tried to make a copy of a Japanese roof. But we did try to pick up the basic qualities of Japanese architecture — its lightness, its transparency, the scale of its details, its texture. This is what Japanese architecture is about. In fact, in some cases it is so light that it almost becomes immaterial. Also, breaking down the scale to fabric, to texture. And this is the reason why this huge building has been built in pieces. It has been broken down, even the structure, into parts. So the Japanese aspects of the building are the spirit of the way in which it has been constructed. It has lightness and it is almost temporary in spirit, although the building itself is very strong and not at all temporary in that sense. But the spirit is almost one of the temporary building, just like a traditional Japanese building — light and broken down into a number of partsæthese are the Japanese aspects of the building. But the other aspects of the building are much more global, belonging to the earth, and it is an airport which is part of a network.

Suzuki: So the whole composition and scale of the building is related to the earth.

Piano: Yes, but the building is also in the spirit of the machine, a gentle machine, it's a soft machine. When you create an airport I think you

Renzo Piano is the Architect of Renzo Piano Building Workshop Paris.
レンゾ・ピアノ：レンゾ・ピアノ・ビルディング・ワークショップ・パリ主宰

Roof shape of the Main Terminal Building, sketch by Renzo Piano

はそれが立地する都市や国に属しますが，同時に空港は多くの空港間のネットワークの1つでもあります．したがって空港はより一層ユニバーサルな存在になります．空港が，ある土地に建つ大きな学校や住宅と同様の，単に大きなだけの建物や施設ではない理由がそこにあります．それは世界の一部です．駅舎をもう一度考えてみるとわかりますが，ホーム上屋は鉄道そのものに属し，建物は都市の一部です．しかし駅は全体として都市の一部であると同時に，ネットワークの一部でもあります．空港は空を飛ぶ飛行機と国々を結びつける絆です．その意味で空港は地域性と普遍性を併せ持つものです．ある場所に付属するが，同時に地球そのものに属している，という意味で，鉄道駅とはスケールが全く異なります．

このように考えていくと，ある意味が見えてきます．これをよく考えてみました．関西国際空港の場合は，ある意味で日本を反映しています．それは単に日本的な建物にするということではありません．日本的な形態をコピーするということでなく，日本建築のもつ軽さ，透明さ，ディテールや素材の独特のスケールといった基本的な特質を拾い上げることです．私たちはその点に努力しました．実際，日本建築はときとして非物質的ともいえるほど軽く，また身近な要素や素材のスケールにまでみごとにブレークダウンされています．関西国際空港の巨大な建物をいくつかのピースに分けて建てている理由もそこにあります．構造でさえいくつかのパーツに分けています．建物の日本的な特質というのは，ある意味では建設の過程での精神です．軽快さと同時に，意識としては仮設と考えることです．実際の建物は決して仮設ではなく，恒久的でがっしりとしたものですが，精神的には，日本の伝統的な建物がそうであるように，仮設というか，軽快でいくつものパーツに分解できるという日本建築独特の特質をもっています．空港にはもう1つの，よりグローバルな，世界に属しているという側面，ネットワークの一部であるという特質があります．

鈴木　全体の構成やスケールは地球に関係してくるわけですね．

ピアノ　そうです．建物は機械，それもやさしいソフトな機械でもあります．空港を計画しようとするとき，それが非常に複雑な機械であることを認識させられます．空港は決して空を飛びませんが，それと同様の複雑で精巧な機械であるといえます．電気や空調設備の図面などをちょっと見ただけでも，空港がいかに精密な機械と同様の複雑な建物かが分かります．まるで電子機器のマイクロチップのようです．これが空港という施設がもつ，そのデザインの裏にある意味であり，フィロソフィです．こうした巨大な機械のような建物は，人間的であるものもあればそうでないものもあります．関西国際空港は，よりヒューマンであってほしいと考えました．

しかし同時に，空港施設はいい意味でのモンスターでもあります．ラテン語でモンスターのことをモンストゥラムといいますが，これは悪い意味ではありません．その意味は「目に見える」「知覚できる」「驚異」ということで，イタリア語のMOSTROでもフランス語のMONSTREでも怪物という意味と同時に，巨大なとか豪華なといういい意味をもつ言葉でもあります．

鈴木　語源的には同じルーツですか．

ピアノ　そうです．ラテン語ではいい意味です．だから私がモンスターという言葉を使うときは，なにか強力で重要な，という意味で使っています．いいモンスターも悪いモンスターもつくることは可能ですが，いいモンスターを生み出すことはなかなかむずかしい．たしかに巨大なスケールだが，そのことを恥じてはいいモンスターはつくり出せません．関西国際空港のように1日数十万人もの人々が使う施設は，非常に複雑な機械であることを避けられない．しかし，そのこと自体はなにも悪くないわけです．それ自身のロジックやスケールを受容し，そこからデザインしていかなければなりません．空港に降り立つ人々は，空港ターミナルを外から眺めて，羽根を休めている凧のようなやさしいオブジェを期待します．それは攻撃的であってはいけません．そして内部に入ると明るく軽快であることが大事です．昨日，私は数か月

have to be careful because you are about to build an immensely complex machine. It doesn't fly but nevertheless it is a machine and a very complex one. We only have to look at some of the drawings, an electrical floor plan for example, to know something of the complexity of the building. The building is like a "macro-chip", not a micro-chip. So this, too, is part of the logic behind the design of the building, part of the philosophy and such a building is like a gigantic machine, sometimes human, sometimes not. I hope this one will be human. But, it is also a monster in this sense, but a monster in the good sense of the word. The word monster in Latin, *monstrum*, is not bad, it is good. The meaning is "visible", something which is "identifiable", a "marvel" (*monstro* point out, show, inform, appoint, denounce; *monstratus* distinguish). It becomes *mostro* in Italian, *monstre* in French, and "monster" in English.

Suzuki: So etymologically the words have the same root?

Piano: Exactly. In Latin it has a positive meaning, so when I use the word "monster", I am implying something strong and important. You can make a good monster or a bad monster but to make a good monster is very difficult. It is something of enormous scale but we should not be shy about it. A building like Kansai Airport is for a hundred-thousand people a day, so inevitably it is a very, very complex machine, and there is nothing wrong with that. We have to accept that logic and we have to accept the scale and work within it. When you land at the airport, the building from outside looks like a sleeping kite, a gentle object. It is not aggressive. And when you are inside it's light. Not having been there for several months, I was very surprised, when I went there yesterday, to find that the space inside is, in fact, very calm and not at all aggressive. This was what I had hoped for. But, nevertheless, it was something of a surprise, because when you see a building it is different from what you imagine.

Suzuki: That's very interesting. It means that even the designer can be surprised about his own work.

Piano: That's right. When you design a small house for the country, for example, there is no surprise. You know what to expect. But when you design something unconventional that has never been done before, you are groping about in the dark. You don't really know what is going to happen. I'm not implying that you don't know what to do. We have known for six years what we want in terms of design. But there is a lot of difference between trying to do something and actually doing it. So I was quite surprised, because the scale is immense. It's not really the scale of a building, it's a geographical scale. You cannot see the end of the building. You only see the whole building when you fly. But, when you are inside, because of the atmosphere, the light, the details, the structure — I think it is quite gentle.

Suzuki: When I went to see the building, I felt a sense of unity or wholeness, because so many airport terminals or other huge buildings are a simple addition of small parts, or a mechanical multiplication of units. But in the case of your building, there seems to be an organic core. You seem to have achieved an organic unity, which impressed me.

Piano: I am very pleased, because this is what we wanted to do. We wanted to have a building with a sense of unity. If you design a large building and break the design up into a number of small pieces, you don't humanize the building. You just create chaos.

Suzuki: Chaos or mechanical repetition.

Piano: Exactly. You loose the identity of the building and this is anti-human. What happens in some buildings is that people get lost psychologically, even physically sometimes. But with the Kansai Airport building you know immediately where you are. It is more simple æ you go right or left, no problem.

Suzuki: It's interesting because you have been able to link several different aspects of the design in a new way æ human scale and the scale of the planet, the invisible mechanics of the building and visible human elements æ many differing and difficult aspects or considerations have been brought together.

Piano: Yes, I hope so. But we must acknowledge the fact that the general concept which was part of the competition brief in the beginning was not at all bad. It was drawn up by ADP on the bases of Paul Andreu's (ADP) concept program. It already had the logic of a unitarian building.

Suzuki: You are being quite generous.

Piano: Not at all. It helped a great deal. We didn't start our design based on a misguided concept. It started from quite a unitarian concept, which we worked out poetically, in a sense. Of course, it is possible to spoil everything however good the brief is. But in this case we were able to work it out giving it even more cohesion. The building had to be coherent and to have cohesion.

Suzuki: But it's very difficult to put differing aspects of our civilization together, combining mechanical aspects with human ones, for example. But how did you realize your original

ぶりに関西国際空港に行ってびっくりしました。非常に落ち着いて攻撃的でないやさしい空間になっていたからです。これこそ私が望んでいたことです。しかし、それはまた驚きでもありました。自分がイメージしていたものとはちょっと違っていたからです。

鈴木　非常に興味深いことですが、デザイナー自身でも自分がイメージしたものと違ってできるということがあるんですね。

ピアノ　いつものことではありません。田園に小さな家をデザインしても、そんなことはありません。イメージしたようにできます。しかし、それまで経験したことのない新しいものをデザインし、つくり出すことは、暗闇の中を進むようなものです。なにが待ち構えているかだれにもわかりません。それはなにをしようとしているかがわからないということではありません。私たちは6年間ずっとその設計に携わってきたわけですから。しかし、しようとしてきたことと実際とは大きな違いがあります。だから実際のスケールの大きさに私は改めてびっくりしたわけです。これはもう建物のスケールでなく、地理的なスケールです。だれの目にも建物の端から端は見えません。建物の全貌が見えるのは唯一上空からだけです。しかし、内部に入ると軽快でディテールも構造も非常にやさしい雰囲気にでき上がっています。

鈴木　しかし、私は実際に見せていただいて、建物の統一感というか全体性のようなものを感じました。というのは、他の多くの空港施設や巨大な建物は単に部分の寄せ集め、あるいは設備的なユニットの積み重ねのように思えるからです。関西国際空港はそうした意味で、なにか有機的なコアというか、有機的な統一感が感じられたことを覚えております。

ピアノ　それを聞いてたいへん嬉しいです。というのは、それこそ私たちが望んだことだからです。私たちは空港にある種の統一感をもたせようとしました。大きな建物を設計し、それらを細かく分割していく段階で、うまく人間的にしていくことに失敗することが多々あります。ただ混乱を生み出すだけのことがあまりに多いのです。

鈴木　混乱というか、単なる機械的な繰り返しですね。

ピアノ　そうです。建物の本質を見逃すと、それは非人間的になります。そこで起きることは人々が心理的にどこにいるかを見失い、物理的にも見失うことです。そうならないことを常に心がけました。関西国際空港ではどこにいるかが一目でわかります。右か左かで非常にシンプルで、全く問題なしです。

鈴木　ここであなたがおやりになった、いくつか異なるデザインの階層を新たな方法で結びつけていかれた手法は、非常に面白いと思います。ヒューマンスケールと宇宙的なスケールの結合、目に見えないメカニックと目に見える人間的な要素の結合といった、異種で相互に困難な問題や配慮を同時に解決していかれ、全体性のあるユニタリアン的な建物にまとめられた。

ピアノ　はい、その通りです。しかし、当初の国際コンペ時の応募要項にまとめられていた全体概要のコンセプトはまあまあよくできていました。それは、ポール・アンドリュー氏（パリ空港公団）のコンセプトをもとに、フランスの空港施設計画の権威であるパリ空港公団や日産設計、日本空港コンサルタンツによってまとめられたものですが、すでに建物のユニタリアン的なロジックができていました。

鈴木　非常に寛大でいらっしゃいますね。

ピアノ　いいえ。それは大助かりでした。計画の発端を間違ったコンセプトで始めるということがなかったからです。計画を全くの始めからユニタリアンなコンセプトで始められ、それを詩的に仕上げていくことができたわけです。もちろん、いかにすぐれた概要でも、そうした概念をすべて無視して計画することも可能でした。しかし、この場合は、それまでの経過との一貫性が大事であると考え、建物もそうした一貫性の中で設計を進めました。

鈴木　コンセプトを実現していく過程での困難あるいは予期せぬことがなにかありますか。さきほどの、実際に空港の中に入って、そのやさしい感じに驚かれたということ以外にもなにかありますか。

ピアノ　建物が完成し、いろいろな人とお話しした後で、自分がなにをしたかが分かってくるものです。しかしボブール（ポンピドーセンター）のときには、あまりはっきりとわかっているわけではありませんでした。この仕事は単純ではありませんから、私は原始的な人間にアピールしようとは思いません。デザインプロセスではしばしば知

concept and were there any surprises in the process of realizing you concept for the new terminal building? You said already that when you went in the building that you felt very happy and surprised when you saw how your ideas were being realized. But were there any other things?
Piano: After the building was up and after talking with people like yourself, then you realized what you have done. When we did Beaubourg, or the Pompidou Center, it was not clear at all what we were doing. I don't want to appear to much of a primitive man, because it's not that primitive. But you work a bit by instinct and you don't know exactly what is going to happen. In the design process, sometimes generalities are more important than intelligence. You need to be able to "jump" but you need the tools with which to jump — the design capacity, the competence. But in making these jumps you don't really know what the final outcome will be. The picture is very out of focus. When we did Beaubourg, it was instinctively a reaction against the institutional building and everything was quite confusing. And then when it was finished, we realized exactly what we had done. It was the same with the building for Kansai Airport, because at the beginning, generally speaking, the idea of creating this building was to do something organic, almost geographical, almost geological; and also to be a machine. It's a piece of corrugated (folded and up-lifted) land. It's also a geological construction, because of the seismic movement which is implied. This is what was done with Peter Rice, implying a very organic structure to withstand the forces; and at the same time it is a machine. So all of these things were already there. And now the building is finished, you realize that this is the most important point, this kind of complexity. The building is not completely predictable. It's not just the result of a simple calculation. But the complexity is there from all points of view — functional complexity, symbolic complexity, spatial complexity; and this is probably the most important point about this building. If we talk about spatial complexity, there is the Canyon, the big space (International Check-in Lobby), and then the Wing. The Canyon is a meeting point, it's a crossing point, it's like a street in a city. And then there is the big space and the Wing, which is like a gigantic boarding bridge. The main spaces are all under the one roof which provides unity. There are at least three different spaces under the one roof so there is quite a lot of complexity, one floor within another.

I was talking to Umberto Eco and he said the Canyon is like a horizontal Tower of Babel, not a vertical one. This is the place were people of different nationalities meet. Different people, coming, going, staying. Eco has not seen the building yet but I have talked quite a lot to him about it.
Suzuki: I met him while I was teaching at Harvard. He certainly has an interesting interpretation of space.
Piano: He also said that he thought the section of the terminal building looked like an old topographical map done by a sailor. On old maps, islands were shown in elevation, not in plan with contours, because they were not interested in that. So Eco sees the building as if it were an elevation of an island done by a sailor.
Suzuki: In a sense, therefore, it's very human and not mechanical.
Piano: Yes, maybe. In fact, you are probably

Hiroyuki Suzuki is the Professor of Tokyo University, Department of Architecture.
鈴木博之：東京大学工学部教授

quite right. Because instinctively people draw things in elevation or in profile the way they see them. They don't draw contours of an island, for example. That is the kind of thing you do by computer. It's a rationalization but profiles and elevations are instinctive and more primitive.
Suzuki: A very "noble" primitive.
Piano: Yes, but I would not want to stress these "primitive" aspects. It's just not true, because in the end we are very cultivated. Nevertheless, there are primitive instincts sleeping within us.

I think it was Claes Oldenburg who once said that when you are a child you have already done everything and invented everything. Then you spend the rest of your life digging for what you did when you were young. Because, when you are a child, you accumulate many primitive, basic sensations.
Suzuki: By the way you are talking now, it would seem that you are not under the control of the mechanics of contemporary technology and neither do you control them. You simply enjoy mechanical systems and the like. It's a pleasure.
Piano: It's enjoyment, that's for sure. In fact, it's quite surprising that we can do a job like this. It is a pleasure to do. It's a bit tiring, too, but it's a pleasure.

Coming back to the building, what I was talking about before is very fundamental. When someone approaches the terminal building, I think they will feel these fundamental qualities — it being like an island etc.
Suzuki: I'm sure all the passengers who pass through the building will feel what you describe and will be able to share in the pleasure of the design.
Piano: Even if they don't understand completely, they will feel something. After all, it is not necessary to explain everything. Good music is good music: there is no need to explain it. There are things you don't have to explain, you just feel them, which is quite important.

But what I want to emphasize is that the building is complex inside. It's not just one thing. It's made up of two or three things — the Canyon, the big space and the Wing, which is fluid. And in each space the experience is different. The Canyon is a Tower of Babel, but in a good sense. I think the International Check-in Lobby is a serene, calm space which puts you in the right frame of mind to travel. And then, when you are in the Wing you are, in a sense, already on the plane.
But the space is immense and the sense of perspective is exaggerated. The space looks even longer than it is.
Suzuki: That's interesting because if you try to make something look longer than it actually is, it usually produces a feeling of inhumanity — a very long corridor can make people feel very uncomfortable. But in this case, I personally don't feel any sense of awkwardness about the space. I wonder why this is?
Piano: I think this problem is misunderstood. Some people believe that in architecture in order to be human you have to be domestic, in other words small. But it is not true. Some small spaces are very inhuman. But the contrary can be true. It is possible to be in a very human space which is endless. If, for example, you are in a forest it is not inhuman. It may be frightening but it is still human. I don't think the sense of humanity comes from the dimensions. It comes from the details and from the atmosphere of a space.
Suzuki: One critic described the building as a "second nature", in a good sense that is.
Piano: But architecture is a second nature. Architecture is not natural. Let's be honest. Architecture is exactly the opposite. It represents man's capacity to manipulate materials, to make something artificial, so I think we should be honest about that. Architecture is not nature. It is the product of the very instinctive capacity of man who, starting with raw materials, manipulates them and makes things. It is a basic activity of man, it's even fundamental. But it is not natural. After all, nature is not a friend. You have to fight nature to produce a shelter. If you don't you will be killed by nature. You would soon die if you were exposed to the elements for too long. Nature is something you fight all the time. However, I don't want to become too philosophical about this.
Suzuki: That is a very European way of interpreting nature. The Japanese tend to view nature as something more friendly.
Piano: But it is not. In Japan you have earthquakes. Are earthquakes friendly? (Laughing) But what is true about Japanese architecture is that the fight between architecture and Mother Nature is very gentle. This is what is so wonderful about Japanese architecture. If we consider almost any traditional Japanese house or building, they are so beautiful because the fight is almost mathematical. A good Japanese building is almost a geometrical theorem. It's not natural but it's gentle, it's very subtle. It's not aggressive, that's the point. But you don't have to be aggressive to defend yourself from nature. In that sense I hope the Kansai Airport terminal building is going to be Japanese, because it's not aggressive. Nevertheless, it is defending people from nature, from the elements — rain, wind,

るでしょうし、またそこにデザインの楽しさを見出すでしょう。
ピアノ　完全に理解しなくても、なにかを感じとるでしょう。いずれにしても、すべてを説明する必要はありません。説明するまでもなく、いい音楽はいい音楽です。説明の必要はなく、感じるだけで充分ということが大事です。
しかし、強調しておきたいのは、この建物は非常に複雑であるということです。ただ1つの空間でなく、2つも3つもの部分からできています。キャニオン、大空間、ウイングが流れるように続いていきますが、それらから感じられることはそれぞれ異なっています。キャニオンは快適な「バベルの塔」であり、チェックイン・ロビーは旅に出かける前にくつろぐ場所にふさわしい静かで落ち着いた空間です。一方ウイングは、もうすでに飛行機の一部のような雰囲気の空間です。しかし、ここでは広がりと見通しが強調されて、実際以上に長く見えます。
鈴木　もし、ある空間を実際以上に長く見せると、長い廊下は居心地が悪いように、大抵その空間は非人間的な雰囲気になってしまうと思うのです。しかし、関西国際空港のウイングでは、私は決してそんな感じを受けませんでした。それはなぜでしょう。
ピアノ　長ければ居心地が悪いなどと考えるのは誤解からきています。建築においては身近なというか、スケールが小さいことがヒューマンであると間違って信じられているようです。しかしそれは本当ではありません。ある種の狭いスペースは非人間的でさえあります。この場合は逆は真なりです。無限の空間が非常に人間的であり得るのです。例えば森の中はちょっと怖いかもしれませんが、非人間的であるとはいえません。人間性ということは、空間の大きさから決められるものでなく、ディテールや空間の雰囲気から決まってくると思います。
鈴木　ある評論家が、この建物をいい意味での第2の自然と評していました。
ピアノ　建築はすべて第2の自然です。建築は自然そのものではあり得ません。正直になりましょう。建築は自然とは対極の存在です。いろいろな素材を工夫して用い、人工的なものを生み出す人間の能力を象徴しています。建築は自然ではなく、自然の素材を用い、工夫して使い、なにかをつくり出す、人間の本能的な能力の産物です。基本的な人間活動です。また、自然は人類の友ではありません。自然と戦うためにシェルターをつくります。そうでなければ自然に殺されます。自然に長い間さらされているだけでも人間はそのうちに死んでしまいます。自然は人類が常に戦い続ける相手です。しかし、私は自然に対して理性的になりすぎることのないようにしています。
鈴木　それはたいへんヨーロッパ的な自然感です。日本人はもう少し自然を身近なものとして見ています。
ピアノ　しかし、本当はそうではありません。日本には地震があります。地震に親しめますか。日本の建築についていえることは、建築と自然の戦いが穏やかなことです。そこが日本建築のすばらしさでもあります。日本の伝統的な民家や建物はすべて、自然との戦いが非常に数学的であるが故に美しいともいえます。すぐれた日本建築はすべて幾何学的な理論に則っています。自然ではないが穏やかで巧みだし、攻撃的でないのもポイントです。自然から身を守るために攻撃的になる必要はありません。関西国際空港のターミナルビルは、攻撃的でないという意味で日本的であるといえます。なおかつ人々を自然、雨風、地震などから守ります。地震時には、建物は非常に軽い構造であるため、ゆるやかに揺れます。攻撃的でもなく、自然も殺しません。だから自然も建物を殺さないのです。
鈴木　いま、日本建築についてのご意見を伺いましたが、関西国際空港のコンペに入選なさってからこのお仕事を進める中で、何度か日本を訪れられて、それまでの日本の印象と変わった点はありますか、あるいはそれまでの見方をさらに強められましたか。
ピアノ　まず、私にとって日本はそれほど未知の国ではありませんでした。なぜなら1970年に大阪万博のイタリア工業館の設計の仕事ですでに日本にきていました。さらに私の事務所には長年にわたって何人もの日本人のスタッフがいますし、ある意味では日本は私の生活の一部になっていました。だからすでにたいへん馴染みのある国だったのです。関西国際空港のコンペに着手するまでにすでに私の中には日本の認識がしっかりとできておりました。
鈴木　コンペを始められる前にすでに、日本

earthquakes. In an earthquake, because the building is very light, it will just rock gently. It's not aggressive, it's not killing nature. Also, nature will not kill it either.

Suzuki: Finally, although you have given us your interpretation of Japanese architecture, since winning the Kansai Airport competition you have visited Japan on several occasions and I was wondering if your impressions of Japan have changed while you have been working here, or maybe your instinctive view was strengthened?

Piano: First of all, I must say that I was not that unfamiliar with Japan, because I was here in about 1970 to do a small building (Italian Industrial Pavilion at the Osaka Expo). There have also been a number of Japanese working in our offices for many years, so Japan has been part of our daily life, in a sense. I was therefore already quite familiar with Japan. I already had a picture of Japan before I came for the competition.

Suzuki: So even before you began work on the competition design, you were already aware of the principle elements of Japanese architecture — lightness, transparency, and the scale of the details.

Piano: Yes, I already understood these things. However, what I have learnt since setting up the office here and having been here quite often, is that the system of communication is very difficult for a European. Gradually I began to understand, but this was made easier by the fact that Nori (Noriaki Okabe) has been in charge of this job from the beginning, so communication now is very easy. We had some battles because normally in Japan the architect does not do the site work. They do the design and then they go away. But in the case of this job, I must say that we have had a good client — intelligent and sensitive, and therefore they accepted having us on site. So the job became more and more Japanese as we became more closely united.

I could not say that my understanding of Japan was deep, it was quite superficial compared to what you may understand about Japan, because you have Japan "inside". But I have a bit of Japan inside me now, so I am quite sensitive to everything.

Suzuki: You must be congratulated for that.

Piano: There is one thing I would like to add about Japanese architecture. You were saying about the lightness, transparency, fabric, sense of texture, and the scale of the details of Japanese architecture. But for me there is something else and that is a sense of permanence, or eternity in construction in Japan that doesn't come from the construction of mass like the Colosseum in Rome. In Japan this sense of eternity perhaps comes from the way monuments are made "constantly" (repetitively). There is a sense of temporality in Japan which is deeply rooted in the culture and is even evident in traditional architecture. It is not only true of Japan. All Pacific culture is about temporality. In Japan, it may be due to the fact that the seismic environment has always created a need for light construction, temporary construction.

Suzuki: Could we say that it is a cyclic culture?

Piano: It's a cyclic culture. And the proof of this is that Japan is certainly the only place in the world were a craftsman is considered like an historical monument and they are protected.

Suzuki: What we call a "Living National Treasures".

Piano: In Europe you don't project people you protect the monument, the building. In Japan you project people as well because it is the repetition of the same gestures that is important. It's cyclic: doing the same thing many times is important and this is eternity.

Suzuki: And it is handed down from one generation to the next.

Piano: Exactly. This is eternity. This sense of permanence through lightness and through temporality is an eternal temporality. This is something even more subtle that for me is quite important. So next time you go inside the terminal building, think about that, especially in the main, open space. Not in the "Tower of Babel". We wanted to do that like a crossing point.

Suzuki: Thank you very much for granting us such a long, interesting interview, which I have enjoyed immensely.

Trees, Wind, Light and Sound of Piano
by Hiroyuki Suzuki

樹木・風・光 そしてピアノの響き
鈴木博之

The New Kansai International Airport is revitalizing the city of Osaka. With the opening of the airport just around the corner, the city of Osaka is holding various events that are boosting the economy. Trains that travel directly into the airport were designed, and the areas around the terminal train station will be expanded to include historic downtown, in anticipation of the flow of people. The New Kansai International Airport is breathing new life into the city.

Construction of the airport was completed almost six years after Renzo Piano won the international competition for the best design of the airport, in December 1988. Was six years a long time or a short one? It is impossible to say. Six years is an extremely short period to complete a modern, ultralarge-scale structure, but it can be done if everything progresses smoothly. However, when we think about changes in economic and international environments, six years might also be a fairly long time. When Renzo Piano was chosen to be the designer after winning the international design competition, I welcomed him to Kyoto, because he also received the Kyoto Prize as a result of his past achievements. I spoke to him about his image for the new airport. He said he wished to create a building that emphasizes the memory of space. Now that the airport buildings have been completed, the appropriateness of Piano's six-year-old idea will be examined.

The New Kansai International Airport was built on a man-made island on the Inland Sea of Japan, close to Wakayama Prefecture. It was designed to allow access from Osaka, Wakayama, Nara, Kyoto and Hyogo Prefectures. The new airport is literally a new airport for the entire Kansai region. All major functions are concentrated in Tokyo, the capital of Japan, causing overcrowding. This situation also diminishes other Japanese cities. Osaka has traditionally been a center of commerce; Kyoto, a historical and sightseeing city; and Kobe, located in Hyogo Prefecture, a international port town. However, even combined, these three cities created a political and economic zone inferior in importance to the Tokyo region. Because the Japanese economy places great importance on close relationships with government offices, it is natural that companies see Tokyo, where the central government offices are located, as the most logical place for their headquarters. Therefore, companies operate mainly in Tokyo, and production and information facilities are also located chiefly around the capital.

Of course, there has been criticism of the centralization of politics, economics and urban functions in Tokyo. There have also been attempts to correct the situation. The city of Kobe built a group of man-made islands, the best-known of which is Port Island in the Inland Sea of Japan, and continued to expand the area and create new commercial districts. Osaka hosted the Expo in 1970, and Kyoto has been constructing a new central station. However, compared with these efforts, construction of the New Kansai International Airport is unequaled in significance.

As mentioned earlier, the new airport is directly connected to Osaka, Wakayama, Nara, Kyoto and Hyogo Prefectures. Moreover, it is not a temporary event like the Expo, but a facility that will permanently function. The new airport is also a symbol of the united Kansai region, which can compete with the Tokyo metropolitan region economically and culturally, and in terms of urban functions. Airports are not built by a single city. They are jointly held by several cities and give those cities a shared feeling of commonality.

In Japan, each prefecture has built its own stations, universities, art galleries and museums. Also, of course, each prefecture constructs its own governor's offices. Prefectures realize that

関西新空港は、大阪の町を活気づけている。開港を目前に町では、すでにさまざまな催し物を行ない、前景気をつけている。空港に直行する電車は新しくデザインされ、その電車の発着するターミナル駅周辺は、新しい人々の流れを期待して、盛り場の拡大を計画している。国際空港は都市に新しい風を吹き込んでいる。

関西新空港の計画は、1988年12月にレンゾ・ピアノがこの空港のための国際設計競技に最優秀賞をとってから、6年近いの歳月の後に、完成を迎えた。この6年という時間がながいものであったのか、みじかいものであったのか、単純には計れない。現代の超大型建築を完成させるための期間としては、これは極めて順調に時間が経過した期間だと考えられるだろうし、経済状況や国際状況の変化を考えると、この6年間はずいぶんながい時間だったともいえるだろう。ちょうど国際設計競技で設計者に選ばれたとき、そうした業績によって京都賞を受賞した彼を京都で出迎え、新しい空港のイメージを彼にインタビューした私は、彼が「空間の記憶(Memory of Space)」を大切にした建築を作りたいと述べるのを聞いた。空港の建物が完成して、6年前の建築家のアイディアの正当性が、今こそ検証されるのである。

関西新空港は、人工の島の上に建設された。島は瀬戸内海の和歌山よりに作られ、大阪、和歌山、奈良、京都、兵庫から利用できるように計画された。文字通り、関西の新空港なのである。日本の首都である東京には、あらゆる機能が集中し、東京の過密を生み出すとともに、その他の都市の地盤低下を招いてきた。大阪は伝統的に商業の中心地として知られ、京都は伝統と観光の都市として、兵庫県の神戸は港町として有名だった。けれどもこれら3都市を併せても、東京圏に対しては見劣りのする政治経済圏しか形成できていなかった。日本の経済が官庁との緊密な連携プレーの上に成り立っている以上、中央官庁のある東京に対して企業群が大きな意味を見いだすのは当然であり、企業群は東京を中心に活動し、生産も情報も東京を中心にして展開していくのである。

無論、こうした東京一極集中の政治・経済・都市構造に対して、批判がなかったわけではないし、その是正を試みる企てがなかったわけでもない。神戸市はポート・アイランドを代表とする人工島群を瀬戸内海に建設して、市域の拡大と新業務地区形成の試みを続けてきたし、大阪では1970年に万国博覧会が開催されたし、京都も新しい中央駅の建設を進めている。けれどもこれらの試みに比べて、新国際空港の建設は比較にならないほどの重要性をもっている。

さきほど述べたように、この空港は大阪、和歌山、奈良、京都、兵庫の各県に直接結び付く施設であり、しかも博覧会のように一時的なイベントではなく、永続的に機能しつづける施設なのである。首都圏に対抗しうる関西圏というまとまりを、経済・文化・都市の面で形成してゆくためのシンボルでもあるのだ。空港は都市単位にもつものではなく、複数の都市連合体が共同でもつ施設なのであり、空港によって、複数の都市連合体は共同体意識をもつことにもなるのである。

我が国では、県庁は当然としても、駅も大学も美術館も博物館も、みなそれぞれの県がひとつずつ建設してきた。公共の施設を拡充してゆかなければならないという意識は、県単位で実現されてきたのである。けれども現在では、県という単位はあまりに小さすぎると感じはじめられてきた。ちいさな日本を40以上の単位に分割している県という地方自治体の制度は、本来はもうすこし大きな単位に再統合されるべき時期にさしかかっているのであろう。とはいっても、これまでの経緯を無視してすべてを一度に再編成しなおすのはむずかしい。

空港はその点で新しい利用範囲による地方単位を生みだすものであり、単なる施設以上の、地方の広域的な核なのである。それはちょうどヨーロッパ古代の円形競技場のようであり、ヨーロッパ中世の大聖堂のようであるといえるかもしれない。そしてまた空港は、円形競技場や大聖堂と同じように、そこから世界に向かって大きな窓が開かれている。

イタリアのジェノヴァからやって来たレンゾ・ピアノは、関西という土地に上陸するための空港のターミナル・ビルを、水夫たちがはじめて目にする島のような姿に設計したという。中央部がゆるやかにたかまってゆく建物の姿は、おおきな海原に浮かぶ小島に例えるにふさわしい。それを目にした人々は、きっとそこに安息の地がひろがり、ゆたかな暮らしがあるという思いに胸をふくらませる。空港は国と国をむすびあわせ、その国への第一歩を体験する場所であり、その意味で、いまも

public facilities must be improved. However, many people today have begun to feel that the prefecture is too small of a unit. A local autonomous government system is based on the division of prefectures. Japan, with is tiny land area, is divided into more than 40 prefectures. It is probably time for Japan to reorganize these divisions into larger units. However, reorganizing these prefectures all at once and disregarding the old system would be difficult.

Airports, in that sense, create regional unity as they define a new scope of utilization. Airports—no longer simple facilities—have become the centers for wider regional activities. They are like the ancient colosseums of Europe, or perhaps they function as the cathedrals found in medieval Europe. And airports, similar to colosseums and cathedrals, are open to the rest of the world.

Renzo Piano of Genoa, Italy, said that he designed the airport arrival terminal building in such a manner as to make as if fisherman were seeing an island for the first time after a long voyage. The gently undulating center of the building can be aptly compared to small islands floating on a vast ocean. People who see the building will certainly experience the comfort and feeling of an affluent lifestyle. Airports connect one country to another, and are the places where people take their first steps in a foreign country. In that sense they still evoke the image of an island, so it is an interesting fact that the New Kansai International Airport was actually built on an island, bringing to life the metaphor.

The fact that the airport was built on a man-made island is auspicious from another perspective. All Japanese cities retain some past memories, and these places are not entirely free from impressions created by such memories. In the Nara, Kyoto and Osaka regions, where Japanese capitals were located in ancient times, there are hardly any places that are not associated with some historical event that took places in the last 1,000 years or so. The airport, which was meant to create a sense of integration in the region, was appropriately built on a new island that is free from past memories.

The planning of a new airport on undeveloped land that has potential for future expansion was an expression of Kansai's determination to build a new channel directly connecting the region with the rest of the world.

However, new sites pose major questions concerning construction. The issues were what kind of architectural context would be created on a brand new site and what kind of architectural story would develop.

What Renzo Piano created was architecture that provides visual inspiration. In an age where modern-day gigantic airports are like labyrinths without any overall image, what is important is not a structure in which people can reach their destinations with the help of signboards, but a building where people can walk to the destination while intuitively knowing their positions. In my personal experience, there are no examples of large airports that inspire an overall image. The Charles de Gaulle Airport in Paris is architecturally simple, but I'm not sure the overall image that the airport inspires in people is the correct one. Although the layouts of O'Hare in Chicago and Heathrow in London are partially easy to understand, they do not inspire any overall image. Narita Airport in the Tokyo region is a typical one in which people move through the building with the help of signboards. Haneda in Tokyo is a newly renovated airport. The structure up to the check-in counter is comfortable, but past that point the airport is just a series of mazes in which people must rely on signs to find their way.

There are some smaller-scale airports that enable people to see the entire structure at a glance. There are also some small airports that are beautifully constructed. Stuttgart Airport and Dulles in Washington D.C. create such impressions. However, when airports exceed a certain size, we assume that it is impossible to move through them intuitively. Like the norm of modern civilization, people are just beings that move along according to instructions they are given, without understanding anything.

All organizations and forms of the modern culture of the 20th century are based on machines. Machines have tasks and comprise all of the components necessary to execute the tasks given to them. Their functions are universally implemented as long as they are operated correctly. Machines are the prime power that built modern civilization, and modern civilization gradually reorganized its social organizations and forms, based on machines, which are its parents of modern civilization. The philosophy of Taylor system pragmatism is more or less based on machines. People have begun to think that the world can be understood based on machines.

Machines were the Spirit of the 20th Century

Around the third quarter of the 20th century, machines went through elemental changes. There were two important changes. One was the shift to electronics. Many machines were re-

なお、島のイメージをもっている。関西新空港が島に建設されたことは、比喩が現実のものになっているという点でも、興味深い。

この空港が人工の島のうえに建設されたことの意味は、別の観点からも興味をひかれる。なぜなら、日本の都市にあっては、あらゆる場所には、かならずなにかの過去の記憶がまつわりついているのであり、それから自由ではありえないからである。とくに古い都のあった奈良や京都や大阪では、千年以上にわたる歴史的連想に染め上げられていない土地は、どこにもないといってよい。新しい地方のまとまりを生みだすべき新しい空港は、そうした各地のそれぞれにもつれあった土地の記憶から解放された、新しい人工の場所に設けられるのがふさわしかった。

何もなく、すべてがこれからはじまる土地、そこに新しい空港が計画されたのは、関西が世界と直接むすびつくための新しい回路を築こうとする、決意の表明だった。新しい場所であるから、大阪、京都、兵庫、奈良などは、どこが中心になって建設する空港なのかを必要以上に問題にしなくともすんだ。新しい酒は新しい皮袋にいれられたのである。

新しい場所は、しかしながら、大きな課題を建築につきつける。何もなく、何の手掛かりもない土地に、どのような建築のコンテクストを作り上げるのか、どのような建築のストーリーを書き上げるのか。

レンゾ・ピアノが生みだしたのは、すべてを視覚によって読み解ける建築である。現代の巨大空港が、全体像のつかめない、迷路のような構造物になってしまっている時代に、もっとも必要なことは、標示板のサインによってようやく目的の場所にたどりつける建築ではなく、人間の五感によって自分の位置を感じながら、目的にむかって歩いてゆける建築をめざすことである。個人的な体験では、ある程度以上の規模の空港で、その全体像が感じ取れる例はない。パリのドゴール空港はやや解りやすい空港だが、全体の空港イメージが正しいものなのかどうかは、まったく自信がもてない。シカゴのオヘア空港、ロンドンのヒースロー空港は、一部分は明快だけれど、全体はなにがなにやら解らない。東京の成田空港も、サインだけで人を移動させようとするタイプの空港である。東京の羽田空港は新しく作り直された空港で、チェックイン・カウンターまでの構成は気持ち良いが、そのあとの通路空間部分はサインだけがたよりの、延々たる迷路の連なりになってしまう。

ちいさな規模の空港であれば、一目で全体が見渡せるものもあるし、美しい構造体によって作られている例にも出会う。シュツットガルトの空港、ワシントンのダレス空港などはそんな印象の空港である。ある程度以上規模が大きくなると、われわれは自分たちの五感だけを頼ることは不可能なのだと、ながらく思い込まされてきた。ちょうど現代の文明そのもののなかにおけるように、われわれは指示に従って、わけも解らずただ動いてゆくだけの存在に貶められていたのである。

20世紀の近代の文化は、あらゆる組織、あらゆる造形において、「機械」を1つのモデルにしてきた。「機械」は、目的をもち、その目的遂行のために必要にして十分な部品からなる構造を備えている。そして、その機能は、機械を正しく操作するかぎりにおいては、普遍的に遂行されるのである。「機械」は近代文明を築きあげた原動力であり、近代文明はやがて、社会組織や造形を、みずからの生みの親である「機械」をモデルにして、組み立てなおしていったのである。機械の美学、テーラー・システム、プラグマティズムの哲学などは、みな多かれ少なかれ、「機械」をモデルにしている。世界は「機械」をモデルにすることによって、明確に把握できるのではないかと考えられるようになっていった。

「機械」は20世紀の時代精神であった。

その「機械」が、本質的に変質したのは、20世紀の4分の3世紀をすぎた頃からである。このとき、「機械」は、ふたつの重要な変質を遂げた。そのひとつは、電子化である。多くの機械が電子機械化していったのである。電子化した機械には、かつての機械のような、「その目的遂行のために必要にして十分な部品からなる構造」は、すでにない。電子部品には、古典的機械におけるような、構造はすでにないのである。もうひとつの重要な変化は、機械のロボット化である。ロボットの定義は「リプログラミング可能な機械」というものなのだそうである。つまり、プログラムを組み替えることによって、さまざまな機能を遂行できる機械をロボットとよぶのである。そこには、機能から解き放たれた機械の姿がある。

構造も機能も、かつての機械とはまったく異な

modelled into electronic ones. These new machines no longer have all of the components necessary to execute their assigned tasks, as machines in the past had. Electronic components no longer have the structure found in classic machines. Another important change is the creation of robots based on machines. The definition of robot is reprogrammable machine. In other words, machines that can carry out various functions through reprogramming are called robots. Robots are machines that are freed from their conventional functions.

Today's machines are entirely different from conventional machines in terms of structure and functions. Today, machines are no longer the models used for philosophy. This is because the actual state of the machines is no longer visible. Machines that have invisible parts have made the civilization they control invisible. Modern airports where people need only to rely on signboards to find their way are an accurate reflection of today's invisible civilization.

However, we do not want a lifestyle in which we must rely on signboards and instructions to make progress. As we live life, we want to be able to accurately understand the places in which we are standing through our own observations. It is a natural and sound desire for human beings. In actuality, however, our lives consist of simply operating machines whose underlying principals we do not understand. We believe the machine is functioning correctly because its results are correct. Under this kind of thinking, we use machines every day. We do not understand why computers are able to display the functions we desire, why facsimiles are able to accurately convey information, what kind of structure a color copier has and how our car navigation system is functioning. Without accurately understanding them, anyone can operate these systems. In fact, we only operate them; we do not understand them.

In that sense, airport buildings are similar to modern-day machines. Although we do not understand the structure of the airport, we reach the boarding gate of the aircraft by following instructions. When we arrive at our destination, our luggage is discharged from the belt conveyors, and we simply have to follow directions to find it. Then, we reach the taxi terminals located at the airport exit. Almost all airports are constructed in this manner, which forces people to go through systems, or rather invisible structures. If we visualize the route through an airport we have visited, we soon realize that building such a system is very difficult.

Architecture gives visual form to the invisible.

Canyon, the first large space. 第1の大空間であるキャニオン

The fourth floor, the second large space.

ってしまったのが，現代の機械なのである．いまや，「機械」はかつてのようなモデルではありえなくなってしまった．機械の実態は目には見えないものになってしまったのだから．不可視となってしまった機械は，それが支配する文明の姿をも不可視のものにしていってしまった．サインをたよりに歩くしかない現代の空港は，現代の不可視の文明の正確な反映なのである．

だが，われわれはサインと指示だけをたよりに進んで行くような生活を望んでいるわけではない．われわれは自分たちが立っている場所を，自分たちの目ではっきりと確かめながら生活を送ってゆきたいと考えている．人間として，それは当然の欲求であり，健全な欲求でもあるはずだ．けれども現実には，われわれは原理のわからぬ機械を，ただ操作するだけの生活を送っている．結果が正しいのだから，おそらくこの機械は正しく機能しているのだろうと考えて，機械を使う毎日なのだ．コンピューターがなぜ望む機能を発揮してくれるのか，ファックスがなぜ情報を正確に伝えてくれるのか，カラー・コピーの機械はどのような構造をもっているのか，カー・ナビゲーション・システムはどのように自動車のなかで機能しているのか．これらをすべて正確に理解しなくても，これらのシステムを操作するだけなら，誰にでもできる．そして現実には，われわれは操作だけをしている．

空港の建物は，その意味で，なんと現代の機械に似ていることだろう．どのような構造になっているか解らぬまま，指示に従って歩くうちに，搭乗すべき飛行機のボーディング・ゲートにたどりつく．到着したときには，やはり指示に従って歩かされているうちに，荷物がベルト・コンベアから吐き出されてくる．そして出口のタクシー乗り場にたどりつく．ほとんどの空港はこうしたシステム，つまり目にみえない構造のなかを通過するタイプの建築でできている．ためしに，利用したことのある空港を取り上げて，そのなかでの歩行経路を頭のなかで復元してみれば，それがいかに困難な作業であるか，すぐに気づくであろう．

建築とは，本来，目にみえないものを可視化する術であった．目にはみえない宗教的な力を教会や寺院や神殿の姿に可視化し，世俗の権力を宮殿や官庁の建築として可視化し，民主主義の理念を議会の建築に可視化し，建学の精神を校舎に可視化してきたのが，建築であった．それが，20世紀にはいって，「機械」をモデルにすることによって機械を可視化できると気づいたときに，機械の美学に則った建築へと，雪崩を打ってむかっていった．しかし機械が不可視の電子機械になり，機能から解き放されたロボット機械になっていったとき，機械の美学による建築は，従来の表現を続けるだけでは，単なる不可視の迷路を生みだすだけのものになってしまったのである．現代の一般的な空港の建築に端的に現われているのは，スムーズに使えるけれども，さっぱり解らないという，不可視の機械のもつ特性である．

建築こそ，「機械」が不可視になってしまった時代にあって，新しいモデルになるべき存在なのである．すでに，たとえばコンピューター技術者たちのあいだでは，感覚的には捉えられなくなった

Architecture has given a visible structure to invisible religious authority through churches, temples and shrines, encapsulated political power in the form of palaces and government offices, crystalized the concept of democracy in parliamentary buildings, and embodied the spirit of architecture in school buildings. The 20th century brought a realization that we could create visual images using machines as a model, causing architecture to lean in this direction. The advent of virtually invisible electronic machines and then functionally-liberated robots has resulted in machine-based architecture which has continued to produce the same expressions and therefore has created invisible labyrinths. This invisible machine character is manifest in modern airport buildings, which are functionally effective, but structurally incomprehensible to most people.

Architecture should be the new model in this era of invisible machines. Computer engineers employ the concept of architecture to understand computer structures which are difficult to comprehend. Architecture is replacing machines as a new world model, but we must never forget that architecture can also visualize complex programs. We must never forget that architecture has this significance.

Renzo Piano experimented with the manifestation of architecture's power to visualize concepts. He used an overall image to create the structure of a gigantic international airport. Upon arriving at the airport, people pass through a large canyon-like area, then to a second expansive space containing the check-in counters, and finally to a long hall of waiting areas and boarding gates. A strong impression is created by passing through the carefully structured series of spaces, from arriving at the airport to boarding a flight. While in this airport, people will receive strong visual impressions as they move through each stage of the process, toward their final goal of departing. Piano employed the original meaning of architecture to redefine the conventional airport labyrinth of signboards.

The airport's architectural expression incorporates many natural elements. Trees play an important role in the canyon, the first large space. Vast numbers of advanced trees create an atmosphere of artificial and nature coexistence. The canyon is the most urban space in the airport, where arriving and departing people pass each other in the air. The rationale for using large numbers of trees on bridges in the canyon is to reinforce the concept that cities are intrinsically linked to the earth. People arriving at the airport will feel that they have entered a new country when they see the glisten of tree leaves.

The check-in counters are arranged within a

第2の大空間，4階国際線出発ロビー

Wing, the third large space. 第3の大空間であるウイング

しまったコンピューターの構成を把握するために，「アーキテクチュア」という概念が用いられている．「建築」こそ，「機械」に替わって新しい世界モデルになりうる概念である．しかしそのためには，建築が複雑なプログラムを可視化することができるものであるという，重要な性格をもつものであることを片時も忘れてはならない．

レンゾ・ピアノが試みたものこそ，建築が本来もっている，ものごとを可視化するという力の顕現である．彼は巨大国際空港を，目にみえる全体性をもった構造にまとめあげた．空港に到着した人々は，キャニオンと名付けられた大きな吹き抜けの空間を通って，カウンターのならぶ第2の大空間に導かれ，そこから搭乗口のならぶ長大な待合の空間に至る．ここには空港到着から登場までのプロセスごとの空間が，印象的な表現をもって連続的に用意されている．人は，自分がいま出発するためのどのような段階に進んでいるのか，これからどのようなプロセスを経て飛行機に乗り込むことになるのかを，視覚的に実感しながらこの空港を利用することになる．サインの迷路だったこれまでの空港を，本来の建築的空間にとりもどすことこそ，ピアノが試みたことなのだ．

従ってそのための建築表現は，自然の要素をできるだけ取り入れたものになっている．具体的には，第1の大空間であるキャニオンでは，樹木が重要な役割をはたす．木々はできるだけ大きく，できるだけ多く持ち込まれ，この大空間を人工と自然の交錯する場となるように演出される．空港にやってきた人，空港から出てゆく人が，空中で交差する場所であるキャニオンは，空港のなかで，もっとも都市的スペースである．そこに樹木をできるだけ多く配したのは，都市は大地の上に営まれるものだからであろう．空港に到着した人々は，木々の葉の煌めきに，新しい土地への到着を実感するだろう．

第2の大空間である，チェックイン・カウンターのならぶホールでは，風がモチーフになる．人工環境である室内空間に風を感じさせるために，オープンエアダクトとよばれる，吹き出し口から風が天井にむかって空中に吹き抜けてゆくシステムが開発された．風の道は白い滑り台のようなかたちで天井に設けられていて，視覚的なアクセントともなっている．モビール彫刻がさらに風を視覚化する．天井の鉄骨の架構もまた，風の流れに沿うかのように，搭乗口の方向にむかって大きくうねっている．この風の流れにのってゆくかのように，人々はチェックインをすませて，奥の搭乗口へとむかって進んでゆく．ターミナルビルの中央部にあるこの大空間に風を吹き抜けさせることが，レンゾ・ピアノにとっての夢だったのではないか．ヨットが趣味だという彼は，風にのって自在に航海する楽しみを，飛行機に乗るという行為に重ね合わせたのではなかったか．

最後に，ボーディング・ブリッジがならぶ長大なウイングの空間では，光がモチーフになる．全長1.6キロメートルにも及ぶというこの空間は，壮大ではあるけれど，非人間的な場所に転じてしまいやすい．そこでまた，うつろう自然の要素が取り入れられる．開放的なこの空間は外側に飛行機の姿と滑走路が見える明るい場所である．外界の変化が，この場所をいきいきしたものにする．しか

second void. The theme for this space is wind. Wind is created in this artificial environment by an open air duct system which directs air from low-level outlets towards the ceiling, giving people the feeling that the wind flows through this indoor space, although it has been artificially created. The white wind channel, shaped like a slide in the ceiling serves as a visual accent, while the mobile sculpture embodies the nature of wind. The iron railing on the ceiling forms a large wave rolling toward the boarding gate, as if following the wind flow. People will also feel as if they are being carried along by the wind as they complete their check-in and move toward the boarding gates. Perhaps Renzo Piano envisaged this concept of wind wafting through a large void in the core of the terminal building. Piano's hobby is yachting, and he may have tried to associate the fun of sailing with the process of boarding an aircraft.

Light is the theme for the great hall of aligned boarding bridges. This space extends for 1.6 km, an impressive expanse, but one that is not of a human scale. Natural elements have therefore been incorporated. The space has a bright, open feel and enables people to view the aircraft and runways outside. The constant movement taking place outside the building vitalizes the atmosphere of this area. The external brightness will change with the hour and weather conditions. Soft early morning light, bright daylight and night darkness will add dynamic change to this part of the New Kansai International Airport, which will operate 24 hours each day. This space will offer a different impression each time it is used; that is the power of nature.

The incorporation of natural elements such as trees, wind and light as themes for the large spaces provides the terminal building with a feeling of organic integration within and between its great expanses. This stimulates the senses while people moving through the building toward their aircraft. The framework of gigantic iron bars, which are the building's structural foundation, smoothly envelop the building, providing a shroud which blankets the movement of people. This building was constructed on an artificial island, subject to strong maritime winds. Careful consideration was given to providing protection against salt damage and the forces of wind and rain. The roof's sweeping curve is beautiful, but also provides an aerodynamically effective shape which can withstand the wind.

I visited the construction site about six months before the scheduled completion. It was fun to climb on the vast roof, which reminded me of a metal ocean, and view the fluctuating curves spread out before me. The roof's brightness changes dramatically each time the sunlight changes or a cloud passes overhead. A bright patch would appear on one part of the roof, spread across it, then disappeared in the opposite direction. It was just like an ocean whose colors change with the sunlight. Few people will be able to climb onto the roof after the airport has opened, but I wanted to share the pleasure I gained from this experience. As aircraft land and take off, their passengers will be able to view this magnificent structure, and witness these dramatic changes in brightness.

The roof appears to extend into the nearby sea, emphasizing the vast scale of the terminal building. While on the roof, we were able to determine our position over the check-in counter because of the shape of the curves. Architecture is designed to visualize programs, and although the airport building is gigantic, its structure can be understood.

A comparison with other large modern constructions will help us understand the nature of the New Kansai International Airport. The New York Convention Center (1986) was designed by I.M. Pei, while the Japan Convention Center (Makuhari Messe 1989) was designed by Fumihiko Maki. Although these buildings have very different natures, they both show the characteristics of their age, in terms of how the large spaces are structures.

The New York Convention Center has evenly-spaced joints throughout its vast space. This mechanical arrangement gives the impression of endlessly multiplied cubes. The expression of the space largely depends on the accuracy of the joints, which are precise elements. This building reflects an attempt to build in the image of machines.

The Japan Convention Center is not designed to multiply a basic unit. A large, undulating arched roof covers the entire building. The roof is curved in only one direction. This was an attempt to create a building as a coordinated entity with dynamic movement. As this building is a venue for trade fairs and is not viewed from above, a simple curved roof was able to create an impression of integration with rich variety.

The roof of the New Kansai International Airport comprises two curves. This roof has a more complex shape than that of the Japan Convention Center. The design considered that the roof would be viewed from the ground and from

も時刻や天候によって、この外界の明るさは刻々と変化するはずである。24時間空港となる関西新空港の場合、朝のひかり、昼のひかり、そして夜の闇は、この場所にダイナミックな変化を与えるに違いない。利用するたびに、この場所の印象は随分ちがったものになるであろう。それが、自然のもっている力なのだ。

巨大な建築を可視化するにあたって、樹木、風、光という自然の要素がそれぞれの大空間のモチーフに据えられることによって、ターミナルビル全体に有機的な一体感が生まれた。それは人々が飛行機にむかって進んでゆくプロセスを、五感を通じて実感させるものである。建築の構造体である巨大な鉄骨の骨組みは、こうした人々の動きを包み込む覆いとして、なめらかに建物をカバーしている。海風の吹きつける人工島のなかの建物であるから、雨や風に対する耐久性とともに、塩害に対しても十分な配慮がなされなければならなかった。大きくうねる屋根の曲面は美的であると同時に、風に対しても無駄な抵抗なしに建つ有効な形態をビルに与えているのであろう。

竣工よりも半年ほど早い工事途中にここを訪れた際、この屋根面に登れたのは楽しい体験だった。金属製の海原という感じのひろびろとした屋根は、つぎつぎに曲率を変えながらひろがっていた。陽のひかりが変化するたびに、屋根はそのかがやきを大きく変える。しかもひろい屋根の上を雲が走り抜けるのが、屋根のかがやきの動きかたに現われるのだ。いっぽうに屋根面にかがやきが現われると思うまもなく、そのかがやきは屋根全体にひろがり、やがて反対の方角に抜けてゆく。陽のひかりによって刻々と色を変える大海原の姿と、それはまったく同じものだった。屋根の上に登ることのできる人は、開港以後はあまりないだろうが、この屋根の上の悦楽は伝えておきたいもののひとつだ。けれども、離陸した飛行機のなかから、あるいは着陸寸前の機内から、この屋根の変化に富んだかがやきは、多くの人の目にふれるにちがいない。

周囲の海にそのままつながってゆくように見える屋根は、その上に立つ者に、改めてターミナルビルの巨大さを感じさせる。しかし、ちょうどチェックイン・カウンターの上の屋根に登ったわれわれには、屋根のうねりを通じて、自分たちがいま建物のどの辺りの上にいるのかが、よく解ったのであった。建築が、本来、プログラムを可視化するものであることを、このときにも実感したのだった。巨大ではあるが、明快さは失っていない建物だ。

関西新空港の性格を考えるために、現代の大空間の例を、ここでいくつか比較しながら取り上げてみよう。ひとつはI. M. ペイの設計によるニューヨーク・コンベンション・センター（1986年）であり、もうひとつは槇文彦設計の日本コンベンション・センター（幕張メッセ、1989年）である。性格のちがう建築ではあるが、大空間の構成法における時代の特徴が見られるように思うからである。

ニューヨーク・コンベンション・センターは、精密に考えられたジョイントが空間を作り出している。キューブを基本としたひとつひとつの単位が、無限に増殖してゆくようなメカニカルな空間がここには見られる。そこでの空間表現は、精密機械のようなジョイントの正確さに多くを負ったものである。ひとことで言えば、ここには機械のイメージを建築化する試みが見られるのである。

日本コンベンション・センターの場合は、基本単位を増殖させるのではなく、大きくうねる弧状の屋根が建物の全体を覆っている。それは大空間を、ダイナミックな動きのある「統一された全体」として表現する試みであった。だがこの屋根は一方向にだけ曲がる曲面である。この建物は見本市会場であり、上空から眺めたりしないから、1次曲面の屋根が架けられれば十分に変化のある全体性を表現できたのである。

関西新空港の屋根は2次曲面の構成であり、日本コンベンション・センターの屋根面よりもさらに一段と複雑な形をしている。地上からも、空中からも眺められることを意識した造形である。この複雑さは、建物が複雑だから選ばれたのではなく、建物を「有機的な全体」として明快に表現するために選ばれているのである。そこにこの建物の現代的表現をみることができる。3つの大空間に窺われる1980年代後半から90年代にかけての建築の変化は、技術的な進歩の結果というよりは、むしろ「機械」に代表される時代精神が変質していった結果だと思えるのである。ニューヨーク・コンベンション・センターのようなタイプのメカニカルな表現は、現在はすでに時代の精神を宿らせた造形とは言えないものになってしまっているのである。

the air. The complex shape was not chosen because the building itself was complex, but to express the building as an organic entity. This embodies the expression of modern buildings. This change in architectural emphasis, illustrated by three buildings constructed during the second half of the 1980s and the early 1990s, appears to result from changes in the spirit of the times, as represented by machines, rather than any technological development. Mechanical expression, embodied by buildings such as the New York Convention Center, can no longer be described as a form which captures the spirit of the times.

The creations of Renzo Piano could not be called high-tech architectural expression. His architecture employs structural technologies to give organic expression. It is evidentially different from high-tech approaches in the sense that technologies develop expressions. In high-tech buildings, we can experience the architect's expressive ability and see beauty, even when we look at only a fraction of the structure. On the other hand, viewing only a portion of the New Kansai International Airport does not allow us to comprehend Piano's organic entity.

If we see modern architecture as inhuman, it is probably because a building is based on the repetition of a single unit. The unlimited repetition seen in these building has no mountains or valleys, but contains an eerie atmosphere, like fluid flowing without pulsating. In this modern age, all functions should be smooth, with no breaks. Such a system actually controls humans, causing people to feel oppressed and revolt. Buildings where all elements are completely smooth are actually strange, unnatural buildings.

Unfortunately, smooth buildings abound throughout the world. Supermarkets are a world where language is not necessary, and international airports reflect the same nature. People move without uttering a word, passing from entrance to exit without gaining an understanding of where they are. People only realize that their goals have been achieved without any major problems when they exit the space.

Renzo Piano adds a pulse which reflects human rhythms to buildings designed to smoothly execute functions. He describes this pulsation as organic. It is irrelevant that we may criticize the building by saying that it looks like a glider, or like a dinosaur bone. Piano did not create the building with an emphasis on the expressions, but tried to visualize the invisible flow. The flow refers to the flow of people, the flow of cars, the flow of trains, the flow of aircraft, the flow of sea winds, the flow of information and the flow of time.

A number of cities, including Osaka, have high hopes for the New Kansai International Airport. They may feel the structure of the airport building reflects the winds of this age, which blow from the city into the sky. Although the opening of an airport does not change our lives, people expect the airport to breathe life into a new age. Piano has created terminal buildings that meet these expectations. Although we live in an era described as the information age, people's dreams have remained basically unchanged since former times. Airports, where people take off to other countries and where foreigners come to a new land, are places that fulfil people's dreams for the sky.

I walked through the deserted terminal building before the opening of the airport. I heard test broadcasting announcements and music. I wondered if most airports use sound a loud bell before announcing flight information. The moment I heard the bell, I felt that this airport was already functioning and had joined the worldwide network of airports. I was filled with an urge to jump on a plane headed some unknown destination.

Before I realized, the test broadcast had ended and a Debussy piano piece was gently playing. Suddenly it struck me that this building had been designed by an architect called Piano. Once the airport is open, the terminal building music will flow like the spirit of the architect. The sound of the piano will continue to flow with the trees, wind, light, people and information which move through the building; I wonder if the story of the new airport is just too perfect.

Hiroyuki Suzuki is the Professor of Tokyo University, Department of Architecture.

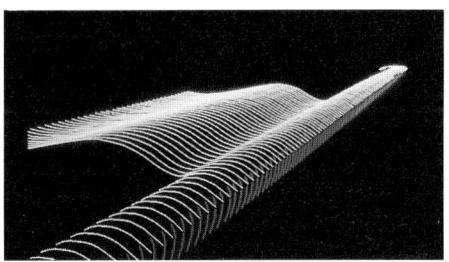
Geometrical drawing of roof, looks like a glider.
グライダーのような屋根のジオメトリー図.

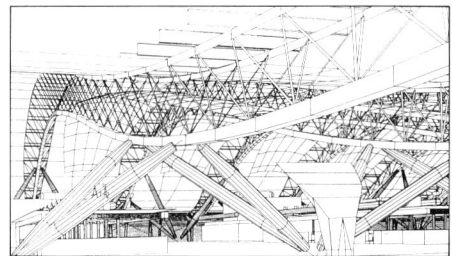
Truss of MTB, looks like a dinosaur bones.
恐竜の骨のようなMTBの屋根トラス.

レンゾ・ピアノの表現は,いわゆるハイテクの建築表現ではない.彼の建築では,有機的表現のために構造技術が駆使されるのであり,技術が表現を切り開くハイテクとは明かに異なる.ハイテクの建築では,建築の一部分あるいは断片だけをとっても,十分建築家の美意識と表現力が味わえるけれど,関西新空港の場合は,一部分だけを見ていたのではピアノの構想した「有機的な全体」を理解できない.

現代建築の形態が非人間的なものに見えることがあるとすれば,それはその建築が基本的に同一の単位の無限の繰り返しに陥っているからであろう.そこに現われる無限の繰り返しは,山もなければ谷もなく,鼓動なしに流れる液体のように不気味なものとなる.現代において,あらゆる機能は一瞬の淀みもなしにスムーズに遂行されるべきであろうが,そのシステムが直接ストレートに人間に覆いかぶさると,人は圧迫され,悲鳴をあげる.スムーズに機能だけが遂行される建築とは,実はそのような不気味な建築のことなのだ.

残念ながら,世界中にスムーズな建築は満ち溢れている.スーパーマーケットは,言語を必要としない世界だし,国際空港もおなじ性格の建築なのだ.そこでは人々が無言で流れ,入口から出口へと訳の解らないうちに通過してゆく.そこを通過してはじめて,どうやら無事に目的が達せられたのだと納得するような世界.

レンゾ・ピアノはそうしたスムーズな機能遂行のための建築に,人間のリズムにあわせた鼓動を打たせる.彼自身が「有機的」というものの中身は,この鼓動のことだ.結果的にこの建物の形態を「グライダーのようだ」とか「恐竜の骨のようだ」などと評しても,ほとんど意味はない.彼は表現主義的に建築をまとめあげたのではなく,むしろ目にみえない「流れ」を可視化しようとしたのである.それは人の流れであり,車の流れであり,電車の流れであり,飛行機の流れであり,潮風の流れであり,情報の流れであり,時代の流れでもあるのだ.

関西新空港に期待している大阪をはじめとする多くの都市は,この空港の形のうちに,都市から大空にむかって吹き上げてゆく時代の風を感じるのではないか.時代が空港の開設だけで変わるものではないが,少なくとも人々の期待は空港から新しい時代の風が吹いてくると思い込んでいる.建築家はそうした人々の夢に応えたターミナルビルを実現した.情報化時代とは言われても,人々の夢は大きくは変わらない.外国に飛び立ってゆく場所であり,外国からの人々が舞い降りて来る場所である空港は,空への夢の出会う場所なのだ.

開港以前の誰もいないひろいターミナルビルを歩いているとき,試験放送のためのアナウンスや音楽が聞こえてきた.フライトの情報を放送する前に流れるチャイムの音は多くの空港で共通なのだろうか.その音を聞いた途端,すでにこの空港は世界中の空港群のネットワークのなかにはっきりと組み込まれ,その一員となっているのだと感じた.同時に,この空港からどこか知らない国へ飛び立ってゆきたい気持ちで,いっぱいになった.

気がつくと試験放送は終わっていて,ドビュッシーのピアノ曲が静かに流れていた.それを聞きながら,この建物の設計者の名前はピアノなのだと改めて気づいた.開港してからこのターミナルビルに流れる音楽は,きっと設計者の精神のように流れるのであろう.樹木と風と光,そしてそのなかを流れてゆくさまざまな人や情報のなかに,ピアノの響きもまた流れつづけるのだとしたら,これはあまりにでき過ぎたストーリーではないかと思った.

鈴木博之:東京大学工学部建築学科教授

The Glamour of Complexity
by John Thackara

複合の魅力
ジョン・サッカラ

Introduction

The world''s airlines carried more than one billion passengers on scheduled flights in 1993, equivalent to one sixth of the world's population. They also carried 22 million tons of freight - almost a quarter of the value of the world's manufactured exports. To achieve these loads 12,184,000 aircraft departures took place around the world. This traffic grows, steadily - so between now and the year 2,000 some $200 billion will be spent on new airports. It is a stupendous investment of money and expertise in what are the most complex environments made by man. But their complexity is hidden: you go through the system, not it through you.

The complexity and sophistication of airports, and the sheer economic and logistical scale of their operations, make them a paradigm of the main challenges facing design in the coming 25 years. Airports are more complicated in many ways than cities; they exist within a global aviation system - or operating environment - which is distributed not just in space, but also in time. Airports exist at the intersection of airways - the space through which aircraft pass - which are densely criss-crossed, in three spatial dimensions, by the routes planes are flying, did fly, and will fly. Air travel space is also saturated with electronic information from humans and machines - some of it integrated, much of it not - which offer directions to thousands of aircraft at any one moment. Aviation's operating environment is intensified by the irregular distribution of traffic, of time zones, and countless other non-spatial factors. The whole system is made more dynamic by the fact that people - in the form of passengers, aircrew, ground staff, air traffic controllers and the like - are part of the system, too.

Airports, then, are the most advanced "smart buildings" on earth. They pose a stark challenge to architecture itself: what power does the lone architect or small team have to influence how these "cities of the air" evolve? Can any individual, or architectural team, impose a concept and a vision on such environments? What possible design methodology can be employed when so many factors are invisible, and hard to describe; so much energy is contained within the system; and there is so little prospect that anything will stay unchanged?

It is this context, and these questions, that make the story of Kansai International Airport so exciting. This introductory text therefore examines the economic, spatial and temporal background against which this remarkable enterprise has taken place. The fact that this stupendous project clearly *is* the clear expression of an architectural vision is proof, against all the odds, that design has a future.

Blasts from the past

It seems not so long ago that airports were best known for individual masterpieces of architecture, such as Eero Saarinen's TWA terminal in New York, work on which began in 1956. Before it even opened in 1962 the concept of this monument - glamorous air travel for the elite - was obsolete. The TWA building was designed for fleets of propeller-driven Lockheed Constellations, but by the time it opened the first jets, the Comets and Boeing 707s, were in use and the terminal's airside had to be encrusted with jet-blast deflectors. Airport design has lagged behind the realities of an exponentially exploding market almost continuously since then. Under frantic pressure from rapidly increasing numbers of people, and informed by the growing complexities of a dynamic global aviation system which never stops changing, airport design became little more than the configuration of large boxes. Airports have evolved continuously, too - master-plan after master-plan becoming outdated before the blue ink was dry. International

はじめに

世界の航空輸送では、1993年の1年間に約10億人の旅客を運んだという。これは世界人口の約6分の1という大きな数字である。また総重量2,200万トンの航空貨物を運んでいるが、これは世界の工業輸出額の約4分の1に当たる。こうした数字を達成させるために世界中16,000の空港からなんと1,220万回航空機が離陸していることになる。航空輸送は確実に伸びており、今後西暦2000年までに新たな空港整備に約2千億ドルが費される予定だ。人類がつくり出す最も複雑な環境のための、莫大な費用と高度な技術を要する投資である。しかしシステムが人を通すのではなく、人が複雑なシステムをマスターしていくという具合に、この複雑さは実は隠されているのだ。

空港の複合性と精巧さ、そして空港事業運営の厳しい経済的あるいは論理的スケールは、空港が今後25年間にデザイン界が直面する重要な挑戦の実例となっていくことを示唆している。空港はいろいろな意味で都市以上に複雑である。空間だけでなく時間も含めて、地球全体を対象とする航空システムあるいは運営的な環境の中に存在している。空港は、航空路の交点に位置し、過去も現在も未来も飛びつづけるであろう航空機が3次元空間の中を非常に高密度に交差し合う場所に存在する。航空機の運行するスペースには、人からも機械からも両方からの膨大な電子的情報が飛び交い、それらはどんな一瞬も数千機の飛行機に、それぞればらばらの指示を与え続けている。航空管理を取り巻く状況は、変則的な交通網、時間網、数えきれない非空間的な要素によって、さらにその複雑さに拍車がかかる。全体のシステムは、旅客、乗組員、地上のスタッフ、整備員その他すべての人々を包含することにより、いっそうダイナミックなシステムとなる。

空港は、地上で最もスマートな最も進歩した建物である。空港は建築への挑戦そのものである。空中の都市を出現させるために、孤独な建築家や設計組織にこれほど大きな影響を与えるものは他にない。このような複雑な環境に対して独自のコンセプトやビジョンを通せる建築家や設計組織があるだろうか。これほど、その条件や要素が見えてこない、読み取れない状況で、莫大なエネルギーをシステムに内包し、なにがそのまま生き続けるかの予想も全くつかない状況で、設計手法は存在し得るのだろうか。

関西国際空港の劇的な出現という筋書きにこそコンテクストがあり問題が存在している。したがって、ここでは一大事業が実現された経済的、空間的、時間的な背景を検証してみる。このとてつもないプロジェクトは明らかに建築的なビジョンの明快な表現そのものであるという事実が、諸々の事象はさておき、そのデザインが未来性を有していることの証でもある。

過去からの訣別

1956年のニューヨークのエーロ・サーリネン設計のTWAターミナルのように、空港施設がそれぞれすばらしい建築作品として知られたのは、それほど古い昔のことではない。1962年のTWAの完成オープン以前に、空の旅がエリートだけの優雅なものであった時代はすでに終わっていた。TWAはプロペラ機のロッキード・コンステレーションのためにデザインされたものだが、それが完成したときにはすでに最初のジェット機であるコメット機やボーイング707機が就航しており、ターミナルのエアサイドをジェットの爆風徐けで覆わなくてはならなくなっていた。それ以来ずっと、空港のデザインは発展し続ける航空業界の現実から常に遅れていた。非常な勢いで増え続ける旅客やとどまるところを知らないダイナミックな地球規模の運航システムの複雑化の状況下にあって、空港デザインは大きな箱という域を脱することができないままであった。空港の建物は大きくなり続け、マスタープランを引いたインクが乾く間もなく、次のさらに大きな施設が出現していった。国際空港は個別の施設の集まりではなくなり、旅客の増大、旅客機の大型化、チャーター機といったさまざまな圧力に応え続ける中で、有機的な成長を遂げ、まるで複雑なミニシティのようになってしまった。

空間、時間をデザインする

すべての建築では時間と空間を分けて考えることはできない。しかし、人類の歴史において空港ほどそれらの要素に大きく影響を受ける環境はないともいえる。私たちの世界が交通網だけで成り立っているのではなく、地球規模の情報網によっても成立していると考えると、空港は未来の時間軸をベースとしたデザイン戦略のテストケースである。

航空機の運航システムは地球全体の空間と時間のマトリックスに基づいて組み立てられる。離陸や着陸の場所は、地球各地の時差を飛び越えてのフライトの時間数によって決められる。自転車の車輪のように中心となるハブ空港から放射状に支線が広がるという空港ネットワークの概念である「ハブ&スポ

airports stopped being discrete buildings and became complex mini-cities that grew organically in response to continuously changing external stimuli: passenger numbers; bigger planes; charter airlines; environmental pressures.

Designing in space and time
All architecture considers time and space to be indivisible - but no other environment in man's history is so influenced by such immaterial factors as is the airport. To the extent that our world is being transformed not just by transportation, but also by global communications, airports are a test-bed for time-based design strategies of the future.

Aviation systems are conceived and planned in relation to a global matrix of space and time. The configuration of take-off and landing slots is based on the journey-times of international flights that cross the world's time zones. The so-called "hub-and-spoke" network of airports, pioneered in the USA, where there are about 30 huge ones, is a planning concept based on the interconnection of journeys that may be distributed throughout a continent and over whole days. The density of aircraft traffic, which varies through the day, will affect the average likely delay to landing or take-off and thus the taxiway capacity required at a particular airport. A branch of the software industry has grown up simply to calculate efficient taxi routes for aeroplanes on the ground. So called "inter-modal" transport concepts (the integration of air and railway or road routes), adds further to planning complexity. Someone has to calculate traffic figures and then factor in likely changes over at least a ten or twenty year period. All that before a single building has been designed. Passenger flows through terminals, which you would imagine to be a safe starting point, cannot simply be calculated according to numbers of people who are projected to travel. The time they spend at different stages will vary according to the type of flight, and the proportion of late vs early checkers-in. Nor have anthropologists systematized the fact that airport behaviour varies from culture to culture: in some countries, more well-wishers accompany departing passengers than in others; the cultural diversity of the "goodbye" ritual - and its duration -is enormous. At bigger airports, many hundreds of thousands of people visit annually just to sightsee, or to shop.

Airport operators who commission new buildings are also driven by contradictory agendas. They compete against each other for business, and must do so in a market swirling with an uncontrolled proliferation of customers - the airlines. And not just in de-regulated North America: the breakup of Aeroflot spawned 100 new airlines by itself; the Soviet state carrier used to carry more than 85 million passengers a year. To commercial managers, eager to separate transit passengers from their dollars, the concept of "passenger discretionary time" is viewed as an asset; to the engineers and operations people, an idle passenger is evidence of inefficiency in the people-moving infrastructure. For many years, when they were public services, design efforts did indeed focuss on efforts to reduce the time taken by passengers to reach the airport and take-off. Now, when more of an airport operator's profits come from concessions than from landing fees, there is insidious pressure actually to increase the time spent in the terminal. Between 1950-1990, the proportion of time spent in the air by passengers on a journey has steadily decreased.

Towards the meta-airport.
"Extraordinary things are happening to airports" says John Worthington, an expert in the "software" of building design; "they are becoming places". At London Heathrow, over 30% of the passengers on the ground at any one time are changing planes and never leave the airport. These international transfer passengers spend on average three hours within terminals, creating a captive market for retail, leisure, and business facilities. International airports are competing to attract such passengers. At Frankfurt, for example, which is designing and promoting its connection with Germany's high-speed rail network, property developers have provided over 100,000sm of office, hotel, and conference facilities associated with the air and rail intersection. A similar development strategy has been employed at Schiphol and Charles de Gaulle.

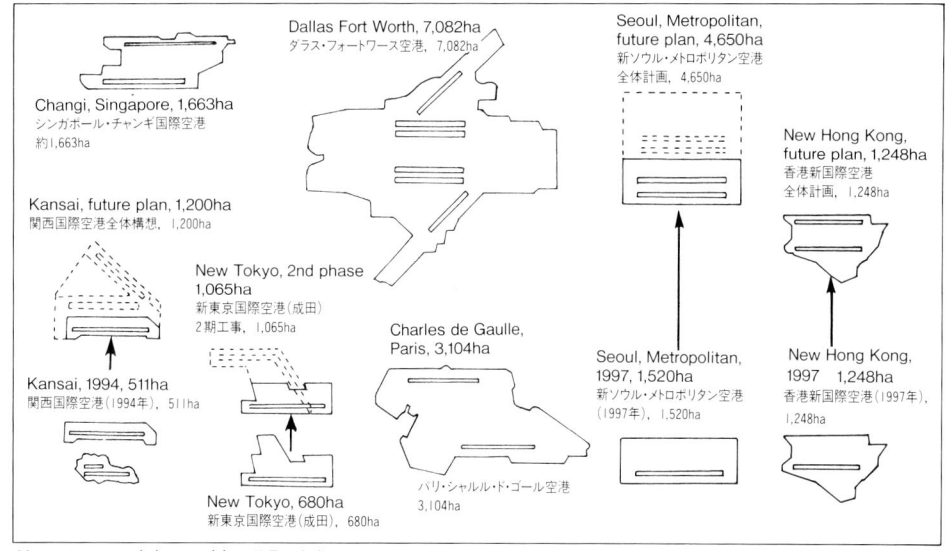
Airports around the world. 世界の空港

ーク」はアメリカで始まり，全米で現在約30か所ある．丸1日かけて大陸全域に乗り換え可能なネットワークというコンセプトである．運航の密度は時間によっても変わるが，離着陸の遅れに影響し，特殊な空港では誘導路の収容力が必要になる．ソフトウエア産業の特殊分野の成長で，航空機が地上でどのような誘導ルートが最も有効かといった計算が簡単にできるようになった．いわゆる「インターモダル」*という輸送の概念（空路，鉄路，道路合わせて）によってさらに計画が加速度的に複雑になった．だれかが今後10年ないし12年という時間軸での交通形態や実態を予測する必要がある．それは施設をデザインする前にしなければいけない．旅の始まりが安全にスタートする場としてのターミナルにおける旅客の流れは，これから旅をしようとする人々の数だけで決して単純に計算できるものではない．人々は，フライトによって，あるいは手続きを早くすませるかどうかなどによって，さまざまなすごし方をする．人類学者が，空港における行動の違いを文化ごとに体系化してみせるように単純でもない．ある国々では旅に出る人を見送る人の数は他の国より多く，また別れの儀式やその時間の長さも千差万別である．大空港では年間数十万人の人々が，ただ見学あるいは買い物のために空港にくる．

新空港建設に携わる空港管理者は，いろいろ矛盾する課題に取り組まなければならない．彼らはビジネスとして相互に競い合い，多くの顧客，つまり航空会社が限りなく急増する中でそれをしなければならないのであり，これは規制をはずした北アメリカに限らないことである．崩壊前のソビエトでは年間8,500万人以上の旅客を運んでいたが，アエロフロートが分割してそこから結果として100の新たな航空会社が生まれている．商業施設としては，空港を通過する客と彼らの使うお金は別に分けたいと考えている．つまり旅客が自由に過ごす時間は全くドル箱というか資産なのだ．しかし，逆に空港の技術者や管理者から見れば，人々が動くことが前提の施設でのんびりとすごす人々は，非効率そのものなのである．長年，空港が公共施設として存在していた間は，いかに人々を早くスムーズに空港を通過して出発させるかに焦点が当てられてきた．しかし現在では，空港ビルの収益は航空機の空港使用税よりその施設からの収益のほうが多くなり，ターミナルでいかに人を滞留させるかといった工夫が密かに進んでいる．1950年から1990年にかけて，飛行機で移動する時間のうちの滞空時間の割合は確実に減少してきている．

超空港に向けて
ビルディング・デザインのソフトウエアの専門家であるジョン・ワーシントンは「異例なことは空港で発生する，空港は広場になった」といっている．ロンドンのヒースロー空港では，地上の旅客の30％以上が飛行機を乗り継ぎ，空港から外には出ないという数字がある．こうした乗り継ぎ客は平均3時間をターミナルビルの，店舗や遊戯施設あるいはビジネス施設の虜になってすごす．国際空港はどこでもこうした旅客を魅きつけようと必死である．例えば，目下，高速鉄道網との接続を推進しているドイツのフランクフルト空港では，空港と鉄道の交点に土地開発業者が10万m²ものオフィス，ホテル，会議施設をつくり出した．同様の開発戦略はオランダのスキポール空港でもパリのシャルル・ド・ゴール空港でも採用されている．新しい香港空港（チェクラプコック新国際空港）はフランクフルトの5倍ものそうした付属施設を計画中である．

これこそ超空港の出現であり，従来の単純に空港という機能だけのターミナルは，国境を超えて発展・成長する，いわゆる「ニュー・エコノミー」という大きな経済のインフラストラクチュアの中に吸収されてしまいつつある．空港ビルを実際に動かすのは多

Inter-model is a technical expression which means 'air/rail/road/pedestrian/boat' or whatever, that are connected to each other.

インターモダル：空路，陸路，海路など含めて，輸送・交通機関が相互につながっていること．

The new Hong Kong airport will have five times as much of this new ancillary space as Frankfurt.

It is in this sense that we are seeing the emergence of the "meta-airport" - a trend in which the discrete airport terminal is absorbed in planning terms into a spatial-economic infrastructure for the growing amount of business carried out across national boundaries in the so-called "new economy". Virtual corporations are big users of airports. Such businesses tend to be innovative and concerned with the application of knowledge, sensitive to market trends and customer service, and highly dependent on global connections. Being involved with high value goods, they need easy access to a changing roster of clients, suppliers, and subsidiaries. Hence the proliferation of meeting rooms, exhibition and showroom facilities, business centres and other non-travel-specific spaces inside, next to, under, and on top of, most new airports. Even so, says Professor Worthington, "although high-tech and intelligent, such buildings must be people buildings to succeed". Their design quality is important.

Sixteen thousand competitors

Having once been managed as public service utilities - rather like the roads, or the water supply - airports are being transformed into economic activity zones of strategic importance. Nor is this only true of international airports and the 30 major hubs in the United States; these big facilities interact with a network of 16,000 other airports of which 6,000 are for regular public use. Hundreds of de-militarized airbases are also joining the commercial market. Competition between all these smaller airports is intense. And in post-Cold War Europe, more than 300 emerging cities or regional entities, all competing to attract ever more mobile capital and jobs, view a nearby airport as a strategic priority for their economies. The World Development Survey in Airports International magazine reveals dozens more projects around the world: from Macau (new $400 million terminal), Netherlands Antilles ($1.3 million terminal upgrade) and Estonia's Tallinn (new cargo terminal) to Orlando (100-gate "Worldport 2000" complex) Qatar (new $15 million airport) and Waterford, Ireland ($5 million terminal). The list goes on for page after page.

Even the smallest airport is a big investment. A single 747-capacity runway can cost $200 million; passenger terminals range from $150-600 million and more (as against $150 million for airplane). Add to these starting figures the cost of building road and rail links between airports and adjacent cities, baggage handling systems, and air traffic control systems with relay stations and cabling dispersed over hundreds of miles, and the total cost of an international airport runs to several thousand million dollars.

Airports are also expensive to operate. Workforces are large, for a start. Frankfurt has 41,000; Paris Charles de Gaulle 29,000, Paris Orly 27,000; Atlanta 32,000; Los Angeles International 35,000. London's Heathrow, one of the biggest international airports, employs 48,000 people in support of an operation handling more than 1,000 airliner movements each day, or more than 363,000 a year. Meteorologists, air traffic controllers, pilots, cabin crew, cleaners, caterers, check-in staff, baggage handlers, engineers, firemen, police, security guards, dogs, shop staff and the like all have to be charged as overhead costs. At Atlanta's Hartsfield, more than 100 staff are involved in operating 200 pieces of motorized maintenance equipment; their plant inventory includes 25 blowers, sprayers and other de-icing devices used only a few times a year. A whole department is occupied making and maintaining more than 500 signs. The scale, cost and complexity of this staff and hardware side alone is stupendous.

These large workforces, when added to passengers, well-wishers, cab drivers and so on, generate surprising volumes of vehicle and mass transit traffic on the ground. LAX carried out a study in the early 1980s which discovered that the airport generated more than 120,000 daily vehicle trips in and out of the central terminal area alone - that is excluding long-stay car parks, warehouses, nearby hotels and their suppliers. Designing a traffic and people movement system of this magnitude is similar to designing a city of more than 500,000 inhabitants.

In the coming five to 15 years, airports will also have to invest heavily in environmental measures. Although most people associate airports with noise pollution, other environmental problems are becoming more pressing. These include the impact on water quality and waste management, and the growing concern over the effect of aircraft emissions on air quality. Manchester Airport in the UK has alone spent some $50 million on environmental work over the past five years; this level of spending is sure to increase sharply for all major airport.

From service to business

These enormous costs, compounded by the fast increasing size of international airports, is one of the factors behind the privatization and commercialization that began to accelerate during the 1980s, and which has radically changed the eco-

---

くの空港使用者である．したがって，そこでのビジネスは必然的に革新的であり知識をいち早く応用し，市場の動向や顧客サービスへの鋭い感性をもち，地球規模のつながりを強く意識したものとなる．これらの高度な事象に対応して，会議室，展示室，ショールーム，ビジネスセンターなど，旅行に直接関係しない施設が，空港の隣接地，新しい空港ビルの地下や屋上などに計画される．先述のワーシントン教授は「いかにハイテクでインテリジェントな建物であろうと，それを引き継ぐのは人間であり，したがって，デザインの質が大事である」といっている．

16,000の市場競争

道路や下水道のように，空港はかつて公共サービス施設として管理されてきたが，戦略的に重要な経済活動の場に変身しつつある．これは国際空港や，全米約30カ所のハブ空港に限ったことではない．大きな施設は，世界中16,000の空港すべてのネットワークの中で相互に作用し合っている．その中でも約6,000の空港は民間施設として存在している．数百の軍関係から脱却した空港も商業施設の市場に参入しようとしている．これら小規模空港間も激しい競争を起こしている．冷戦後のヨーロッパでも，300カ所以上の新興の都市や地域が近くの空港を彼らの経済活動の戦略的拠点として，資本や仕事の機会が増大をねらって，しのぎを削っている．国際空港関連の世界開発調査によると，世界で1ダース以上のそうした開発計画が打ち出されているという．例えばマカオ(新ターミナルの総予算4億ドル)，オランダ・アンティール(ターミナルビル改築に130万ド

ル)，エストニアのタリン(新貨物ターミナル)，オーランド(ワールドポート2000用に100ゲート整備)，カタール(新空港に1,500万ドル)，アイルランドのウォーターフォード(ターミナルビルに500万ドル)などがある．取り上げだすとリストは長大なページになる．

空港の運営は高価なものだし，第一に作業量も膨大である．従業員の数で比較するとフランクフルトは41,000人，シャルル・ド・ゴールが29,000人，オリーが27,000人，アトランタが32,000人，ロサンジェルス国際空港が35,000人，世界最大の国際空港の1つであるロンドン・ヒースローが48,000人で，1日1,000便以上，年間363,000便以上の運航を司っている．気象学者，管制官，パイロット，乗組員，清掃員，食料調達関連，出入国管理や税関関連職員，手荷物取扱い者，技術者，消防署員，警察署員，保安要員，麻薬犬，店員等々のすべての費用が間接経費としてかかってくる．アトランタ・ハートフィールドでは，年に数回しか使わない氷を解かすための設備のメンテだけのために100人以上のスタッフが自動化されたメンテナンス用の設備の200カ所の管理にあたっている．こうした全部署をサインで示せば500以上になるだろう．スタッフのスケールもコストも複雑さも，機器だけをとってみても巨大である．

こうした膨大な作業員に，旅客，見送り人，タクシー運転手などを加えると，地上の自動車や鉄道などで移動する量も膨大となる．ロサンジェルスLAXでは，1980年代はじめに調査を実施し，ターミナルの中央部分だけでも1日に12万台以上の車の出入りがあったということが判明している．これは，長時間駐車の車や，倉庫や配送センター用の車，ホテルや関連施設への出入りの車は除外しての数字である．このスケールで交通手段や人の動きをデザインすることは，50万人規模の都市をデザインすることと同じである．今後5年から15年の間に，環境保全に対しても大きな投資を迫られるだろう．騒音対策は従来から真剣に取り組まれているが，その他の環境問題も大きな課題となってくる．水質汚染，ゴミ管理，航空機からの放射による大気への影響なども浮上してくる．英国のマンチェスター空港では，過去5年間に環境対策だけで5千万ドルをかけている．こうした費用は主要空港では今後確実に増大する．

サービスからビジネスへ

国際空港の短期間の規模拡大に伴う膨大なコストは，1980年代に加速した民営化や商業主義化の結果であり，空港の経済性やデザインを根本から変えることになった．1945年から1970年にかけて，それまでは花形であった小規模な公共サービス用の民間空港では，空港使用料や航空会社にかかる関連費用が，空港の収益全体の95％以上であった．1970年代から1980年代前半にかけて，空港は駐車料金，飲食店舗やその他の施設からの収益によって，旅客から収益を得るようになった．今日では，ロンドン・ヒースローをはじめとする，ほとんどすべての民間空港で，空港利用料などの直接収益は全収益の50％をきっており，その数字はさらに落ち続けているという．

こうした経済的な背景の変化は，旅客の増大，ジャンボ・ジェットの登場などと同様に，空港デザインに大きな影響を与えた．ナポレオンいわく「小売り商人の国」といわれる英国は，商業主義化のパイオニア

nomics and design of airports. From 1945 to the 1970s, in the smaller public-service airports which predominated until then, landing fees and associated charges to the airlines made up 95% of an airport's operating income. In the 1970s and early 1980s, airports began to extract income from passengers via parking charges, restaurants and bars, and assorted concession services. Today, in the most commercial airports, like London's Heathrow, less than 50% of airport earnings come from landing fees. And even that percentage is still falling.

This economic change is having as much impact on airport design as increased passenger numbers or the arrival of jumbo jets. The British - whom Napoleon described as a "nation of shopkeepers"- have been pioneers in commercialization. Until the early 1990s, each air traveller in the US usually spent about $3 at an airport, compared with $35 at Heathrow. True, the London figure are distorted by the inclusion of duty-free goods, and by the fact that most American transit passengers have one hour to kill at the airport, compared with an average of one and a half hours to three at Heathrow. But that's not the point: dollars spent by passengers *not* flying are becoming one of the powerful new drivers in air transport economics. Of those that do fly, a growing number will be leisure travellers; Airbus predicts that in 2000 only about one in five travellers will be making a journey for business. Total numbers will grow dramatically too; Boeing reckons air travel will increase by 6 per cent a year to 2000 - and that numbers travelling will double between now and 2005.

Air travel purists and romantics, appalled by these commercial trends, face even worse developments in the future. London's Gatwick International, for example, has just unveiled plans for a $40 million "airport theme park" which, when it opens in 1996, will be visited by one million people a year who have no intention of travelling anywhere except to the airport itself.

The irony is that even today, before the dreaded theme park has been built, some 500,000 people visit Gatwick each year on day trips unconnected with seeing off departing friends or meeting arrivals. Around the world, despite the cultural impoverishment of an industry able to describe a Boeing 747 as "equipment"; and despite the spread of airport complexes that resemble piled up boxes; nonetheless, millions and millions of people are still drawn to aviation epicentres like moths to a flame. Air travel and its facilities continue to exert a visceral hold on the public imagination.

Space as sign

Big airports are best understood as gigantic adaptive software programmes operating continuously in three or even four dimensions - the ultimate wide area network. No individual understands the intimate workings of the whole system. But that fact is no justification for perceptually opaque airports: it may suit technocracy that travelling by air is like travelling in hyperspace; but the experience does not suit humans. A sense of place, and a sense of movement if we are moving to another place, is integral to our understanding of the world. Take that away and we are literally dehumanized. Nor are signs and information systems, however rational, a solution by themselves to cluttered, incoherent space and inhuman procedures. If the classic definition of design is "intelligence made visible", then airports need design with a vengeance.

But intelligence made visible is not the same as architecture made visible. Too many airport buildings of the 1970s and 1980s were designed to look modern and high-tech but perform badly and look a mess.

It is the combination of scale and architectural clarity that makes Kansai International so significant. The project represents a moment of control by humanity over rampant techno-science. The airport is functional - the journey from town to plane is, if not painless, then at least coherent. The architects have tried to make an "explicit and self explanatory space rather than a layout that must rely on signs", in Noriaki Okabe's words. Those 150 metre long main beams will afford travellers the pleasure of being part of a moving throng in a great space To its great credit, the airport has segregated most commercial activities on another level.

The design story of Kansai International Airport is quite fascinating, and beyond the scope of this introduction. But it is appropriate that the geometry of the main roof should have been inspired by the design of an airflow, and developed by reference to fractal geometry. The fact that architecture, confronted by an immeasurable volume of data and limitless complexity - not to mention a vast, fast building programme - has responded with a coherent concept, is highly encouraging. Kansai represents an advanced evolution of the modern airport - but the more exciting possibility is that the design skills involved may be transferable as we take our first steps towards an architecture of experiential information.

John Thackara is the Director of the Netherlands Design Institute, Amsterdam.

である．1990年はじめ頃までは，アメリカ国内では空港1か所で平均3ドルの消費額がヒースロー空港では35ドルであった．実際には，この数字には免税品の金額が加算されていたり，アメリカ国内では乗り継ぎ客は通常，空港に約1時間滞留し，ヒースローの場合は1時間半から3時間近く滞留するという背景からも，正しい比較にはならないが，それは大した問題ではない．旅客以外の人たちが使うお金が，航空業界を支える大きな支えになっているという事実である．もちろん旅客の中でもレジャー客の増大も見逃せない．エアバス社は，西暦2000年には航空旅客のわずか5分の1がビジネス客と予測している．旅客数はトータルでは増加し続けるだろう．ボーイング社は2000年まで年間約6％という割合で増加すると予測している．とすれば航空旅客の数は西暦2005年には現在のほぼ倍になる．

航空機での旅を追求する純粋主義者やロマンティストは，こうした商業主義的な改悪に対して，あるいは将来展望に顔をしかめている．例えばロンドンのガトウィック国際空港では，先頃4千万ドルかけたエアポート・テーマパーク計画を発表したばかりである．1996年にオープンすると，空港へは来てもどこにも旅行しないという来場者を年間約100万人の来場者を集めることになる．

このおそろしいテーマパークができなくても，現在のガトウィック空港には，見送りでも出迎えでもない年間約50万人の来場者があるという皮肉な数字がある．世界を見れば，ボーイング747でさえ単なる装備といってしまう，産業の文化性のなさにもかかわらず，あるいはまるで箱を積み重ねただけのような空港の普及にもかかわらず，数百万という人々が蛾が明かりに吸い寄せられるように空港という中心地に引き寄せられている．航空機による旅やその施設は，人々の想像にとっての本能的な部分に影響を及ぼし続ける．

サインとしての空間

大空港は，3次元ないしは4次元の，つまり究極の広範用ネットワークとして継続的に動き続ける巨大な適合性のあるソフトウエアのプログラムそのものである．システム全体の緻密な作業の全貌は個人で把握できる性質のものではない．しかし，だからといってこの事実が，空港が知覚的に不明瞭であることを正当化する理由にはならない．航空機による旅は超空間への旅のようなものだということは，技術至上主義にはふさわしいが，その体験は人間的ではない．自分がどこかに移動しようとしたときの場所や動きの感覚は，私たちがその世界をどのようにとらえているかということの総合である．それをなくせば，私たちは文字通り非人間化されてしまう．サインや情報がなければ，いくら合理的でも，結果として混乱し，支離滅裂な空間となり，非人間的な運営となってしまうのは明らかである．デザインの古典的な定義にもし「知性を視覚化したもの」という定義があるとすれば，空港は間違いなくデザインを必要としている．しかし，知性の視覚化は建築的な視覚化と同じではない．1970年代から1980年代の多くの空港ビルは，モダンでハイテクなものとしてデザインされたにもかかわらず，醜悪で混乱そのものの建物ばかり であった．

関西国際空港をこのように意義深い建物にしているのは，スケールと建築の明解さである．このプロジェクトは，世の中に蔓延しているテクノサイエンスを人道的な思想でみごとにコントロールして完成した．空港は機能そのものである．街から航空機への移動は，骨折りでなく首尾一貫したものでなくてはならない．「設計者としては，サインで示さなくてはならないようなレイアウトより，明確で説明力のある空間そのものをデザインする努力をした」と岡部憲明はいっている．150mのメインビーム（主梁）は，人々に自分たちがこの大空間を構成する動く雑踏の一部である喜びを与える．この明快さが，ほとんどの商業施設を他階に分離配置する結果になった．

関西国際空港のデザインにまつわる話は非常に魅力的であり，また私の論文をはるかに超えるものである．しかし，メインルーフの幾何学的な形態は，空気の流れをデザインし，フラクタル幾何学を発展させたものとしてふさわしいものである．無数のデータや限りない複合に直面した建築が，首尾一貫したコンセプトにみごとに呼応しているという事実は本当にすばらしいことである．関西国際空港は，近代空港の最も進歩した展開例の代表である．しかし，さらに興味深い可能性がある．私たちが，経験から学ぶ建築への第一歩を踏み出すために，関西国際空港で展開されたデザイン手法が転用できるということである．

ジョン・サッカラ：アムステルダムのオランダデザインセンター館長

Gateway to a Different World
by Teiji Matsumasa

異界への開口
松政貞治

Camus observed that the value of travel lies in its anxiety. Travel brings us back to ourselves. Today, with aircraft criss-crossing the skies, the sensation of the traditional rite of passage has been lost, and the realistic passage of the journey has replaced the rite: the crucial displacement is not in the rite, but is inherent in the journey. That which transports us into ecstasy and brings about a metamorphosis is no longer a rite. It is travel indeed that unfolds a strange parade and magnificent spectacle in the skies above the earth.

The traveller's anxiety intensifies his sensitivity to the world, awakens his self-reliance and lends substance to his individuality. Travel serves to separate you from the confinement of your mother's womb. In other words, human permanence and settlement is a precondition of travel. The dialectical experience between normality and the journey as a departure from that normality does indeed influence the richness of the journey. However, the contrast between permanence and mobility exposes the antagonism between national and international characteristics. The airports of today are fated to maintain a delicate balance in terms of the twin difficulties of the over-actualization of nationalism and prosaic internationalization.

Travel not only has power over the individual but also exerts influence on the group. When travel offers opportunities for cross-cultural contact, new cultural self-consciousness and group self-awareness are born. The self-identity of the individual and the group is born of mutual reflection and understanding between humans. Relationships with others stimulate transformation. By making contact with the worlds of others, one becomes conscious of one's own identity. In a modern world interconnected by economics, transport and information, our national and state consciousness is unexpectedly strengthened, and we begin to examine our identity as a group and as an individual, searching for those irreducible differences that set us apart. Travel brings such differences into existence. Departing on a journey from our familiar and intimate surroundings, we establish links and a feeling of unity with new human relationships with foreigners as we move through space, and experience an arrival that unifies what had formerly been differences between the self and a new context. The airport provides the stage for the departure, mobility, and arrival, and is the most crucial node of "change", which today bears the burden of "the production of differences".

Earth and Place

Creating "an island in harmony with nature" is the fundamental concept of the competition-winning Kansai International Airport Passenger Terminal Building (PTB), designed by Lenzo Piano and Noriaki Okabe. Its intention was to celebrate the balance between nature and technology through the unique characteristics of the place that comprise an island. This island seen from the air resembles Venice, or a Noh stage. An artificial island created by the modern-day violence, which is reclamation on a massive scale in a very short period of time, is, as it were, Mother Earth flowing and subsiding, serving as a "graft" onto the land of the Kansai District and its climate. This district embraces the cities of Nara, Kyoto, and Osaka, which were formed by sedimentation and stratification over countless years. This floating "earth" is a miniature of the Japanese archipelago itself, its very existence symbolizing Japan. Completely unlike the Pompidou Center, this island has no specific historical traces, only an isolated diachronic and synchronic context. Because it is on the threshold of the most historical district of Japan, the emergence of this island will intensify its topological characteristics. The PTB actualizes the significance of such meanings of the place. An

旅の価値はその不安にある、とカミュは述べている。旅は我々を自分自身へと連れ戻す。航空機が飛び交う現代においては、伝統的な通過儀礼に対する感覚は失われ、旅の現実的通過が儀礼にとって代わり、重要な変位が儀礼にではなく旅の中に書き込まれる。我々を夢中にさせ、変容をもたらすのはもはや儀礼ではない。旅こそが世界の空を舞台に異様な行進と壮観を繰り広げているのである。

旅人の不安は世界に対する感受性を強め、自立性を喚起して旅人の個性を実体化する。確立と幽閉の働きをする母胎から自我を切り離す旅は、逆に言えば人間の定着性、定住性を前提としている。常態とそこからの逸脱としての旅との弁証法的経験こそが旅の豊かさを左右する。しかし定着と移動の対照は、民族性と国際性の対立をあらわにする。民族性の過剰な顕在化と平板な国際化という二重の困難の上に微妙な均衡を保たねばならない宿命を、現代の空港は負っているのである。

個人への旅の力は集団にも影響する。旅によって文化間に接触が生じると、新たな文化的自意識や集団的自覚が生まれる。個人と集団の自己同一性は、人間同士の相互反映や了解、つまり他者との関係から生まれさらにそれによって変容を促される。我々は他者の世界に触れることによって自らの同一性を意識する。経済や交通、情報によって世界が連結された今日、民族や国家の意識が逆に強められ、集団や個人の同一性、還元不可能な差異が求められている。旅はそうした差異を産出する。我々は慣れ親しんだ環境から旅立ち、空間を移動し、異人同士の新たな人間関係の中に絆と一体感を確立し、自我と新たなコンテクストとの間にそれまでとは異種の統一性を生み出す到着を体験する。旅立ち、移動、到着を演出すべき空港は今や「差異の産出」を担う「変化」の最も重要な結節点である。

大地、場所

関西空港ＰＴＢ（旅客ターミナルビル）のレンゾ・ピアノと岡部憲明によるコンペ当選案の基本コンセプトとして、「自然と共生する島」をつくることがうたわれていた。「島」という特殊な場所性を舞台に、自然と技術とのバランスを謳歌することが意図された。空から見るとこの島はヴェネチアや能舞台のようにも見える。極端に短い期間での広大な規模の埋立という現代のバイオレンスによって造られた人工島は、いわば流動し沈下する「大地」であり、長い歴史的時間をかけた沈殿と成層化によって形成された奈良や京都、大阪を擁する関西という土地とその風土への「接ぎ木」である。浮遊する「大地」は日本列島そのものの縮図であり、存在そのものが日本を象徴する。ポンピドーセンターの場合とはまったく逆に具体的な歴史的痕跡は何もなく、通時的にも共時的にも隔絶されたコンテクストしか持たないこの島の現出は、それが日本の最も歴史的な地方の敷居となる限りにおいて、そのトポロジー的特性を一層強く浮かび上がらせる。このＰＴＢは場所のこうした意味を顕在化させる。人工島上の空港という均質で無性格になりかねない敷地に、没場所的でない個性的なＰＴＢが生み出された。不同沈下は永遠に完結しない不断の修復を共示し、ジャッキアップ・システムの制御による支持の関係性は大黒柱の不在を象徴する。ウィングを決定するジオメトリーの半径16.4キロの円は、大地を貫き、今にも飛び立とうとするＰＴＢと浮遊する土地を、視覚的にも哲学的にも大地に根づかせている。このＰＴＢで展開される旅は、移動と定住の対照を鮮明にし、空への出発と空からの到着を可能にさせる大いなる大地を見事に意識化させるのである。

テクノロジー、自然

岡部によるとコンペ案の構想当初から、旅客のためにオリエンテーションを明瞭にすることが重要なコンセプトと見做されていた。そのため、空間を分割するのではなく、全体を一体として1つの航空機のような大きなオブジェにするという発想が生まれた。短辺、長辺のスパンの差を大きくとり、ランドサイドからエアサイドへの方向性が強調された。コンペ案ではＭＴＢ（メイン・ターミナルビル）の大屋根は対称的に3分割されたアーチ構造だった。中央の大空間を空調する際に生じるコールドドラフト現象を回避するために、オーヴ・アラップ社との協議の中で、エアの動きに屋根の形態を合わせることが考え出された。そのため、大屋根の構造体が変形アーチになり、エアサイドへの方向性が明確にされた。基本設計を経て、機能上の要求と屋根構造の軽量化及び施工の効率化によるコストダウンの必要から2つのアーチにされた。シェル構造に変えられていたウィングのブーメラン・ビームは、大アーチのトラスと一体化さ

individualistic PTB which is not "placeless" has been created on an artificial island airport site which should be homogeneous and characterless. Irregular subsidence symbolizes a never-ending restoration and the support of a jack-up control system connotes the absence of central pillars. The circle with a diameter of 16.4 kilometers that determines the shape of the wing penetrates the earth, and forms the roots of the PTB, which looks like it will fly away, and the floating land both visually and philosophically. The journeys enabled by this PTB create a sharp contrast between the mobility and settlement of journeys and the gigantic earth that allows us to enter into and arrive from the air.

Technology and Nature

According to Okabe, clarifying the traveller's orientation was seen as a crucial concept of the competition draft from the beginning. This brought about the idea that the entire space is not divided, but is actually a giant object like an aircraft. The directionality from the land side to the air side was emphasized by magnifying the difference between the spans of the long and short axes. In the competition draft, the main roof of the Main Terminal Building (MTB) was constructed of arches which divided it symmetrically into three parts. To avoid the cold draft phenomenon which occurs when the central vault is air-conditioned, a plan was devised with the collaboration of Ove Arup & Partners to match the movement of the air with the shape of the roof. For this reason, the structure of the main roof comprises deformed arches, defining the direction to the air side of the building. Through the course of the basic design process, functional requirements, lightening of the roof structure and attempts at cost reduction through efficient construction led to the two arch design. The boomerang beam of the wing, which features a shell structure, was united with the grand arch trusses, creating continuous vaults. As a result, the air side direction has been emphasized by the even greater increasing spaces.

To Piano, the Pompidou Center (1971-77), designed jointly with Rogers, was an ironic comment on the existing culture and established building technology and also a criticism of the concept of technology for technology's sake that was gaining prominence. For him, technology was a means and not an end: He abhorred being labelled a high-tech artist, although he himself employed high-tech craftsmanship. He remarked of the IBM travelling pavilion, "I examined the issue of high technology, which is not necessarily divorced from the limpidity of natural techniques." According to Piano, referring to nature, which is a fertile source of curiosity and inspiration, is not simply a matter of imitating its forms. It is possible to create a naturalistic structure by pushing a research project to its limits in accordance with the rules and discipline of nature, so the simple perfection of such a structure can be achieved. To Piano, technology is the means of this great journey to the Arcadia, which is nature.

Metaphor

Eero Saarinen's TWA Building (1962) at Kennedy Airport is representative of early airport passenger terminal building designs that were only for special people travellig by airplane. The intention of the design of the reinforced concrete shell of this building is to express the notion of a bird as it takes flight as a simile, rather than in a straightforward manner. It is of great interest that from the start of the project, the Kansai International Airport PTB has been the subject of a variety of metaphors, though they are not straightforward, either. From the start of the competition, it was represented as "an aircraft or glider landing on an island rich in nature, and coexisting in harmony with the light and greenery, though it has its own technology." Subsequently, too, in Piano and Okabe's words, representations of birds, undulating geological strata, and trusses shaped like dinosaur bones can be detected. For some, the structure will bring to mind waves, the mountains, mist, rays, and bows, while others will associate the wings with passages, streets, and Gothic churches. The structure is expressed as the shape of the flow of jet air in inner space and a wing cutting through strong winds in outer space. This is a metaphor combining nature and wind, the flow of air, and aircraft.

Many metaphorical expressions have been used extravagantly in Piano's works. Such metaphors are not only for use in simply explaining the works, but are believed to be steeped in the conceptual process, vigorously playing an important role in the concept. In response to the criticism that holds that the Pompidou Center is like a factory, he counters that "it is a mobile dynamic instrument like a ship". He has designed a number of yachts, and when conceptualizing buildings, the elegance and structure of ships are often referred to and used as metaphors. Examples of this include the musical instruments and ship in a musical space for the opera "Prometheus", the cargo vessel crane in the 1992 Columbus International Exhibition, the shell of the Ravenna Sports Hall, the butterfly of

Prometheus Opera Space 「プロメテオ」上演スペース

Columbus Intl. Exhibition
コロンブス大陸発見500年記念国際博覧会

St. Nicola Football Stadium 聖ニコラス・フットボール競技場

れ，連続した大空間として構成された．その結果，エアサイドへの方向性は一層加速度的な空間によって強調されている．

ロジャースとの共同によるポンピドーセンター(1971—77)は，ピアノにとっては既成の文化や固定化した建造技術に対するアイロニーであると同時に，台頭しつつあったテクノロジー至上主義への牽制でもあった．彼にとってテクノロジーは目的ではなく手段である．彼はハイ・テクというレッテルを貼られることを嫌い，自らをハイ・テク・クラフツマンシップであると規定している．またIBM移動巡回パビリオンについて「ハイ・テクという問題が自然技術の持つ明快さから，必ずしもかけ離れたものではないということを立証してみたかった」と述べている．彼によれば，好奇と霊感の肥沃な源である自然を参照することは，単純にその形態だけを模倣することではない．自然の規則と規律に従って探求的な計画をその極限まで推し進めることによって，自然的な構造の創出が可能となり，そうした構造の簡素な完全性が了解される．ピアノにとってテクノロジーは，自然というアルカディアへのこの大いなる旅の道標なのである．

隠喩

飛行機による旅がまだ特別な人たちだけのものであった初期の空港PTBの代表的なものに，エーロ・サーリネンのケネディ空港のTWA社棟(1962)がある．鉄筋コンクリートのシェル構造のこの作品は，構造を率直に表現することよりも全体の形態の強烈な直喩表現によって今にも飛び立とうとする鳥を明示することが主題とされた．関西空港のPTB場合は，直截的なものでないにしろ計画の当初から様々な隠喩の対象とされてきたことは興味深い．コンペの当初から「テクノロジーを有しながら，自然にあふれる島に降り立ち，光や緑に調和して共存する飛行機あるいはグライダー」と表現され，その後もピアノや岡部の言葉には，鳥，隆起した地層，恐竜の骨のようなトラス，などが見い出される．その他，波，山並み，霞み，えい，弓などを連想したり，ウィングをパッサージュや街路，ゴシックの教会と結び付ける者も多いだろう．内部のジェットエアの流れをそのまま形態化し，外部の苛酷な気候である強い風を切る翼のようにしたという表現も，自然や風，空気の流れ，飛行機などを複合化した隠喩であると考えられる．

これまでのピアノの作品についても，異様なまでに多くの隠喩表現が用いられてきた．そうした隠喩は単に作品の解説に用いられているのではなく，コンセプトに強く関与して構想の過程に入り込んでいるように思われる．ポンピドーセンターを工場のようだとする批判に対しては「可変的で動的な船のようなもの」と反論している．彼自身幾つものヨットを設計しているが，建築を構想する上で船の優美さと構造がしばしば参照され隠喩に用いられる．オペラ「プロメテオ」上演スペースの楽器と船，コロンブス大陸発見500年記念国際博覧会の貨物船のクレーン，ラヴェンナ・スポーツホールの貝殻，自然繊維構造研究所の蝶，聖ニコラス・フットボール競技場の花びらと火口，ベルシー・ショッピングセンターの宇宙船，ニューポート・アメ

the Research Laboratory for Vegetal Structure, the petals and craters of the St Nicola Football Stadium, the space ship of the Shopping Center Bercy II, the magic carpet of the Museum of American Contemporary Art at Newport Beach and, the most straightforward of all, the dolphin of the passenger liner Crown Princess. Notwithstanding the plea that these were not a direct imitation of nature's forms, they were monistic metaphors. This is because Piano's designs contain detail and are characterized by a variety of articulations, while generally constituting a complete form. This PTB does not deviate from that pattern and composes Prägnanz (excellent forms). However, unlike his other works, voluptuous metaphorical readings are possible with this PTB because it exhibits a complex multiplicity of meanings and ambiguities. The richness of the connotations does not have the dual meaning of a post-modern naive reference to past words, nor the semantic double meaning mentioned by Venturi. It also differs from Paul Ricoeur's "vivid metaphor as semantic innovation" as created by Le Corbusier's Chapel at Ronchamp (1954). However, as an airport which evokes different images, the rich metaphors of this PTB which has no equal also facilitates a journey around connotative meanings and paradigms.

Historicity and Type
Piano tackled the Pompidou Center holding to the doctrine that the architect's professional role must be updated. He recognized a great significance in the decoding of the context of history and place. However, that pursuit was limited to the periphery of the "here" and "now" of individual projects. He said, "I'd like to contribute to the search for a language hat expresses our world, which is so rich in technical and social innovations. I believe that conceiving architecture as a quotation of the past means giving up something important". His thoughts on history differ substantially from the thoughts of those who give emphasis to patterns and prefer their deformation, such as Aldo Rossi, who is influenced by the style of Croce and Argan. In Piano, the loathing of post-modernism weakens the self-awareness of the ideality of type. Despite the success of the Pompidou Center, Piano subsequently refused to reproduce it and unexpectedly accepted a commission from UNESCO to tackle a series of restoration and reclamation works. Through this, he reminisced, "Working with old architecture made me more sensitive to the historical context". For him, the history, as well as the site, are subjects for further studying and listening, and are no more than a "rule for creation".

In the idea of this PTB however, that historicity went one step further. His attempt was not such a citation or imitation of the historical forms he loathes, but was a "inscription" of the balance between nature and new technology, premised on a reference to and transcription of history. That is unmistakably a "invention" which is supported by typological historical consciousness. Okabe also speaks, and the reference to and the transcription of history go back to Boullée and Ledoux in the 18th century. While being monuments to the ideal of the Age of Revolution, and the sublime unreality of the Stone Age which had attempted to give rise to gigantic internal spaces, the fruits of the Industrial Revolution in the bridge construction sector flowed into the academism of architecture and was crystallized in several excellent works. These include Paxton's Crystal Palace (1851), Labrouste's Bibliothèque Nationale (1875), Wyatt and Brunel's Paddington Station (1854), and the Eiffel Tower (1889). Most notably, in terms of the space of the three 74-meter paths and the impression of the internal spaces, and the role played by stations in the journeys of the day and their symbolic nature, in Paddington Station, the clear referent relationships with the competition draft for the PTB can be understood, although the difference in the axial directions of the internal space forms a 90 degree. In addition, in Saarinen's TWA building and Utzon's Sydney Opera House, the struggle between the architectural form and technology, the epidermis and the geometry of the structure have been sought.

Argan had this to say about the relationship between history and creation, between type and invention: "The moment of the invention is only that of the replication of the requirements of the actual historical situation, beyond criticism and the overstepping of the past, sedimented and synthetic soluitons in the schematic character of the type." The attempt to create a new "inscriptions" and responses to the various requirements of actual historical situations for this PTB has begun with a journey into the past, which means going back according to the movement of type.

Scale — the whole and the parts
"Consequently, one of the basic laws of architecture is that people should actually feel the dimensions or magnitude of a building." Alain stated that in his Essays on Art. Choisy said, "if form is changed, everything else must also be changed." For example, if we want to double a beam span, we must more than double the

リカ現代美術館の魔法の絨毯、そして最も直截的な客船クラウンプリンセス号のイルカなどである。自然の形態の直接的な模倣でも引用でもないという弁明にも拘らず、これらは一義的な隠喩であった。ピアノの作品は、ディテールを含めて多様な分節を特質としているが、全体としてはまとまった形になっているからだろう。このPTBもその例にもれず、プレグナンツ（良き形）を構成している。しかし既に観たように、このPTBはこれまでの作品とは異なり豊饒な隠喩的読みが可能であり、複雑な多義性、曖昧性を呈している。その共示義の豊かさはポストモダン的な過去の語彙の素朴な引用の複義性でもなく、ヴェンチューリの言及した意味論的両義性でもない。あるいはル・コルビュジエのロンシャン礼拝堂が生み出すような、ポール・リクールの「意味論的革新としての生きた隠喩」とも異なっている。しかし様々なイメージを喚起させる空港としては他に例のないこのPTBの豊かな隠喩は、共示的意味やパラダイムを巡る旅をも可能にしているのである。

歴史性，類型
「建築家の職能的役割は時代に適合したものでなくてはならない」との理念をもってピアノはポンピドーセンターに取り組んだ。彼は歴史と場所のコンテクストの解読に大きな意義を認めている。しかしその探求は個々の計画の「ここ」と「いま」の周囲に限定されている。「私は、技術的、社会的創造性に富んだ世界を表現する言語を探求したいのです。建築が過去の引用として説明することは何か重要なことを放棄しています。」と語っている。彼の歴史についての考えは、クローチェやアルガンの流れを汲むアルド・ロッシなど、類型を重視した上でその変形を志向する人たちとは本質的に異なっている。ピアノにおいてはポストモダニズムの嫌悪などが類型の持つ理念性の自覚を弱めている。ピアノはポンピドーセンターの後、その成功にも拘らずそれを再生産することを拒み、意外にも、ユネスコの依頼を受け入れて一連の修復・再生の仕事に取り組んでいる。これによって「古い建物を相手にすることで、歴史的コンテクストに対して一層気を使うようになった」と述懐している。彼にとっては歴史は敷地と同様に「聞く」対象であり、「創造のためのルール」以上のものではない。

しかしその歴史性もこのPTBの構想においては、そうした姿勢から一歩踏み出したものになっている。彼が嫌悪する歴史的な形態の引用や模倣ではなく、歴史の参照と転記を前提とした、自然と新たな技術との平衡の「登録」が試みられている。それは紛れもなく類型学的な歴史意識に支えられた「創出」である。岡部も語っているが、この歴史の参照と転記は18世紀のブレやルドゥーに遡る。革命時代の理想の記念碑であると同時に巨大内部空間を現出しようとした、石の時代の崇高な非現実性は、橋梁土木の分野での産業革命の成果が建築のアカデミスムに流入するとともに幾つもの優れた作品として結晶化された。パクストンの水晶宮(1851)、ラブルーストの国立図書館(1875)、ワイアットとブルネルのパディントン駅(1854)、エッフェル塔(1889)などである。とりわけパディントン駅については、74メートルの3径間と内部空間の印象、そしてこの時代の旅において駅の果たした役割や象徴性の点で、内部空間の方向性は90度異なるが、このPTBのコンペ案との明確な参照関係が見い出される。またサーリネンのTWA社棟やウッツォンのシドニー・オペラハウスに、建築の形態と技術のせめぎ合い、表皮や構造の幾何学の典拠が求められている。

アルガンは歴史と創造、類型と創出の関係について次のように述べている：「創出の契機は、類型の図式的性格における過去の、沈殿された、そして総合された解決策の批判と止揚のかなたの、歴史的現実的状況の諸要求への応答の契機に他ならない。」このPTBの歴史的現実的状況の諸要求への応答と新たな「登録」の試みもまた、類型の運動を遡行する過去への旅とともに始められたのである。

大きさ，部分と全体
「それゆえ、建築の基本法則の1つは、大きさを実感させるということであろう。」とアランは「芸術論集」の中で述べている。またショワジーによれば形が変わればすべてが変わるのであり、梁間を2倍にする場合、梁成は2倍以上にしなければならない。こうした大きさと比例の微妙な関係を司る「スケール」の問題を重要視するフィリップ・ブドンは、ヴァレリーの次のような一節を引用している：「どのようなものでも大きさで変わってくる。形はそれほど簡単に増大に従うものではない。材料の強さも、方向を決める仕掛けも、増大をそのまま引き受けることはない。あるものの一性質が

beam's depth. To attach importance to scale, which determines the delicate relationship between dimensions and proportion, Philippe Boudon quoted a phrase of Valéry's: "Everything changes according to its dimensions. Form does not change as easily as dimensions. If we want to change a dimension, other factors such as the strength of materials and their placement, must also change. When one of the properties of an object is increased by an arithmetic ratio, all of the other properties must also increase, but in a different manner." This paragraph reminds us of the fact that Renzo Piano designed a ship that imitated the morphology of a dolphin, except on a larger scale. The Kansai International Airport PTB, however, is not an enlarged abstraction of any natural form. This terminal is a successful realization of that basic law of architecture — letting us feel the magnitude, while impressing us with the lightness of the roof coverings. The huge trusses of the MTB and the building's two wings, which stretch and seem to disappear in the distance, are breathtaking, yet they are in harmony with every hierarchy of the architectural details. We are not merely overwhelmed and surprised at how huge it is; we feel the very size of the building. Those who cross the airport bridge are first led into a "human-scale" area on the land side, and then *pass* through the MTB and move into a "super-scale" area of airplanes of the air side. And as your plane leaves the ground, the majestic appearance of those roofs and wings soon start to look like a tiny speck in the ocean, shining in silver colors. Here, with airplane travel, we can also experience various scales.

As a young architect, Renzo Piano strongly thought that architecture meant figuring out how to put together ultra-lightweight parts and materials. But after his encounter with Jean Prouvé, Piano was awakened to a view of the whole picture of designing a building. After that, Piano became more oriented toward the "whole" in his professional work. He believed that we had to proceed on the general and detailed levels simultaneously and that we had to start working on the details right from the beginning, together with the project. He likes neither the repetition of details taken from historical references nor details that conform to a particular style or order. His works employ details that are brought forth during the process of, and as a result of the efforts of, meeting the mechanical accuracy and precision required in each project. Details are continually renewed on the basis of experience gained from his precedent works. The details thus refined are, in the end, visually integrated into the whole. This concept is consistent throughout his works, even in the handling of large elements or space. In the Kansai International Airport PTB, not only in the structure but particularly in the roof claddings and the glazings, small elements that have the same specifications are integrated, according to the geometry of the building, into a large-scale structure. Piano said, "To construct a building is to collect elements of materials and assemble them into a whole." Anyone who travels through this airport can appreciate not only a significant "figure" as a whole, but also the play delicately intertwined by the parts on a variety of structural levels.

Louis Kahn and Renzo Piano

Although it is generally unknown, Piano worked under Louis Kahn in the latter part of the 60's. In those days, Kahn was introducing plastic top lights into the Olivetti factory, so Piano was introduced to him through Olivetti. He only stayed at Kahn's office for a few months. Apparently, there is little in common between these two artists, in terms of their temperaments and architectural works, and Piano himself says very little about his life with Louis Kahn. In connection with the discussion of the Kansai International Airport PTB, it would be interesting and meaningful to probe into the referential relation of these two architects. According to Louis Kahn after the 60's, form became a universal idea belonging to "beginning world." A form itself has no shape and no dimensions; it is through feeling and thought that the space order is realized. Visualizing this form is what we call designing. A particular form is made possible by a structure, and through modification, the form can further be liberalized into all shapes. According to Kahn, a structure itself must also be perceptible, and designing is a way of materializing a form in terms of substance; that is, organizing various spaces according to their properties, using a structural system, and then filling that space with natural light. A structure allows natural light to enter, and with light, a form is given its dimensions. In this way, for Kahn, architecture was the art of integrating spaces in the light.

On the other hand, Piano used to say, "an architect is a man who is cooperating as a partner of nature." An architect should endeavor to discover the laws of nature — not imitate nature. Nature is, as it were, reconstructed in our technical processes. It would be reasonable to think that nature in Piano's mind is very close to what Louis Kahn terms the "nature of nature," which may even lead to "a beginning world." If this assumption is correct, the structure of the Kansai

International Airport PTB is a medium of its form and natural light.

The distinction between a "served space" and a "servant space" had been realized by Kahn before the arrival of Piano. These concepts materialized in the buildings of the Richards Medical Research and Biology Laboratory (1957 - 64), where a "servant space" and a "served space" were allocated by vertically partitioning the area for the principal functions. At the Salk Reserach Institute (1959 - 65), the concept of a "horizontal servant space" was introduced; all such services as water pipes, duct work, and wiring, were located in a space underneath the floor. At Olivetti-Underwood factory (1966 - 69) and the Paul Mellon Center (1969 - 74), the piping and duct works that have been concealed are exposed and are made of costly materials such as stainless steel. Although it is uncertain whether Piano's distinctive style of allocating space by its function (as exemplified by the Pompidou Center and other structures) is derived from Louis Kahn or if Piano's presence influenced the works of Kahn in his later years, it is certainly true that notions of nature and structure were transmitted from Kahn to Piano. A tale about the erection of the Menyl Collection Museum (1981 - 86) proves this point. Kahn initially received the commission for this museum in 1973, but because he died in 1974 before he could complete the design, Piano took over the project and redesigned everything. Piano himself studied elements of the Kimbell Art Museum (1966 - 72) as the point of reference, and some elements of his art museum (i.e. considerations of the natural environment and location, and his brilliant way of using natural light) are commonly found in Louis Kahn's works, but the light of this museum is apparently different in nature from that of the Kimbell Art Museum, which notifies "beginning world." With the Kansai International Airport PTB, on the other hand, the relationship between the lightweight construction and natural light of the Menyl Collection Museum is homologicaly embodied despite the difference in scales. Since Piano was always inspired by natural light, thinking it the "nature of nature," he began a search for his own "primitive light."

Characteristics of Various Spaces
Piano and Okabe have been partners since the Pompidou Center was first designed. This PTB, jointly designed by Piano, an Italian, and Okabe, a Japanese, on an artificial island, gives us a strong impression of the "tradition and mobility" of the type or the architectural idiom — in a manner similar to the British architect Stirling's museum in Stuttgart, Germany — in a classically Italian style. As it were, this "traductibility" is a moment of correspondence between architectural nationality and internationality. We must specifically examine whether such styles truly do correspond. Piano and Okabe were mainly responsible for designing the large roof of the building that houses the departure lobby, the canyon (an open ceiling built in an evident sandwich structure, enabling vertical movement through the space), the wing floor and its roof.

In the large MTB space and the large truss, the designers eliminate the feeling of oppression superbly, by differentiating various details of the eaves, end walls and check-in counters, while Piano utilizes his unique skill in articulating the space and scale. However, the departure lobby for international flights does not allow passengers to see the runway. This presents a major problem. I must also point out that the airport's design was revised because of a reduced budget and several excellent plans selected during the bidding were not fully implemented. For example, plans to landscape along the wing and the MTB was either scrapped or minimized. The trees in the canyon look rather uncomfortable in a corner on the land side. A feeling of coordination is not present in the canyon because the space incorporates too many elements, including stairways. The numerous transparent handrails and partitions located throughout the PTB are positioned vertically. Therefore, the space creates an effect of confusion, diminishing the feeling of openness the designer originally intended. This is particularly evident in the canyon. In order to eliminate reflections, these objects should have been angled slightly, as is usually done in museums and other buildings. The elimination of top lights in the MTB truss makes it impossible to see the sky or the aircraft overhead. This presents another major problem. Furthermore, the domestic lobby and the international arrival lobby are laid out as one gigantic, uniform space. Here, we see little evidence of Piano's concepts of varied details or the articulation of scales.

The lib of the wing inclines toward the building center, locates 16.4 kilometers underground. All of the parts are standardized into the same dimensions by keeping the inclination within the range of construction deviation. The chairs come in a wide range of colors and are separated into different zones. However, the fact that these chairs are arranged in the same direction and in the same order throughout the lengthy wing with safety and functionality taken into consideration, detracts from the attractiveness of

術館(1981—86)の計画がそのことを象徴的に物語っている．この計画は当初(1973)，カーンに委嘱されたが計画の途中でカーンが死去したため(1974)，ピアノがすべて設計し直した．ピアノ自身，カーンのキンベル美術館(1966—72)を参照していたためか，自然環境や場所性についての配慮や自然光の見事な取り入れ方などはカーンと共通するものがあるが，「原初の世界」を告知するキンベル美術館の光とは異質のものである．しかしこのメニルコレクション美術館で展開されている軽快な構造と光の関係性は，ＰＴＢにおいてもスケールの相異にも拘らず相同的に具体化されている．ピアノは「自然の本性」としての光に照らされて以来，「原初の光」を求める旅に出たのかもしれない．

諸空間の特性
ピアノと岡部はポンピドーセンター以来，20年近くパートナー関係にある．イタリア人のピアノが日本の人工島に日本人の岡部と計画したこのＰＴＢは，イギリスのスターリングがドイツのシュツットガルトの美術館をイタリアの古典言語で構成したのと同様に，類型のあるいは建築的イディオム(固有語)の「伝承と移動」を強く印象づける．このいわば「翻訳可能性」は建築的な民族性と国際性の交感の契機である．そうした交感が成功しているかどうかを具体的に検討しなければならない．ピアノと岡部が担当したのは主にＭＴＢの出発ロビーを含む大屋根，キャニオン(サンドイッチ構造を明示し上下の移動を可能にする吹き抜け)，ウィングのフロアと屋根などである．

ＭＴＢの大空間や大トラスにおいては，ヒューマンスケールのディテール(庇やエンドウォール，チェックイン・カウンターなどのディテール)の差異化によって威圧感は見事に回避され，ピアノ特有のスケールの分節がもたらされている．しかし国際線の出発ロビーからは直接滑走路が見えないことは大きな問題だろう．また予算縮小などのため設計が変更され，コンペ当選案の幾つかの良さが弱められたことも指摘しなければならない．例えばウィング及びＭＴＢの緑が削減あるいは縮小された．キャニオンの樹木もランドサイドの端部ですまなそうに佇んでいる．キャニオンは階段など余りにも多くの要素が突出していて一体感が弱められている．ＰＴＢ全体の無数の透明な手摺やパーティションは，床面に垂直に立てられているために，その設計意図に反して様々な光景が乱反射し透明感を弱めている．キャニオン部分は特にそれが顕著であり，大空間そのものを不透明なものにしている．美術館などで工夫されるように斜めに立てて反射を避ける必要があっただろう．ＭＴＢのトラス部分のトップライトがなくなったことで，空や飛行機が感知できないのも大きな問題である．また国内線ロビーや国際線到着ロビーは巨大な均質空間になっており，ディテールの多様性や空間のスケールの分節というピアノのコンセプトに対する配慮はここではほとんど見い出せない．

ウィング部分については，リブは地下16.4キロに眠る中心に向かって傾斜され，あらゆるパーツの傾きを施工誤差の範囲内に収めることによって同一寸法で規格化している．数多くの椅子は色彩豊かにゾーニングされているが，安全性や機能性を考慮した結果とはいえ，長大なウィング全体にわたって画一的に同一方向に同一の秩序で並べられている様は，ディテールの多様性が巨大スケールを和らげていることとは異なり，ウィングそのものの内部空間の魅力を弱めている．しかし旅客にとって，これから乗り込もうとする飛行機を，陸側の風景，ほんの少し前に渡ってきた橋や青々とした海，そしてこれから飛び立とうとする滑走路を背景にしながら広々と見渡せることは，日本の建築の特性である内外空間の連続性を強く感じさせるに違いない．管制塔からの視認領域に基づく建築可能な領域の限界の中で決定された9万平方メートルもの屋根を覆う同一規格のステンレスパネルは，管制塔からの視界で過度に輝かないように表面に特殊仕上げが施されている．その淡い光り方や横に連なる鱗状の模様は，奈良や京都の寺院の甍や町屋の瓦屋根の連なりを想起させる．基本構想に従った結果とはいえ，何の障害もなく快いテーパーがかかったウィングの長大なスケールは，平行する滑走路に着陸したりそこから離陸する飛行機のスピードに照合されたかのような効果をもつだろう．高速道路の車のスピードとの照応がコンセプトにされたパリのベルシーのショッピング・センターの計画を容易に想起させる．

空港全体を明確なデザイン理念をもって統括する者がいないために(ピアノと岡部はＰＴＢのみに関与した)，管制塔や，ＭＴＢの中心軸を構成する駅やホテルは，魅力的な固有性を持っていないばかりでなく，複合的な都市的統一性をも構成し

the wing's interior space, while the variety of detail is intended to tone down the gigantic scale. Nonetheless, passengers will have an excellent view of the airplane they are about to board, with the island, the bridge over which they recently crossed, the sea and the runway in the background. This gives a strong sense of continuity between the interior and exterior spaces, which characterizes Japanese architecture. The stainless steel panels covering the 90,000-square-meter roof, which have a uniform appearance and which reach architectural limit in terms of visibility from the control tower, are specially treated so they do not create excessive reflections in the range of the control tower. The subdued light reflected from the panels and the overlapping pattern remind us of the pattern of the roof tiles of temples and the homes of townspeople in Nara or Kyoto. The scale of the lengthy, smoothly tapered wing will give an impression of speed that parallels the landing and take-off of airplanes, despite being an integral part of the basic planning process. This is reminiscent of the architectural style employed in the Shopping Center Bercy II, that was designed to coordinate with speeding cars on the highway.

Because the total project of this airport lacks a clear total designer (Piano and Okabe were only in charge of the design of the PTB), the train station and the hotel, which form the main axis of the MTB, as well as the control tower have no singular, unique attraction. Nor do they have a coordinated urbanized integration. Furthermore, the groups of buildings on either side of the MTB, which house various airlines, as well as airport and customs offices separate from the MTB, obstruct visibility from the end walls. Locating these buildings a little further away from their current sites and landscaping the area would not only allow the light and greenery to be seen from the MTB's interior, but would also further enhance the MTB's characteristics as a "figure" of Prägnanz (excellent forms) surrounded by nature. The color chosen by the workshop for the control tower and the accessory buildings is a light gray. In terms of materials, structure and details, the buildings are not much different than the large number of stations, hotels and office buildings found throughout the country. The contrast between the PTB and these buildings is quite evident. The artery into the PTB, particularly the area between the train station and MTB, is too commonplace architecturally — it is difficult to call the area an urbanized space. Those who come to the international departure lobby by car may miss seeing it. But is there any justifiable reason for forcing air passengers to feel as if they are passing under highways that crisscross the city of Osaka? This reveals the limits of the entire project — priority was given to the functions of the civil engineering work and only the architectural design of the PTB was selected through competition as a face for the airport. Ironically, this fact reveals to travelers from around the world the standard of Japanese urban design.

More about Traveling

Traveling is not only a means of separation, but it also enables new forms of participation for travelers. Once the airplane takes off, we feel that we have a common destiny with our fellow passengers. Traveling sharpens our sensitivity, and our heightened awareness causes us to notice not only the strangers around us, but also such things as chairs and glasses, and to memorize them. At the MTB and the wing, the overall image of the space, including the fragmented space and the architectural details, conveys the feeling that it co-exists with the occupants. This impression will be collectively stored as an individual memory and disseminated as the collective memory of the groups of people who temporarily share this place.

Observations about space when traveling are followed by observations about time. Foreign travel takes us back to what we left behind: our origin, the origin of the group to which we belong, our soul and our past. During our travels, we find a thread leading to what is buried in the depths of our memory. The essentially locational characteristic of airports is evidenced by the fact that airports provide us with an opportunity to look at ourselves objectively in relation to others or to other objects, with synchronic visions and diachronic thoughts. It may not be appropriate to examine the PTB space in search of what we feel at Le Corbusier's Chapel at Ronchamp or what he experienced at St. Sofija and the Parthenon — experiences that guided Le Corbusier for the rest of his life after he returned from the journey to the Orient (Le Voyage d'Orient). However, the PTB signifies traveling itself in that it is attractive, and at the same time marks a historic point in architecture: another milestone in the experience of Piano, and a beginning of a correspondence of architectural nationalities between Japan and Europe, including Piano's country, Italy. There is no doubt that the PTB, more than any other airport, will encourage exchanges among foreigners and cause "changes" resulting in the "production of differences", thereby serving as a gateway to a different world.

Kimbell Art Museum by Kahn
カーンのキンベル美術館　(撮影：岩田尚樹)

Teiji Matsumasa is a research worker and an assistant to professor of Osaka University, Faculty of Technology.

松政貞治：大阪大学工学部環境工学科助手

The New Atlantis
by Thomas Fisher

ニュー・アトランティス
トーマス・フィッシャー

The new Kansai Airport in Osaka Bay is already a landmark. The huge, man-made island on which the airport stands demonstrates the power of civil engineering to create an artificial landscape, a kind of second nature. Likewise, the Kansai Airport's terminal, designed by Renzo Piano Building Workshop in association with Noriaki Okabe, reveals the ability of its architects, engineers, and contractors to construct what is, in effect, a miniature city under one roof. The 1.7 km long terminal has connected office buildings, interior shuttle trains, attached parking garages, elevated highways, a sprawling commercial sector, and adjacent maintenance facilities that are like pieces of a city displaced from the mainland and recombined into a more perfect form.

The conjunction of nature and technology in this project, something that characterizes much of Piano's work, raises some important questions. Is a technologically derived nature, a created island such as Kansai Airport, any less natural than the "real" thing? Does it mean anything anymore to talk about "real nature" when so much of the environment in which we live and experience has been altered through technology? Or, put another way, has technology become the new nature, providing the context and resource for human actions? And what are the social, political, and psychological implications of this merging of the natural and the technological?

A key to answering such questions lies in another island off the coast of Japan, an island that, although it is fictional, is not unlike that of the airport. Sometime between the years 1614 and 1617, the English philosopher and essayist, Francis Bacon, wrote *The New Atlantis*, a fable about European explorers who come upon an island called Bensalem in a "South Sea," near Japan. Bacon describes the people of this imaginary island living comfortably because of their pursuit of science and development of technology. The architecture of the island is mostly designed with science in mind: there is a tall tower for observing the skies and heavens, large glass-walled buildings in which animals and plants are kept for study, and a "stranger's house" in which the wayward explorers are indoctrinated into the benefits of life in this technological utopia.

There is a superficial resemblance between Bensalem and Kansai Airport. Both operate with an efficiency and orderliness unlike that of the mainland and both provide for people's needs with an array of sophisticated technology. Both also have physical traits in common, including a high observation tower in which to study the skies and a great glass-walled building filled with people and plants. Even the giant wave-like form of the Kansai Airport's terminal brings to mind the inundation that destroyed the mythical civilization of Atlantis, whose greatness Bacon thought we could recreate through the pursuit of scientific knowledge.

But beneath this resemblance lies a more profound connection, which may shed some light on the questions raised above. One aspect of life in Bensalem, for example, that Bacon evades is politics, leaving the reader to wonder what sort of political system is needed to operate a technological society. The Kansai Airport suggests one answer. While it has the population and size of a small city, the terminal operates like a big machine, processing passengers, moving aircraft, providing for staff, all of which requires a high degree of security, scrutiny, and control. We have come to accept, even to welcome, such measures in airports in order to ensure our safety. But we can begin to see, at Kansai Airport, that were it not just a place of passage, but a place of habitation, such control and scrutiny could become oppressive.

This may seem a tangential point, something not really related to this building, but that is not entirely true. For while this is a big building and

大阪湾に完成した関西国際空港はそれ自身がランドマークである。巨大な人工島に建つ空港施設は、ある種の第2の自然ともいうべき人工のランドスケープをつくり出したシビル・エンジニアリングの力を誇示している。このように岡部憲明を代表とした、レンゾ・ピアノ・ビルディング・ワークショップのチームの設計による関西国際空港ターミナルビルは、建築家、エンジニア、建設技術者がその力を発揮して、大きな1つの屋根の下にミニチュアの都市を出現させた。都市の構成要素である管理施設、鉄道駅、駐車施設、高架自動車道路、関連商業施設、整備施設などを本土からばらばらにもってきて、より完結した形態に再結合させたかのように、1.7kmに及ぶターミナルビルを中心に全体を配置している。

この計画における自然とテクノロジーの結合は、ピアノの作品の共通の特徴であるが、ある重要な問題を投げかける。関西国際空港のような人工島に技術的につくり出された自然は、本当の自然とどう違うのかという問題である。私たちが住む環境や経験するもののほとんどが技術によって大きく変遷してきた現代において、本当の自然といい続けることに意味があるのか、あるいはテクノロジーは人類にとってコンテキストや資源となる、新たな自然あるいは本質となり得るのか、と。

これらの疑問に答える鍵は、日本を少し離れた島、空港と似ていなくもない想像上の島にあるように思う。1614年から1617年にかけて、英国の哲学家であり随筆家であったフランシス・ベーコンが書いた「ニュー・アトランティス」は、日本に近い南海の小島である「ベンサレム」に偶然たどりついたヨーロッパの探検家たちの話である。この想像上の島の住民は、彼ら独自の科学的探究と技術開発によって快適に暮らしていると書かれている。島の建築は、心に描くものが科学的にデザインされており、大空や天国を眺める高い塔、動物も植物もその中で観察し得る大きなガラス張りの建物、心を閉ざした探検家たちにこの技術的なユートピアにおいて生活の利便について教える「異人館」などが建っている。

ベンサレムと関西国際空港は表面的によく似ている。両者ともそれまでの環境とは異なり、効率よく秩序正しく運用され、また高度な技術によって人々のニーズに応えている。両者とも大空を観察する高い塔や人々や植物でいっぱいのガラス張りの巨大な建物がある、という実際の特徴でも非常に共通点が多い。しかも、関西国際空港の大きな波のような形態は、洪水の氾濫で消滅した伝説上のアトランティス大陸の文明は、科学の力でもう一度創出することが可能だとベーコンが考えたことを想起させる。

こうした表面的な相似は、実は先述の大きな疑問にある回答を与え得る、もっと深い関連があるのだ。たとえば、ベンサレムの生活の一面で、ベーコンが巧みに回避して触れていないことに政治がある。この技術社会がどのような政治システムで維持されているかは読者の想像に任されている。この疑問には、関西国際空港が1つの解答を与えてくれる。ターミナルは1つの小さな都市程度の人口と規模を有している、なによりもまず、そ

れらのすべての高度な安全性や正確さ、制御性を確保した上で、旅客を移動させ、飛行機を運行し、スタッフを動かしている巨大な機械である。私たちは、自身の安全のために、空港のこうした特徴を認め、むしろ歓迎している。しかし、関西国際空港は、空港が単なる通過の場所でなく、人が住む場所としては、制御や秩序が重苦しいと感じる機会をつくった。

これらは、建物に直接関係しないことで、的外れだといわれるかもしれないが、実はそうではない。空港は大きな建物であるが、都市ではないが故に、スケールそのものが大きな要素となる。近代建築の中心教義の1つであり、しかもレンゾ・ピアノ・ビルディング・ワークショップが設計を通じて追求していることは、都市や建築や家具のデザインにも共通のデザイン原理である。この、デザインはスケールを超越するという仮定は、ル・コルビュジエやフランク・ロイド・ライトなどの建築家が彼らの建築論を都市のデザインに適用したときに判明したように、社会的、政治的には非常に悲惨なものになり得る。また、心理的に予期せぬ影響を起こす。オーヴ・アラップ＆パートナーズの故ピーターライスとの協同作業で生まれた関西国際空港の屋根の構造は、図面や模型では非常にエレガントである。しかし、実物を観察すると、特に上階のランドサイドのエントランス近くなどでは、この屋根はむしろ脅威に思われる。写真で見るかぎり、巨大なカーブを描くトラスは、ものすごい重量にたわんでいるようにも感じられるし、それを支持している大きな部材は、倒壊を防ぐのよう

not a small city, the politics of scale still enter into it. One of the central tenets of Modern architecture – and one that Renzo Piano Building Workshop clearly adheres to in much of its work – is that the same design principles obtain whether one is designing a city, a building, or a chair. This presumption that design transcends scale, however, can be disastrous socially and politically, as happened when architects such as Le Corbusier and Frank Lloyd Wright applied their architectural ideas to the design of cities. Likewise, it can have unexpected effects psychologically. The roof structure at Kansai Airport, which was worked out in conjunction with the late Peter Rice of Ove Arup & Partners, looks extremely elegant in drawings and models. But when you see it full scale and close up, as on the upper level near the landside entrance, the roof structure seems rather threatening: the enormous curving trusses look as if they are sagging under some tremendous weight, and the bulky support members appear somewhat precarious, leaning in toward each other as if to prevent the other from falling — at least, that is my impression from the photographs I have seen. While such psychological responses may seem irrational, they point out the danger of disregarding the effect of scale shifts. (More pragmatically, those responses suggest that when the scale of something is enlarged in a building, the distance between it and the viewer should increase. On the lower levels of the Kansai Airport's terminal, the trusses and supports do not seem nearly so threatening.)

In Bacon's Bensalem, the explorers were at first disoriented in the strange surroundings, which raises another issue relevant to Kansai Airport. In the terminal, there is a logical stacking of circulation systems, with international and domestic departures and arrivals careful – and cleverly – separated. The view of and movement between these various levels occurs primarily at the "canyon," a four-story well along the terminal's landside that is crisscrossed by bridges, escalators, and elevators. This vertical slice through the building was probably necessary to orient visitors; it certainly is a memorable and dramatic space. But I wonder if it is enough to prevent people from feeling lost, given the size and complexity of the terminal.

To achieve maximum flexibility and a minimum of obstruction to people's movement, the architects have created largely open floors with elements set among grids of columns. This free-plan approach was probably the right response to a program in which considerable flexibility was needed. But because of the size of the building, I can see some people feeling adrift amidst so much fluid space. Here, the analogy of the building as a small city might be of some use, since at this scale, traditional urban cues, such as streets, blocks, and plazas might help some people find their way more easily. Once again, what looks orderly on a drawn plan does not always look that way in real life, the effect of shifting scale that is particularly a problem in large, free-plan buildings.

A third scale-related issue has to do with the airports international context. Bacon's hope for a technological society was that differences among nations would no longer matter, that there would arise an international culture that would unite humankind. When one considers a project such as the Kansai Airport, it certainly seems as if Bacon's dream has materialized. Although meant to serve the population that lives in and around Osaka Bay, the airport an extension of a global network of air travel and a place of arrival and departure for passengers from around the world. This internationalism is evident in the derivation of the airport's design: Renzo Piano's firm, based in Italy, won the competition to design the terminal among an invited group of internationally known architects from several countries. And such globalism is reflected in the design of the terminal itself: its sleek tapered shape, its daring use of materials such as steel and glass, and its expressive (and in places oppressive) structure are all transcultural gestures, forms that are as universal as the airplanes on the tarmac.

This is to be expected. Airports, like convention centers, stadiums, and similar public facilities, have come to represent cities to the world and as such, their design has come to be measured by global standards. Kansai Airport represents Osaka well to the world. But I wonder if the architecture could not have made at least some reference to Osaka as a place. Piano has shown himself adept at creating technologically advanced forms that somehow seem related to a particular context. In his design for the DeMenil Museum in Houston, for example, he used a cladding whose scale and color effectively linked the building to the wood-sided houses that surrounded it. On this island in Osaka Bay, there is no immediate context, of course, and nothing easily referred to. Nevertheless, might some connection have been made beyond the rather abstract one of the tidal-wave roof?

Finally, there is the scale of technology itself to consider. In *The New Atlantis*, Bacon has the citizens of the island engaged in various small-scale empirical observations and experiments, a community of scholars and scientists that seems to fore-

---

に斜めに寄り集まって、いかにも不安定に思える。こうした心理的な反応はばかげているかもしれないが、スケールの転換による影響を無視した危険をも暗示している(実際、この感覚は、建物のどこかのスケールを拡大したときは、建物と見る人の距離を広げるべきということを示している。その証拠にキャニオンの下の方では、トラスやサポート材はそれほど近くなく、脅威にも感じない)．

ベーコンのベンサレムでは、探険家たちはこの風変わりな環境に当初は戸惑うが、同様のことが関西国際空港でもある．ターミナルビルは、論理的に人々の動線を多層に分けている．国際線・国内線、到着・出発と注意深く分離されている．これらの動線はターミナルのランドサイド側の4層吹き抜けの「キャニオン」空間で、ブリッジ、エスカレーター、エレベーターを介して一堂に集まる．こうした垂直方向の区画は、おそらく人々を有効に導くために必要な措置であろう．確かに、この吹き抜けは印象的でドラマチックな空間である．しかし、人々が道に迷わず、ターミナルの大きさや広さ、複雑さを認識するのに、この空間で充分かどうか、私には少し疑問である．

人々の動きに対する最大のフレキシビリティと最少の障害を計画上達成するために、建築家は柱の林立する空間のあちこちに、間仕切りのない広いオープンなスペースつくり出すのが常である．かなりのフレキシビリティを必要とする計画への対応としては、このフリープランという方法は適切であろう．しかし、これだけ建物が巨大になると、この大きな流動的空間では、人々は方向性を見失って漂流しているように感じるのではあるまいか．ここで小都市としての建物という考えが生きてくる．ストリート、1ブロック、広場といった伝統的な都市の中にある手がかりが、人々が自分の行くべき方向を見いだす手助けとなる．図面上に描かれたものがいかに秩序だっていようとも、実際にはそうなるとは限らないということである．ここに、大きなフリープランの建物に特有のスケールのシフトの問題がある．

第3のスケールに関する問題点は、国際空港であることに由来する．ベーコンの技術社会の理想は、それぞれの国による違いでなく、全人類を結びつける国際的な1つの文化を生み出すことであった．関西国際空港のような施設を計画する人間なら誰しも、ベーコンの夢が実現できる、と考えるだろう．大阪一帯に住む人々にとって空港の完成は、飛行機による世界中への旅行、あるいは世界中からの人々の往来によって、グローバルなネットワークの拡大を意味する．国際化が、空港のデザインの根本にあることは明らかである．イタリアを本拠とするレンゾ・ピアノ・ビルディング・ワークショップは、世界中の国際的に著名な指名建築家たちによるターミナルビルのデザインコンペを勝ち取った．したがって、こうしたグローバリズムが、ターミナルのデザインそのものに反映されている．滑らかなテイパーのついた形、スチールやガラスなどの大胆な材料の使い方、表情豊かな(ある意味では重苦しい)構造といった要素はすべて、滑走路の上の飛行機と同様にユニバーサルな、複合文化を象徴した表現であり、形態である．

予測されることだが、国際会議施設や競技場などの公共施設同様、空港施設は世界に向けてその街を代表するものであり、そのデザインもまたグローバルなスタンダードをもって考えられる．関西国際空港は世界に向けて大阪を代表している．しかし、この建築は大阪にあって、大阪らしさが全くないように思う．ピアノは独特のコンテキストに基づいた、技術的に非常に進んだ形態を生み出すことにかけては名人である．例えば、彼のヒューストンのメニル美術館のデザインでは、周辺のウッド・サイディングの住宅群に実に効果的にマッチする外装材のスケールや色彩を採用している．もちろん、大阪湾に浮かぶこの人工島では、直接的なコンテキストは存在しないし、容易に参考にできるものもない．それでもやはり、波のうねりのような屋根という抽象的な関連以上の関係づけはできなかったのであろうか．

最後に、テクノロジーそのもののスケールの問題がある．「ニューアトランティス」でベーコンは、さまざまな小規模の経験的な観察や実験に従事する島民、現在の大学の研究期間を予告するような学者や科学者のコミュニティを描いている．ピアノの組織もこれと同じような性格を有している．彼とそのスタッフはワークショップをもち、そこでは建物の材料や構成要素を実際に則して組み立ててみることで、性能や見え方を検討している．ベーコンの時代では、技術が発展していく唯一の方法は個人の小規模の実験であった．しかし、現代のように大企業が何億もの費用をかけて製品を開発する時代には、ピアノの事務所のやり方は、

shadow the modern research university. Piano's firm has much the same character. He and his staff have a workshop where mock-ups of building materials and components are constructed to test their performance and appearance. In Bacon's time, such small-scale experimentation by individuals was the only way technology was developed. But in our own era, when large-scale companies spend millions to develop products, the work done in Piano's workshop seems almost like a protest against this corporate control of invention. In that regard, Piano's methods recall those the Arts and Crafts movements of the late 19th Century, in which controlling technology and the means of its production was seen as critical to the empowerment of people and the beautification of the built environment.

The Kansai Airport, however, reveals the quixotic nature of that ideal. There is in this building, as in most of Piano's architecture, an attempt to show how the building works: the structure and mechanical systems, for example, are revealed as much as possible. Seeing such technology, however; does not mean the ordinary person can control or even necessarily understand it. At Kansai Airport, much of the equipment that makes the airport function – the baggage handling equipment, the airplane service vehicles, the control tower, the mechanical plant – must remain, for security reasons, invisible and beyond the public's access. Whether the appearance of access to and control of technology is better than no such appearance at all is a question we might ask. But we should not confuse the look of control with the actual lack of it.

Clearly, much of the technological world envisioned by Bacon in *The New Atlantis* has come to pass some 380 years later, amply evident in this real south-sea island off the coast of Japan. But we can see in the Kansai Airport that, for all of the promise of Bacon's utopia, it has turned out not to be as benign as he hoped. Life in a highly technological environment, such as the airport, can bring angst as well as comfort, confusion as well as clarity, alienation as well as amazement. Accordingly, we have generally embraced Bacon's utopia and yet kept it within bounds and somewhat apart from everyday life. The location of the airport provides a metaphor for that simultaneous attraction and repulsion: the island is tied to the mainland by a bridge and yet that single link also seems like a very stiff arm, keeping the airport at a distance.

One of the curious facts about *The New Atlantis* is that the tale remains unfinished. Bacon never tells us whether the explorers, who were so impressed by the achievement of the people of Bensalem, stayed on the island or returned to Europe. If the Kansai Airport represents a kind of modern-day Bensalem, then I would place bets on their return. This airport is an impressive achievement, destined to take its place among the major terminals of our time. But, for all of its formal power and technical brilliance, it is the sort of environment that one wants to experience, but not inhabit for too long. And for all of the inefficiency and disorder of life on the mainland, be that in Osaka or on some distant shore, it is just the sort of environment that everyone at Kansai Airport is eagerly boarding busses, trains, and planes for.

Thomas Fisher is the Editorial Director of Progressive Architecture magazine.

こうした大企業の新しい開発に対するコントロールへの抗議のように思える．ピアノの手法は，技術や生産方法の管理が，人々の可能性を拡大し，まわりの環境を美しくすることにつながらないと考えて起こった19世紀後半のアーツ・アンド・クラフツ運動を思い起こされる．

関西国際空港はしかしながら，ドン・キホーテ的夢想を現実化した．ピアノの他のほとんどの作品同様，ここでもいかに建物が機能しているかを構造システムも設備システムも含めて，最大限に見せている．しかし，こうした技術を見せることが，一般の人々がコントロールし，必然的にそれを理解するということにはつながらない．関西国際空港では，バゲージ・ハンドリング設備や航空機サービス用の乗り物，管制塔，設備プラントといった，空港を機能させている設備の多くは，安全性の面から，一般の人々からは見えないし，近づけないところにある．近づけたり技術の管理が見える方が，全く見えないよりいいのかどうか，ということも私たちが今後考えなければならない点である．しかし，目に見えるコントロールと，管理の欠如を混同してはならない．

ベーコンが「ニューアトランティス」で描いた技術社会の多くの事がらが，380年後に現実の大阪湾に浮かぶ島のの上で実証された．しかし，関西国際空港で私たちが見るように，ベーコンが彼のユートピアで描いた事がらの多くは，彼が望んだようにすばらしいものではなかったということが判明したともいえる．空港のような，高度に技術化の進んだ環境での生活は，快適さと同時に不安を，明快さと同時に混乱を，驚きと同時に疎外感をもたらす．したがって，一般的にはベーコンのユートピアを私たちは受け入れるが，自分たちの領域に入れつつ，毎日の生活からは少し距離をもたせているのだ．空港の立地は魅力と反発が共存することのメタファーである．人工島は連絡橋によって本土と連絡している．このたった1本の連結は，空港を離れたところに置いておくためにしっかりと腕を伸ばして緊結しているように見える．

「ニューアトランティス」の中で興味深いことは，話が未完で終わっていることである．ベーコンは，ベンサレムのさまざまな出来事に深い感銘を受けたこの探険家たちが，最終的に島に残ったのかヨーロッパに帰ったかを書いていない．関西国際空港が現代のベンサレムであるなら，私は絶対に，探険家たちはヨーロッパに帰った方に賭ける．空港は，現代の主要なターミナル施設としては抜きん出たものとして，たしかに非常に印象的な作品である．しかし，空港のさまざまな特徴や輝かしい技術の数々を計算に入れても，ここでは体験はしてみたいが，長く滞在したり住みたいとは思わない，という種類の環境である．大阪でもどこでも，本土の生活の不合理や無秩序にかかわらず，関西国際空港に到着した人々は，バスや電車や飛行機に乗り継いで我先にとそこに向かっていくという，そうした環境なのだ．

トーマス・フィッシャー：米国建築誌「プログレッシブ・アーキテクチュア編集局長

Down to the Sea I

海へ

Geographic and Geometric Creation

The passenger terminal building for the Kansai International Airport (KIA) has taken shape at an exceedingly rapid pace, based on the design concept by the Renzo Piano Building Workshop Paris chosen in an international competition held in 1988. Throughout the processes of creating the basic and final designs as well as in the actual construction process, the original design concept has been firmly maintained.

The KIA terminal design competition represented a very special stimulus to all those who participated. We were presented with an image of a manmade island (which in fact had not yet even been created at that point, bringing to mind Gaea, the Greek earth goddess and mother of the Titans, who created the land out of the chaos of the seas), which represented not only a geophysical symbol of the island nation of Japan, but the revolutionary achievements of technology through which human beings were about to redraw the map of the earth. The image of this virgin land aroused in us architects the excitement of a voyage to outer space and stirred our imaginations as we stood before an uncharted frontier. The yet-to-be-constructed island offered the ideal conditions in which the dream of flight so long cherished by human beings might truly be given free rein. We were guaranteed a veritable utopia in which to design a totally new kind of architecture. The strength of the stratigraphical and geographical architecture incorporated into the foundation of the airport island as a last resort was estimated.

The artificial island, built in the middle of Osaka Bay, is 5 kilometers from the shoreline, surrounded by waters 18 meters deep and covers an area 1.25 by 4.37 kilometers. In densely populated, mountainous Japan, it has been almost impossible to build airports that can function 24 hours a day without causing severe noise pollution for near by residents. That difficulty was what spurred the adventure of building on a man-made island in the middle of the sea. A Landsat satellite photograph of Wakasa Bay, Osaka Bay, Awaji Island, and Kii Peninsula shows clearly that in terms of geographic scale and topography, such an airport could only be built on such an artificial island. The strength of the stratigraphical and geographical architecture incorporated into the foundation of the airport island, the unknown earthwork, was estimated.
— *Noriaki Okabe*,
Abbreviated as N. O. hereinafter.

ジオグラフィとジオメトリーの生成
関西国際空港(KIA)旅客ターミナルビルは、1988年に実施された国際設計競技の優勝案(レンゾ・ピアノ・ビルディング・ワークショップ・パリ)のデザイン・コンセプトをベースとし、基本設計・実施設計のプロセスと建設過程を通して、コンペ原案のコンセプトを維持しつつ、構築実現へと向かう螺旋状の開発運動が行なわれた。ここでは、コンペの精神的導線と基本的なコンセプトの概要にまず触れたい。

旅客ターミナルビルのコンペは参加者たちに、エモーショナルな刺激を与えた。いまだに水の中にしか存在しなかった人工島(マンメイド・アイランド)のイメージは、カオスの海から生成しつつある万物の女神ガイア(大地)を想起させ、海に囲まれた日本という島を象徴する地勢的な記号、地球における新たな地図の誕生、テクノロジーの革命的軌跡を意味していた。処女地となるガイアは宇宙探険に似た興奮と、空白の大地に1本の線を引く開拓者の自由な想像力を喚起した。

見えない大地は人類が抱き続けた飛翔の夢を解放できるすばらしい条件を提示していた。私たちは新たなターミナル・デザインを展開するのにふさわしい、1つのユートピアの場を約束されたのである。

大阪湾の中央に現われる人工大地は、沿岸から約5km、水深18m、面積511ha(1.25km×4.37km)の規模である。山が多く人口密度が高い日本国土に、騒音公害を避けて24時間機能する空港を建設するのは至難の技である。こうした困難が逆に、海に囲まれた人工島の建設という冒険へと駆り立てたのだ。空港島を囲む若狭湾、大阪湾、淡路島、紀伊半島などをランドサットから撮影すると、その衛星画像に写し出された地理的スケールと特殊な地形条件は、島の建設がこの地域における唯一の解答だったことを示している。未知のアースワークともいえる空港島の基壇と一体化する地層的・地理的建築の力が予知された。

(岡部憲明、以下N.O.)

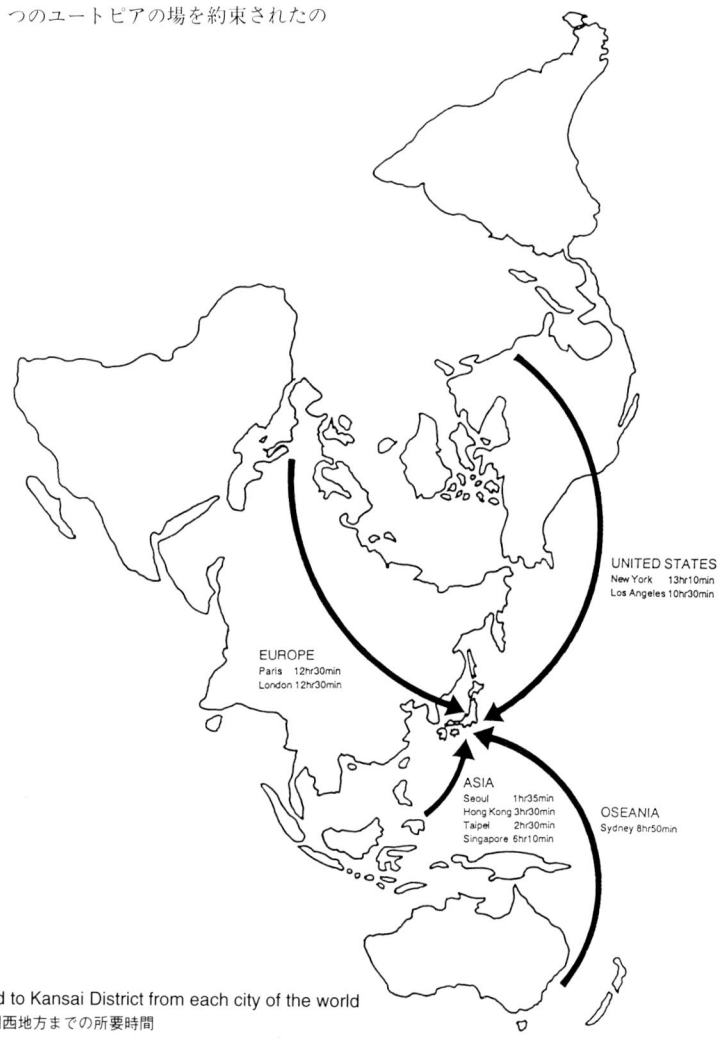

Time required to Kansai District from each city of the world
世界各地から関西地方までの所要時間

The Kansai district seen from landsat.　ランドサットから見た近畿地方

Convergence of Natural and Artificial Ecology

The more we are surrounded by the man-made, the more our aspirations return to nature. So, while the design embraces the image of an "integrated-circuit" island, the competition proposal itself called for the planting of trees and shrubs on the island in a fixed order. Looking again at a Landsat photo of the region's topography from the Japan Sea to the Pacific, we can see that most of the islands have inhabited coastlines on one side and wild shorelines on the other. In fact, this is the case with most islands throughout the world.

Because of the essentially technological nature of the airport island, the area that could be given over to natural landscaping was unavoidably limited. However, the more complete the "integrated-circuit" nature of the construction, the greater the rationale for creating a place where nature can be found on a small scale, growing and changing daily with the advance of the seasons, and offering the unforgettable repose of a remote mountain stream.

The Japanese landscape is a harmonious composite of many faces of nature, from the deep primeval forests that still stand on the nearby Kii Peninsula to the artistic landscaping epitomized in the gardens of Kyoto. Also, greenery is indispensable to establish a linkage with the other, tree-covered islands in the Inland Sea. A plan was drawn up for a series of planted areas in the more trafficked entry areas of the facility. The terminal building is located as a transitional territory between the human-centered, greenery-accented arrival area (or "landside") and the more detached, technology-centered operational side (or "airside"). This zone between the two realms is a station from which we embark from earth, with its wealth of life, into another dimension of time and space. —*N. O.*

原始と人工のエコロジー

人工であればあるほど，自然が希求されてくる．集積回路島というイメージを抱くと同時に，私たちはコンペ案の時から，島に一定の秩序をもった植栽を行なうことを提案していた．衛星からの写真で，日本海から太平洋に続く地勢図を見てみると，存在する多くの島には，居住地の海岸と反対側に自然の海岸が残されていることがわかる．一般に世界の多くの島の自然形成も同様の構成になっている．

空港島はテクノロジカルな本質的役割上，自然の占める面積は少なくならざるを得ない．だが完璧な集積回路島であればあるほど，季節とともに生長し日々表情を変える小さな自然の存在は，山の奥の清らかなせせらぎのような忘れがたい安らぎの場所となるはずだ．

日本の自然は，紀伊半島に象徴される深い原始林にはじまり，京都の庭園に表徴される芸術的人工植栽に至る自然の複合的な混成で成り立っている．瀬戸内海に浮かぶほかの島との関連性を持たせるためにも，自然は不可欠な要素であった．旅客がアクセスするランドサイド側に一連の植栽を施す計画を立てた．ターミナルビルは，小さな自然に恵まれたヒューマンなランドサイドから，テクノロジーが集積したクールなエアサイドへの通過領域として位置している．この境界ゾーンは，私たちが生命に満ちた地表次元から大気の時空間次元へと飛び立つための基地となる． (N.O.)

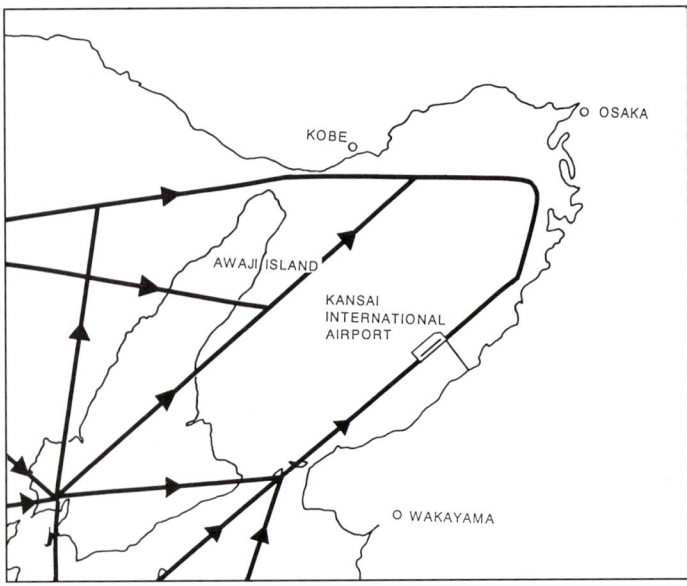

Locational simulation for airplane route.
航空機進入経路検討によるロケーションプラン

37

In regard to the landscape given by climate, Japan is distinguished by the changes in and the delicateness of climate. Both the fertility of changes in the four seasons peculiar to the Temperate Zones and a microclimate given by mountainous geography produce a world interwoven by delicate light and shade, by heat and wind, and by nature in this country.

The mountains of Kii — located near the Bay of Osaka and surrounded by myth and traditions — are in particularly rich depth of nature. The historical cities of Nara and Kyoto are integrated into such nature and still show the remaining tracks which incorporated the human sensitivity. In exchange, the largely citified Osaka and the coastal reclaimed belts show their images as economic machines on their surfaces and accordingly they have small nature at the frontage of houses and in city parks of a limited number. In comparison with the nature of mountains surrounding the Kansai District, the coast lines of Kansai seem as though they had almost lost nature on account of reclamation of the foreshore.

I hope that the "airport island", a hub in ocean, will link the bay areas as the center circulation of people, physical distribution, and information, and at the same time, it will also be position in the link of nature of the coastal areas as the base for resuscitation of nature. Generating green on the upheaving new earth, the "airport island" will have significance as the first step towards resuscitation of nature in the Kansai bay areas.　　　　　—*N. O.*

風土のもたらす景観において、日本はその変化と繊細さによって際立っている。温帯のもつ四季のうつりかわりの豊饒さと山がちな地形がもたらすミクロな気候が、この国土に微妙な光と影、熱と風、自然の織りなす世界を生み出している。大阪湾に近い、神話と伝統に彩られる紀伊の山々は、とりわけ深い自然の豊かさの中にある。奈良や京都の歴史都市はこうした自然と一体化し、人間の感性を組み込んでいった軌跡を今も残している。それにひきかえ、大都市化した大阪や沿岸の埋め立て地帯は、現代の経済のマシーンとしての姿を前面に出し、わずかな軒先の自然とかぎられた都市公園しかもっていない。関西を包囲する山々の自然に比して、埋め立てによって多くの海岸線はまるで自然を失ってしまったかにみえる。

海の中の拠点「空港島」が、人間と物流と情報の

Nature of Japanese mountains. 日本の山なみ

中心となってベイエリアをリンクさせると同時に，自然の再生の拠点としても沿岸の自然のリンクの中に位置することを望みたい．隆起する新たな大地「空港島」に緑を生成させることは，関西のベイエリアに自然を再生する一歩としても意味をもつだろう． (N.O.)

An "Integrated-Circuit" Island

The many complex functions required by an international airport now or in the future are to be contained on the island. Every square centimeter of the land, created at immense cost, will be utilized to its full potential. Both surface and underground space are densely and functionally arranged to avoid waste. These requirements suggest a metaphor of the island as an immense 511-hectare integrated circuit.

Like the creation of the landfill for the island, the construction of the airport terminal had to be accomplished within an extremely short period of time given the scale of the project. Not only did the arrangement of buildings have to be precision-designed to fit the available space but the construction work had to be timed according to a detailed schedule of synchronized planning. In other words, the construction of the KIA terminal building itself was planned and coordinated with the same care and precision required to create an integrated circuit.

The nightscape of this "integrated circuit" airport floating on the dark waters of the bay, as mysterious and intricate as the high-tech control panels of a spaceship, will surely excite the hopes and imaginations of people flying toward its runways in the same manner as a visit to a mysterious space station on some unknown planet, as described in the pages of a cyber-punk science fiction novel.

The construction of the island itself was directed by the Kansai International Airport Company (KIAC). Using the latest engineering technology, construction began in 1987 and was completed by the end of 1991. The soft floor of the bay, extending as much as 20 meters down from a depth of about 18 meters, was first solidified by sinking 1 million sand piles. The reclamation operation then began, during which filling added 18 meters from the sea floor to sea level and another 5 meters above sea level. This amazing project was carried out with formidable speed and resulted in an awesome earthwork that seemed to proclaim the advent of a new age.

—N. O.

Airport island as an airplane's eye view, along an approach.
© SKYFRONT
航空機進入経路から，航空機の目となって見る空港島
写真提供／スカイフロント株式会社

Aerial view of airport island with Kii mountains, Mar. 1993.
紀伊の山を背にした空港島全景(1993年3月).

集積回路アイランド

空港島には現在，また将来必要になる，多様で複雑な空港機能がぎっしりと詰めこまれている．高価な埋め立て地は，全面的にフルに生かさなければならない．表面と地下空間を，無駄なく機能的に親密に配置すること．これらの条件が，511haの島全体を，インテグレイティド・サーキット(集積回路)のように展開することを示唆した．

島の土木工事と同じように，空港ターミナルビルの建設も，その規模に比較して非常に限られた時間の中で進めていく必要がある．施設デザインを空間的に高密度に配置するばかりではなく，建設工事の時間的なプログラムも緻密に同時並行して進展させなければならない．つまりターミナルビルのプロジェクト自体が，集積回路島の中でも，最高密度の時空間のインテグレイティド・サーキットのように計画されるべき条件の下にあった．

真っ暗な海に浮かぶ集積回路空港の夜景は，光と輝きによる精密装置のような精緻さによって，舞い降りる人々にサイバーパンクの未知の宇宙基地との遭遇のような詩的な期待と感興を与えることができるだろう．

島の建設は関西国際空港株式会社(KIAC)の指揮のもとに，最新の土木技術を結集して1987年に開始，1991年末までに完成した．水深18mの海底に約20mの深さで堆積した軟弱層を100万本の砂杭を打つサンドパイル工法によってまず改良する．その後，海水面下18m，海水面上5mの埋め立てを行ない，トータル33mの厚さの土量が投下された．この気の遠くなるような工事は，恐るべきスピードで実現された．それは新たな時代の到来を思わせるアースワークの試みであった．　(N.O.)

Technological Island II

島──テクノロジーの地形

Completion of revetment. Reclamation work of the opposite shore is proceeded in order to shorten the connecting bridge.

The Kansai International Airport is an airport surrounded by sea built on a 511-hectare manmade island. In recent years, airports throughout the world have been reaching their upper limits of with regard to the frequency landings and take-offs as well as available time slots. This trend is the result of an increased volume in air cargo as well as other factors and is particularly true for Asian airport. Airports that serve as transit bases, such as the one in Frankfurt, are known as "hub airports." In the future, five to six hub airports that can host supersonic passenger airliners will be needed worldwide. Accordingly, South Korea and several other Asian countries have started constructing large-scale airports to serve as Asian hubs.

In Japan, the Kansai International Airport is the first airport to be operated around the clock. When it was launched in the fall of 1994 following the completion of the first phase of construction, it had only one runway that allowed for a total of some 160,000 landing and take-off operations per year. When all the planned construction is finished in the 21st century, however, the airport is expected to boast three runways and a combined area of 1,300 hectares.

The need for the Kansai International Airport was first discusses when the Osaka Airport was opened in Itami, Hyogo Prefecture. In 1987, nearly 30 years later, reclamation work for the airport island was started. The sea area subject to reclamation had a depth of 18 to 20 meters. It took 180 million cubic meters of sand and soil to fill up the ground to an average thickness of 33 meters. The first challenge was to reinforce the soft alluvial clay bed so that it could sustain the weight of massive soil. Because the alluvial clay layer was watery, it was bound to cause subsidence as water was squeezed out under the weight of the dumped soil. To cope with this situation, construction authorities used a method called "sand draining." In this method, sand piles that facilitate drainage were driven in to reduce drainage time as well as to solidify the footing. The total number of sand piles used for the "sand draining" method was approximately one million. Meanwhile, two years were spent on completing shore protection. Then, reclamation work began with sand and soil collected and shipped from three hilly points surrounding Osaka Bay (the Hannan district in Osaka Prefecture, the Kata district in Wakayama Prefecture, and Awaji Island in Hyogo Prefecture). The reclamation work was completed in December 1991.

— *Process Architecture*

Over leaf: Site sea, June, 1987
前頁：埋立が始まる前の現場（1987年6月）

護岸が完成したころ．連絡橋の距離を縮めるために対岸の埋立も並行して進む．（1989年8月）

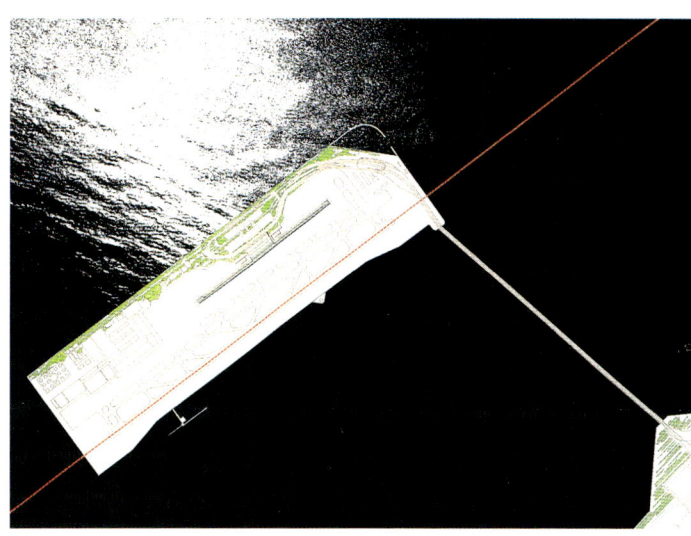

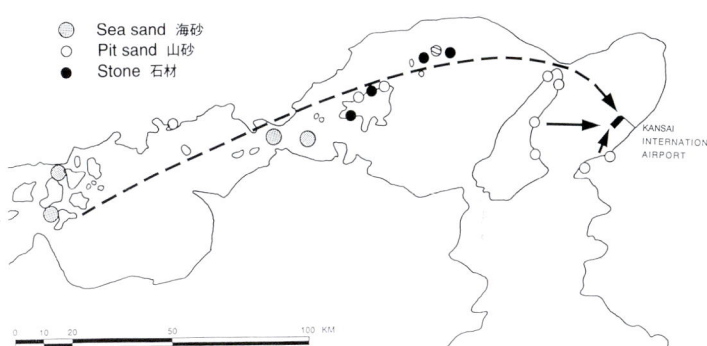

Sand, gravel, and stone materials supplying areas and transporting routes for reclamation of the airport island　空港島埋め立てのための土砂・石材の供給地と搬入経路

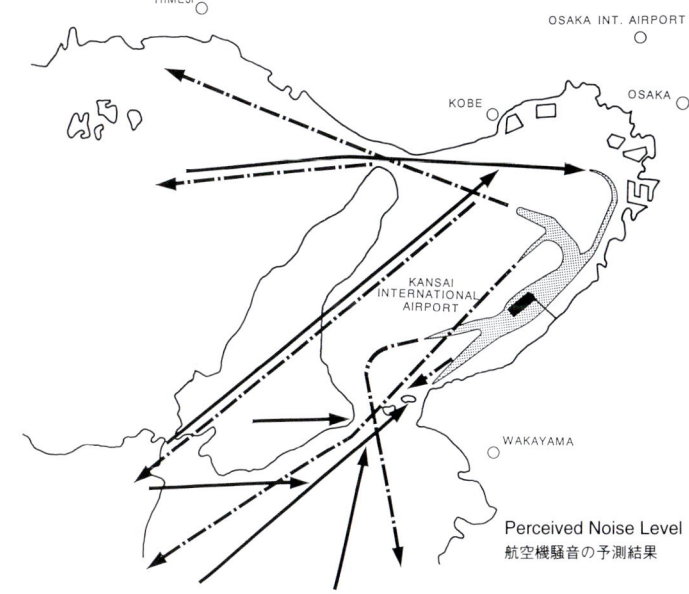

Perceived Noise Level
航空機騒音の予測結果

空港島の造成

関西国際空港は，511ヘクタールの人工島に建設された海上空港である．近年航空貨物の増大などによって，離着陸のできる時間とそれに比例した回数がパンク状態になっている空港が世界中にある．特に，それはアジアで顕著に見られる．現在のフランクフルトなどのように乗り継ぎの拠点となる空港をハブ(基幹)空港という．将来，超音速旅客機の乗り入れが可能なハブ空港が世界に5～6地点必要になるだろうということで，特にアジアを代表する拠点を自国にと，韓国をはじめ数か国が大規模空港建設に着手している．

関西国際空港が日本では，はじめての24時間空港となる．1994年秋，第1期工事が終了して開港するときには，滑走路1本で年間離着陸回数約16万回という規模ではあるが，21世紀を目指した全体構想では，総面積1,300ヘクタール，合計3本の滑走路ができ上がる．

伊丹にある大阪空港が開港するときから，すでに関西国際空港の必要性が語られていた．それから30年近くたった1987年に空港島の埋立工事がようやく始まった．現場の海域は深さ18～20メートルあり，計1億8,000万立方メートルの土砂を投入して厚さ33メートルの埋め立てが実現された．まず，軟弱な海底地盤の沖積粘土層をこの大量な土砂の重さに耐えられるように改良しなければならない．この沖積粘土層は水分を多く含んでいて，埋め立てによる重さによって，水分が抜けると地盤沈下をおこす．ここでは主としてサンドドレーン工法という，排水路となる砂杭を打ち込む方法を使って排水時間を短縮させ，地盤を締め固めた．サンドドレーンのための砂杭は100万本にものぼる．護岸は2年がかりで建設され，大阪湾を取り巻く3か所(大阪府の阪南地区，和歌山県の加太地区，兵庫県の淡路島地区)の丘陵地から土砂を輸送する埋め立てが始まり，1991年12月に完了した．

(文責／編集部)

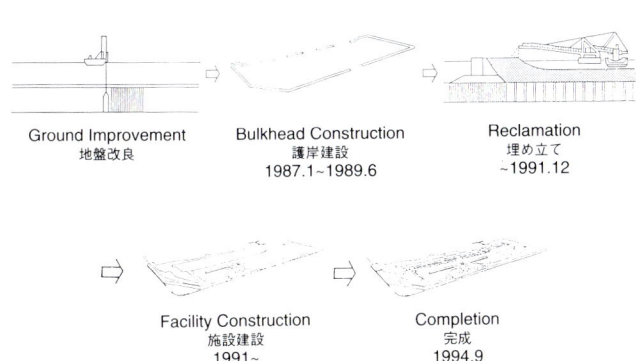
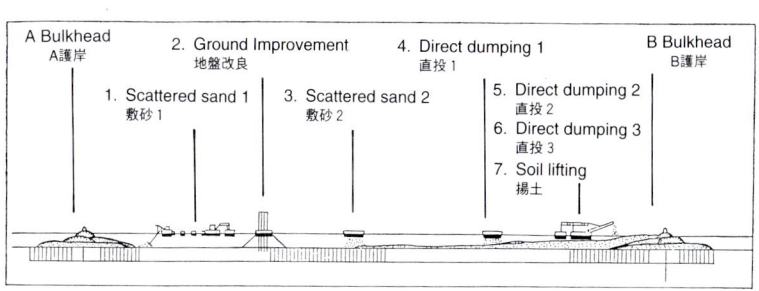

Process of construction of an airport island. 空港島建設工事の進め方

View of Kii peninshura from the connecting bridge. 連絡橋から半島を見る.

View of the airport island from the connecting bridge. 連絡橋から空港島を見る.

View of the PTB from the connecting bridge. 連絡橋から旅客ターミナルビルを見る.

Connecting bridge as an entrance to the airport. 空港への入口、連絡橋.

The airport island facilities
空港島の施設

1. Passenger Terminal Building
   旅客ターミナルビル
2. Runway 滑走路
3. Apron エプロン
4. International Cargo Terminal
   国際線貨物ターミナル
5. Domestic Cargo Terminal
   国内線貨物ターミナル
6. Maintenance Facility 整備施設
7. Supply & Disposal Zone 供給処理施設
8. Administrated Facility 管理施設
9. Railway Station / Parking
   鉄道駅・立体駐車場
10. Sea Access 海上アクセスターミナル
11. Access Bridge 連絡橋
12. Approach Light 進入灯
13. Oil Tanker Berth
    オイルタンカーバース
14. Aero Plaza (Hotel, Office and shops)
    エアロプラザ（ホテル・オフィス・商業施設棟）

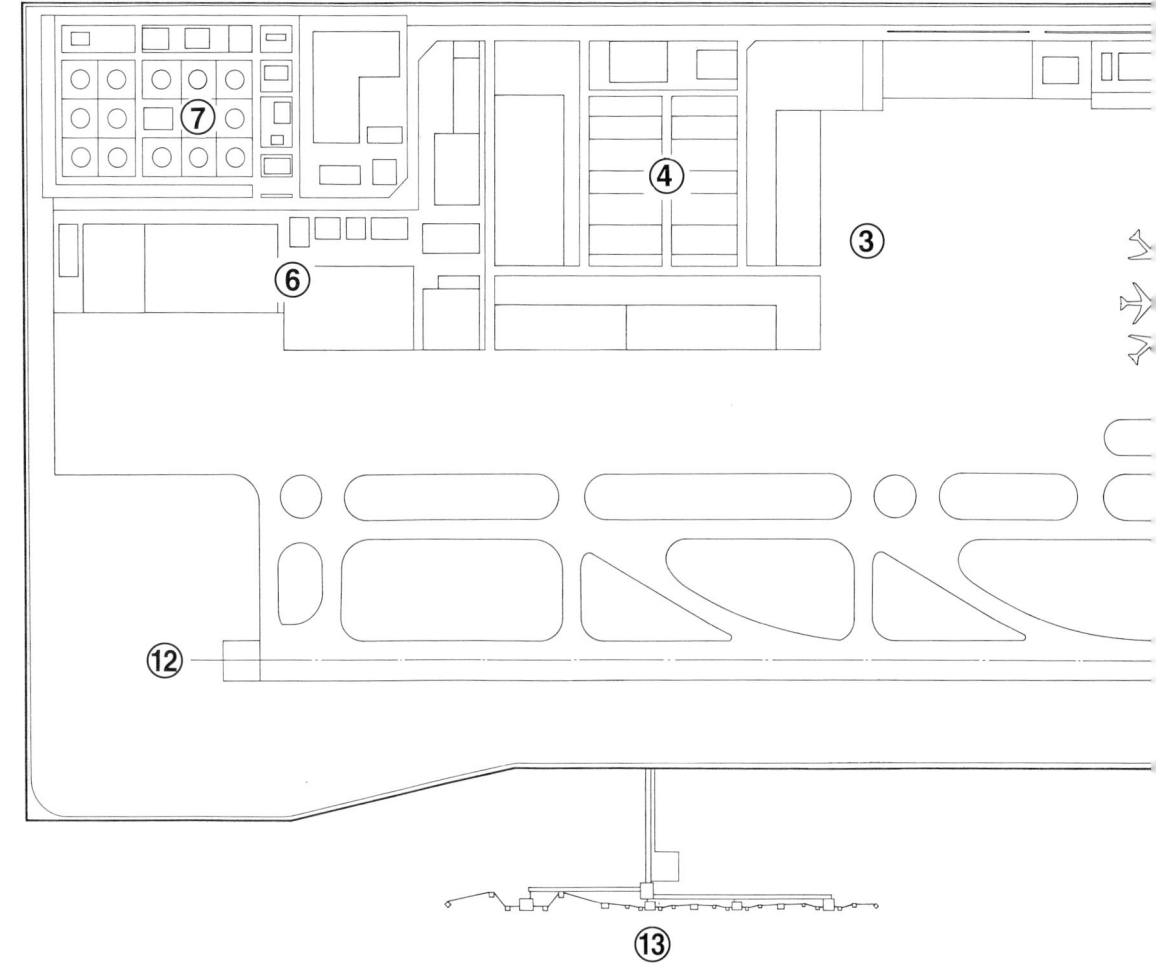

In the beginning of September 1988, I visited the site. The bulkhead work (levee) extending as long as 1 km was almost finished, and the "island without land" (an area of sea surrounded with bulkheads alone) was a gigantic earthwork with an upheaving frame of the island, which, however, made me imagine the image of airport island.

Renzo Piano, standing in front of this unprecedented site, proposed to introduce a vast green zone to the airport island. He entertained a plan to cover with green the whole landside behind the terminal facing the runways. On returning to Paris, we got cooperation of French landscape architect, Michel Desvigne, and put this plan into drawings. A planting method called "Scanner System" which arranges trees regularly and linearly was thought out. Without following the arrangement theory of buildings, we thought out to arrange trees by an independent system similar to a theory to plant trees on mountain side. Wishing to create a landside covered with green in a sharp physical contrast to the airside where airplanes are operated, we presented this important tree planting plan to the master plan for design competition. —*N. O.*

1988年9月初頭，現地を訪れる．1kmにわたる護岸工事がほぼ終わり，「陸地のない島」は，島のフレームが隆起する巨大なアースワーク，空港島の姿を想像させてくれた．この稀有な敷地を前にしてピアノは，空港島におもいきって緑を導入することを提案した．滑走路とターミナルビルをはさんで反対側のランドサイド一面を緑で満たす計画だ．パリに戻るとすぐ私たちは，フランス人のランドスケープアーキテクト，ミッシェル・デヴィーニュの協力を得てこの計画を図面化した．規則正しくリニアに樹木を並べる「スキャナーシステム」と名づけた植栽の方法が考えられた．建物の配置論理に追従せず，丘陵の植林の論理のように植栽を自立したシステムで配置することを考えた．航空機が稼働するエアサイドと対称的にグリーンでつつまれたランドサイドを創成したいと考え，コンペティションのマスタープランの中核に植栽計画を提示した．

(N.O.)

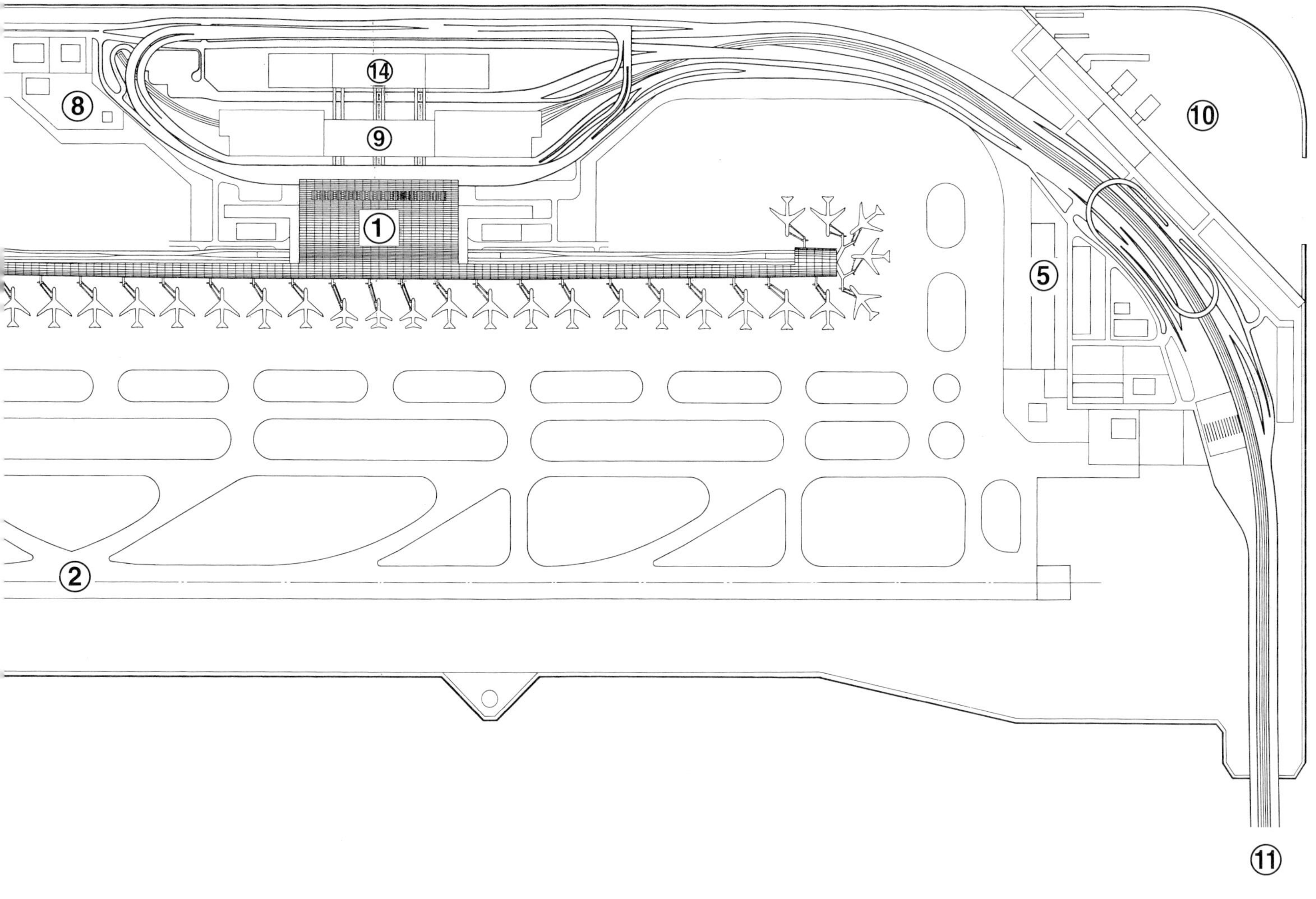

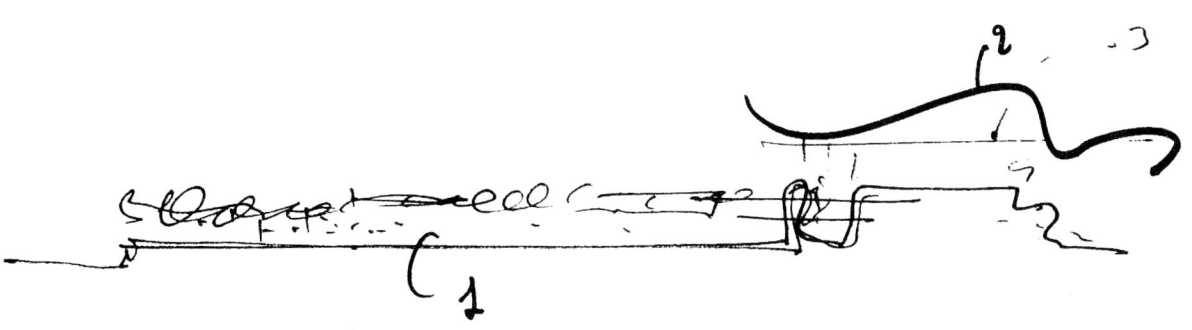

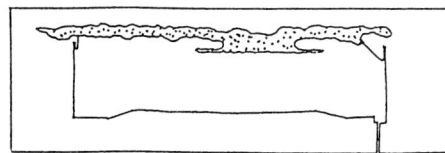

Landscape design concept at the competition, which has an image of a coast line of a verdant island.
コンペ時の景観コンセプト．緑豊かな島の，未踏の海岸線をイメージしている．

Scanner system plan for landscaping. ランドスケープのスキャナーシステム．

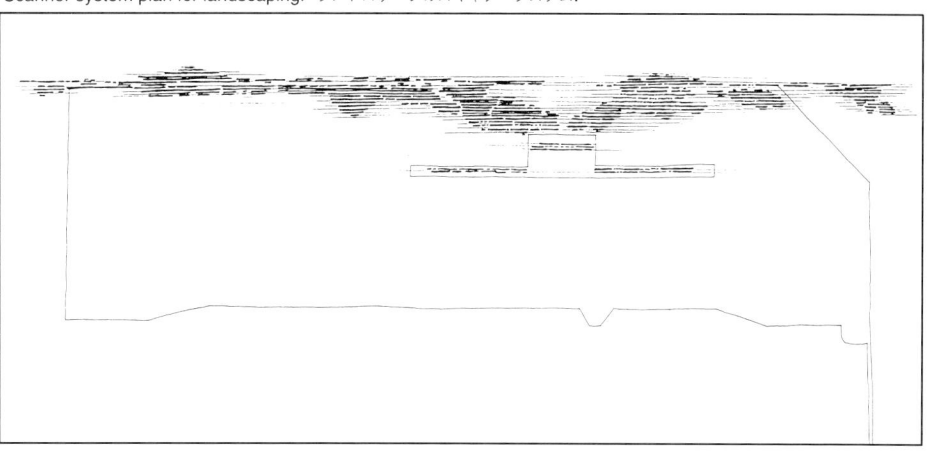

Photo by Kanji Hiwatashi　撮影：樋渡寛治

PTB – The Skin III
Passenger Terminal Building

旅客ターミナルビル――被覆

GEOMETRY
ジオメトリー

Geometry of the Roof

The design of the terminal building was conceived as creating a happy union of high technology, human sensibilities, and the natural environment, combining these elements into a new organic form. For airplane passengers gazing groundward, as well as for people crossing the connecting bridge or arriving by sea from the mainland, the first visual contact is with the island itself fellowed by the roofline of the terminal building,. It is clear that the key to the entire design of the terminal building — with its wings spreading 1.7 kilometers and 41 spots for parking aircraft — is its 90,000-square-meter expanse of roof.

To take advantage of the closely integrated layout of the site while dealing with the shape of the linear wings and pursuing our intention of developing the concept of direct boarding[1], we decided instantaneously on a special hybrid methodology combining geography and geometry for the architectural design of the new airport. Just as the manmade island was planned according to accurate geographic calculations, so the roof would be drawn geometrically from precise figures determined by computer analysis.

The roof shape is not the result of the direct application of fractal geometry but a natural shape formed by self-analogy indirectly influenced by the fascinating idea of fractals, as expressed by computer. Fractal geometry has made it possible for us to attain a new reading of nature, going beyond compositions following only the pure geometry of Plato and instead using solutions of natural fractal configurations — such as trees and lightning —that were once dismissed as manifestations of chaos. Architectural methods of the past either clung to the axiomatic pure forms or patterns of tradition or ventured into the wilds of dramatic expressionism. The revolutionary concepts of fractals have provided a fresh break-through in architectural concepts — freeing them from confining historical precedents. This paradoxically liberating new system of logic provided the energy that opened the way for a freer, more flexible application of geometry in the design of the terminal building. —*N. O.*

1. The layout plan and functional composition of the Program for the International Design Competition for the Kansai International Airport Passenger Terminal Building are based on Aeroports de Paris proposals.

ルーフの幾何学

ターミナルビルのデザインは，高度なテクノロジーと人間の感性と自然環境の表現が，幸せな交配の結果生み落とす，新たな生命的形態として考案されるべきものであった．飛行機の中から眺める人たちをはじめとして，連絡橋を渡ったり高速水中翼船で空港島に向かう人々にとって，空港を視覚的に決定するのはまず島であり，次にターミナルビルの屋根の形状である．41個のリニア駐機スポットのある1.7kmのウイングをもつ，面積9万㎡の広大な構築物をおおう屋根が，ターミナルビルのデザインの鍵となることは明らかだった．

サイトにたくみにインテグレイトしている配置計画の条件を生かし，リニアなウイングとダイレクト・ボーディングの構想を発展させることを前提条件*とした時，私たちは新空港の建築デザインにジオグラフィとジオメトリーの特殊な交配方法を使うことを即断した．人工島が正確な地理的計算によって決定したように，屋根もコンピューター解析による精密な数値からジオメトリック（幾何学的）に導き出されてくることになる．

ターミナルビルの屋根の形状はフラクタル幾何学を直接応用したものではないが，自己相似体として形づくられる自然の形態を，コンピューターが表現しえるというフラクタルの魅惑的な思考を間接的には背景にしている．フラクタルの思考は，私たちに自然の読み替えを可能にしてくれた．つまりプラトンに始まる純粋幾何学による構成を越えて，木や雷の形状といったこれまでカオスの範疇に入れられていた自然にも，フラクタルの形態論的解答を与えているからである．従来の建築作法は，定理となった純粋形態やパターンの様式へと，あるいはその反対にドラマティックな表現主義へと収斂されていきがちだった．フラクタルの革命的思考は，こうした歴史的に挾撃された建築的思考に新鮮な未来への突破口を開いてくれたように思える．この逆説的な解放の論理が，ターミナルビルのデザインのジオメトリーをより気楽でフレキシブルな表現へと開いていく動力になったのだ．

(N.O.)

*関西国際空港旅客ターミナルビル国際競技設計のプログラム（設計条件）における配置計画と機能構成は，パリ空港公団（ADP）による提案をもとにしている．

Other pioneering structures with graceful membrane-covered roofs, among them the white sail-like shells of the Sydney Opera House with its curves drawn free hand by Jorn Utzon, were ultimately adapted using accurate geometry and structures. But the curve of the KIA terminal building roof began with a geometrical approach calculated based on the Building Workshop Paris's experience with an earlier project, the Shopping Center Bercy II in Paris. The actual design process will be described in detail below, but Bercy II, which is shaped like slightly deflated airship that unexpectedly landed, required a whole new methodology of construction technology.
—N. O.

先駆的に実現された美しい構造と被覆をもつ屋根の代表的な建物には、白帆のようなシドニー・オペラハウスがあげられる。だがシドニー・オペラハウスの屋根が、ウッツォンによって直観的なフリーハンドで描かれ、後に正確なジオメトリーと構造に導かれたのとは異なり、ターミナルビルの屋根の流線形は、今回の設計競技に先行してビルディング・ワークショップ・パリが実現したショッピング・センター「ベルシー2」の経験を経て、かつ改良を加えた、計算されたジオメトリーのアプローチからスタートしている。ベルシー2はあたかも飛行船が都市に不時着したような不定形な形態を持つ建築で、その形態を建設にまで展開するには新たな方法論を必要とした。　　　　　(N.O.)

Bercy II the shopping center.
ショッピングセンター「ベルシー2」

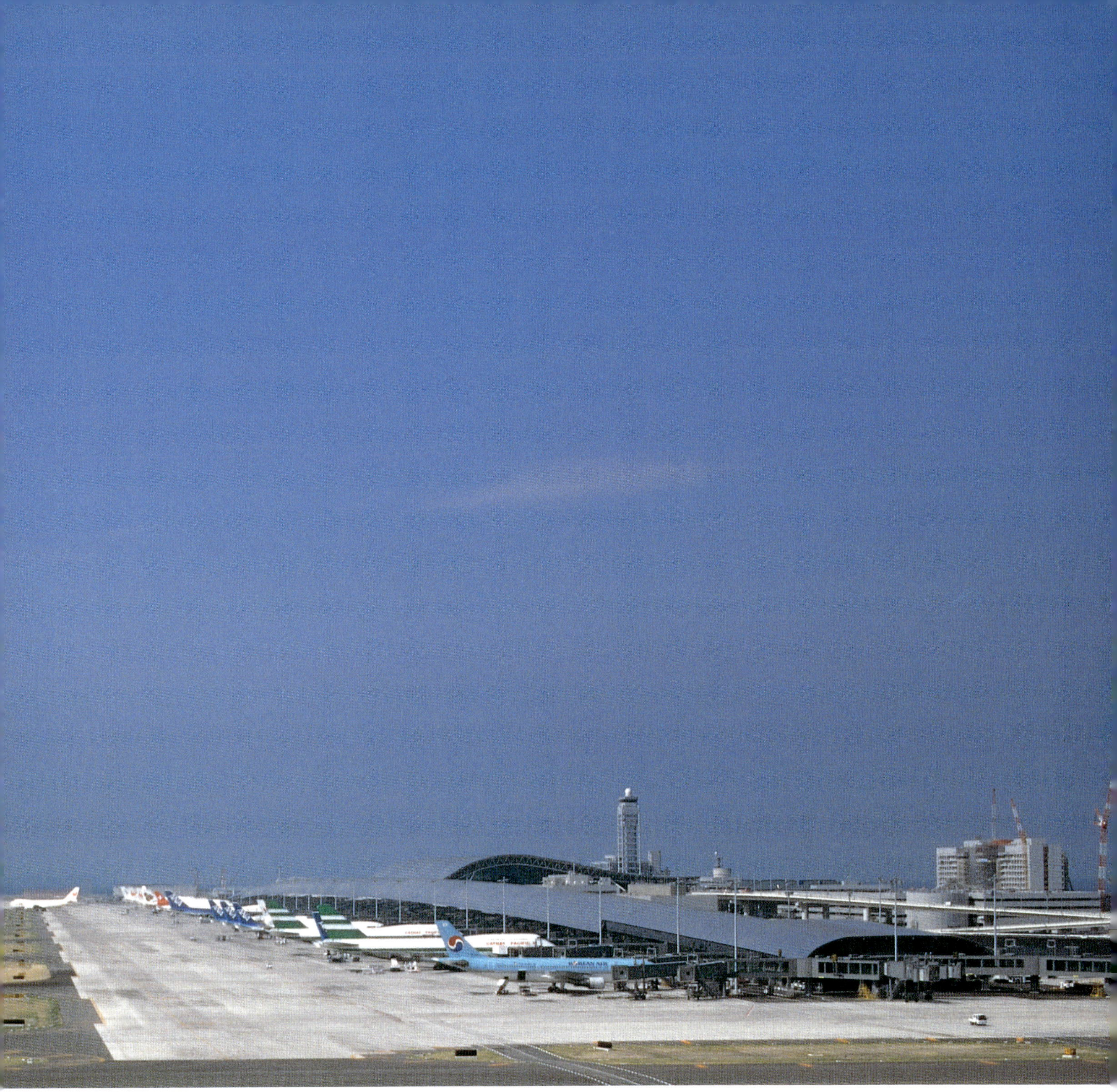

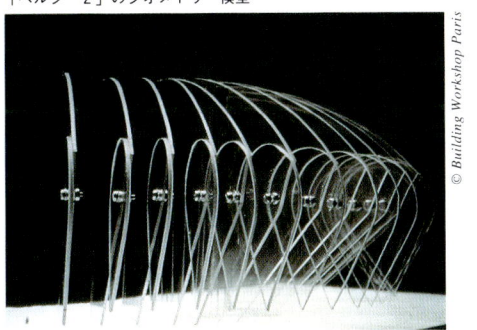

Geometrical model of Bercy II
「ベルシー２」のジオメトリー模型

© Building Workshop Paris

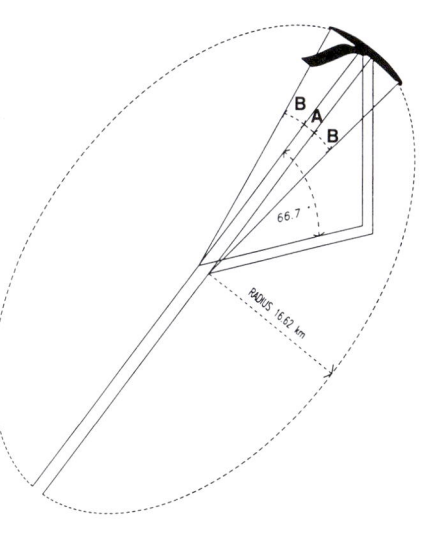

Basic Geometry　基本ジオメトリー

A. Parallel displacement of the MTB reference curve
　ＭＴＢ基準曲線の平行移動
B. Rotational displacement of the WING reference curve
　ウイング基準曲線の回転移動

B
A
B
66.7
RADIUS 16.62 km

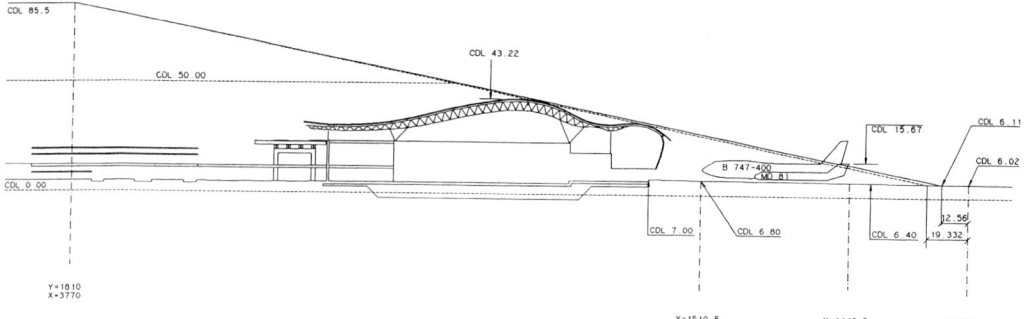

Summary of visibility limits
1. A. C. T.
2. General aviation height limit
3. Maximum height
4. Height of tail
5. Axis of control tower
6. Nose of Aircraft
7. Align tails of Aircraft
8. Axis of taxi lane
9. Control tower
10. Taxi way center

視認制限図

1. 管制基準高さ
2. 航空高さ制限
3. 最高の高さ
4. 機体後尾部の高さ
5. 管制塔中心軸
6. 機体先端位置
7. 機体後尾位置
8. 誘導路軸
9. 管制塔位置 (原設計)
10. 誘導路中心線

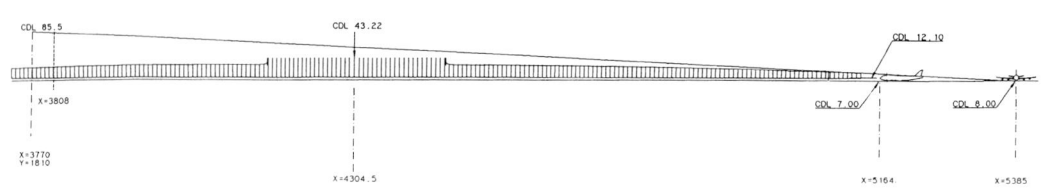

Parameters for the reference curve at the MTB
MTBでの基準曲線のパラメータ

1. Maximize cantilever, over hang and weather protection
2. Low point for rainwater collection
3. Maintain 4 meters minium between Floor level Four and the roof structure for fire clearance
4. Provide rise and fall for structural arch action benefits
5. General form to match macro air system profile
6. Satisfy control tower visibility limits
7. Locate "High Point" to optimize head room at the end of the wing Passerelle
8. Provide optimum curvature for structural gain in "Shell Action"
9. Over hang for solar protection to glazing
10. Control cantilever for structural and floor surface area

1. 片持ち梁，オーバーハング，耐候性保護材を最大にする
2. 雨水収集低地点
3. 耐火のための4階床レベルと屋根構造の間のクリアランス．最小4mは維持
4. 構造アーチを効果的にするために昇降の動きを設ける
5. マクロ空調に沿う一般形態
6. 管制塔の視認限界を満たす
7. ウイングエンド3階の端部の天上高を最適にするための最高地点
8. 「シェル構造」のための最適曲線を与える
9. グレージングの日照保護のための張り出し
10. 構造上また床面積のために片持ち部分を調整する

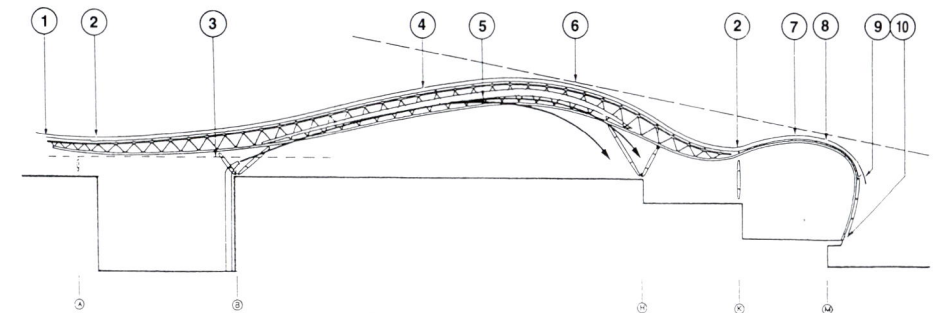

View and Volume from the Control Tower
The entire area of the airport island is supervised from a single, beacon-like control tower. It is the kind of full-surveillance system described by Michel Foucault, a tower that can guarantee a clear line of vision for the radar that monitors the planes as well as the human controllers watching over them; it is the key to safety for the aircraft and their human passengers. An unbendable rule of construction for the airport facilities was that no building other than the control tower be more than 45 meters high and, of course, that no obstacles be allowed in the area where the planes land and take off.

In order to attain a three-dimensional grasp of the scope of visibility from the control tower, we made a simple model at the time of the design competition. What became immediately clear was that the height and volume of the terminal building had to be markedly diminished toward the edges facing the wings in order to assure a clear line of vision.

The curves of the terminal had to be drawn through the space prescribed by these restrictions. The convergence of the gently curving roof, inspired by the metaphor of the glider and the dynamic perfection of the curves of Brancusi's "Bird in Space", was the inevitable result of these conditions. —*N. O.*

管制塔からの視認とボリューム
空港島全域をまるで灯台のように1つの管制塔がコントロールしている．いわばミシェル・フーコーの説いた一望監視システムそのものなのだが，航空機の動きを追うレーダーや視認といわれる管制官の目視を保障することが，航空機と人間の安全を守ることにつながる．したがって空港内施設においては，空からの規制は絶対遵守であり，45m以上の建物は管制塔以外には認められず，航空機の発着の空域は当然無障害とされた．

視認の航空制限範囲を立体的に把握するために，私たちはコンペの初期に簡単なモデルを作った．この時すぐに明確になったことは，ターミナルビルの形態がウイングのエッジに向かって，高さのボリュームを大きく減衰させていかねばならないことだった．

視認制限で切り取られた空の全域にはばたく曲線を描くこと．ゆるやかにカーブする屋根と，暗喩としてのグライダー，そしてブランクーシの『空間の中の鳥』の開かれた完結性は，こうして必然の出会いを遂げることになる． (N.O.)

The Governing Skin: From Geometry of the Skin to Structural Form

Utilizing a shell structure would require complex structural calculations, so at the time of the competition, we proposed a boomerang rib structure which approximates a shell. Peter Rice had promised to design the shells immediately if the plan was chosen in the competition. In any case, the main ribs were situated 7.2 meters apart with section contours and slope along the skin. The sections, computed on the basis of a composition of four circles, are repeated along a circumference line that radius is 16.4 kilometers. The wing consists of these ribs is shaped a tholoid curve, that height of wing are attenuated toward both wing ends. Naturally this meant that most groups of secondary members were repeated pieces of the same length. The pin joints supporting each rib from the floor are of slightly varied angles, but the other main members were designed to permit a standardized production process.

This process means that the geometry of the skin governs the structure itself. In the design, the geometry of the skin shapes that of the structure; when actual construction starts, the latter precedes the former and serves as the basic standard. A perfect conformity of skin and structure, which was not possible in Bercy II, was achieved in ideal form in the KIA terminal building because of its large scale.

Our geometric analysis began with the Building Workshop model and computer work. Based on the structural intersection points drawn by a large computer at OAP, a steel manufacturer drew up the final data for the geometry.

—*N. O.*

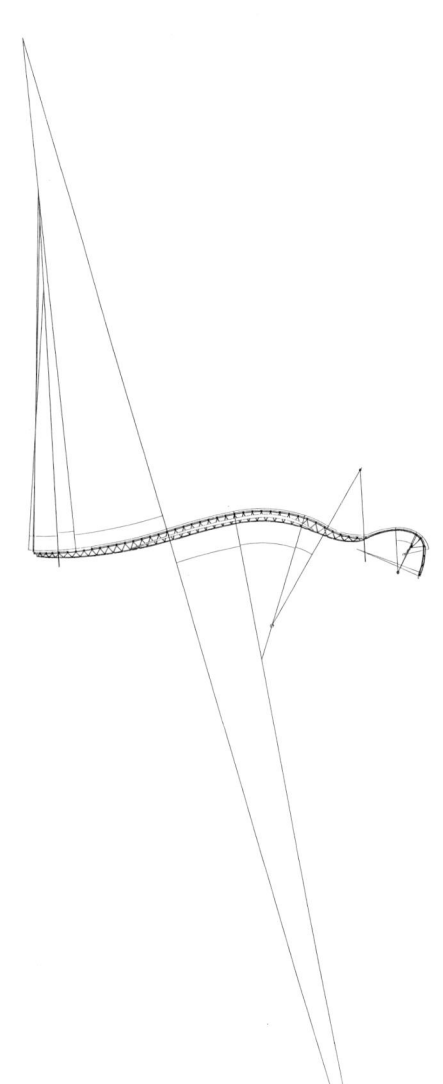

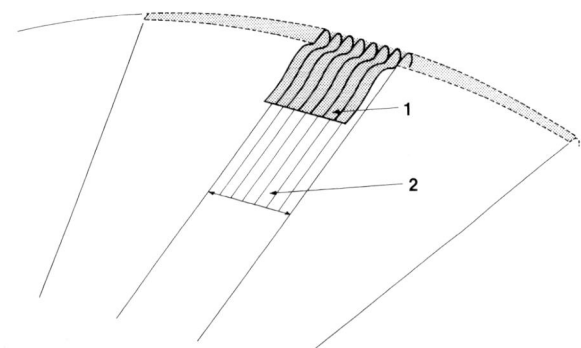

MTB Roof Cladding Geometory
ＭＴＢのルーフクラディングのジオメトリー

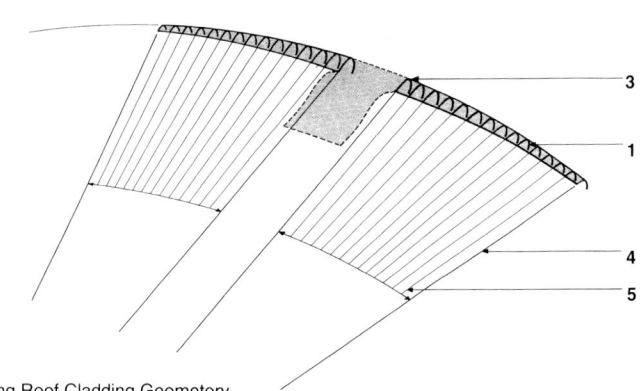

Wing Roof Cladding Geometory
ウイングのルーフクラディングのジオメトリー

1. Pieces with a constant width
   一定幅の一片
2. Parallel displacement of the two-dimensional reference curve
   2次元基準曲線の平行移動
3. Rotational displacement of the two-dimensional reference curve
   2次元基準曲線の回転移動
4. The turning radius is 16.4 km
   回転半径16.4 km
5. Equal rotating angle
   均等な回転角度

GENERATION OF TOROIDAL WINGS
EXTRUSION OF THE 2 DIMENSIONAL SECTION
GENERATION OF TOROIDAL WINGS
GENERATION OF TOROIDAL WINGS
GENERATION OF TOROIDAL WINGS
GENERATION OF TOROIDAL WINGS
GENERATION OF TOROIDAL WINGS

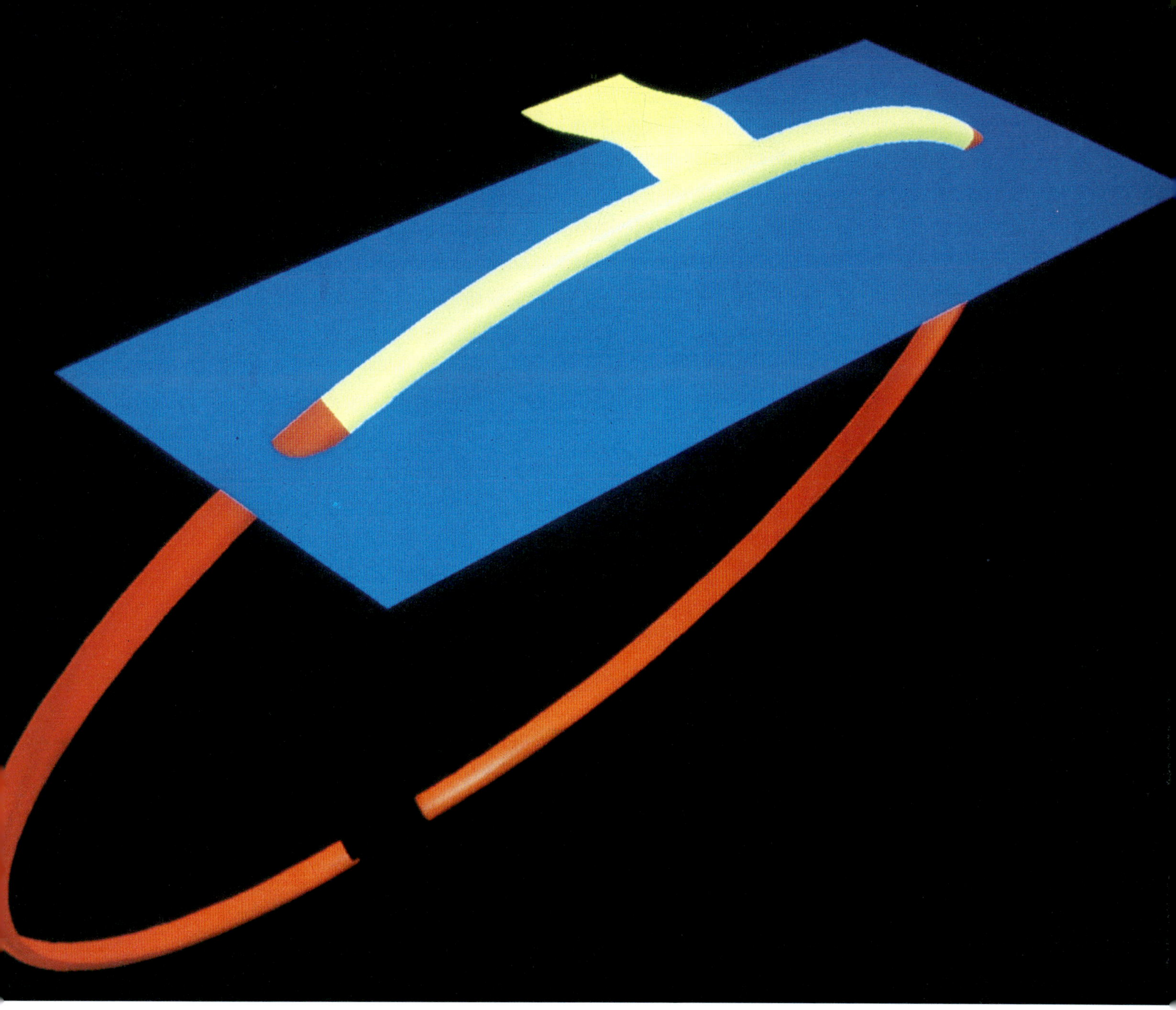

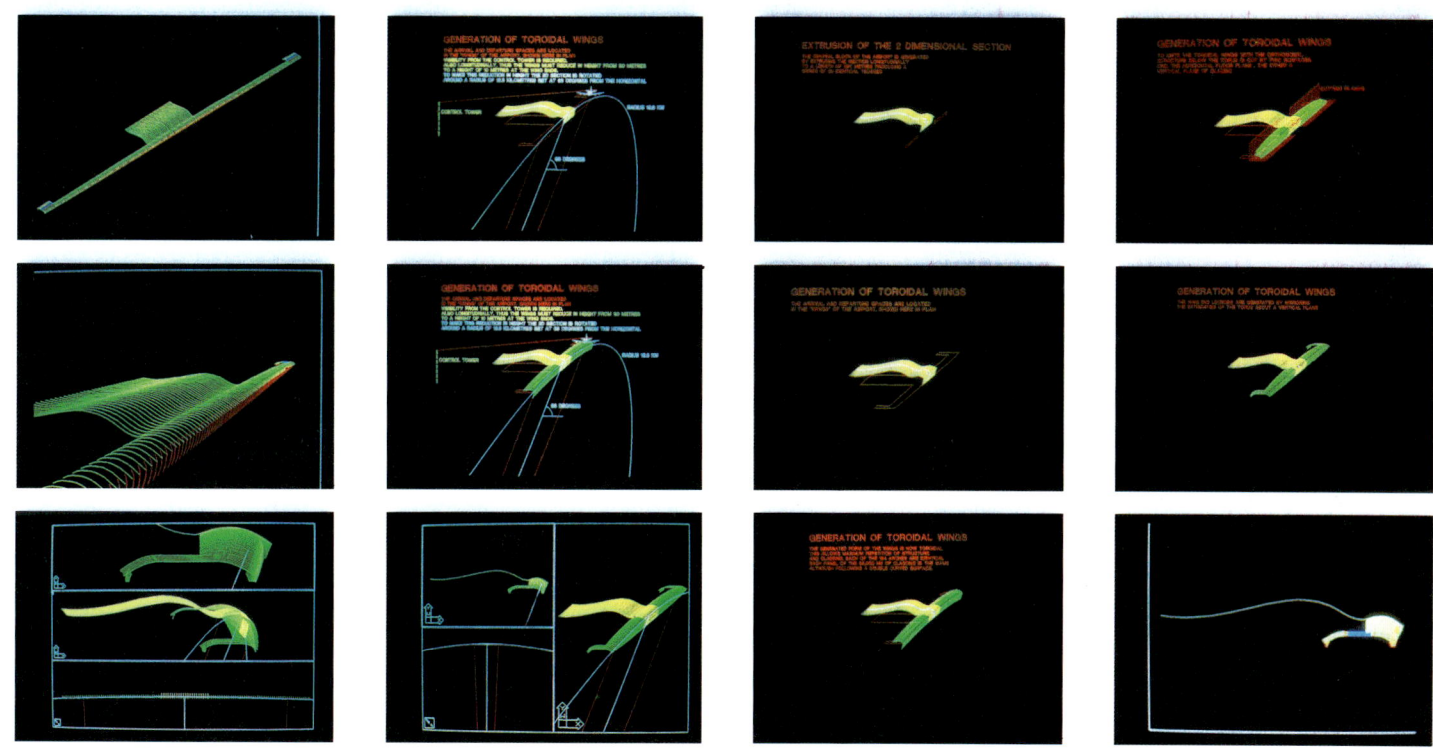

It is possible to see the geometrical shape just when you arrive by airplane.
飛行機で到着するとき、旅客ターミナルビルの幾何学的な形が特によくわかるであろう．

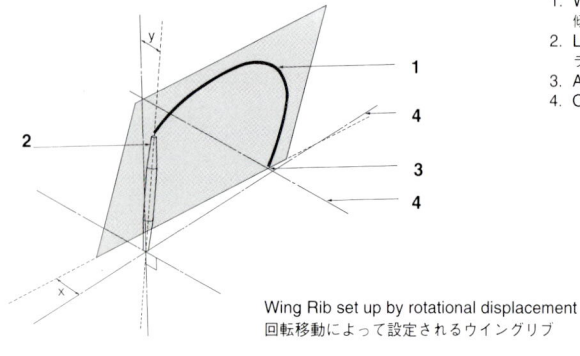

1. Wing Rib included in the inclined surface
   傾斜面に含まれるウイングリブ
2. Landside support
   ランドサイドの支持材
3. Airside contact エアサイドの接点
4. Orthogonal grid line 直交グリッドライン

Wing Rib set up by rotational displacement
回転移動によって設定されるウイングリブ

ROOF CLADDING
ルーフ・クラディング（屋根被覆）

Aerodynamic Roof

The designing of the roof of the main building began with a symmetric arch structure, but as we worked with the drawings, we kept on searching for a method to break away from the boredom of a functionally and structurally integrated arch. Any design oriented to structure has a strong tendency toward established and prescriptive forms. While we did not want the building to be categorized by standard styles, we were aware of the danger that the integrity of the whole might be lost in the breakaway process.

While we vacillated over the shape of the roof, we also faced the major problem of climate control for the 4th floor international departure lobby which lay directly under the roof 20 meters above the ground. Warm air rising toward the ceiling would cool, creating a rapidly descending cold-draft phenomenon, but we did not want to clutter the ceiling with the usual type of air ducts. We wanted to find a way to achieve both macro-scale climate control and micro-scale air conditioning.

The competition design was prepared by the Renzo Piano Building Workshop Paris, the winning team in the Kansai International Airport Terminal Building International Competition, in cooperation with Ove Arup and Partners (OAP), an engineering team in London. In response to the challenge of finding a way to overcome the cold-draft effect, OAP environmental engineering specialist Tom Barker came up with a splendid solution: channel a stream of air from one end. If the ceiling is shaped to accommodate this flow of air, the flow will travel for 80 meters, allowing macro environmental control to be achieved.

The airflow diagram sent in by engineer Tom Barker provided a major thrust forward in the development of the arch design. When a ceiling was drawn along the graceful lines of this diagram, it resulted in a fine asymmetrical arch, and OAP structural engineer Peter Rice immediately accepted the request to create the structural components for realizing this arch. In dealing with the problem of airflows the established shape of the structure was thus transformed and dissolved, bringing into being an entirely new shape. This convergence of elements took place in September 1988, only two months before the deadline for the design competition.

This aerodynamic roof was not conceived as an active mechanical form to resist the forces of air from without, as is an aircraft body, but as an interior-oriented architectural solution to the task of creating a climate hospitable to human beings. Placing top priority on climate control might be considered rather passive and overly modest as far as design methodology is concerned, but it represents an orientation we have always treasured in our approach to architecture. By placing input jets on the landside end and outlet vents at the airside end, the air current contours accelerate upward from landside, determining the curve of the ceiling. By flow originating at one end and terminating at the other, moreover, this airflow emphasizes the physical but invisible directionalism of human movement in the building.

—*N. O.*

Airside Elevation エアサイド立面図

Airside (runway side) view, Dec. 1993.
エアサイド（滑走路側）の外観．（1993年12月）

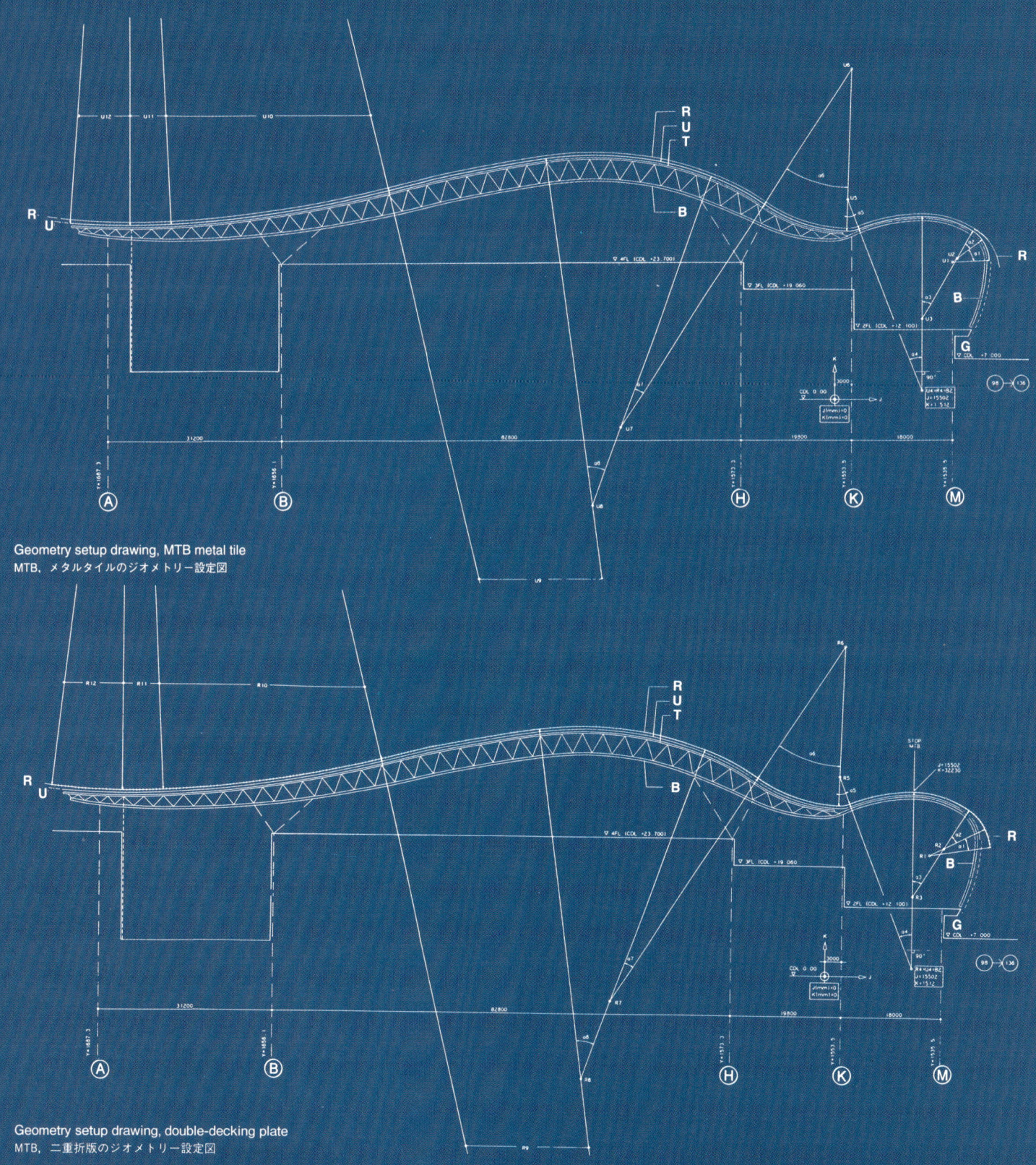

Geometry setup drawing, MTB metal tile
MTB，メタルタイルのジオメトリー設定図

Geometry setup drawing, double-decking plate
MTB，二重折版のジオメトリー設定図

エアロダイナミクス・ルーフ

メインターミナルビルの屋根はシンメトリーなアーチ構造から出発したのだが，ドローイングを見ながら，機能的で構造的な整合性をもつアーチの退屈さをなんとか解体する方法がないかと考え続けた．構造優先のデザインは，どうしても既存の形態へと規範化していく傾向がある．標準的な様式化に組み込まれたくないが，解体操作は全体性を欠いてしまう危険も伴う．

ルーフ形態への逡巡が続く一方で，高さが20m近い大空間になる4階の出発階は，環境制御の面で大きな問題を提出していた．暖まった空気が天井に上り，そこで冷えて急速に落下するコールドドラフト現象が起きるのだ．だが天井に通常のダクトをつけたくなかった．マクロな空調制御とミクロな空調制御の兼ね合いで考えられないかと思案した．

コンペはレンゾ・ピアノ・ビルディング・ワークショップ・パリの関西国際空港ターミナルビル国際コンペチームと，ロンドンのOAPのエンジニアの協力で進められていた．コールドドラフトを克服するための対策の相談をすると，OAPの環境技術専門家のトム・バーカーは次のようなすばらしい回答を出してくれた．

「片側からジェットエアを吹けばいい．天井面がこの空気の流れにそう形になっていれば，空気は80m飛ばせる．この天井にできた空気の流れがマクロな環境を制御できる．」

トムから送られてきた気流のダイアグラムが，アーチのデザインを大きく進展させることになった．美しい曲線をもつこのダイアグラムにそった天井によって，非対称のアーチが現出した．そしてOAPの構造家のピーター・ライスが，即座にこの非対称アーチを構造として成り立たせることを引き受けてくれた．空気の流れが構造の形式を変容し溶解させ，新たな姿を生成させた瞬間だった．コンペの締め切りを2か月前にひかえた1988年9月半ばのことである．

このエアロダイナミクス・ルーフは，航空機などのように外気に対抗する積極的な機械の形態とし

Curve R: Set-out the external metal tiles.
 R曲線　外部メタルタイルを設定
Curve U: Set-out the internal ceiling surface.
 U曲線　二重折版を設定
Curve G: Set-out the Airside glazing.
 G曲線　エアサイド・グレージングを設定
Curve B: Set-out the lower chords of the main terminal building trusses, and Wing ribs.
 B曲線　本館トラスの下弦材及びウィングリブを設定
Curve T: Set-out the upper chords of the main terminal building trusses.
 T曲線　本館トラスの上弦材を設定
Curve F: Set-out the ends of the Landside metal tiles of the wing.
 F曲線　ウイング・ランドサイドメタルタイル先端を設定

1. Reference point for setting up the metal tile (the point is defined in three-dimensional coordinates.)
 ウイング・メタルタイルの設定基準点（3次元の座標にて定義）
2. Reference line for shifting to the Wing Landside fan
 ウイング・ランドサイド側のフィンへ移行する基準線
3. Landside end of the Wing metal tile　ウイング・メタルタイルのランドサイド側先端部
4. Constant against the overall length of the Wing　ウイングの全長に対して一定
5. Geometry symmetry axis at the Wing End
 ウイングエンドでのジオメトリー対称軸
6. Wing End center bay
 ウイングエンドのセンターベイ
7. Adjustment zone for Wing geometry and Wing End center bay
 ウイングのジオメトリーとウイングエンド・センターベイの調整ゾーン

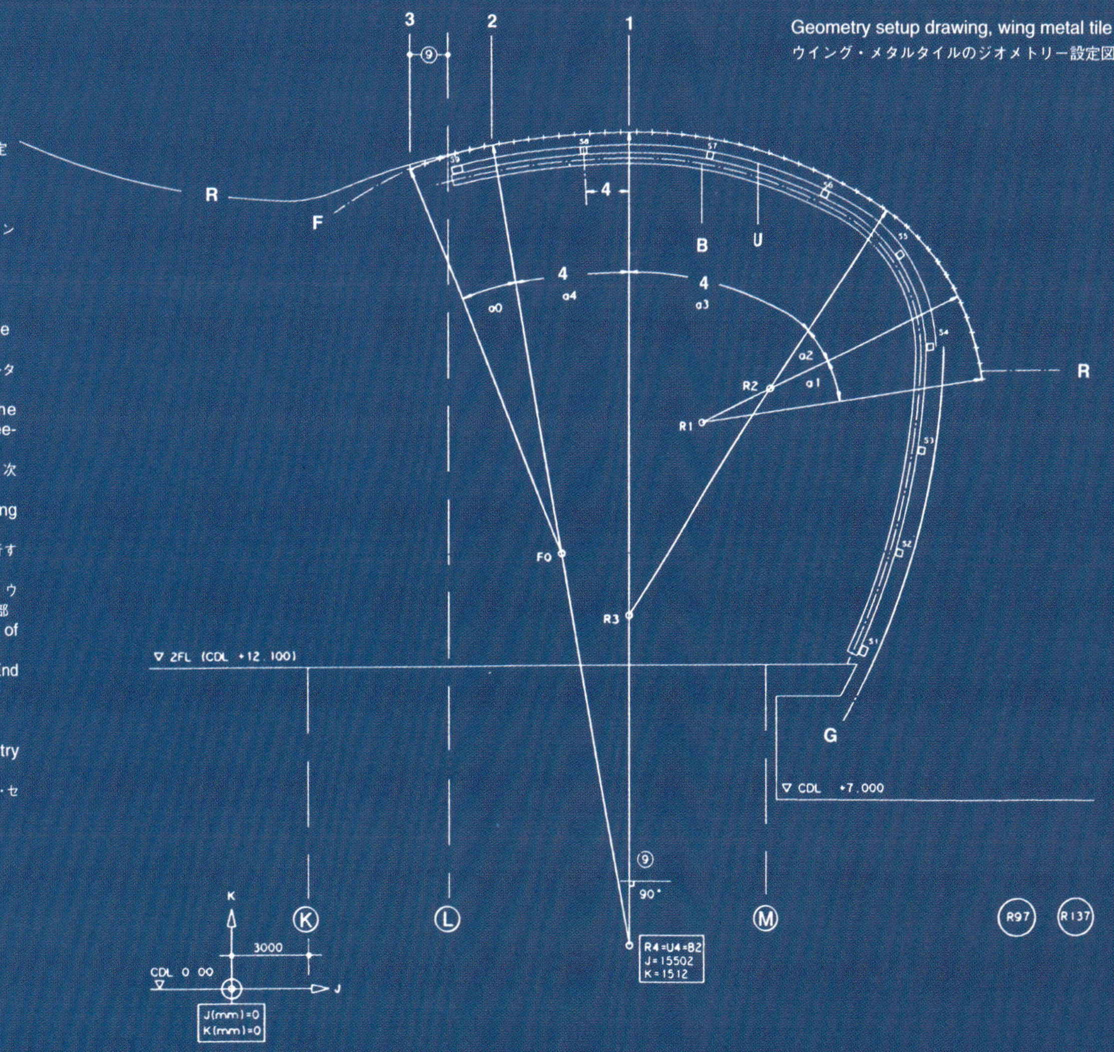

Geometry setup drawing, wing metal tile
ウイング・メタルタイルのジオメトリー設定図

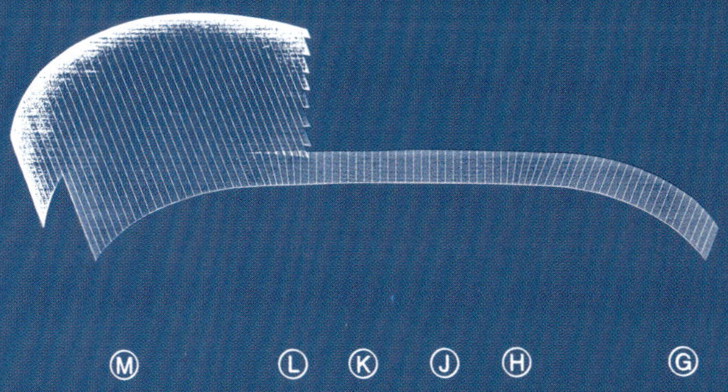

Metal tile of wing end
ウイングエンド・メタルタイル側面図

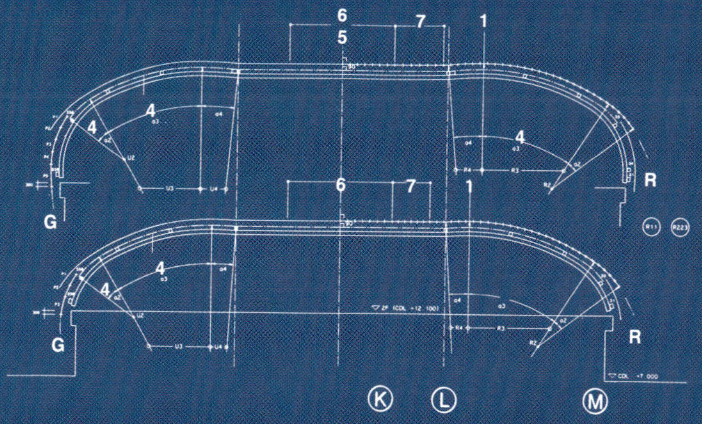

Geometry setup drawing - wing end section
ウイングエンドでのジオメトリー設定図

て構想されたのではなく，人間のための環境づくりという内部からの建築上の問題を解決するために生まれたものである。環境制御を第一におく方法は，デザインの方法論としては謙虚ともとれるが，私たちが建築においてつねに大事にしている方法の1つである。ランドサイド側にジェットの吹出口を，エアサイド側に吸込口を設ければ，空気の流れの形状がランドサイドから加速的に上昇する天井をつくりあげてくれる。始点から終点へと向かうこのゆるやかな気流が，人間の移動にそった目には見えない身体的な方向性を強調することにもなった。
(N.O.)

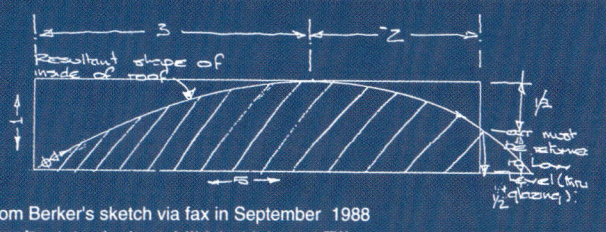

Tom Berker's sketch via fax in September 1988
1988年　トム・バーカーから送られてきたFAXの回答

View of south wing with control tower in left, April, 1994.
南ウイングを手前に見る旅客ターミナルビル．写真左は管制塔．（1994年4月）

View of the opposite shore, Kii peninshura, from manmade island, airport island. April, 1993. 人工島である空港島から、対岸の紀伊半島を見る．(1993年4月)

Chemical fire engines made in Austria. オーストリア製の化学消防車

Boarding bridge of the wing end and a connecting bridge over there. Dec. 1993.
ウイングの先端につけられるボーディングブリッジの建設。遠くに連絡橋が見える（1993年12月）

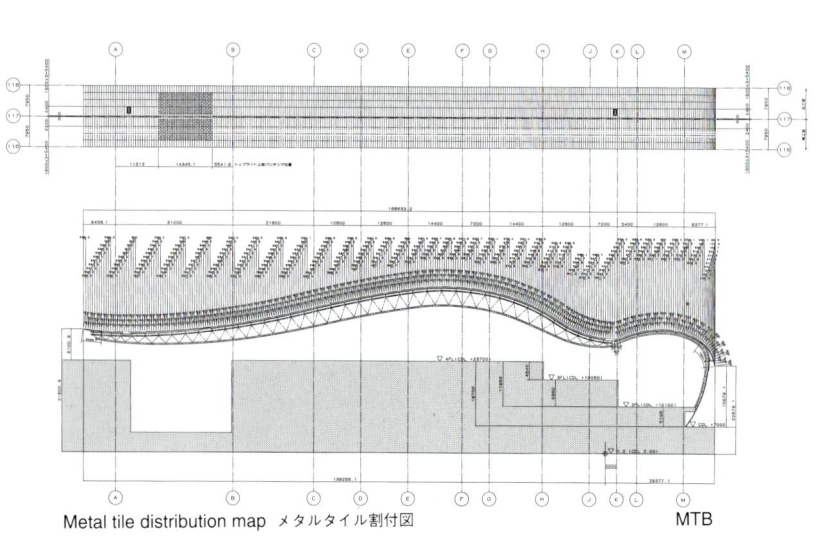

Metal tile distribution map メタルタイル割付図 MTB

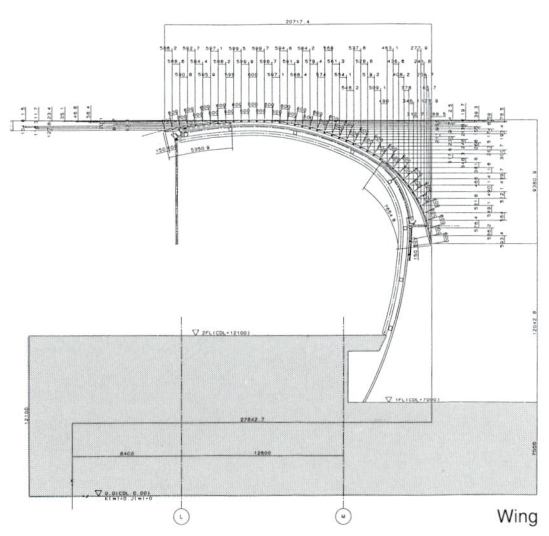

Wing

View toward south wing from central wing front. April 1993.
中央部から南ウイング方向を眺める（1993年4月）.

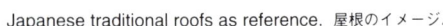

Japanese traditional roofs as reference. 屋根のイメージ.

Close up view of roof panels of the wing.
ウイングの屋根.

View of the north end, control tower in right. Aug. 1994
旅客ターミナルビル北側先端を見る．写真右手は管制塔（1994年8月）．

Airside view of the north end. June 1993　北ウイングのエアサイド（1993年6月）．

Landside view of the north end. June 1993　北ウイングのランドサイド（1993年6月）．

Close up view of the end. June. 1993　ウイング先端部分（1993年6月）．

Landside view of the south wing and AGT vehicle which color was controled by Renzo Piano Building Workshop. Aug. 1994
南ウイングのランドサイド．赤いAGTがウイングを走る．旅客ターミナルビルに関連するものの色彩などはピアノ事務所のデザインコントロールを受けている（1994年8月）．

June, 1993

April, 1994

June, 1993

Nov. 1993

Installation drawing, decking plate upper metal tile　折版上部メタルタイル取付図

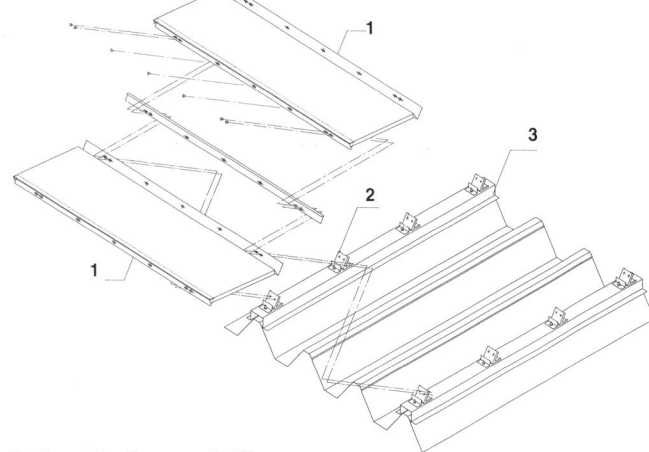

South construction area　南工区

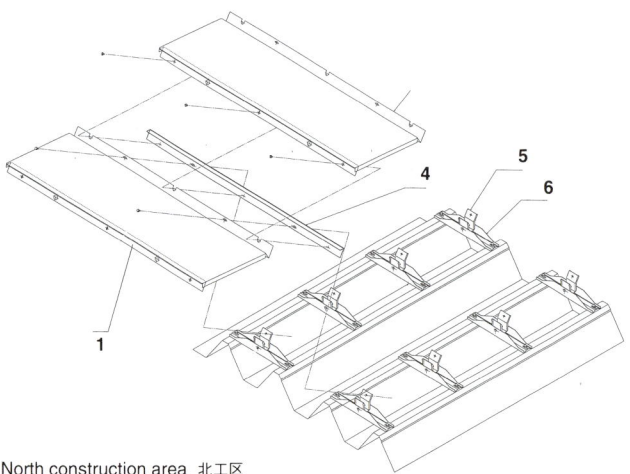

North construction area　北工区

North construction area　北工区

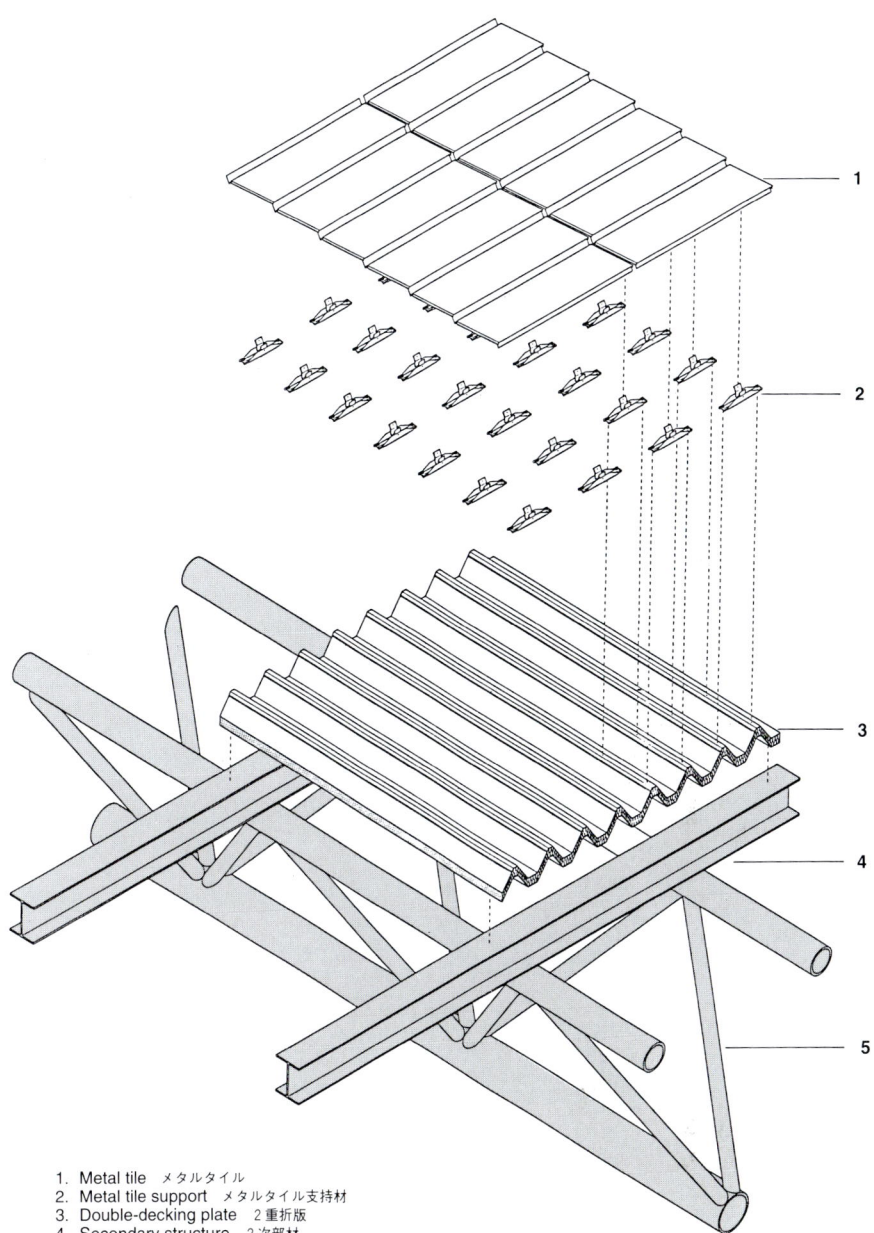

1. Metal tile　メタルタイル
2. Metal tile support　メタルタイル支持材
3. Double-decking plate　2重折版
4. Secondary structure　2次部材
5. Main structure　主体構造

Composition of Roof Cladding (for North construction area)
ルーフクラディングの構成 (北工区納まり)

Installation drawing, fin upper metal tile
フィン上部 (エアサイドのフィン部分) メタルタイル取付図 (南工区・北工区)

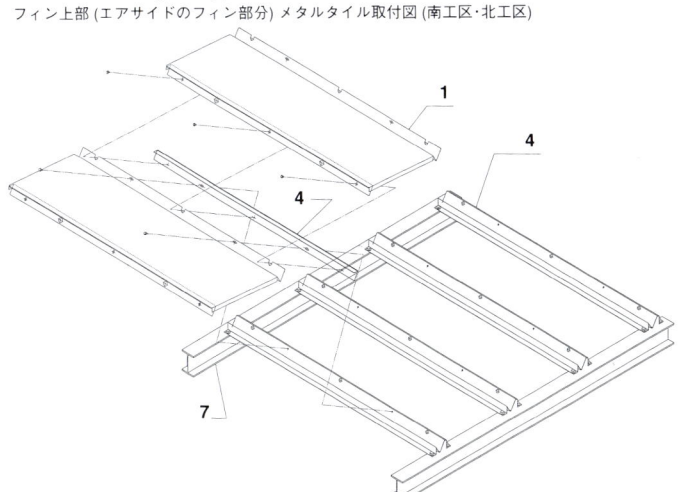

1. Metal tile　メタルタイル
2. Local fixture　部分固定金具
3. Hat rail　ハット型レール
4. Through clip tingle　通し吊子
5. Piece clip tingle　ピース吊子
6. Decking plate band　折版バンド
7. Fin　フィン

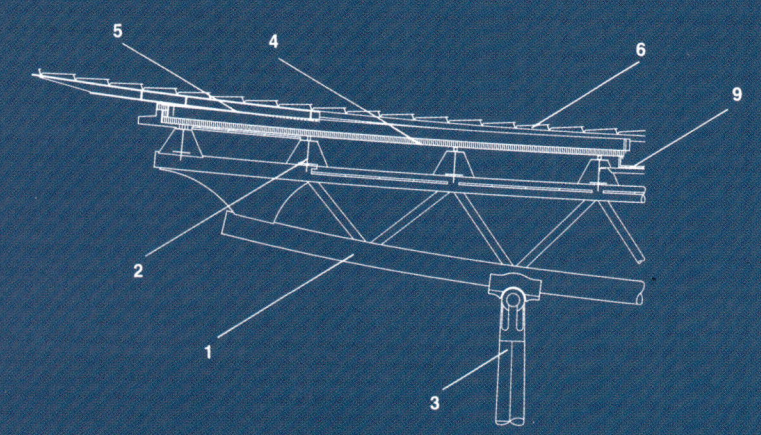

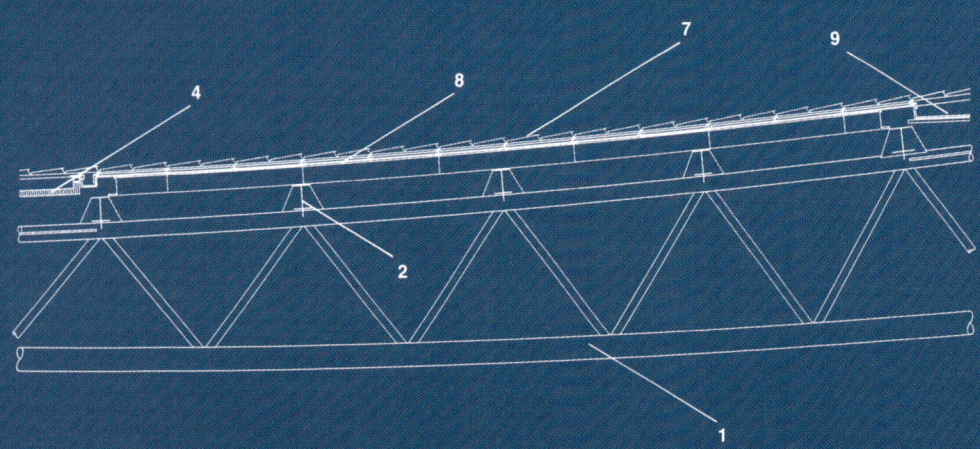
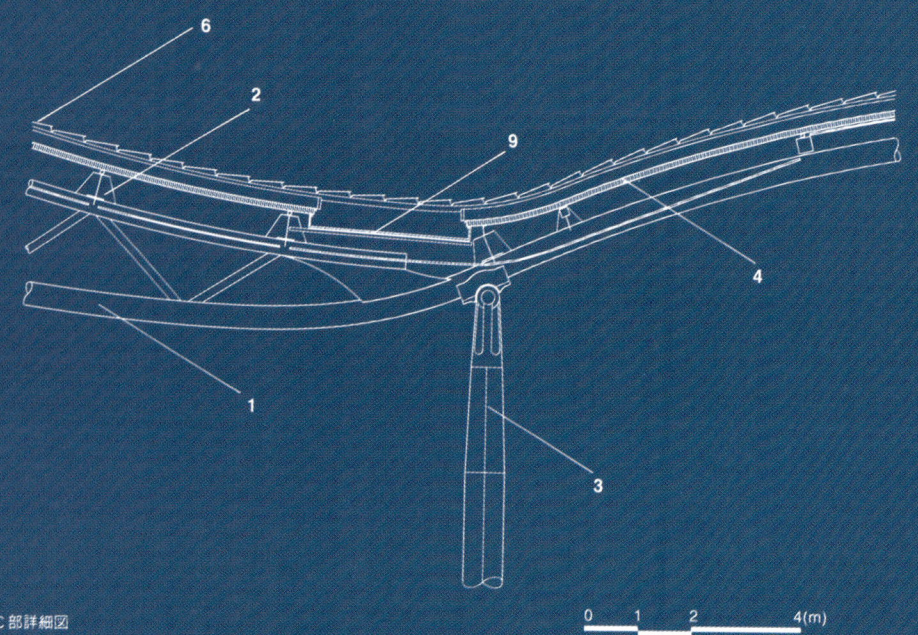

1. Main structure　主体構造
2. Secondary structure　2次部材
3. Fireproof support pillar
   耐火被覆された支持柱
4. Double-decking plate　2重折版
5. Steel fin　鋼製フィン
6. External metal panel　外部メタルパネル
7. Roof perforated metal tile (above the top light)
   屋根パンチングタイル　トップライト上部
8. Canyon upper top light
   キャニオン上部トップライト
9. Drain panel　樋パネル

Detail C　C部詳細図

Passenger terminal building has 11 expansion joints because of its long scale.
長大な旅客ターミナルビルの歪みを補正するため、エキスパンションジョイントが全体で11ヵ所設けられている。

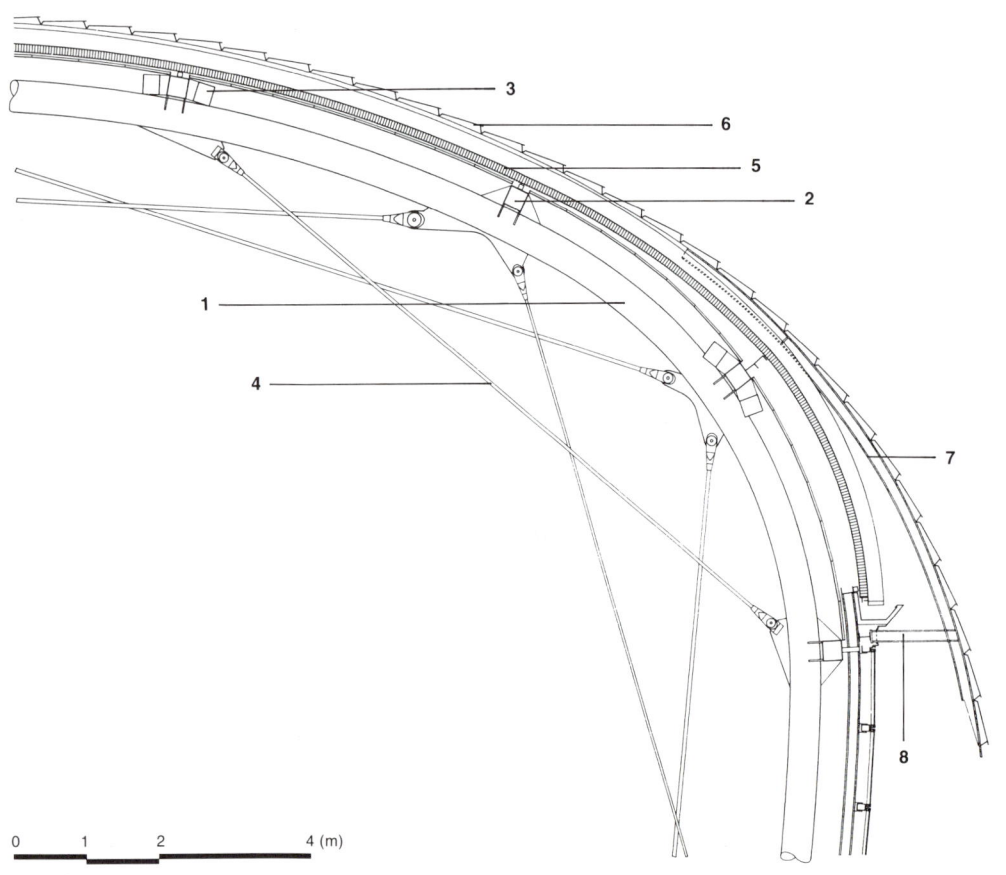

Detail of airside end of roof
ウイングの庇部分詳細図

1. Main structure 主体構造
2. Secondary structure 2次部材
3. Bracing ブレース材
4. Tie bar タイバー
5. Double-decking plate 2重折版
6. Metal tile メタルタイル
7. Steel fin 鋼製フィン
8. Steel fin support 鋼製フィン支持材

AIRSIDE GLAZING
エアサイド　グレージング

Decreasing of height of wing cause change of connection of the passenger boarding bridges with glass.

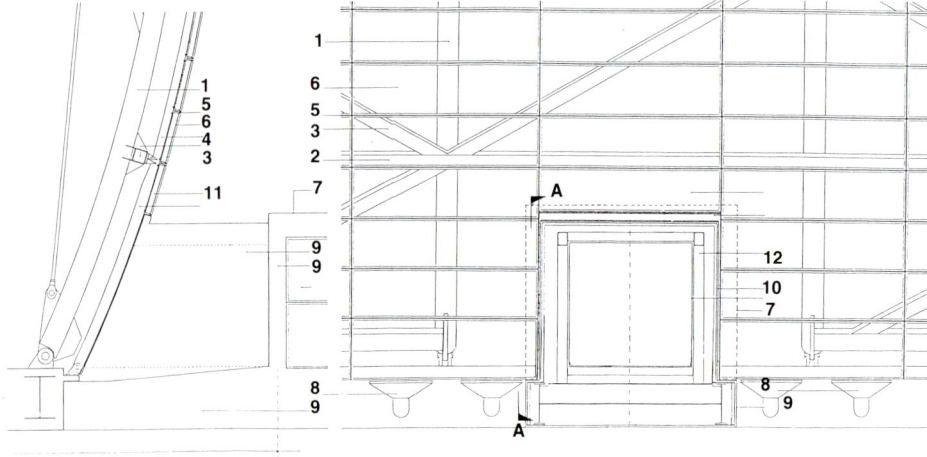

Detailed drawing, the airside glazing at connection of PBB (Working drawing)
エアサイドグレージング搭乗橋貫入部詳細図 (実施設計図)

1. Main structure　主体構造
2. Secondary structure　2次部材
3. Bracing　ブレース材
4. Steel support mullion　鋼製支持マリオン
5. Transom　無目
6. Heat-ray absorbing glass
   熱線吸収ガラス
7. Pssenger boarding bridge　搭乗橋
8. Air outlet　吹出し口
9. Glazing calcium silicate plate with a waterproof design.
   施釉ケイ酸カルシウム板 防水仕様
10. Structural steel column　鋼製柱
11. Deformed glass panel　変形ガラスパネル
12. Drip (aluminum)　水切アルミニウム

A — A section　　R 152 — 153

ウイングエンドに向かって屋根の高さが減る．搭乗橋とガラスの取り付け角度が変わってゆく．

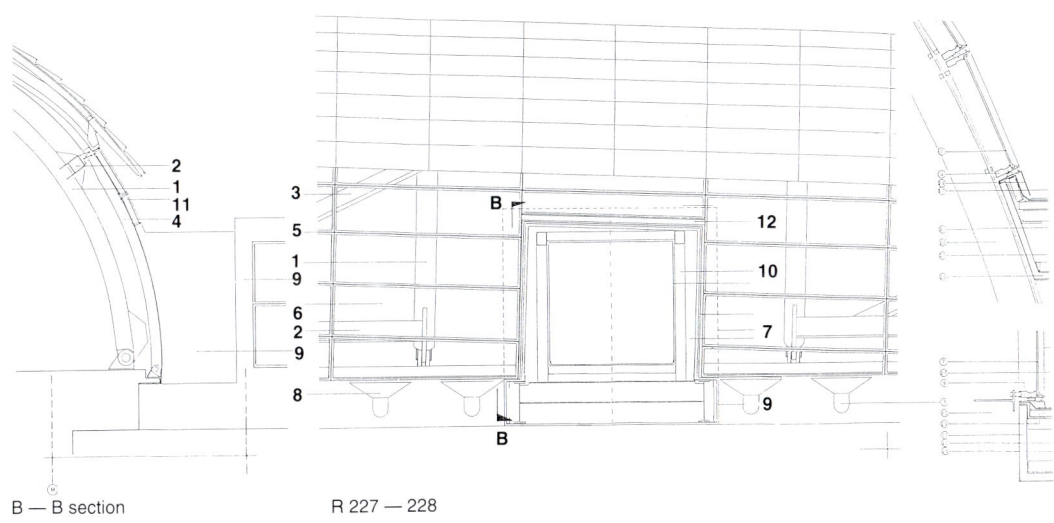

B — B section R 227 — 228

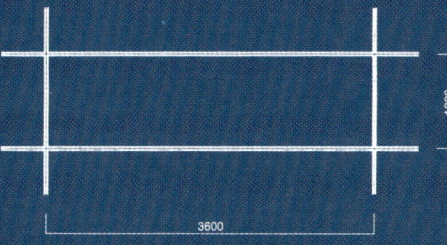

Standard dimensions of the airside glazing panel
エアサイドグレージングユニット標準寸法

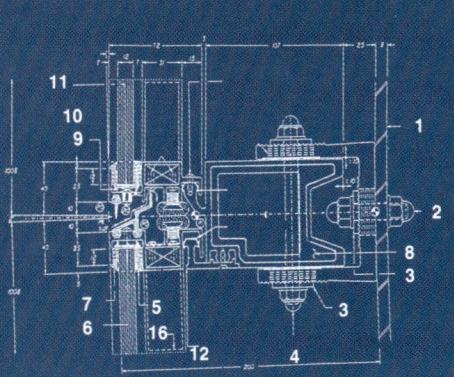

Horizontal section 水平方向断面

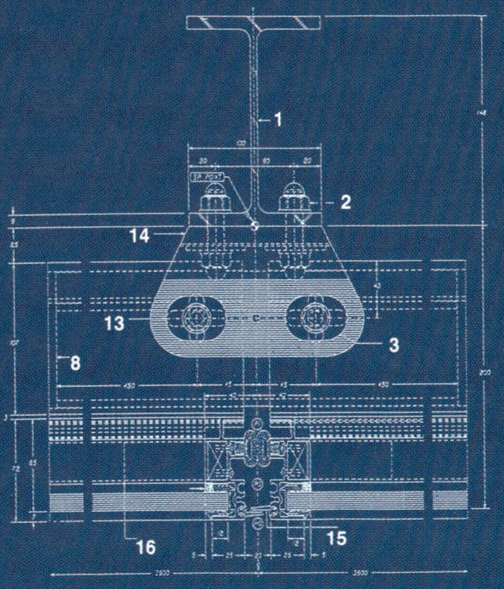

Vertical section 垂直方向断面

Detailed drawing, Airside glazing エアサイドグレージング詳細図

1. H—148x100 Steal mullion サポートマリオン
2. 12 mm DIA SS bolt 45 mm long ステンレス化粧ボルト
3. Extruded serrated aluminium washer ギザワッシャー アルミ押し出し形材
4. 10mm DIA SS bolt 125mm long ステンレス化粧ボルト M10 x 125mm
5. Silicone ガラス回りシール
6. Heat-ray absorbing glass 熱線吸収板ガラス t=12
7. Silicone gasket ガスケット (シリコーン)
8. Transom splice 無目材
9. EPDM material セッティングブロック (EPDM)
10. 12.7 mm Diaweep holes 下枠排水孔位置
11. Weep hole at center of unit spacing in glazing gasket グレイジングビート排水孔位置
12. Rail retainer field installed 無目グリップ
13. Slot for adjustment in transom 長穴
14. Extruded aluminium anchor アルミ押し出し形材
15. EPDM gasket assembly レインバリア (EPDM)
16. Extruded aluminium spline コーナーブロック アルミ押し出し形材

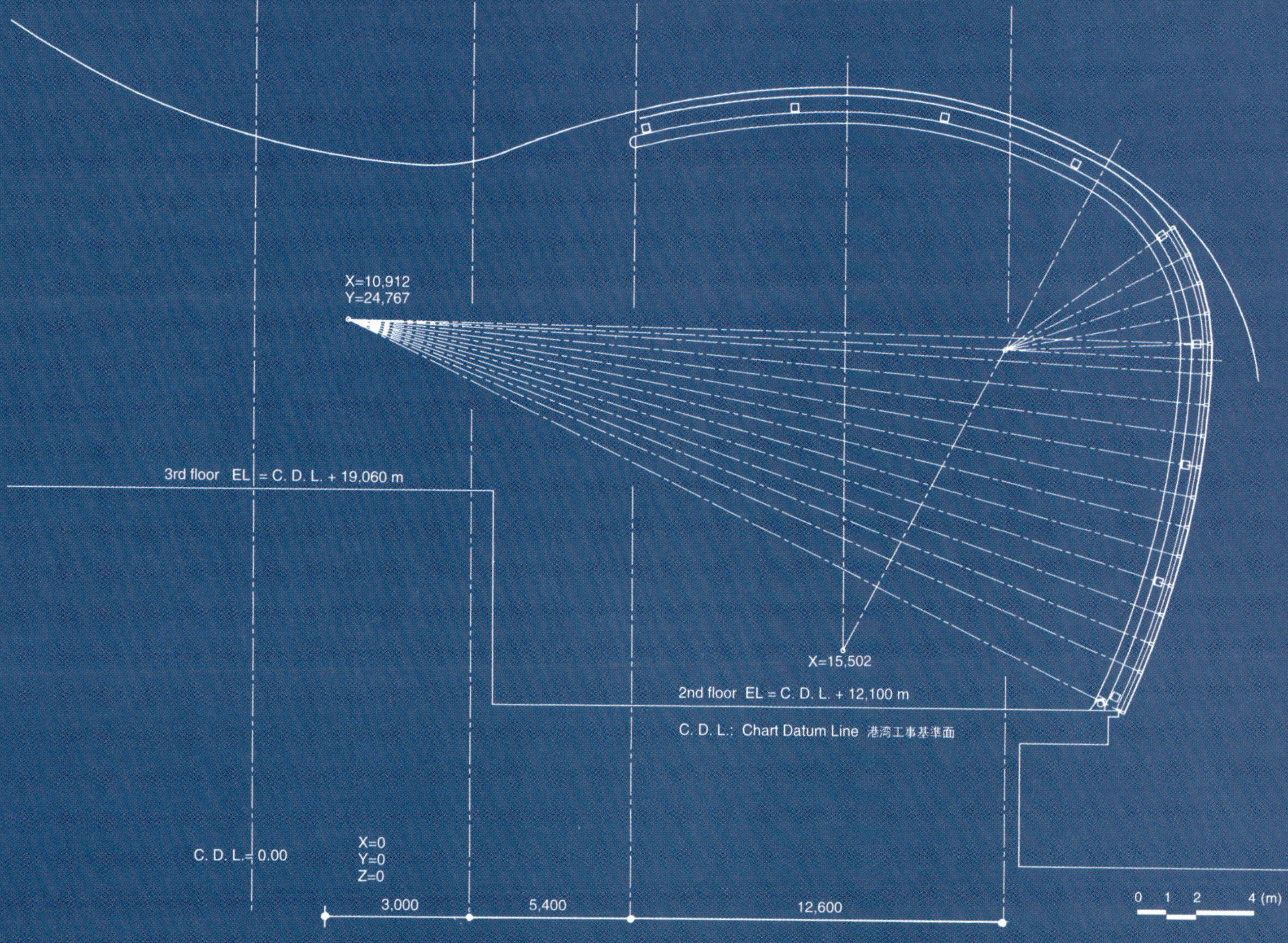

X=10,912
Y=24,767

3rd floor EL = C. D. L. + 19,060 m

X=15,502

2nd floor EL = C.D.L. + 12,100 m
C. D. L.: Chart Datum Line 港湾工事基準面

C. D. L.= 0.00
X=0
Y=0
Z=0

3,000 | 5,400 | 12,600

0 1 2   4 (m)

1. Support mullion　サポートマリオン
2. Secondary structure　2次部材
3. Heat-ray absorbing glass
   熱線吸収ガラス
4. Transom　無目
5. Main structure　主体構造
6. Floor slab　床スラブ
7. Fishtail　フィッシュテイル(空調吹き出し口)
8. Tie bar　タイバー

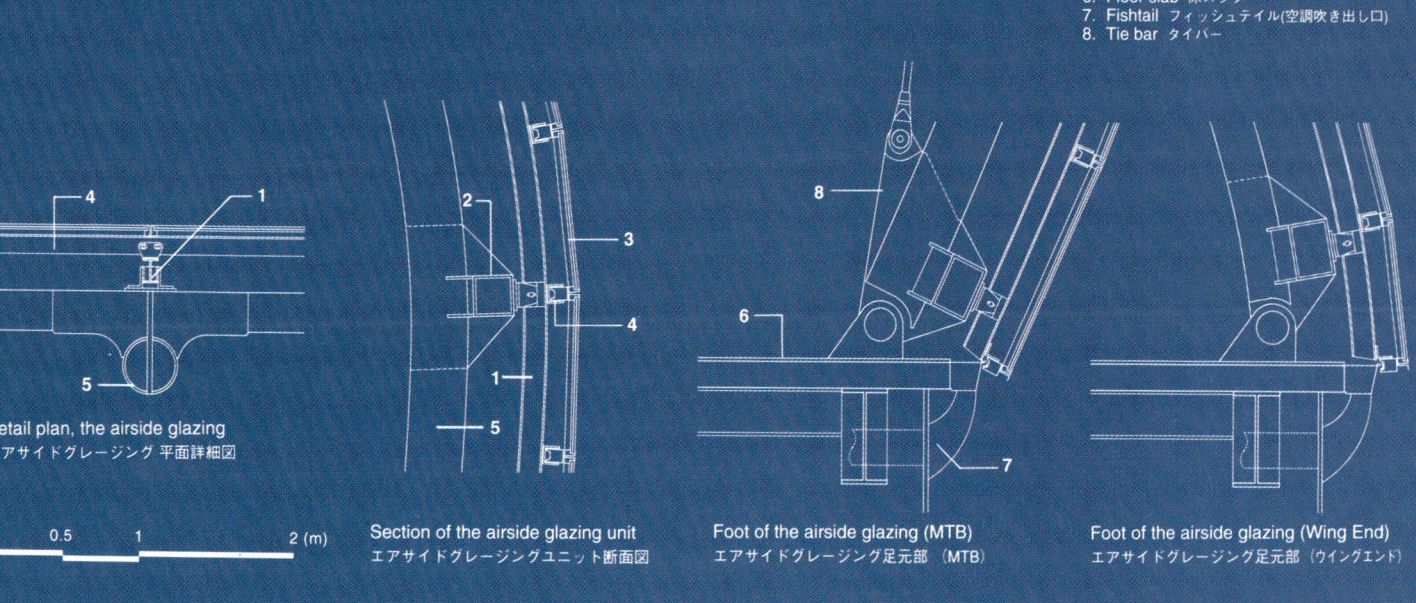

Detail plan, the airside glazing
エアサイドグレージング 平面詳細図

0 0.5 1 2 (m)

Section of the airside glazing unit
エアサイドグレージングユニット断面図

Foot of the airside glazing (MTB)
エアサイドグレージング足元部 (MTB)

Foot of the airside glazing (Wing End)
エアサイドグレージング足元部 (ウイングエンド)

Internal view of airside glazing.
内部から見るグレージングの納まり.

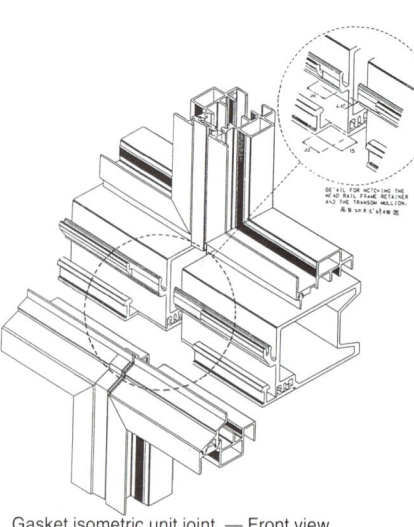

Gasket isometric unit joint — Front view
外観ユニットクロス部アイソメ

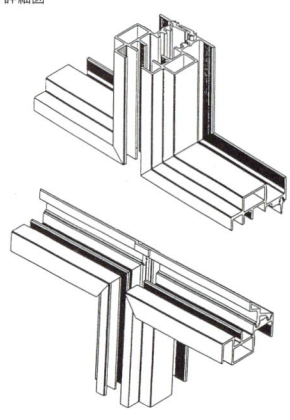

Gasket isometric unit joint — Rear view
内観ユニットクロス部アイソメ

Detail for notching the head rail frame retainer and the transom mullion.
無目切り欠き詳細図

Panorama view of airside under construction from wing. Mar. 1993.
ウイングから見るエアサイド、海、対岸の眺め。（1993年3月）

ENDWALL
エンドウォール

View of the south end wall from approach highway.
高架道路から見る，メインターミナルビルの南側エンドウォール．

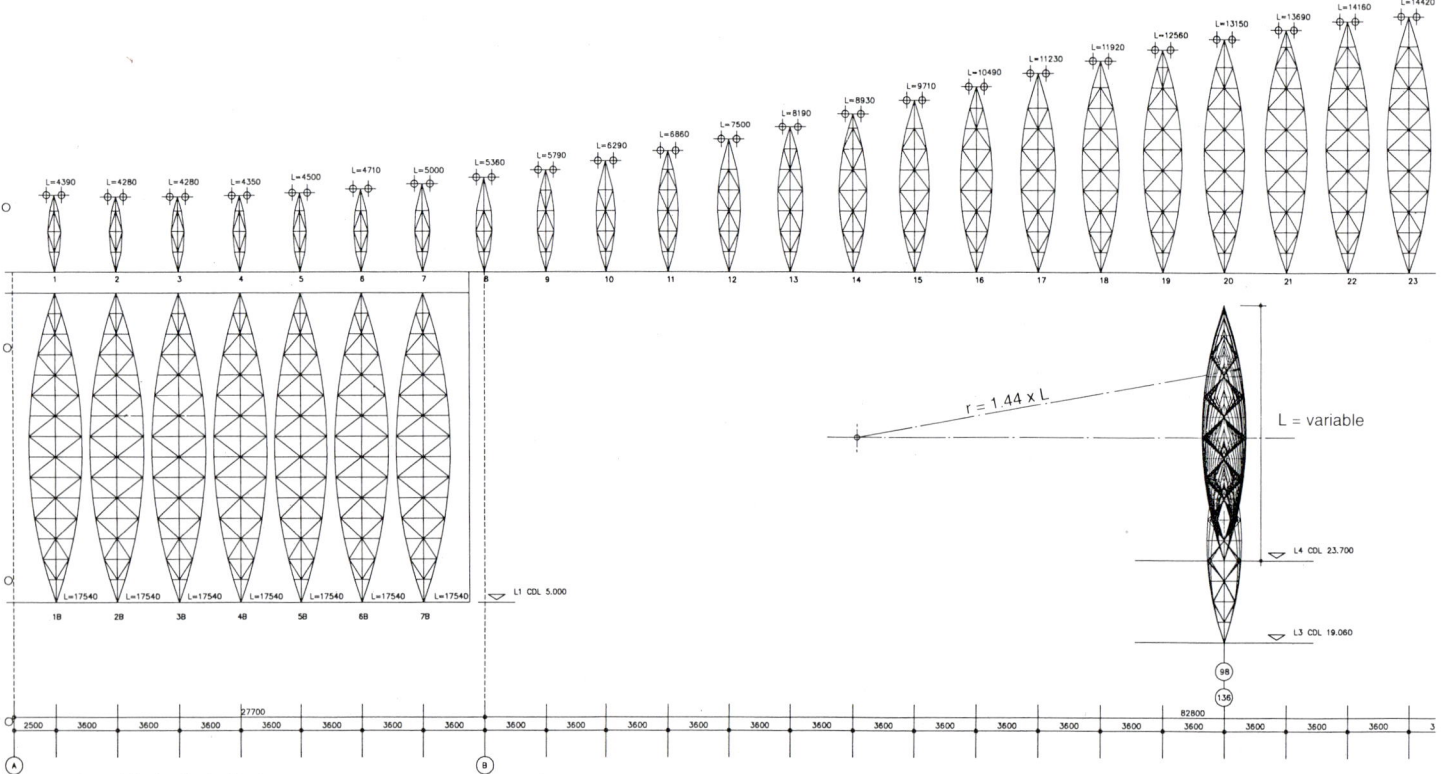

Construction of Endwall glazing bow truss　エンドウォールグレージング・ボウトラスの構成

L=14460
L=14260
L=13830
L=13160
L=12250
L=11080
L=9680
L=6620
L=6620
L=5260
L=4390
L=3980
L=8810
L=10180
L=11310
24 25 26 27 28 29 30 31 32 33 34 35 36 37 38
L4 CDL23.700
L3 CDL19.060
19800
5400
3600
H
K
L

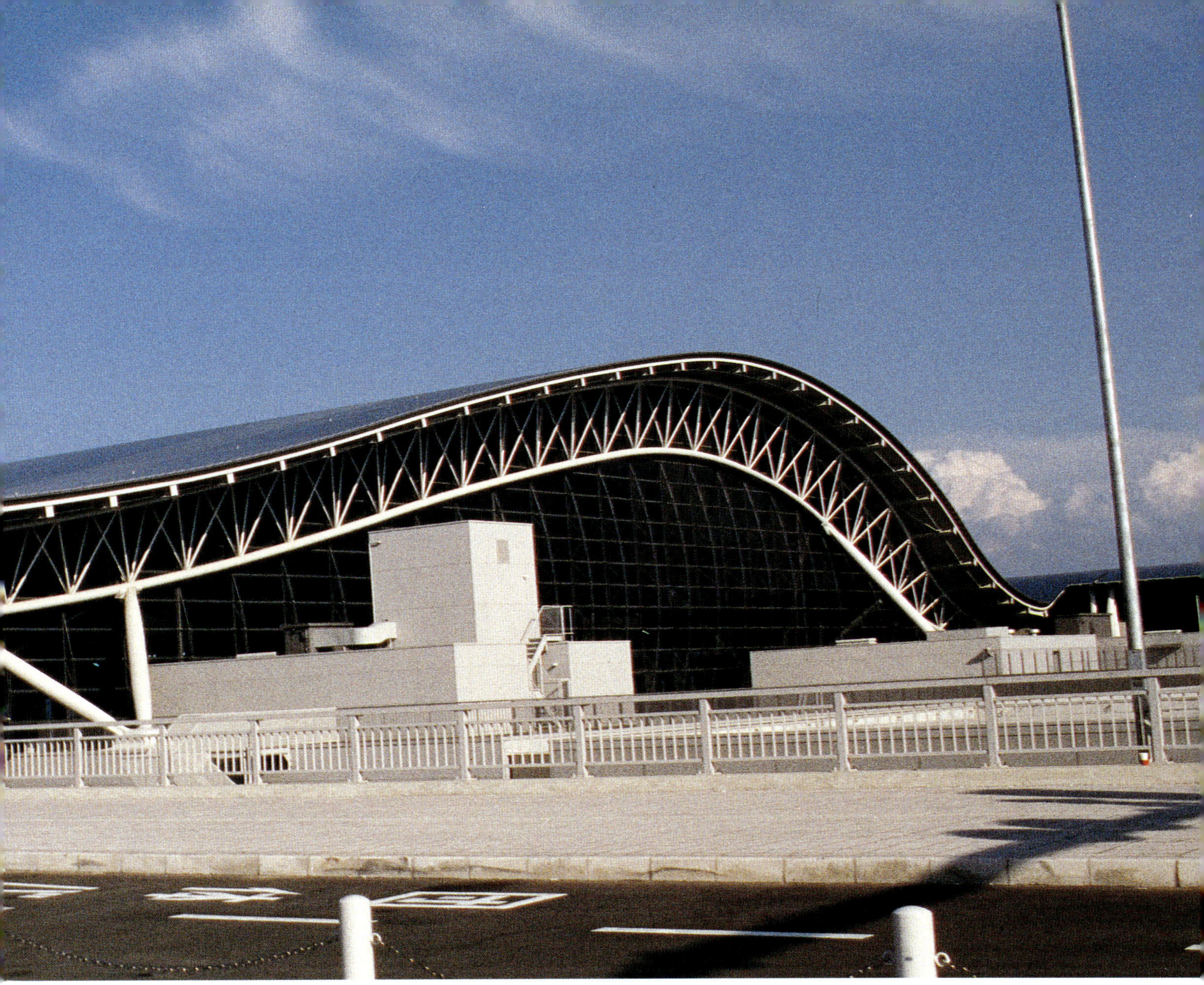

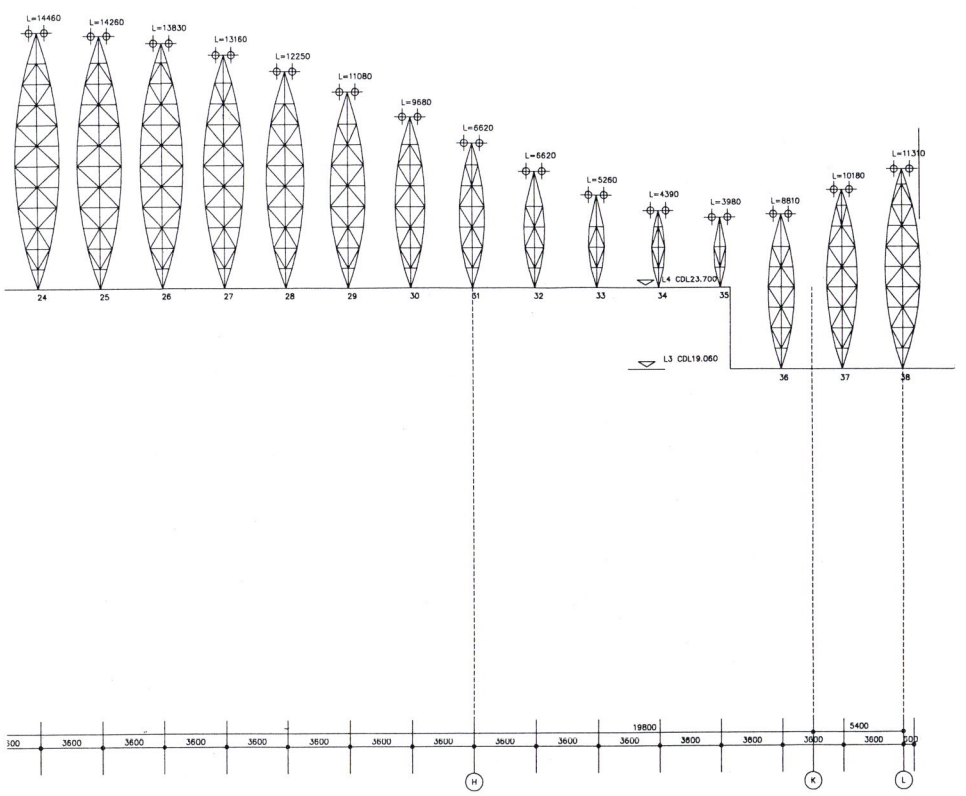

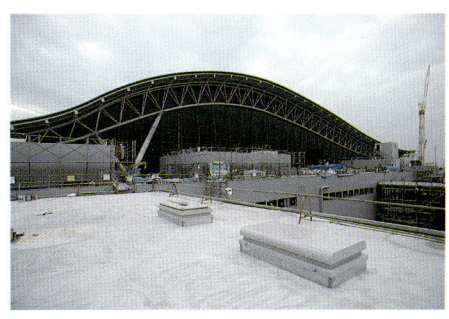

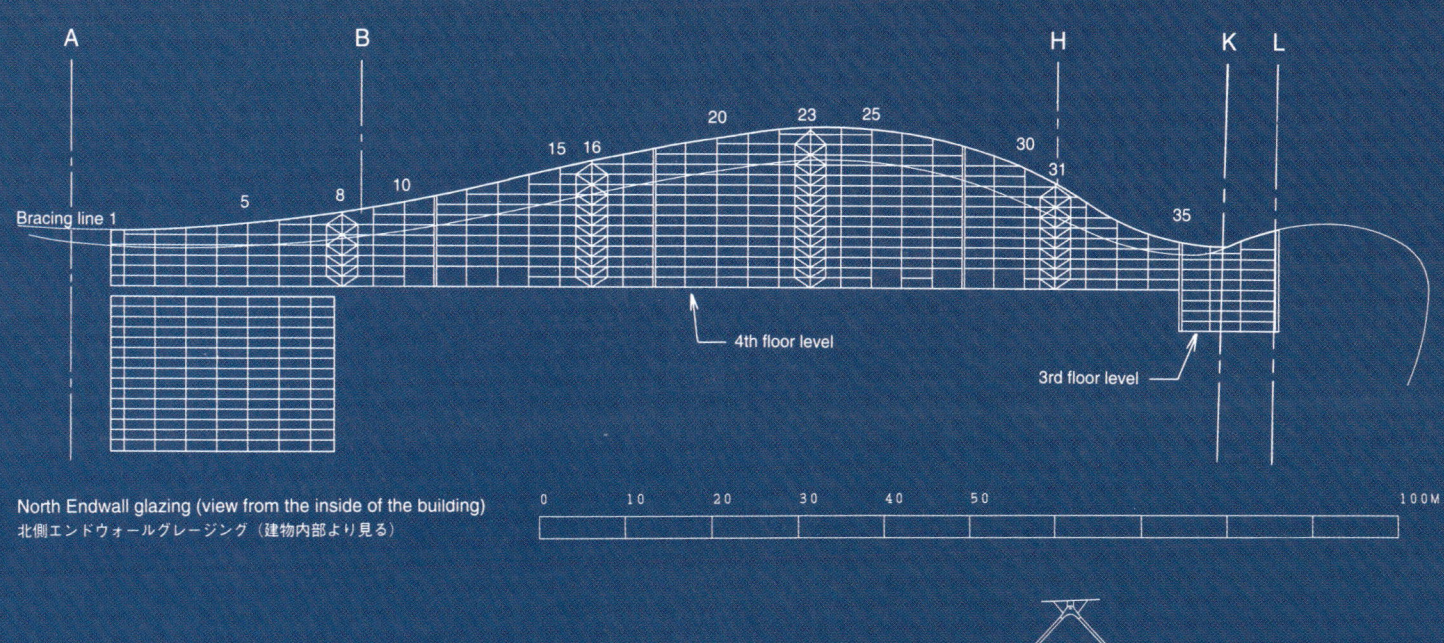

North Endwall glazing (view from the inside of the building)
北側エンドウォールグレージング（建物内部より見る）

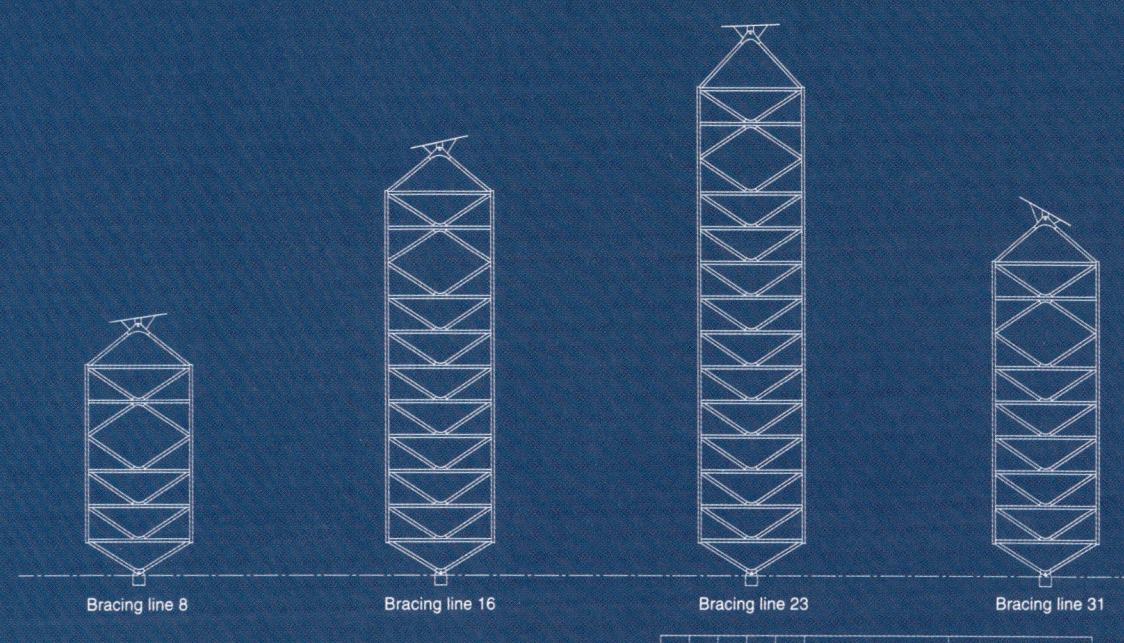

Elevation, blacing of Endwall glazing　エンドウォールグレージング、ブレース材立面図

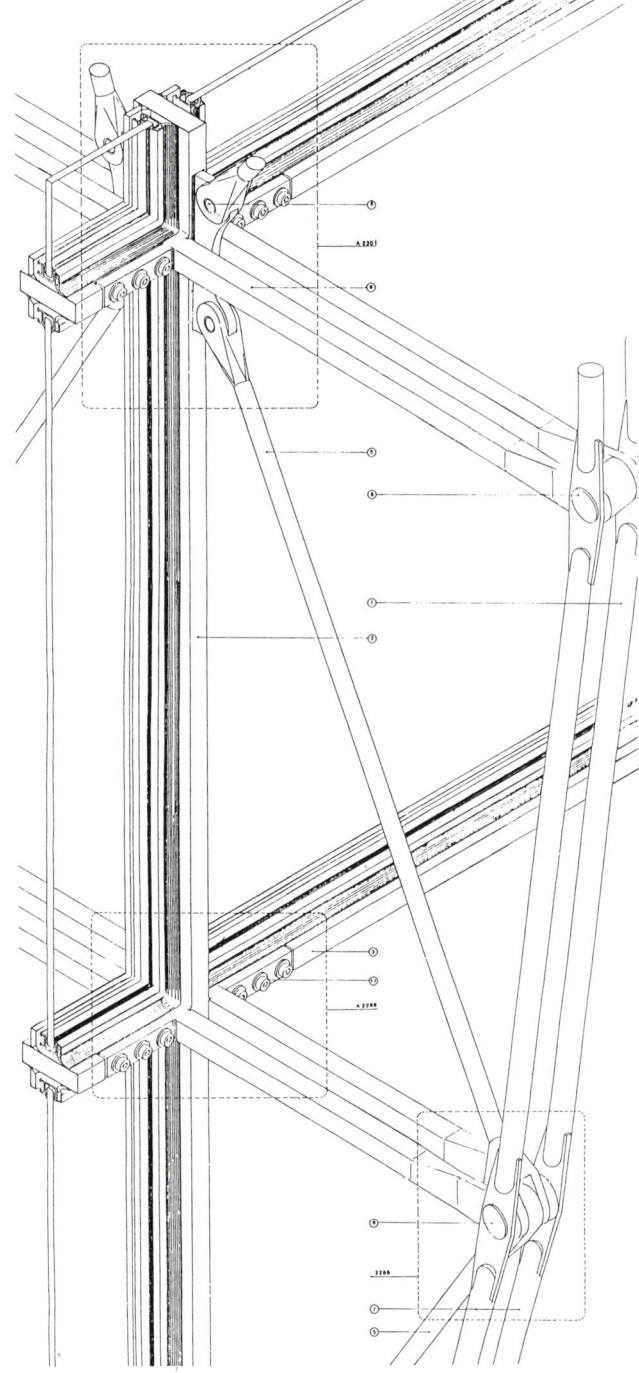
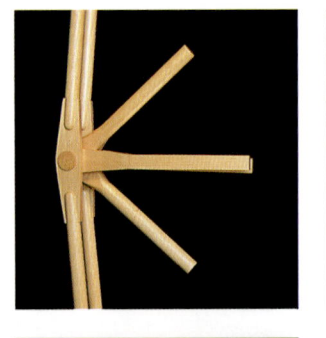

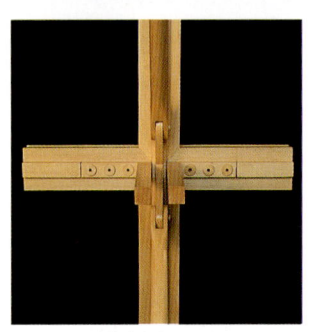

Model photo of Mullion and bow-truss. Right page shows close up view and air supplying boxes in bottom.
マリオン(方立て)とボウトラスの模型．右ページはエンドウォールの内観．下に空調吹き出し(ファンコイルポスト)が並ぶ．

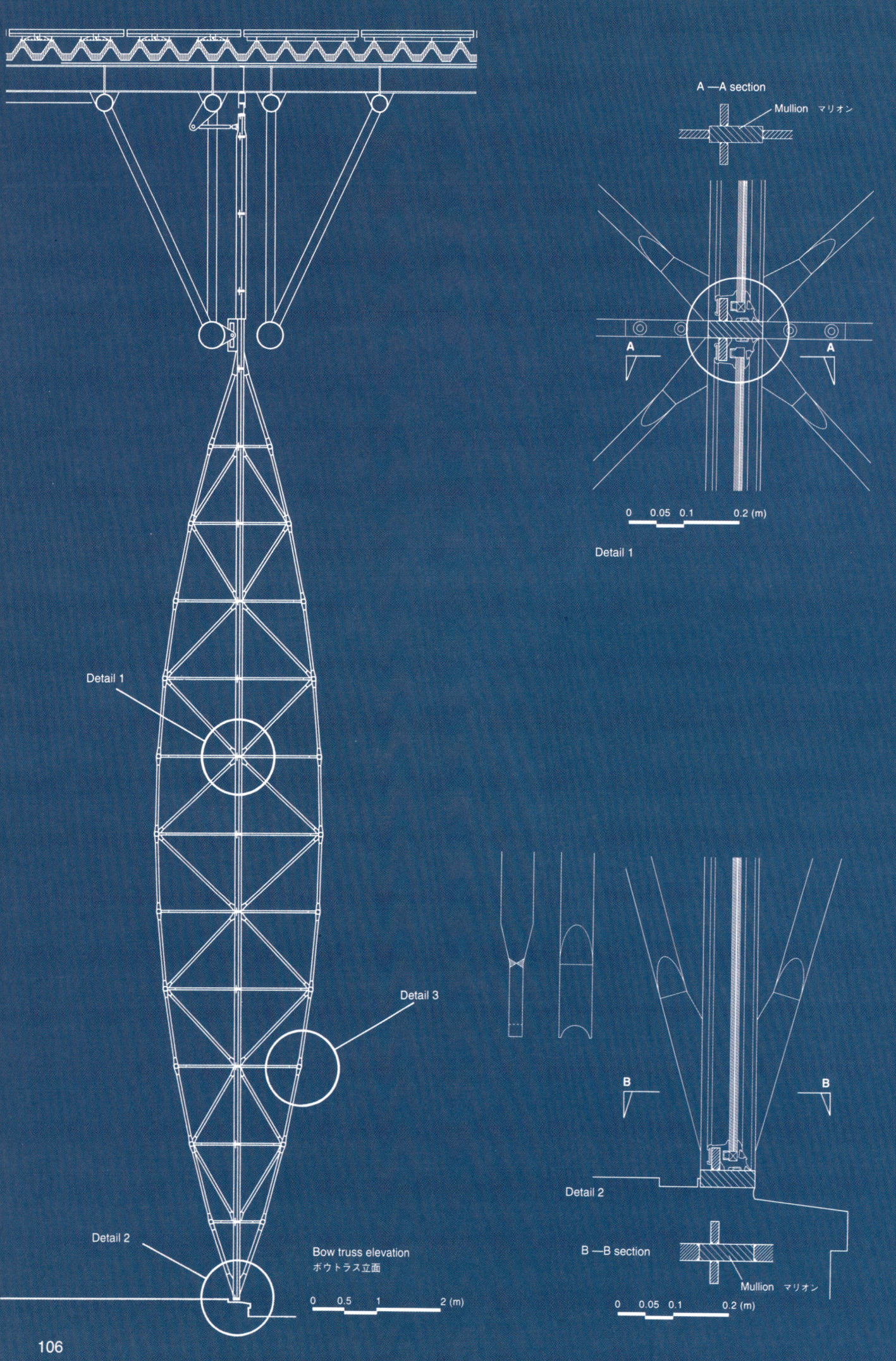

Typical detail of endwall glazing
エンドウォールグレージング標準ディテール

Detail connection mullion — transom
マリオン・トランザム接合部ディテール

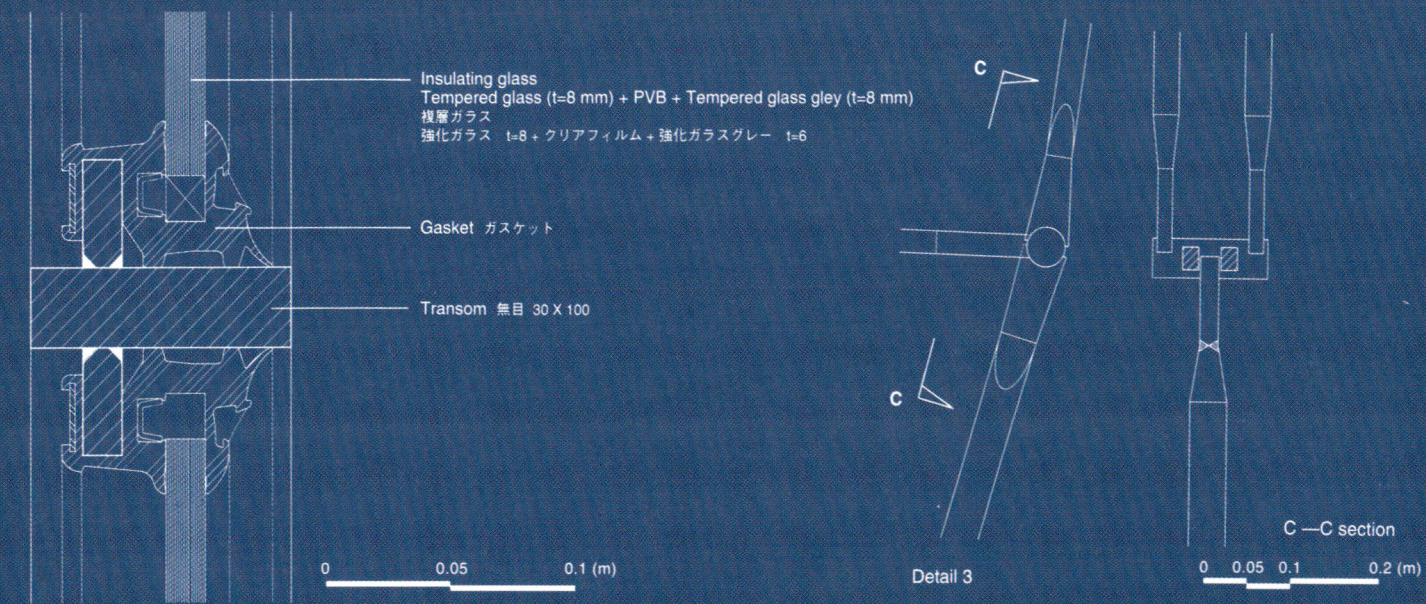

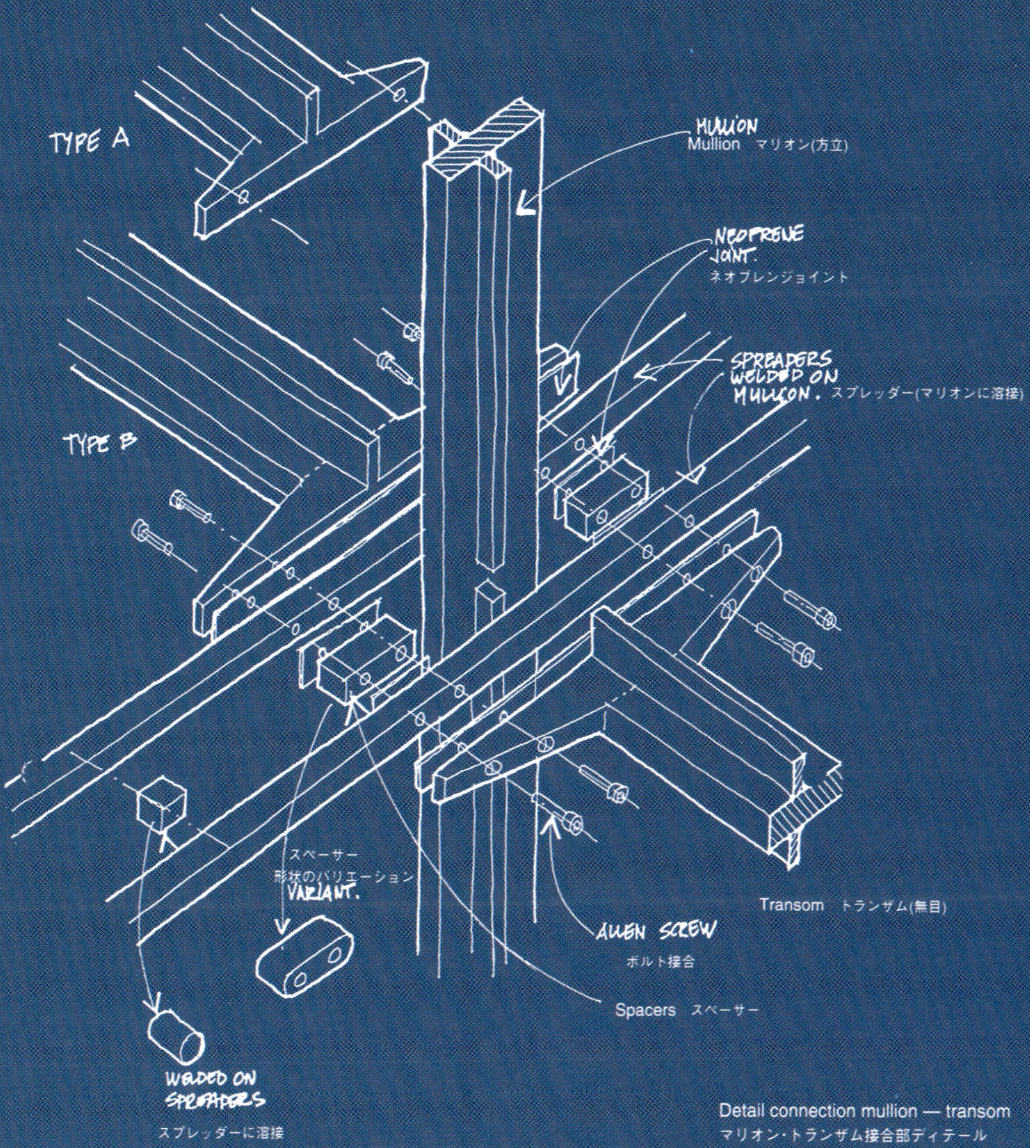

PTB – The Space IV
Passenger Terminal Building

旅客ターミナルビル――大空間

Canyon the entrance hall. Aug. 1994 エントランスホールとなるキャニオン（1994年8月）．

Transparency and Direction

To eliminate the uncertainty human beings experience in moving from one place to another, a design should allow users the ability to get a clear view of the space they are about to move into and give them a firm grasp of the direction they are to take. Often the corridors of airports are difficult to penetrate and involve confusing up and down movements, so that the moment passengers enter an airport, they are thrown into a maze as intricate as an underground metropolitan concourse. They have to move carefully and vigilantly from one sign to the next, which can be exhausting, because even through their feet are still firmly on the ground they feel as if they are drifting in suspended semiotic space.

Any traveler about to set off to another country feels a certain amount of uncertainty in boarding an airplane, even if this anxiety is unconscious. This makes it crucial that an airport, even more than other kinds of places, imbue those who pass through its halls with a sense of trust that is natural and physical. To accomplish this goal, we sought to create space that is explicit and self-explanatory rather than to contrive a layout in which passengers must rely on signs. Even in an airport, there ought to be landmarks that give one a clear sense of direction. In a port city like Kobe, for instance, which is built facing the sea with the mountains at its back, one never loses one's sense of direction no matter what street you are on.

In both horizontal layout and vertical composition, the competition design was deliberately constructed to assure the transparency of the space and to provide users with a clear sense of direction. To do so, a rectangular grid made up of long and short spans was adopted from the beginning. The roof over the 4-story main building consists of an arched structure (14.4 meters on the short side) measuring 82.5 meters from landside to airside. Passengers checking in move through a space that is completely transparent, without visual obstructions for 150 meters ahead. The second-floor domestic lobby is designed on the same principle and it was planned so that the line of flow, from the landside to the airside, was clear. These spatial concepts included in the competition plan are being realized in the final construction.

—*N. O.*

CG line art of inside of MTB with wing. ウイングからMTBにつながる内観.   International check-in lobby, the 4th floor. 4階、国際線チェックインロビー.

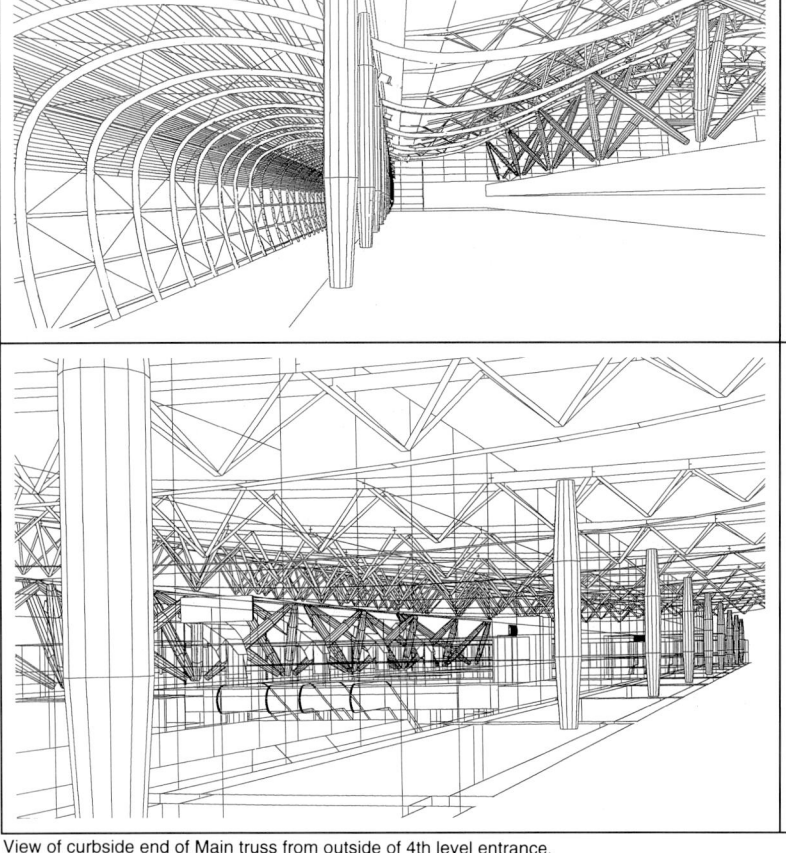

View of curbside end of Main truss from outside of 4th level entrance.
4階入口の外側から見る内部とメイントラス.

Four times height Canyon viewed from ceiling level.
4層吹き抜けのキャニオン.

A Greenery-filled Canyon

Based on the Aeroports de Paris (ADP) basic concept that set the conditions for the competition design of the terminal building, the domestic lobby is located between the international departure lobby on the 4th floor and the international arrival lobby on the 1st floor. We considered this unique composition a real asset, and a fitting symbolic expression for a hub airport built to facilitate smooth changing of planes between international and domestic flights. The only problem was that movement in a vertical direction tends to be confusing for travelers. The solution we adopted in the competition design was to make explicit the character of each floor with spaces for movement in a horizontal direction and to make the landside arrival lobby first entered by visitors in the form of an immense atrium (in the execution drawings, 27 meters wide, 28 meters high, and 275 meters long) where the vertical organization of the terminal is readily apparent and the mechanisms for vertical movement can be identified at a glance. This atrium has been named the "canyon" and contains a generous amount of greenery, making for an oasis-like scene that eases the fatigue of travelers arriving on international flights and provides a spacious and relaxed atmosphere for persons who have come to see off or greet passengers. It seems fitting that the first glimpse of Japan to greet visitors from overseas should be this huge, lushly landscaped atrium.

The other element of spatial composition we proposed in the competition design is the third floor of the main terminal where restaurants, souvenir shops and other concessions are clustered. Concession functions on other floors were kept to a minimum; not only to facilitate the transparency of the space and clarity of pathways but to enhance fire safety by concentrating facilities with high fire load in one area. As a result of this interior structure, which took into account the need for disaster prevention, construction of a large, open space with no partitions under one roof measuring 90,000 square meters became possible. —*N. O.*

空間の透過性と移動の方向

空間の中に視覚の広々としたパースペクティブが与えられていること，そして方向性が明確であることは，移動する人間から不安感をとりのぞく重要な要素となる．往々にして空港は動線が閉鎖的で上下の複雑な移動があることが多く，旅客は空港に足を踏み入れたとたんに，都市の地下街の迷路にはまり込んだようになる．サイン（旅客案内表示）を目で必死に追いつつ歩き回り，地表次元にいながらにして，記号的空間を漂流する疲れを負わされることになる．

海外への旅立ちを前にした人間は，航空機に乗ることに対する一抹の不安を無意識にしろ感じているものだから，どんな空間以上に空港の空間はそのゾーンを通過する人々に，自然で身体的な信頼感を与えることが大切である．こうした空間を実現するためには，サインという記号のレイアウトに頼る以前に，空間そのものに自明性がもたらせられることが望ましい．空港内にいても，山を背景にして海に臨む神戸のような都市の街路を歩いている時のように，方向の必然的な明快さが必要なのだ．

コンペ案は平面レイアウトと断面構成において，空間の透過性と方向性を明確にする意図的デザインで構築されていった．方法として大スパンと小スパンをもつ長方形グリッドの採用がはじめに決定した．メインターミナルビル（MTB）4階の大屋根はランドサイドからエアサイドへ82.5mのアーチ構造（短辺方向は14.4m）が使用され，チェックインする旅客は150mにわたる視覚的障害のない見通しの良い空間の中を移動する．2階の国内線の空間も同様の原則でつくられ，ランドサイドからエアサイドへの明快な方向性の維持が目指された．これらのコンペ案の空間コンセプトはそのまま維持され実現されている． (N.O.)

Open Air Duct　オープンエアダクト　　　　　Main truss viewed toward airside.　エアサイドに向かうメイントラス．

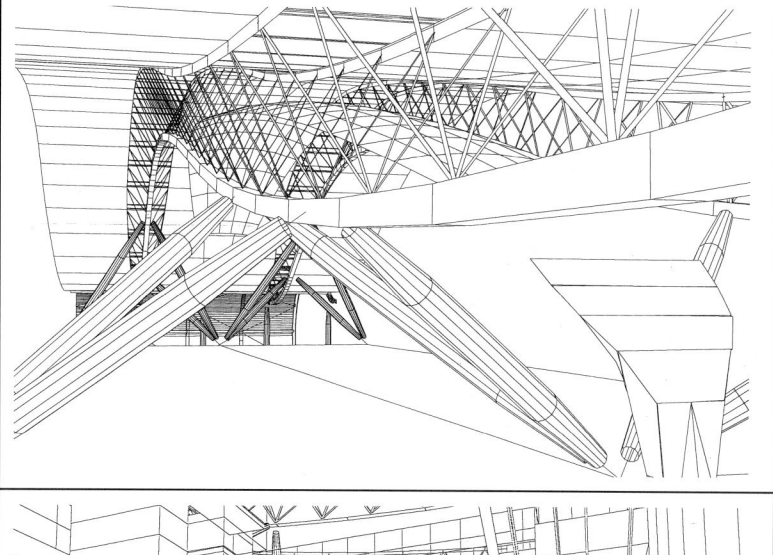

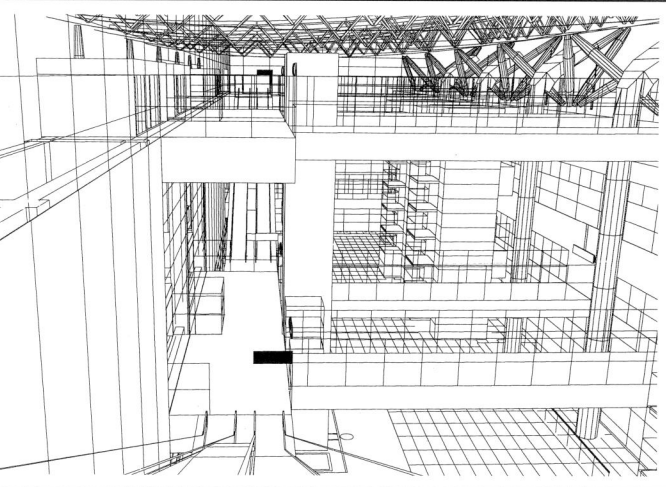

Canyon viewed from the 4th floor level.
4階から見たキャニオン

Canyon viewed on the ground level.
1階から見たキャニオン．

キャニオンの緑

メインターミナルビルはコンペの条件となったADP（パリ空港公団）の提案にもとづいて，国際線出発階（4階）と到着階（1階）の間に国内線（2階）をはさむ構成がとられる．このユニークな構成は国際線から国内線へのスムーズな乗り換えを前提とするハブ空港としてのシンボリックな表現を含めて，魅力的なものに思えた．ただ問題は垂直方向の移動が，旅客を混乱させがちなことである．この問題を解決するためにコンペ案では，水平方向の移動空間にあたる各フロアの性格を明確にするとともに，垂直の移動を選択しなくてはならない到着ロビーは，巨大な吹き抜け空間（実施案では幅27m，高さ28m，長さ275m）を設け，ひと目で必要な移動のメカニズムが知覚できるようにした．

この吹き抜けはキャニオンと呼ばれ，豊かな植栽が施されて，国際線から到着した旅客の旅の疲れをオアシスのようにいやすとともに，見送りや出迎えの人々がゆったりとやすらいだ雰囲気で待ち時間を過ごせるように配慮されている．海外から訪れる旅行者が日本に着いてはじめて目にする風景が，この巨大な吹き抜け空間の生き生きとした植物群なのだ．

この吹き抜け空間以外に，私たちがコンペ案で提案した空間構成は，メインターミナルビルの3階に，レストランやショップを集中配置したコンセッション・フロアを設けることである．他の階のコンセッション機能を最少限にとどめることは，透過性の高い動線を可能にするだけではなく，火災荷重の高い施設を集中させて消火設備を充実させることができるので，防災上有効な構成になる．この結果連続した大空間の安全性を高めることにつながる．こうした防災を考慮した室内構成により9万m²の屋根の下に，仕切りのない連続する巨大空間が可能になった． (N.O.)

CIRCULATION
動線計画

The passenger terminal building at the Kansai International Airport houses both international and domestic terminals measuring a total of 294,000 square meters. This building has a frontage of 1,670 meters and 33 boarding gates, each equipped with a boarding bridge. The most important challenge for designers and builders was to enable users to reach their destinations in this huge and complicated building smoothly and with minimal walking distance. The central Main Terminal Building (MTB) has domestic arrival and departure gates on the second level located between the international departure facilities on the fourth floor and the international arrival facilities on the ground level. As the cross-sectional view suggests, this arrangement is called a "sandwich structure." It enables quick and easy transit from international to domestic flights and vice versa using only vertical movements inside the building. This is one of the main features of this airport. Passengers can also swiftly move to international departure gates located on the airport's north and south wing using a transportation system called as the wing shuttle.

The second floor accommodates the domestic arrival and departure facilities and is linked via eight connecting bridges to a railway station served by both the JR and Nankai lines, as well as to a parking building capable of housing 4,500 cars and a multi-purpose complex called the aero plaza (consisting of a hotel, shops, and offices). The path of circulation here is simple, with no changes in floor level.

In addition to the public areas along the passenger circulation, there are baggage sorting areas on the first floor and a main concession stand (comprising shops and restaurants) on the third floor of the MTB, respectively. These facilities are easily accessible from the second floor (domestic arrivals and departures) and fourth floor (international departures). In addition, the MTB consists of communal areas such as rented out to airline companies, machine rooms, shafts and staircases and areas for governmental use (including customs clearance, immigration, and quarantine checks). Sections inside the MTB are first divided into public and private zones. They are also classified into restricted and unrestricted zones from a security standpoint. Otherwise, they are classified into bonded areas and unbonded areas from a customs standpoint. Entrance to the restricted and bonded areas is strictly monitored.

旅客ターミナルビルは，294,000㎡の国際線，国内線両ターミナルを内包している．33の駐機スポットの固定橋を持つその間口は1,670mにも及んでいる．このように巨大で，さらに複雑な機能を持つビルの中を，旅客がスムーズに短い歩行距離で目的の場所に移動できることが空間づくりの命題である．ターミナルビルの中央部，メインターミナルビル（MTB）の断面は2階国内線フロアを4階国際線出発フロアと1階国際線到着フロアで上下にはさむ構成で，サンドイッチ構造と呼ばれる．上下の移動だけで国際国内間の乗り継ぎができることが大きな特徴である．MTBから南北に伸びたウイングの国際線ゲートラウンジにある各ゲートへもウイングシャトルでスピーディに移動できる．

国内線のある2階は，JR・南海両鉄道の乗り入れる鉄道駅，4,500台収容の立体駐車場，さらに奥のエアロプラザ（ホテル，商業施設，事務所などの複合施設）に8本の連絡橋で結ばれており，レベルチェンジのないシンプルな動線になっている．

MTB内には旅客動線上にあるパブリック部分以外に，旅客の手荷物を目的の航空機別に仕分ける荷さばき場が1階に，メインコンセッション（店舗，レストラン）は3階にあり，2階（国内線），4階（国際線出発）どちらのフロアからも利用しやすくなっている．これに航空会社諸室（ラウンジなど）の貸室，機械室，シャフト，階段などの共用部分に，CIQ（税関，出入国審査，検疫）の官庁部分が加わって構成される．ターミナルビル内は官民区分で明確にゾーニングされるほか，セキュリティによる制限／非制限エリア，保税上のボンドエリア（国外扱い）／アンボンドエリア（国内扱い）に区分され，これらの間の出入りは厳しくチェックされる．　　　　　　　　　　（文責／編集部）

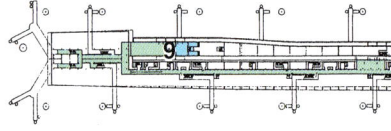

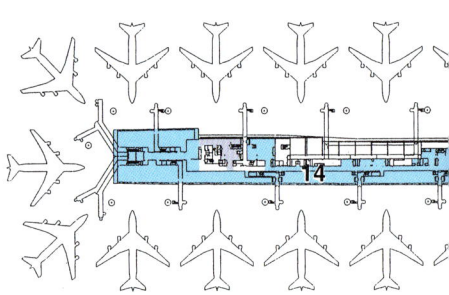

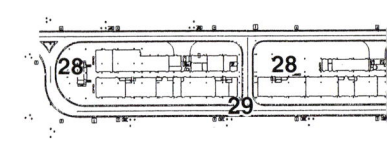

1. Dep. Curbside 出発カーブサイド
2. Canyon キャニオン
3. International Dep. Lobby 国際線出発ロビー
4. Security セキュリティ
5. Airlines Administration Bld., South 航空会社事務棟 南棟
6. Airlines Administration Bld., North 航空会社事務棟 北棟
7. CIQ Administration Building CIQ管理棟
8. Airport Administration Building 空港管理棟
9. Wing Shuttle Station ウイングシャトル駅
10. Concessions コンセッション
11. Machine Room 機械室
12. Immigration 出国審査場
13. Transit トランジット
14. International gate Lounge 国際線ゲートラウンジ
15. Domestic Check-in Lobby 国内線出発／到着ロビー
16. Immigration 入国検査場
17. Baggage Claim バゲージクレイム
18. Domestic Gate Lounge 国内線ゲートラウンジ
19. Swing Gate lounge スウイングゲートラウンジ
20. Arr. Curbside 到着カーブサイド
21. International Arrival Lobby 国際線到着ロビー
22. Customs 税関検査場
23. Baggage Claim バゲージクレイム
24. International Baggage Handing 国際線バゲージハンドリングエリア
25. Domestic Baggage Handling 国内線バゲージハンドリングエリア
26. International Bus Lounge 国際線バスラウンジ
27. Domestic Bus Lounge 国内線バスラウンジ
28. GSE Garage GSE置場
29. GSE Road Area GSE走行帯
30. Airline Offices 航空会社事務室

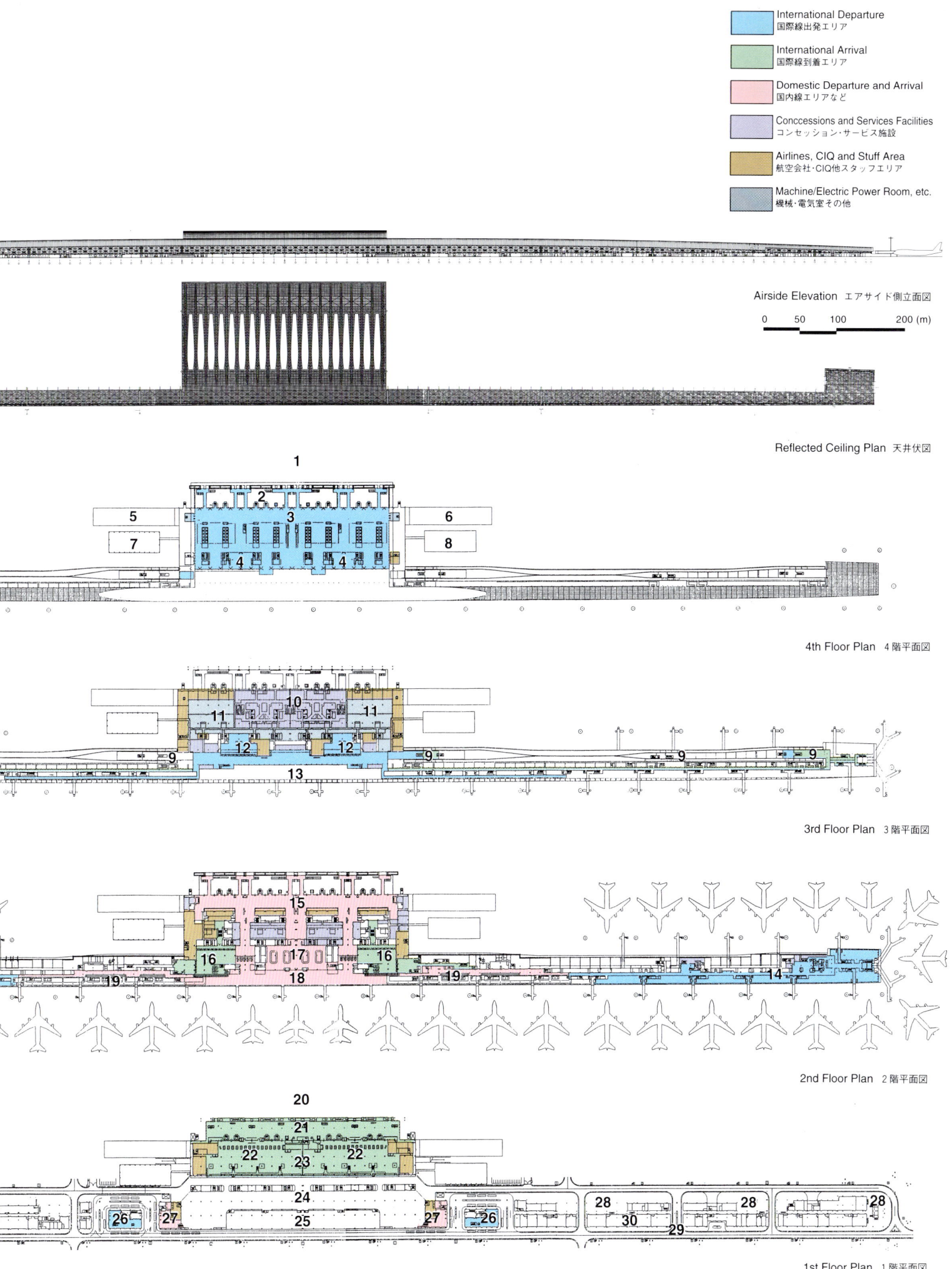

Passenger circulation
旅客動線図

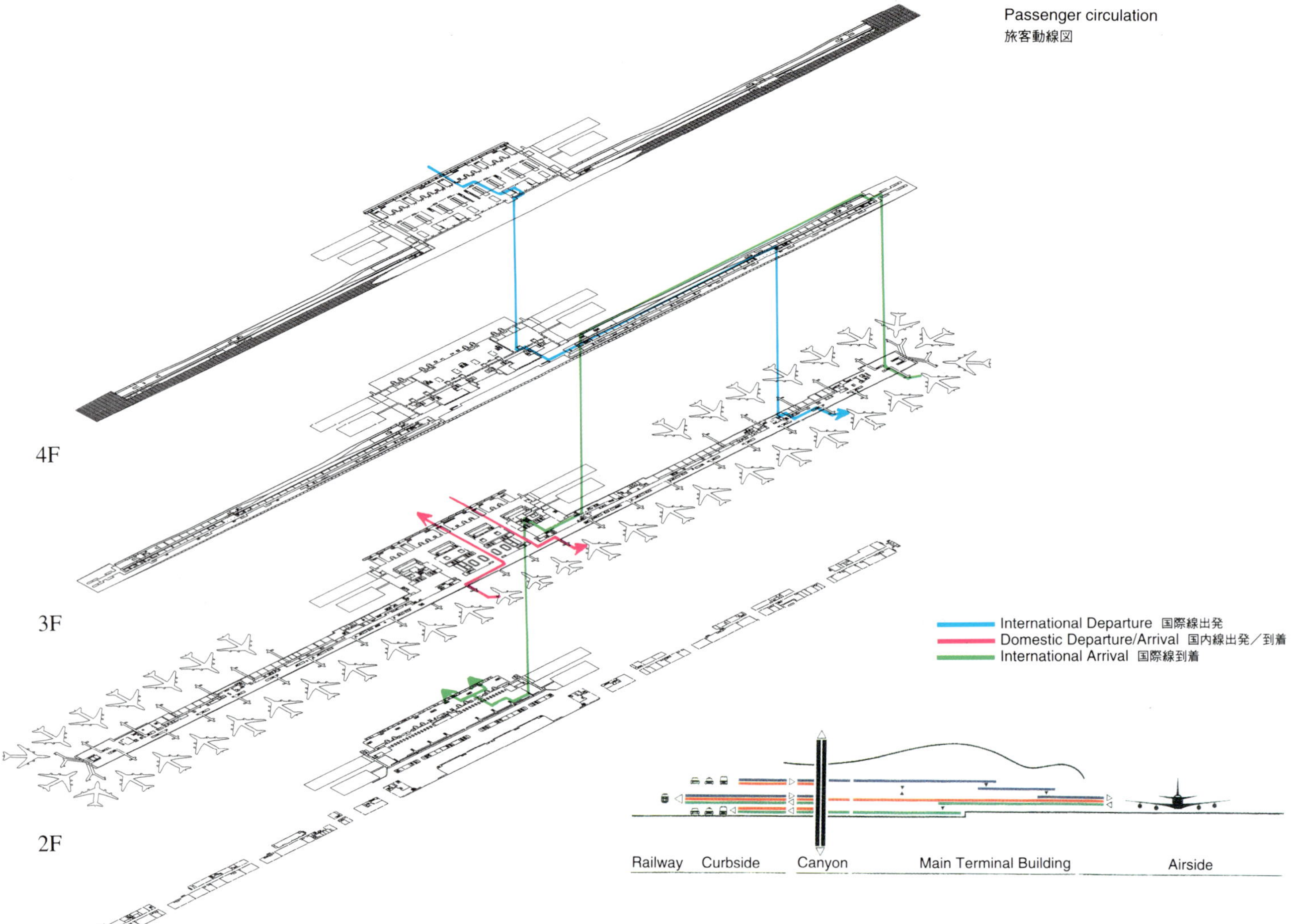

4F
3F
2F
1F

— International Departure　国際線出発
— Domestic Departure/Arrival　国内線出発/到着
— International Arrival　国際線到着

Railway　Curbside　Canyon　Main Terminal Building　Airside

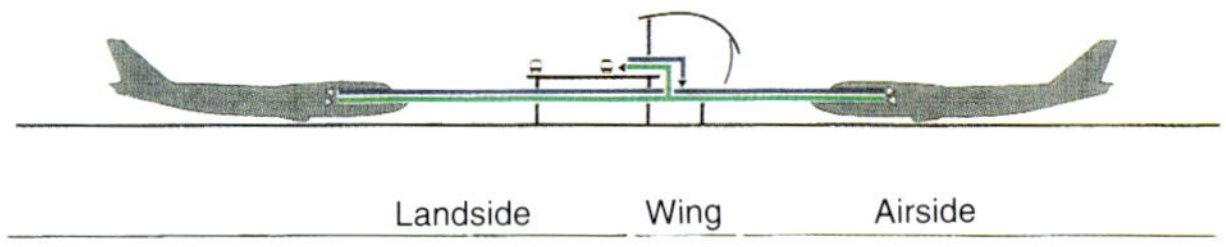

Landside　Wing　Airside

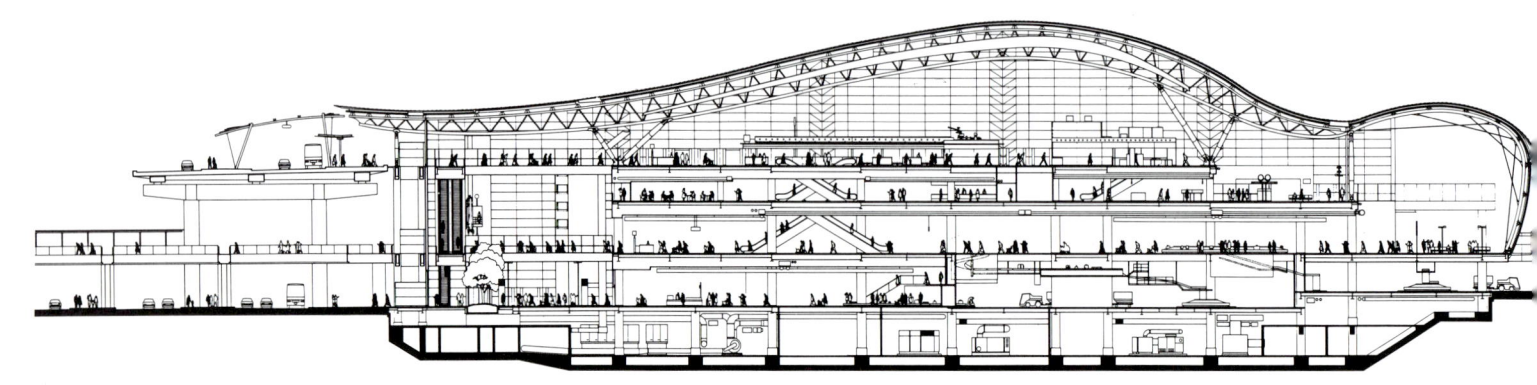

Outgoing international passengers proceed from the fourth floor entrance of the MTB to the departure lobby on the same level by way of Canyon bridges, check in at the counter, and go through security clearance before heading down to the third floor for immigration checks and a ride on the wing shuttle. Passengers arriving on international flights go through the arrival concourse on the third floor of the wing and use the wing shuttle to get to the MTB. On the second floor of the MTB, they undergo quarantine and immigration inspection. Then, they move to the ground level for baggage pickups and customs clearance before reaching the arrival lobby. Trusses for the big roof that flow from the landside (parking side) to the airside (runway side) form a consecutive pattern toward the wings and afford an unobstructed view. The wide, open space along the path of circulation makes it easy for passengers to know where they are and where they are heading. The Canyon located between the rail and bus station and the check-in lobby is a space brimming with natural light. It is also a space for vertical movement where escalators, see-through elevators and glass stairways are concentrated in such a manner as to guarantee an unobstructed view. Passengers boarding domestic flights can walk straight to the boarding area from the railway station, which is expected to be a popular access point, without any changes in floor level. Those arriving on domestic flights will follow the opposite path. The circulation will be simple for both domestic arrivals and departures at the airport.

In close consultation with Osaka Prefecture, airport authorities have implemented comprehensive guide plans covering the terminal building and the adjacent railway station. Their objective is to ensure that physically handicapped people can follow the same circulation as passengers' one. There will be elevators designed to transport the handicapped and information counters for providing personalized services. In a space as big and functionally complex as this terminal building, large baggage alone could obstruct free movement of passengers. In this situation, meticulous consideration for the disabled works to improve the functioning of the terminal building for everyone.

In this sandwich-structured MTB, elevators and escalators are used mainly for vertical movements. The Canyon is equipped with see-through elevators and gently sloping escalators that can also accommodate carts.

Passengers in the check-in lobby can take advantage of connected escalators to reach the second, third or fourth floors quickly. Also, each gate on the wings is installed with elevators and escalators connected to the boarding bridge. They enable passengers to enter the concourse on the third floor smoothly and head for their destination by riding on a wing shuttle.

The wing shuttle is an unmanned, fully automated transport system that runs on the roof at the third floor of the two wings. It offers quick access to gates located on the north and south wings, each of which stretches out 680 meters from the main terminal building. The shuttle can reach the intermediate stations in 60 seconds and the wing terminal stations in 90 seconds. A wing shuttle consists of three coaches. One of the coaches carries up to 82 people and is reserved for departing passengers. The other two are reserved for arriving passengers and have a combined capacity of 161 people. The rubber-wheeled shuttle is powered by electricity.

The baggages checked in at airline counters by passengers departing on international flights descend through spiral shafts to the baggage handling area (baggage handling zone) on the airside of the first floor of the MTB and are automatically sorted by flight. In this section, an automatic sorting system is employed to sort the baggage according to the departure data supplied by airlines at the time of check-in.

— *Nikken Sekkei*

国際線の出発旅客はMTB 4 階入口からキャニオンのブリッジを渡って同じ階にあるロビーでチェックインをすませ，セキュリティコントロールを受けた後，3 階に下り，出国検査を経てウイングシャトル駅に向かう．国際線到着旅客は3 階の到着コンコースを通り，ウイングシャトルをつかってMTBに入る．そこで2 階の検疫，入国審査から1 階のバゲージクレーム，税関検査を経てキャニオン1 階の到着ロビーに至る．MTBのランドサイド（駐車場側）からエアサイド（滑走路側）に流れる大屋根トラスは，両ウイングに向かって連続しているので見通しが良く，動線に沿って広がる空間が，旅客の進む方向，位置確認を容易にしている．鉄道・バスの到着場所とチェックインロビーとの間にあるキャニオンは，自然光あふれる空間であると同時に，上下階への移動空間であり，エスカレーター，シースルーエレベーター，ガラス階段が見通しを確保しつつ集中的に配置されている．国内線出発では，旅客の多くが利用する鉄道駅からレベルチェンジすることなくエアサイドに直進，航空機に搭乗できる．到着客はその反対の流れにのり，国内線は発着双方とも簡潔な動線になる．

これら旅客の動線は，身障者も同様の動線をたどれるように大阪府との綿密な協議を踏まえ，鉄道駅を含めた総合的な誘導計画が施されている．上下移動には，身障者対応エレベーターが配置されるほか，案内カウンターなど適切な人的サービスが受けられるよう工夫されている．ターミナルビルのような巨大，かつ複雑な機能を持つ空間では荷物を携えて来るということだけで移動の障害となってしまいがちである．その意味でもきめ細かい身障者への配慮は，そのままターミナルビル本来の性能を向上させることにもつながる．

サンドイッチ構造のMTBで旅客の上下移動は，主にエレベーター，エスカレーターが使われる．キャニオンには見通しを良くするためのシースルーエレベーターと，カートも一緒に乗り込める緩勾配エスカレーターがある．チェックイン・ロビーではエスカレーターで 2～4 階間を瞬時に乗り継ぐことができる．またウイングの各ゲートには，各固定橋に結びついたエレベーターとエスカレーターが設けられ，スムーズに3 階のコンコースにつながり，ウイングシャトルへ移動することができる．

ターミナルビル南北に伸びるウイング（各680m）のゲートまで短時間に移動できるよう，ウイング3 階屋上に無人自動運転のウイングシャトルが走っている．MTB両端の本館駅から中間駅（所要時間1分），先端駅（所要時間1分半）とシャトル運行する車両本体は，出到着分離のために出発専用1両（82人乗り），到着専用2両（161人乗り）の計3両からなるゴムタイヤ式の電動車両である．

国際線のチェックインカウンターで旅客が航空会社に預けた手荷物は，スパイラル状のシャフトを降りてMTBエアサイド側1階のバゲージハンドリングエリア（荷さばきゾーン）で自動的に出発便ごとに仕分けられる．ここにはチェックイン時の情報に基づいて荷物を自動的に出発便により分けるオートソーティングシステム（自動仕分けシステム）が採用されている．到着手荷物は取り降ろしブレークダウンコンベアにのって1階バゲージクレームに搬送される． （文責／日建設計）

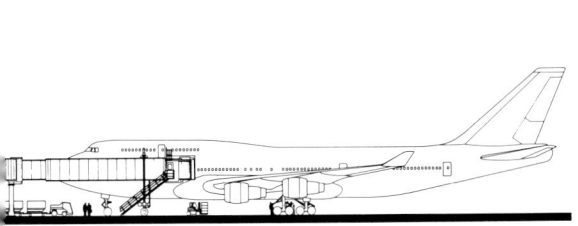
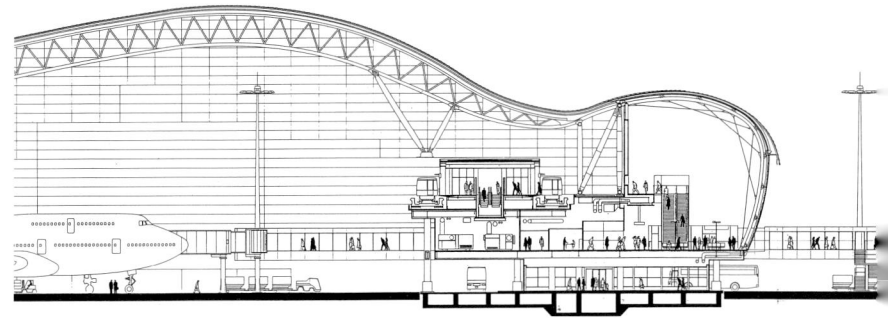

Main Terminal Building, Roof Structure
メインターミナルビル

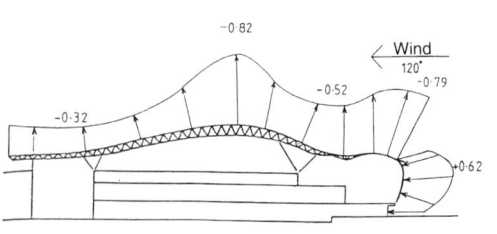
Wind force coefficients of MTB　MTBの風圧係数

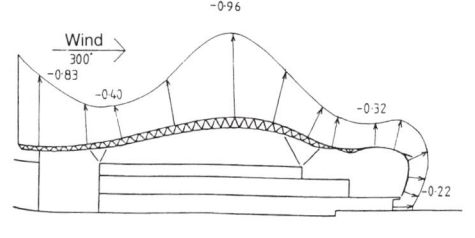

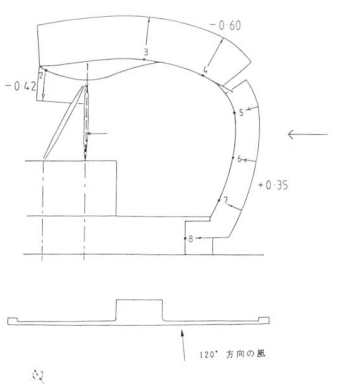
Wind force coefficients of Wing　ウイングの風圧係数

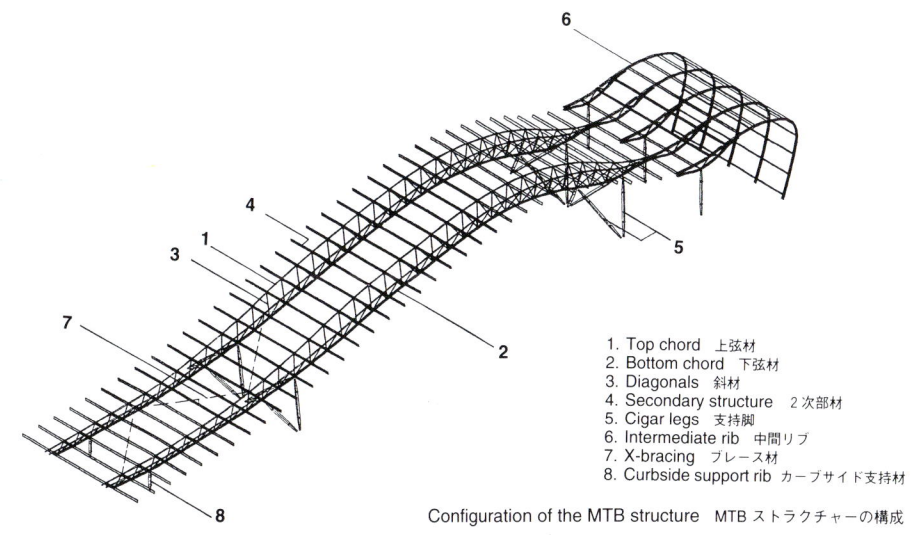

1. Top chord　上弦材
2. Bottom chord　下弦材
3. Diagonals　斜材
4. Secondary structure　2次部材
5. Cigar legs　支持脚
6. Intermediate rib　中間リブ
7. X-bracing　ブレース材
8. Curbside support rib　カーブサイド支持材

Configuration of the MTB structure　MTB ストラクチャーの構成

© 川崎重工業

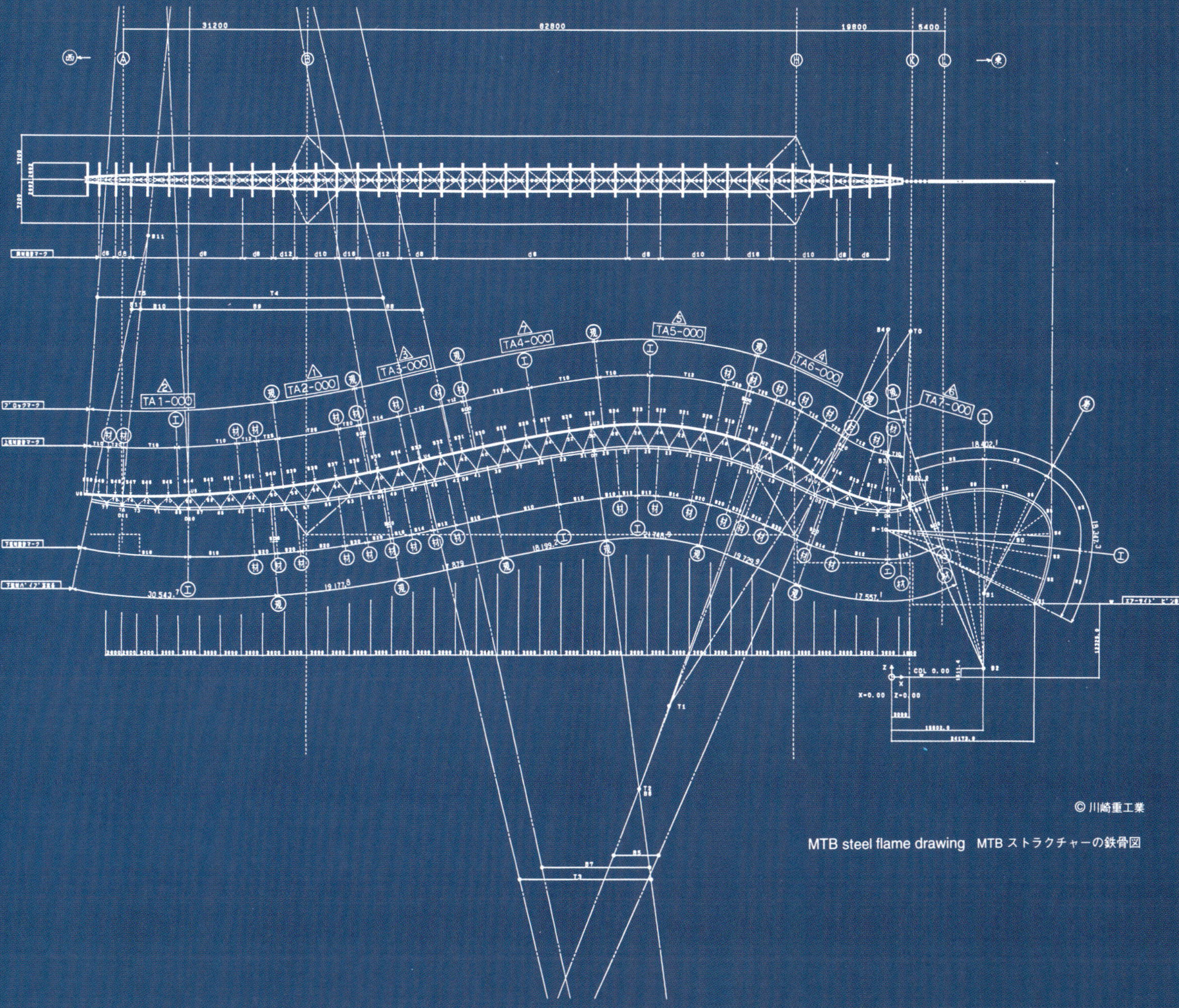

MTB steel flame drawing MTB ストラクチャーの鉄骨図

Result of roof truss, Model Analys's
屋根架構の振動数固有値解析

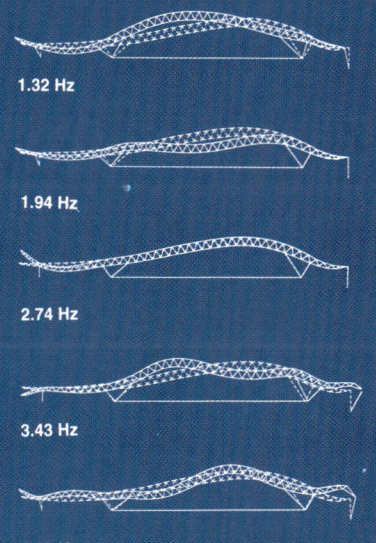

1.32 Hz
1.94 Hz
2.74 Hz
3.43 Hz
4.57 Hz

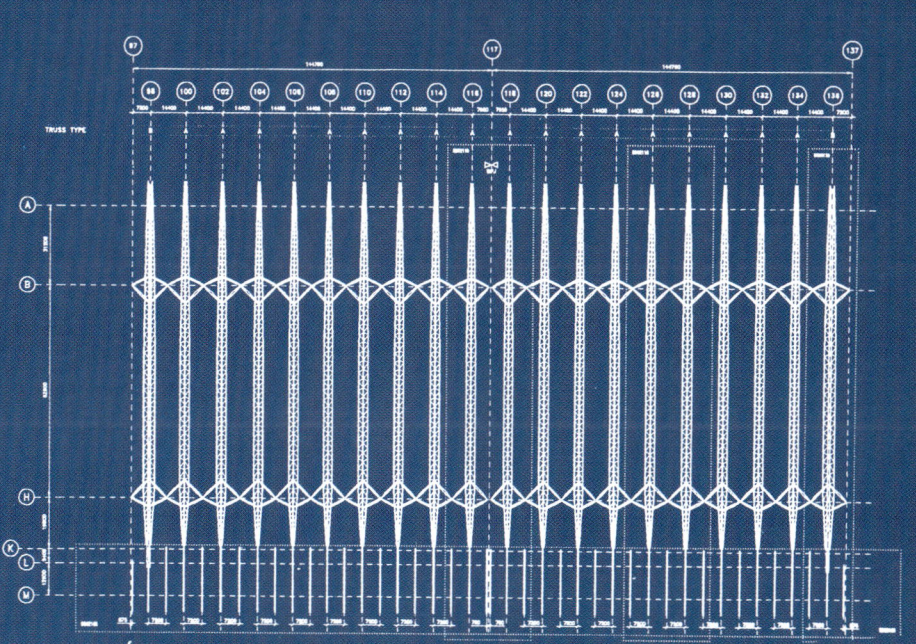

MTB structure flaming plan MTB ストラクチャーの鉄骨伏図

View toward landside at the north end of the 4th floor. 4階北側エンドウォール付近からランドサイド方向を見る．

Left/Close up view of roof truss from the support column on [L] line.
左／手前ウイングから奥の大空間へ向かうトラス（右はL通り）．

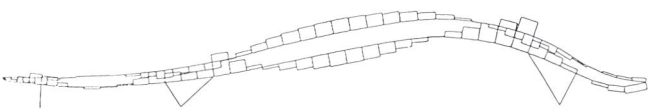

Top and bottom chord stress under vertical loading
鉛直荷重時上下弦材軸力図

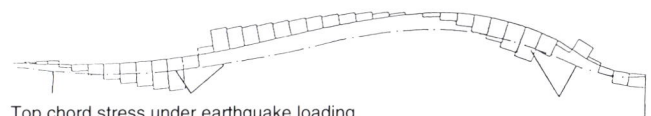

Top chord stress under earthquake loading
地震荷重時上弦材軸力図

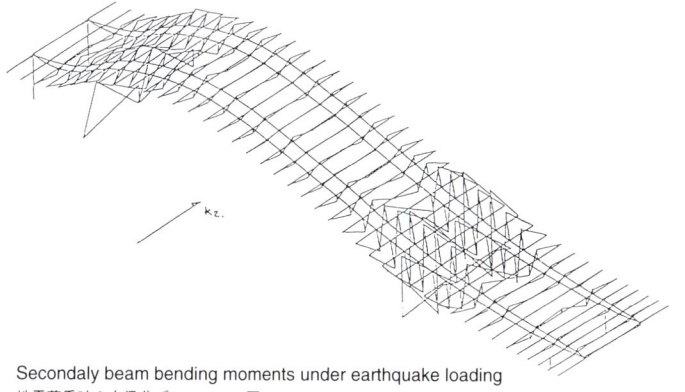

Secondaly beam bending moments under earthquake loading
地震荷重時2次梁曲げモーメント図

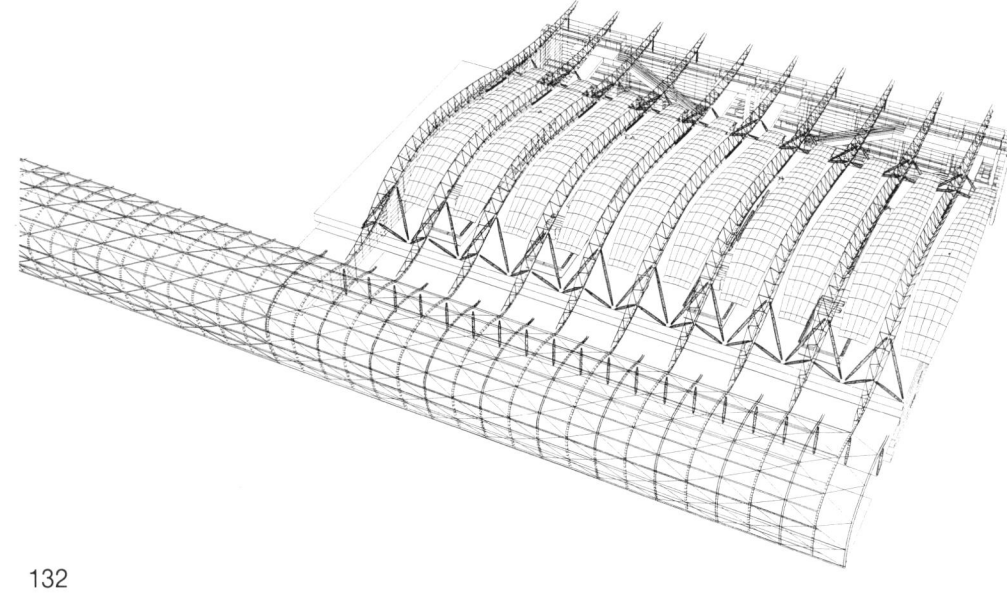

Election of the roof of MTB. Mar. 1993
MTB屋根の建方（1993年3月）

MTB erection MTB建方図

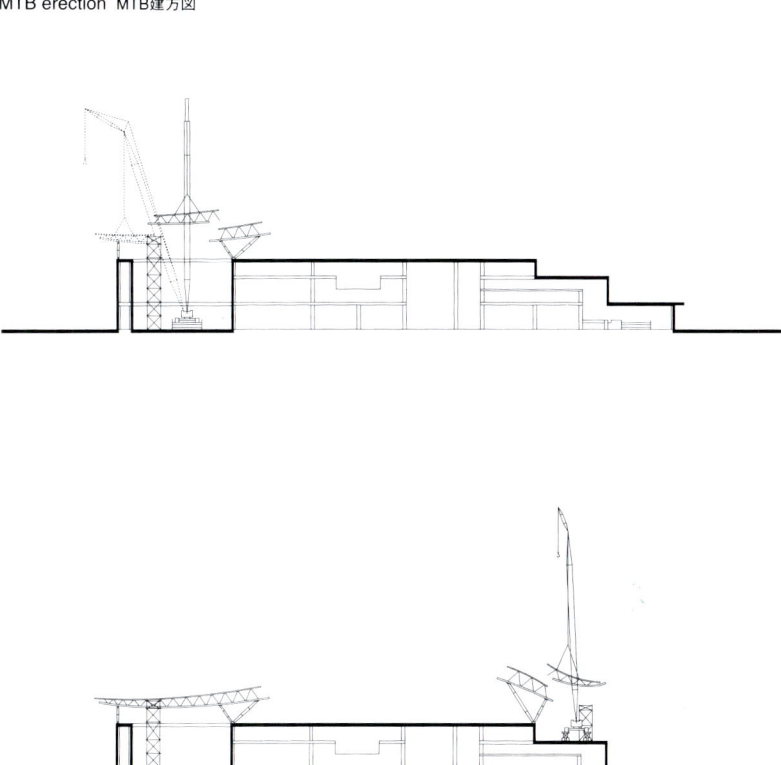
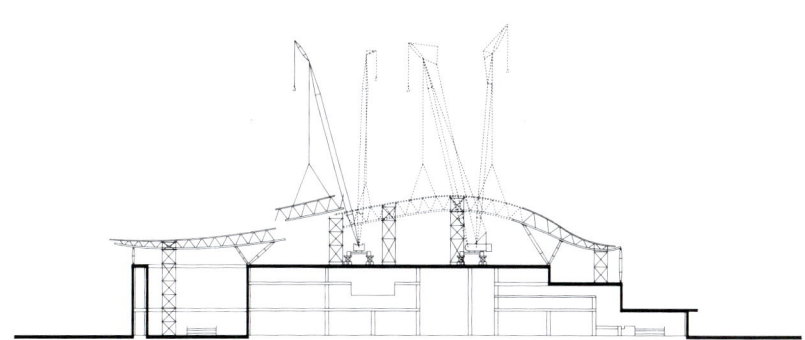
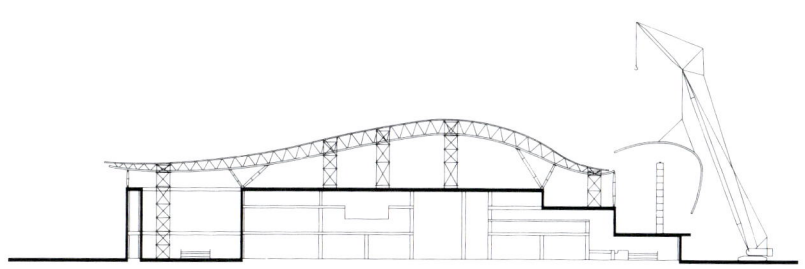

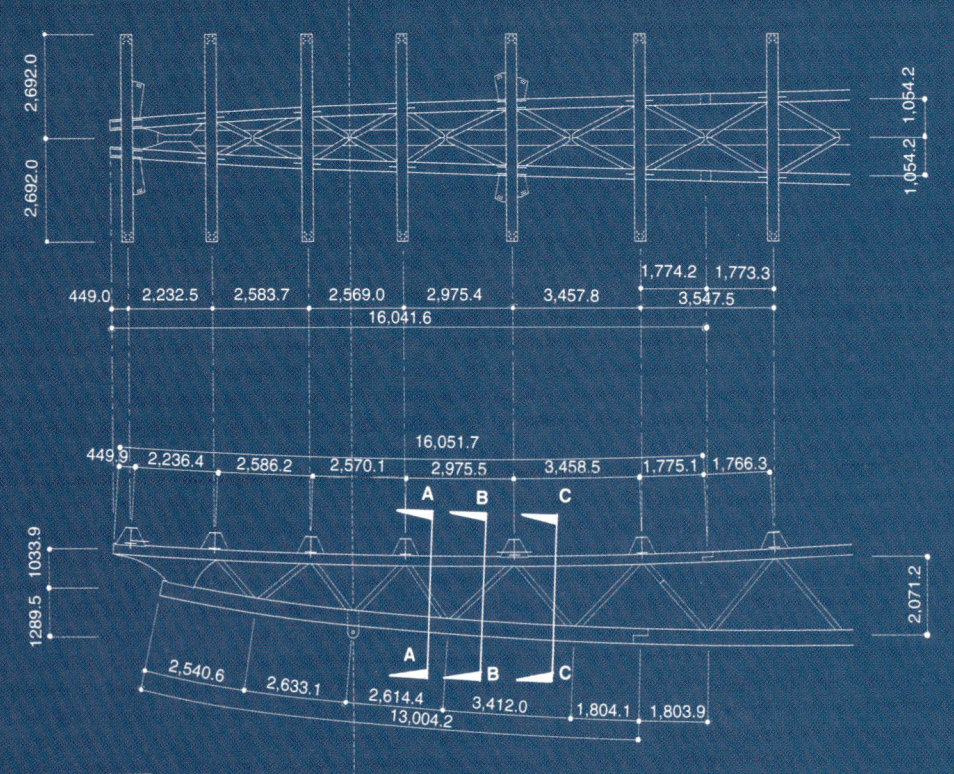 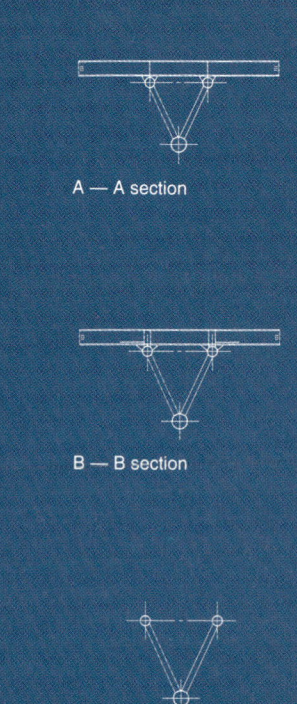

1. Detail drawing, curbside of MTB truss
   MTBトラス（カーブサイド）詳細図

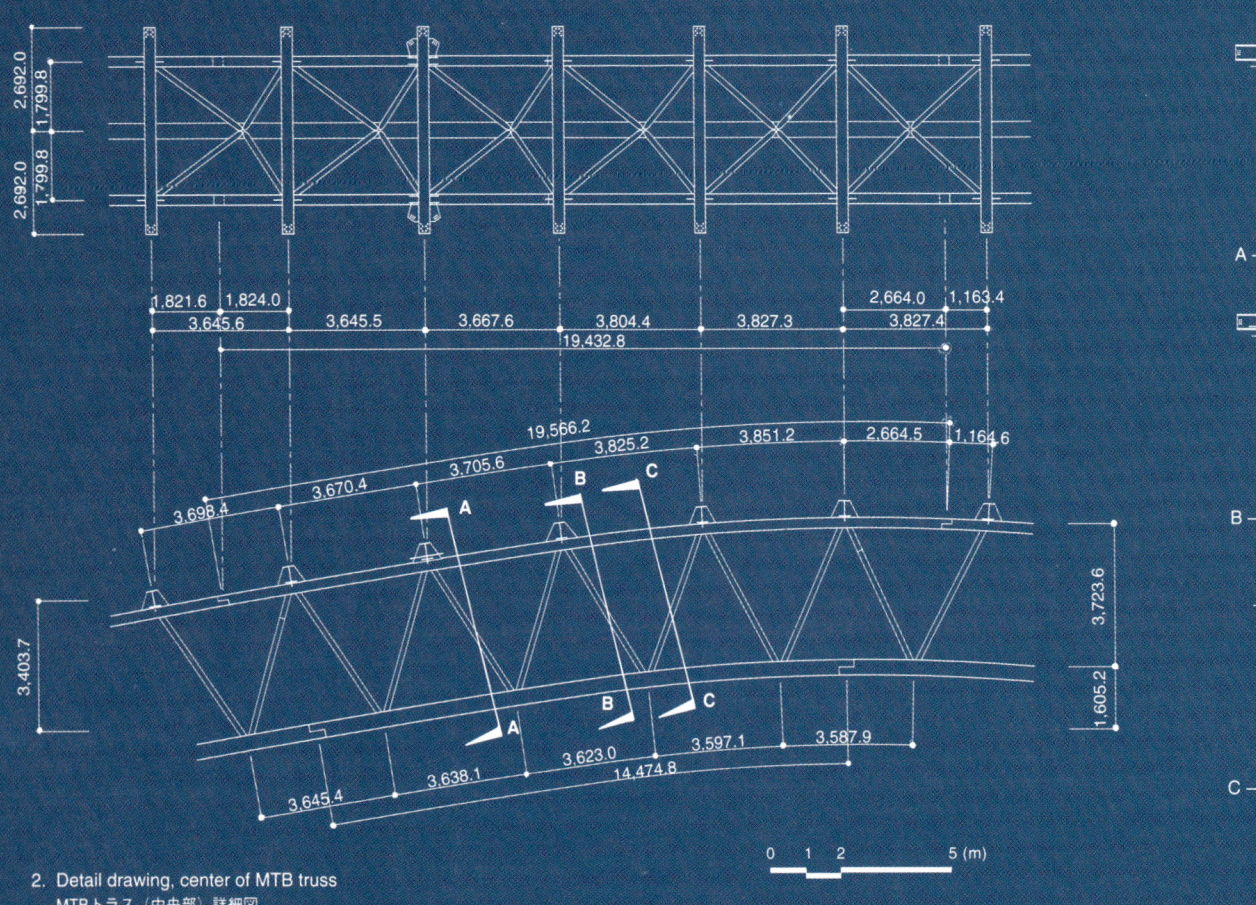 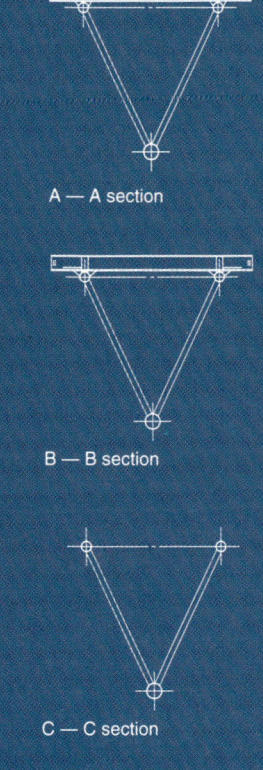

2. Detail drawing, center of MTB truss
   MTBトラス（中央部）詳細図

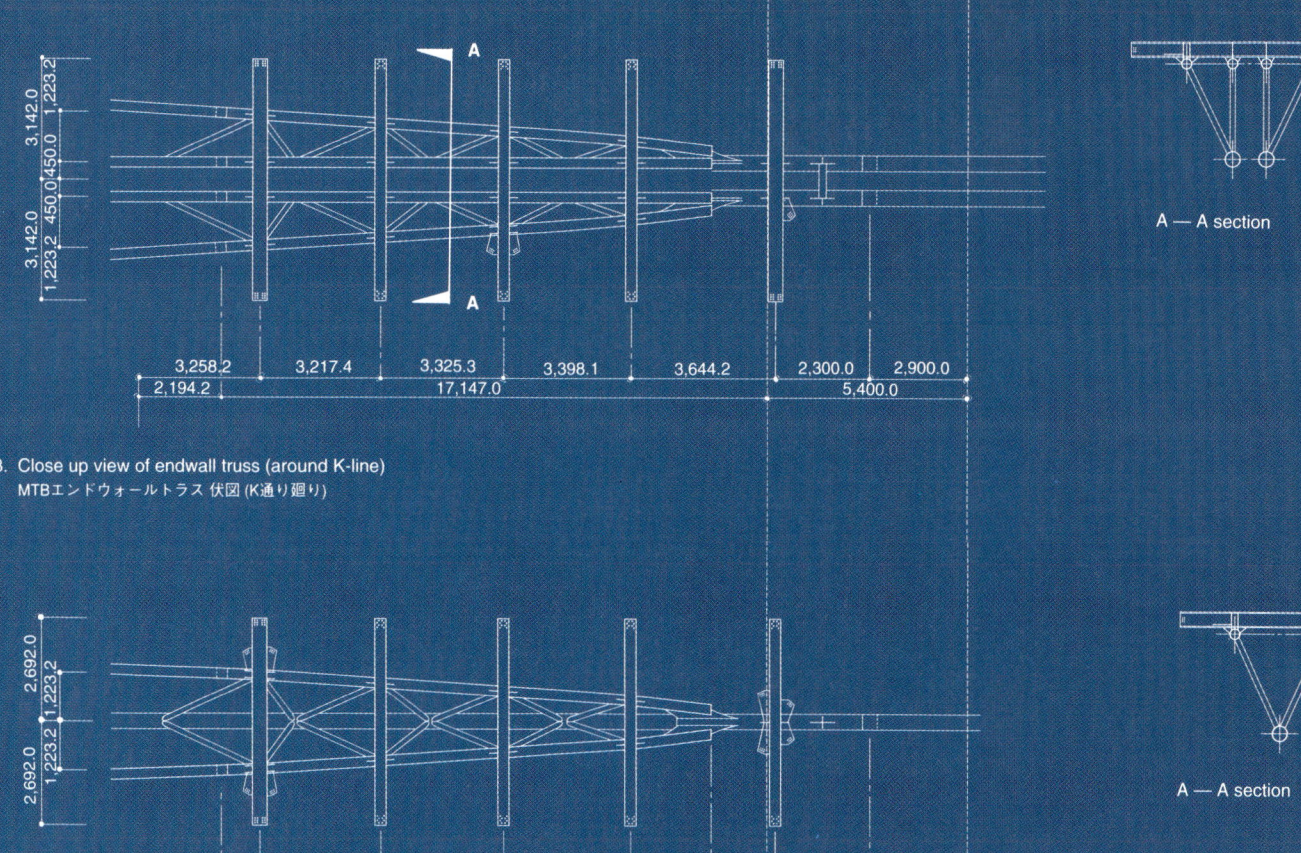

3. Close up view of endwall truss (around K-line)
MTBエンドウォールトラス 伏図 (K通り廻り)

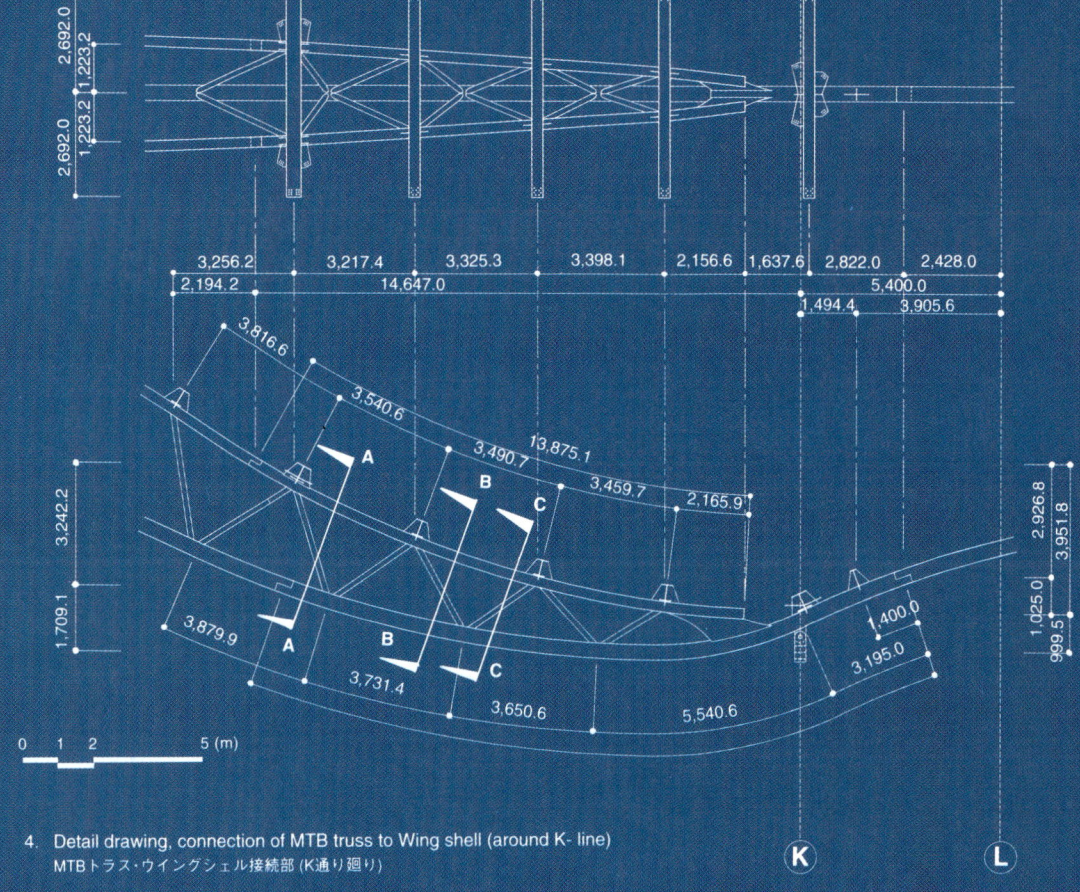

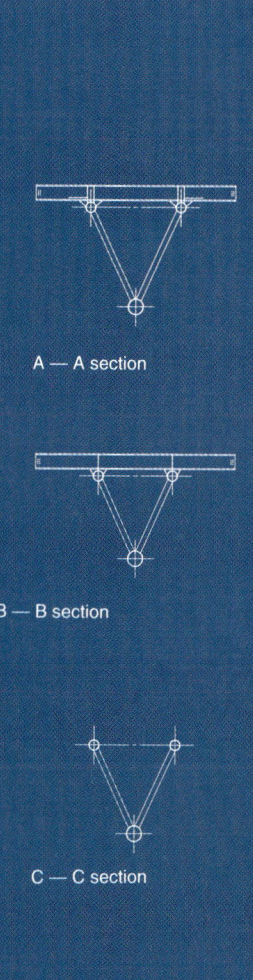

4. Detail drawing, connection of MTB truss to Wing shell (around K-line)
MTBトラス・ウイングシェル接続部 (K通り廻り)

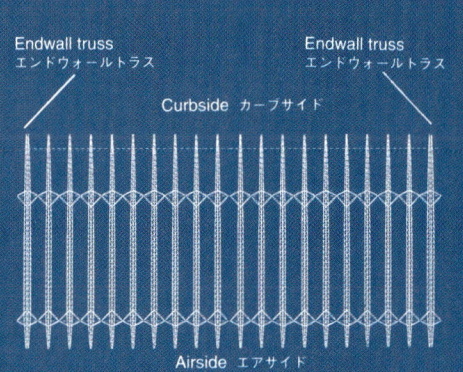

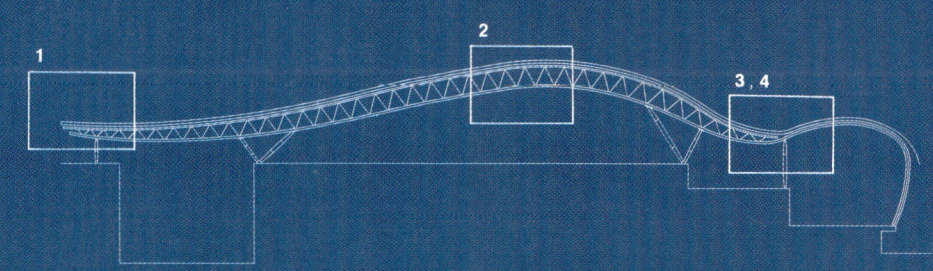

OPEN AIR DUCT
Air conditioning and illumination membranes
オープンエアダクト：空調と照明の白い膜

In order to maintain a smooth flow of air, we devised a set of open air ducts made by suspending a thin membrane from the ceiling in a roughly parallel pattern. Ultimately the skin chosen for the these ducts was a white lustrous teflon, 19 sheets in all, which would not only serve as a conduit for air but also function as part of the indirect lighting by reflecting illumination from below. Lighting originates with the "lighting poles" (technical trees) 3.5 meters high and lights installed in the upper part of the check-in counter and elsewhere. This fluctuation of air currents and flow of light creates a ceiling with a soft but varied expression. This method also eliminated the necessity for any air conditioning or lighting equipment in the ceiling and created a ceiling filled with light and moving air, yet light-weight and requiring no troublesome maintenance. —*N. O.*

なめらかな気流を保つために，天井面にほぼ平行してオープンエアダクトと名づけた薄い膜を吊ることが考案された．オープンエアダクトの膜は最終的に19個の光沢のある白色のテフロンに決定し，空気の誘導以外に下部から照射される間接照明の反射膜としても機能する．照明源は床から約3.5mの高さのライティング・ポール(テクニカル・ツリー)やチェックインカウンターの上部に設置されている．変化のある気流と光の流れによって，天井はソフトで豊かな表情を生み出すことになる．この方法によって，天井から空調機械と電気照明設備が消え，軽量でかつメンテナンスのいらない輝く気流の天井が実現する．　　(N.O.)

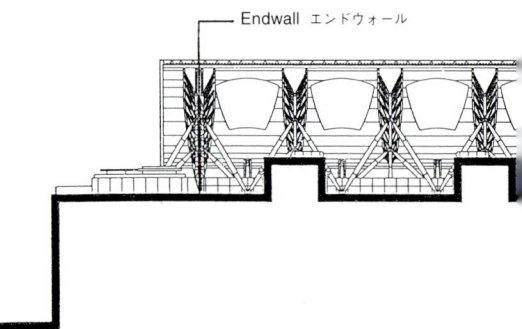

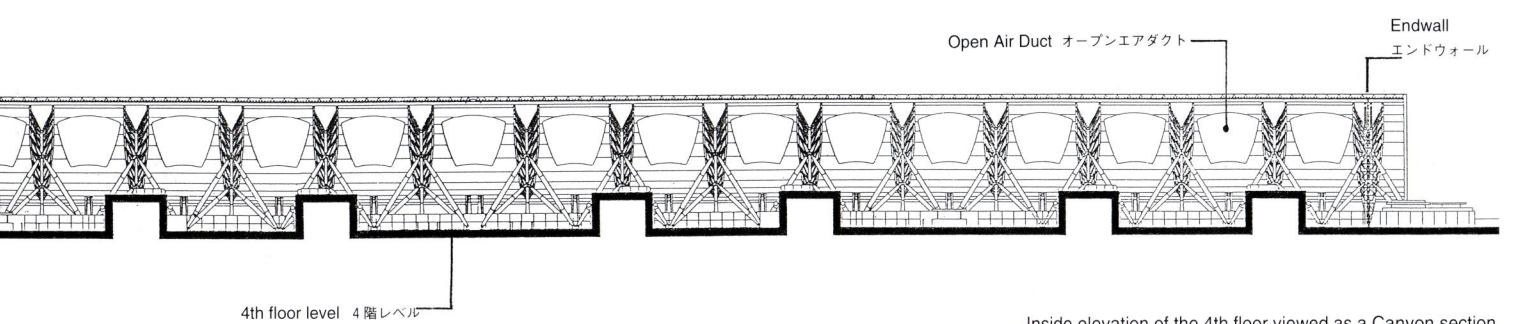

Inside elevation of the 4th floor viewed as a Canyon section
キャニオン側から見る4階大空間

Open Air Duct オープンエアダクト
Endwall エンドウォール
4th floor level 4階レベル

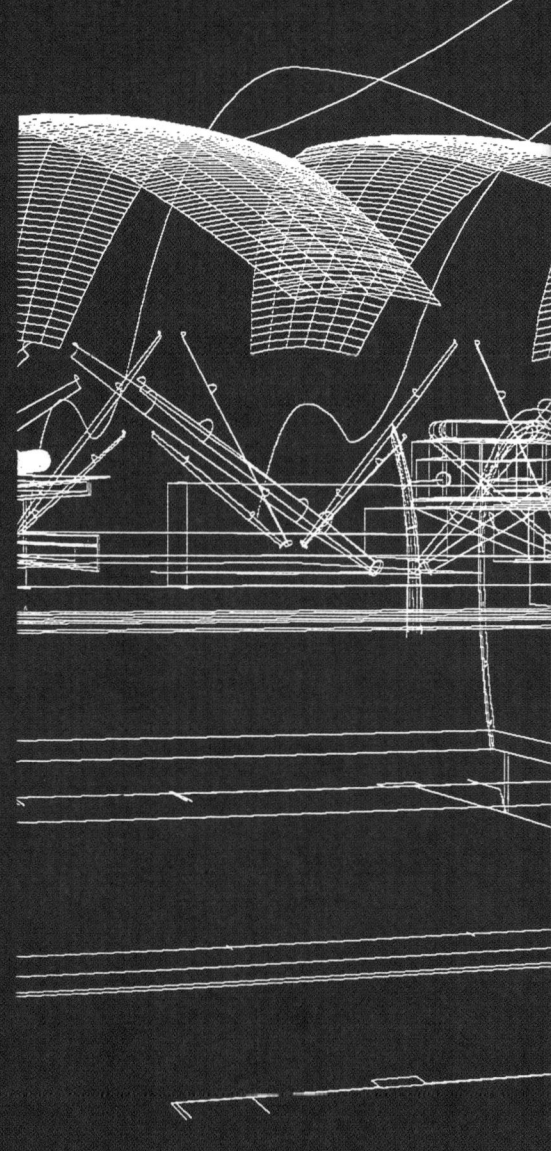

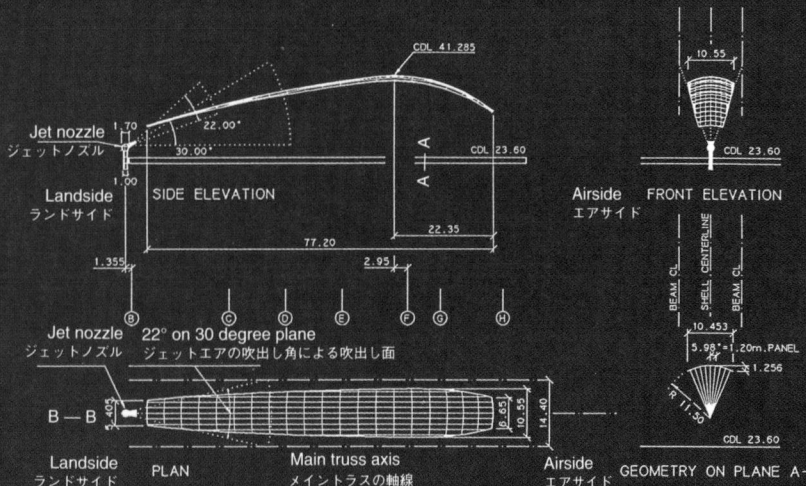

Geometry of the Open Air Duct (Preliminary design drawing)
オープンエアダクトのジオメトリー (基本設計)

Air-Conditioning Plan for Large, Open Spaces

Large, open spaces inside the passenger terminal building (PTB) consist of the international departure lobby on the fourth floor of the MTB (referred to as "MTB's fourth floor" hereinafter), the Canyon or international arrival lobby on the first floor of the MTB, and the gate lounge concourse on the wing of the second and third floors (referred to as "gate lounge" hereinafter). A special air-conditioning system is in place at these large, open spaces, as well as in high-ceilinged locations such as the customs inspection area. This is an example of a system for providing a comfortable environment. This system is based on a program which was proposed by Renzo Piano Building Workshop and Tom Barker (OAP).

MTB's fourth floor has two air-conditioning systems of different sizes, the macro air-conditioning system and the micro air-conditioning system. The macro air-conditioning system features functions for disposing of heat on the roof and supplying fresh air by circulating air from macro jet nozzles (large, horn-shaped jet nozzles) at whole of the fourth floor through open air ducts located along the ceilings. The micro air-conditioning system circulates air from eyeball nozzles (small jet nozzles) installed on decorated, exposed ducts at check-in counters and core elevators. In this way, the system disposes of localized heat burdens in heavily populated areas.

The macro and micro air-conditioning systems incorporate normally used perimeter and interior air-conditioning, as well as general and personal air-conditioning, methods attracting increasing amounts of attention recently, into their architectural designs. To select air currents created by macro jets, such factors as jetting velocity, differences in jetting temperatures, and jetting angles have been studied through numerically-controlled simulations using British and Japanese airflow analysis codes, as well as a British experiment using one-tenth-scale models.

— *Nikken Sekkei*

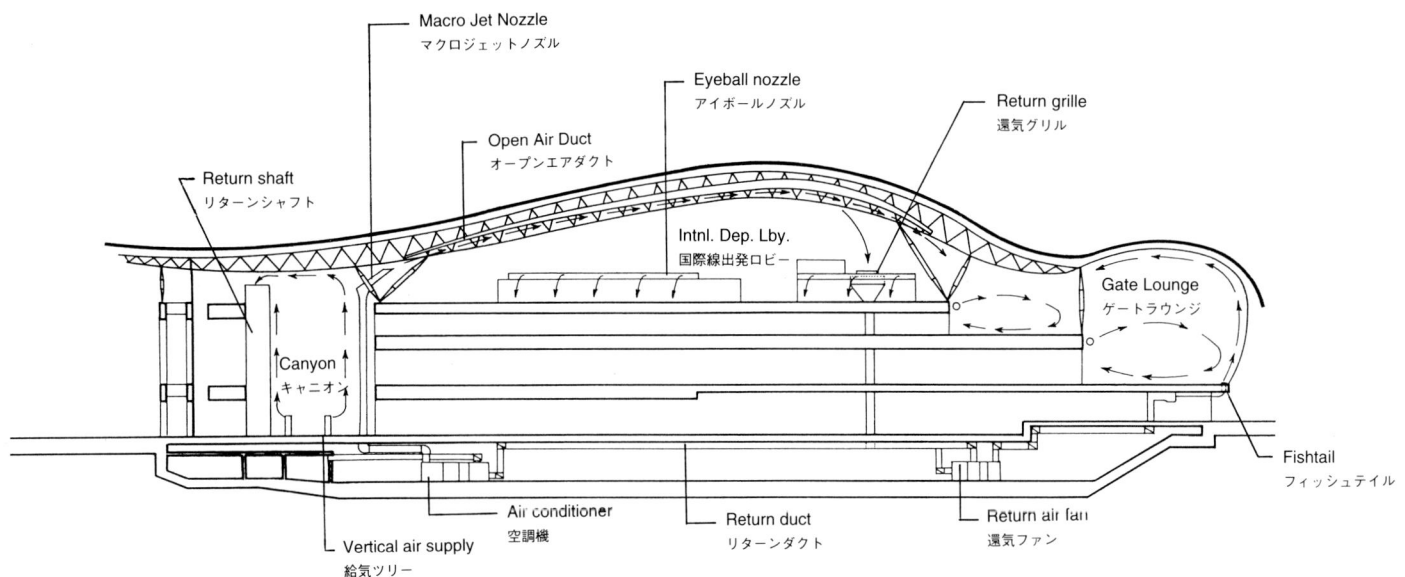

Air-conditioning system　大空間の空調システム図

大空間の空調計画

旅客ターミナルビル（ＰＴＢ）の中の大空間部分は，メインターミナルビル（ＭＴＢ）４階の国際線出発ロビー（以下，ＭＴＢ４階），キャニオン（ＭＴＢ１階，国際線到着ロビー）およびウイング２・３階のゲートラウンジ・コンコース（以下，ゲートラウンジ）の３つのものからなる。ユニットスペースである大空間や，税関検査場などの天井の高いところには，快適な空間を提供する環境システムの例として，独特の空調システムがとり入れられている。このシステムは，コンペ時にビルディング・ワークショップとOAPのトム・バーカーによって提案されたものである。

ＭＴＢ４階には，マクロ空調とミクロ空調と呼ばれる大小２つの空調システムがある。マクロ空調は，マクロジェットノズル（大型角型吹き出しノズル）から吹き出された空調空気を，天井面に沿ったオープンエアダクトに合わせて４階全体を循環させ，屋根面の熱負荷処理と新鮮な外気を供給する機能を持つ。ミクロ空調は，チェックインカウンターとエレベーターコア上部の化粧露出ダクトに取り付けられたアイボールノズル（小型吹き出しノズル）から空調空気を吹き出し，人の滞留域の局所熱負荷を処理する。

マクロ空調とミクロ空調は，通常よく用いられるペリメーターとインテリアや，最近注目されている全体空調とパーソナル空調の考え方を，建築デザインとうまく融合させた形で実現している。マクロジェットの気流性状については，英国及び日本の気流解析コードによる数値シミュレーション及び英国での縮尺10分の1の模型実験により，吹出風速・吹出温度差・吹出角度に関するさまざまな検討が行なわれた。

（文責／日建設計）

Outlet of macro air jet. エアジェットの吹き出し口.

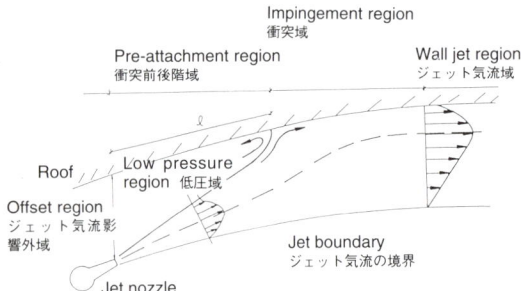

Flow regions of offset jet　ジェット気流分布図

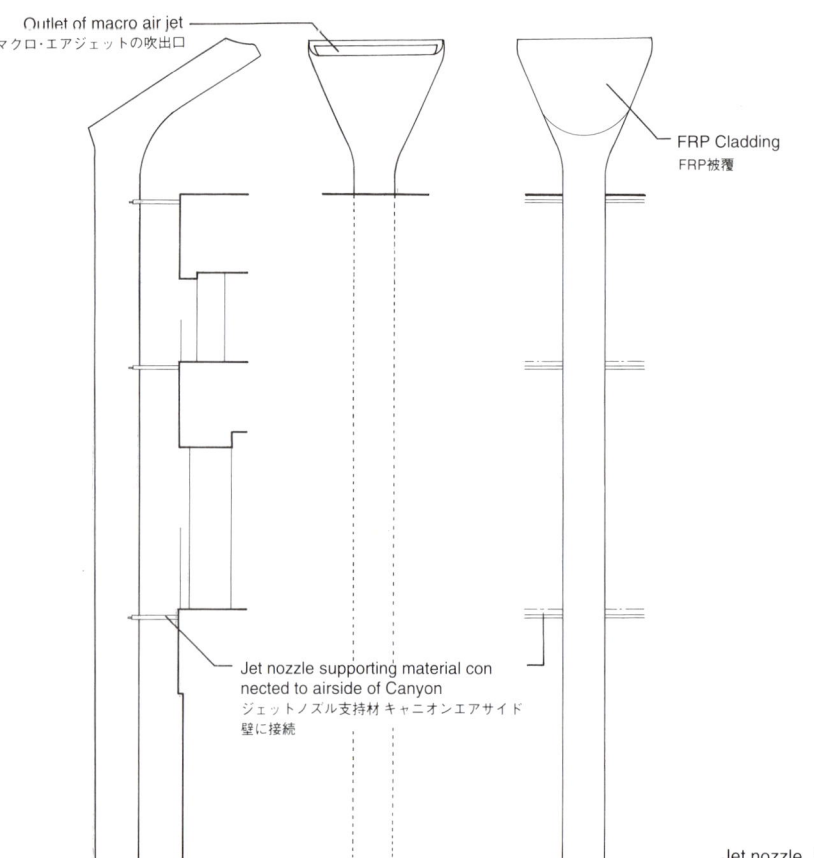

Jet nozzle　ジェットノズル

Jet nozzle　ジェットノズル

1. FRP Cladding　FRP被覆
2. Heat insulating materials　断熱材
3. Steel supply air duct　鋼製給気ダクト
4. Outline supply air duct
　 給気ダクトの外形線
5. Outlet of macro air jet
　 マクロ・エアジェットの吹出口
6. Embedded type diffuser of air-supply duct provided with an angle adjusting mechanism for air-conditioned air flow
　 給気ダクトの埋込み型吹出口 空調気流の角度調整用機構付き
7. Jet nozzle supporting material connected to airside of Canyon
　 ジェットノズル支持材 キャニオンエアサイド壁に接続

Jet nozzle viewed from Canyon. キャニオンから見るジェットノズル.

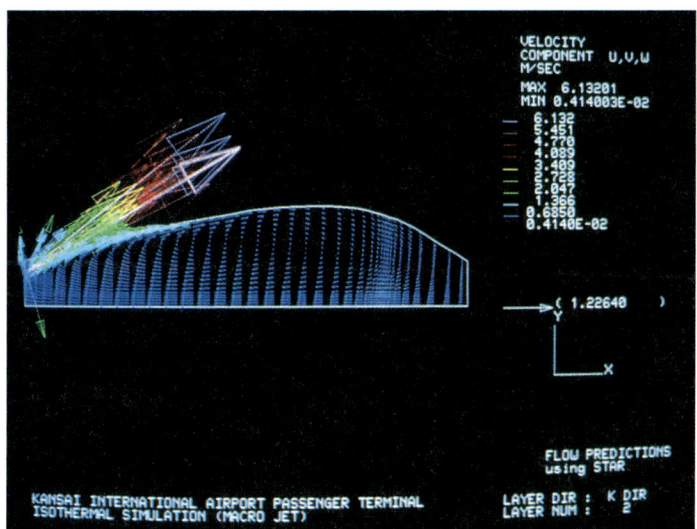

Simulation of jetted air flow by OAP　OAPによる空調シミュレーション

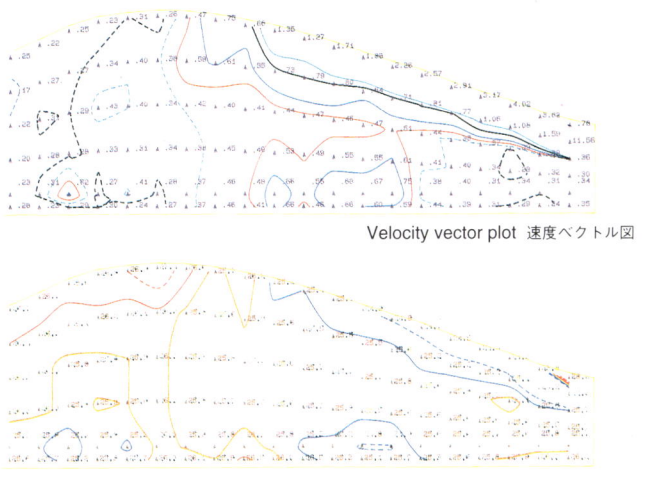

Velocity vector plot　速度ベクトル図

Temperature plot　温度分布図

An average floor illuminance of 200 luxes is the goal of such indirect lighting. Mobiles are designed by Susumu Shingu.
間接照明による床面平均照度は200ルクスである．浮遊彫刻は新宮晋の作．

Illumination Plan

The major characteristics of the terminal building's illumination plan include the illumination of large, open spaces, such as the adoption of indirect lighting on the fourth floor and the illumination control system for public areas, as well as energy-saving methods that take advantage of natural light in such large, open spaces.

To create soft, indirect lighting, light is projected onto open air ducts on the ceilings. In this way, reflected light creates soft shadows. There are other inventive ideas at work, such as the elimination of glare and the prevention of blinding from direct light through the location of light sources on the upper portions of the check-in island and technical boxes.

— *Nikken Sekkei*

照明計画

照明計画の大きな特徴は，4階での間接照明の採用をはじめとする大空間の照明と，パブリックゾーンの照明制御システムと大空間の自然採光利用による省エネルギー化などであった．

天井面のオープンエアダクトに向けて照射したその反射光を使って，きつい影をつくらない柔らかい間接照明にしている．たとえば光源をチェックインアイランド上部とテクニカルボックスに取り付けてグレア（まぶしさ）をなくし，ランプが直接目に入らないようにするなど，さまざまな工夫をこらしている．　　　　　（文責／日建設計）

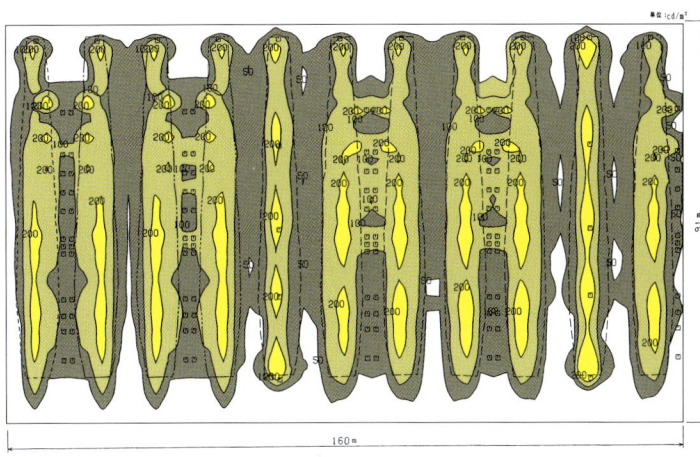

Brightness distribution drawing on Open air duct membrane surface after arrangement of lighting equipment 照明器具配置時のオープンエアダクト膜面における輝度分布図

Metal halide lamps have been adopted as a light source because of their efficiency.
光源は効率のよいメタルハライドランプである．

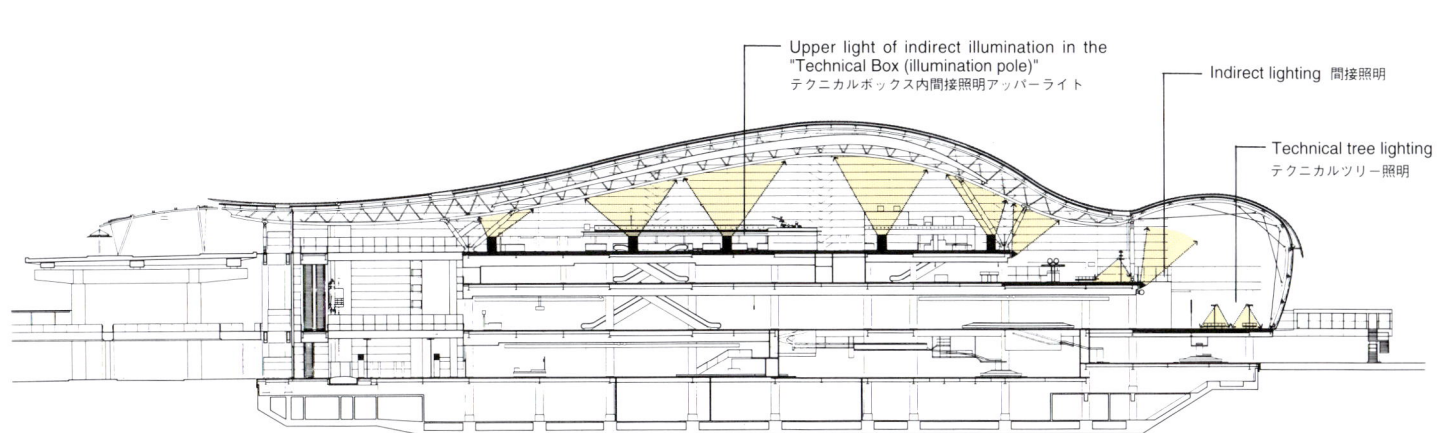

Lighting plan at Canyon, 4th floor and wing. 大空間のライトアップ照明配置

WING
ウイング

Wing Scale

The height of the 1.7-kilometer-long and slender wings tapers down from the center toward the ends in order to assure optimal observation conditions, like the wings of a bird spread out over the ground. We sought to achieve the same sort of dynamic perfection as Brancusi's "Bird in Space," a form that makes one literally feel the flow of air over the contours of the wings as they stretch out gently and symmetrically from the center. Their light weight skin and delicate structure is reminiscent of a glider. Carrying on the continuum of logic and expressing the wings was the next stage of the design.

What specifically determined the form of the wings was a simple symmetric treatment achieved by what might be described as a serial shifting of a section horizontally. We had struggled with a very difficult contour analysis in designing the volumes of the airship-like shopping center on a streetcorner for the Bercy II project in Paris. The initial idea for determining the volume was a revolving paraboloid, but it turned out to be impossible to cover the paraboloid with panels of the same shape. For the KIA terminal building we planned to use stainless-steel tile panels for the skin and conducted many meticulous studies in a search for a method of finding a precise and plain exterior expression to match the irregular volume of the building.

It was in the course of those studies that we asked one of Peter Rice's collaborating engineer, Henry Barsdley, whether the irregular form could be covered by a process of shifting a certain section in a horizontal direction. He found a splendid resolution to the problem of irregularity by parallel movement in horizontal and vertical directions of a section composed of two different-sized circles and one straight line.

Therefore, once the wing volume of the KIA terminal building was to some extent prescribed, it was relatively easy to apply the method we had used for the Bercy II project to create the curve by the section-shifting method. We were fortunate in the KIA design, moreover, in that the wing scale was much larger than in the Bercy II project, giving us 1.7 kilometers in which to graduate the contour. Because of the scale effect of the building itself, the disparities between each section are relatively gradual. It became possible to cover the entire roof surface by simple repetition of a single type of stainless steel panel. This was a detailed resolution made possible by the immense scale of the design.

In the competition plan we created the curves of the wings by rotating a section centering on one focal point, but from the basic design plan onward, in order to avoid difficulties of conformity with the geometry of the main building's roof, we sought a simple horizontal movement of the sections in the linked portion; for the gradually diminishing wings, we drew the curve from a focal point situated at an angle of elevation of 68.2 degrees and a radius of 16.4 km.

—*N. O.*

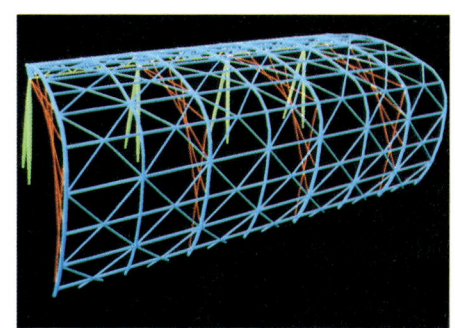

ウイングのスケール

1.7km長の細長いウイングは、視認制限により中央からエッジに向けて高さを減衰させていく。いわば鳥が広げた羽の端を地面に下ろしたような形態になる。中心からシンメトリックにゆったり伸びつつ落ちていく断面のカーブに、空気の流れを感じさせるブランクーシの「空間の中の鳥」のような開かれた完結性を与えたい。そしてグライダーのように軽くて精緻な表皮と構造体を考えること。ウイングにおける表現の連続性と論理の展開が、次の段階のデザイン・ポイントとなった。

ウイングの形態を具体的に決定したのは、「ある断面を移動させることで、形態を構成する」という簡潔なジオメトリックな処理だった。私たちはパリのベルシー2のショッピング・センター・プロジェクトで、道路のカーブにそって立ち上がる不定形の飛行船のような連続ボリュームを手がけた時に、非常に困難な形状解析に直面した経験をもっている。最初にボリュームの解決として放物面の回転体が思考されたが、放物面体を同じパターンのパネルでおおうことは不可能だった。スキンにはステンレス・スチールのタイルのパネルを使用する予定で、精密でかつ生な外装表現と不定形なボリュームをマッチさせる方法を探す難解なスタディが続けられた。

スタディの展開途上のある日、何らかの断面を移行する方法で、不定形をカバーできるのではないかと、ピーター・ライスのコラボレーターのエンジニア、ヘンリー・バーズレーに質問した。彼は異なる2つの円と1つの直線で構成された断面を水平垂直に平行移動することで、不定形の問題をみごとに解決してみせた。

KIAターミナルビルのウイングのボリュームをある程度規定した時、断面の移動による曲面の形成というベルシー2の方法を容易に採用できた。しかも幸運だったのは、ベルシーのショッピング・センターに比較して、ウイングのスケールが1.7kmという規模をもっていたことである。断面から断面への移行のずれと差異は、この長大なボリュームによってごくなだらかなものとなる。建物自体のスケール効果で、たった一種類のステンレス・スチールのパネルを反復させることによって、すべての屋根面積をカバーすることが可能なのだ。巨大さゆえの精緻な解決法を見いだしたわけである。

コンペ案では1つの焦点を中心に断面形を回転させて曲面を形成したが、基本設計以後は、メインビルディングのルーフのジオメトリーとの整合性のために、連結部分は断面の単純な水平移動におさえ、そこから減衰してゆく両翼をそれぞれ半径16.4km、仰角68.2度の距離にある点を焦点として回転していく曲面を形成した。　　　(N.O.)

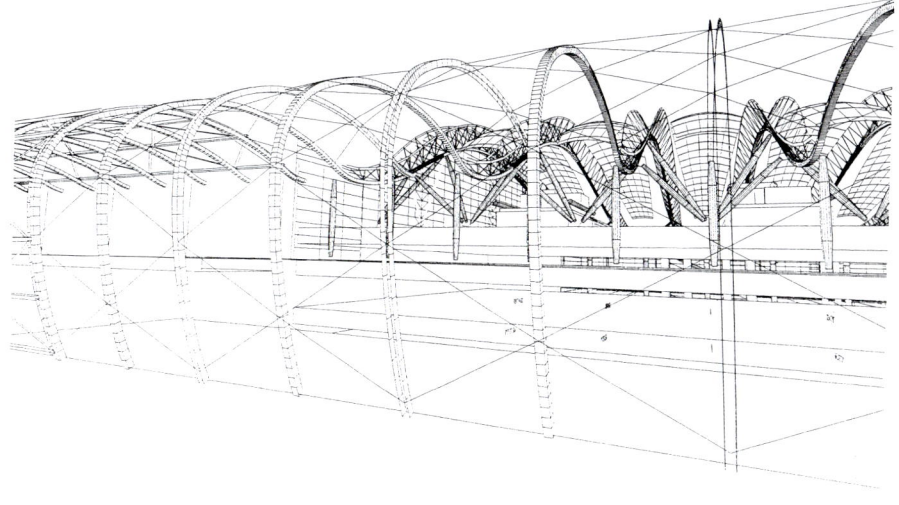

149

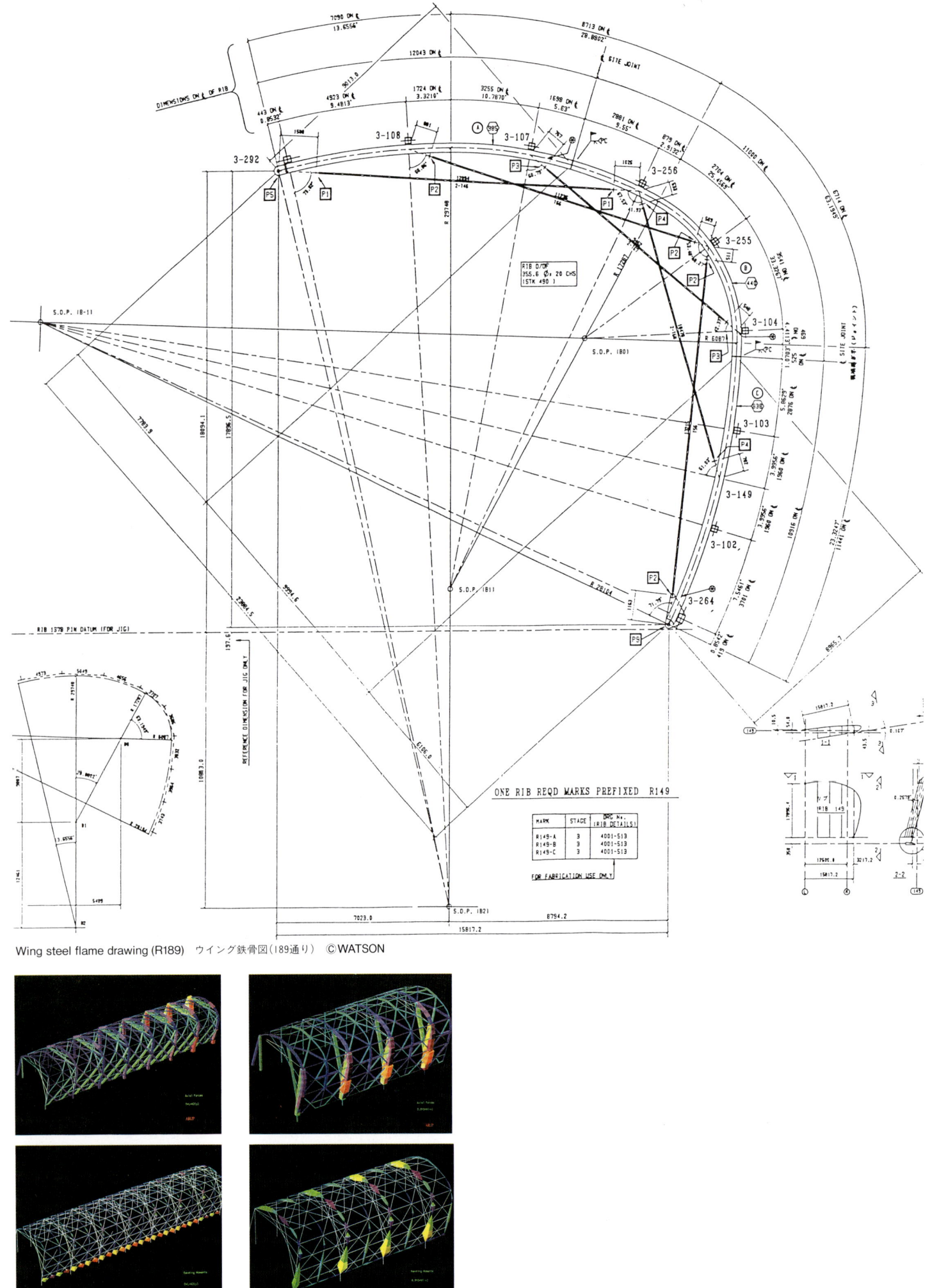

Wing steel flame drawing (R189) ウイング鉄骨図（189通り） ©WATSON

Election of wing ribs (north construction area, March 1993)
ウイングリブの建方（北工区，1993年3月）

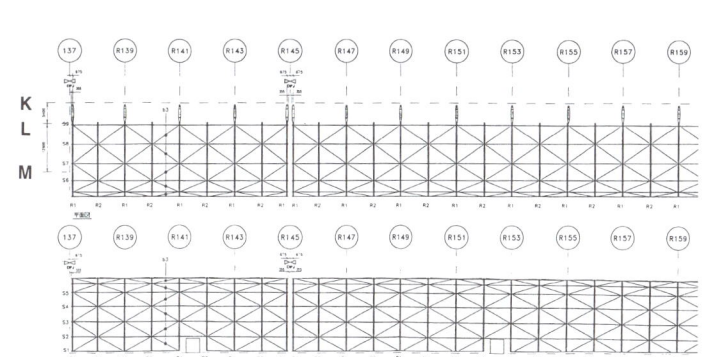
Wing steel flame drawing ウイング鉄骨図

Election of wing ribs (south construction area, March 1993)
ウイングリブの建方（南工区，1993年3月）

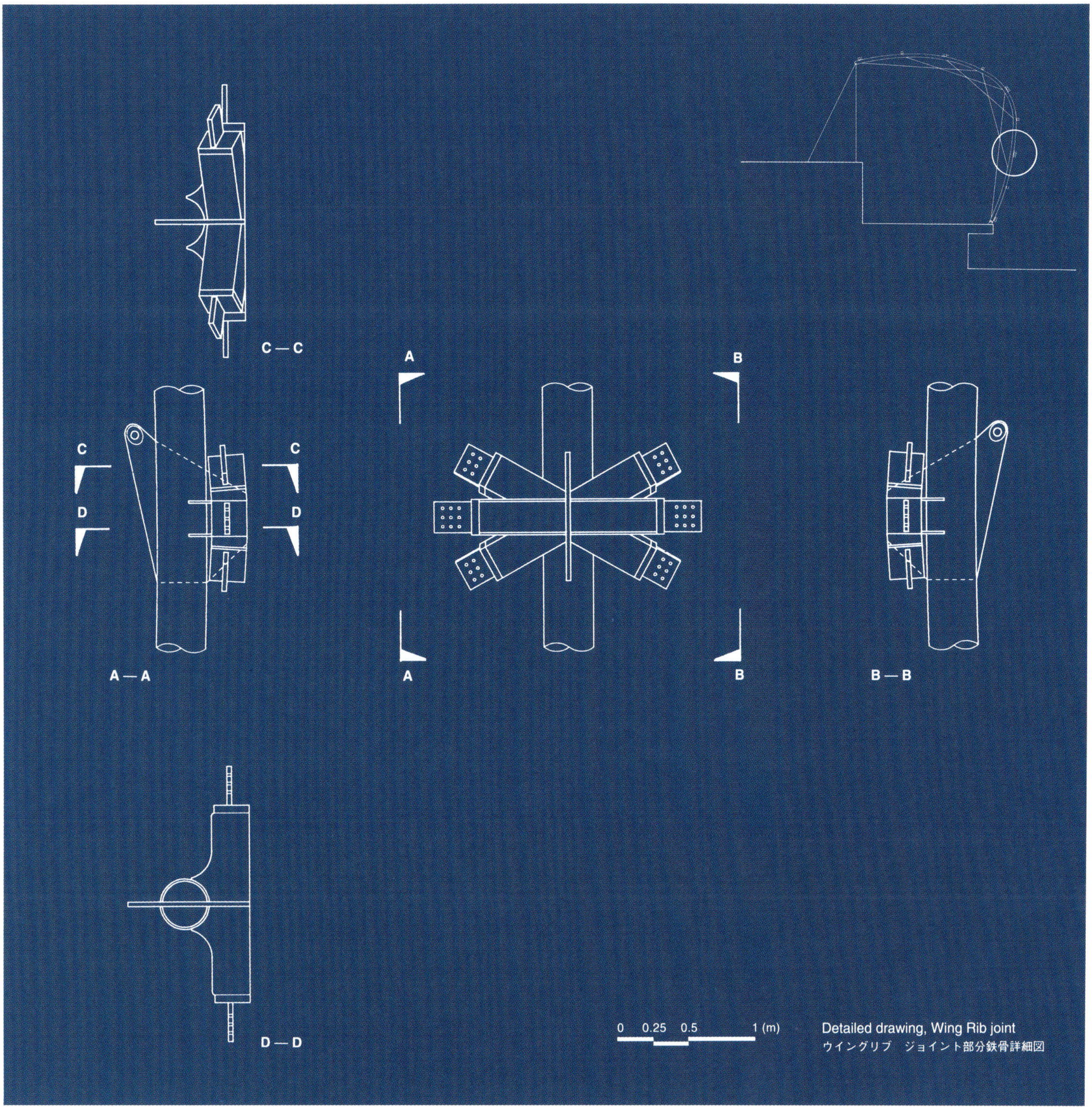

C—C

A—A

D—D

A A

B B

B—B

0 0.25 0.5   1 (m)

Detailed drawing, Wing Rib joint
ウイングリブ　ジョイント部分鉄骨詳細図

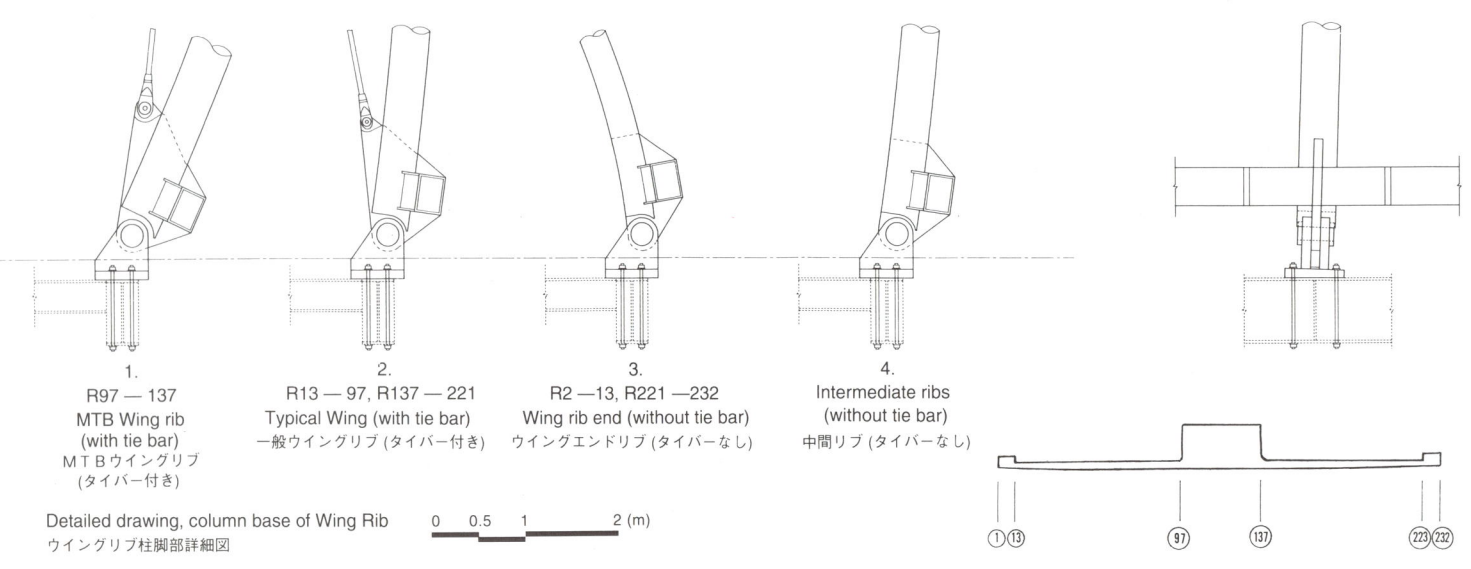

1.	2.	3.	4.
R97—137	R13—97, R137—221	R2—13, R221—232	Intermediate ribs
MTB Wing rib (with tie bar)	Typical Wing (with tie bar)	Wing rib end (without tie bar)	(without tie bar)
MTBウイングリブ（タイバー付き）	一般ウイングリブ（タイバー付き）	ウイングエンドリブ（タイバーなし）	中間リブ（タイバーなし）

Detailed drawing, column base of Wing Rib
ウイングリブ柱脚部詳細図

0 0.5 1 2 (m)

South wing end　南ウイングエンド

Tie bars are set with every other ribs.
タイバーは1本おきのウイングリブにつく．

Central MTB ribs　MTB中央部のリブ

Wing ribs　ウイングのほぼ直立しているリブ．

Wing end ribs　ウイングエンド付近のリブ．

Intermediate ribs without tie bar.
タイバーなしの中間リブ（手前）．

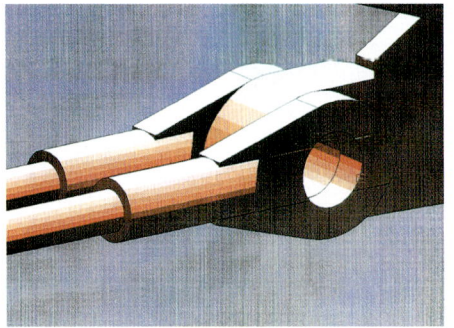

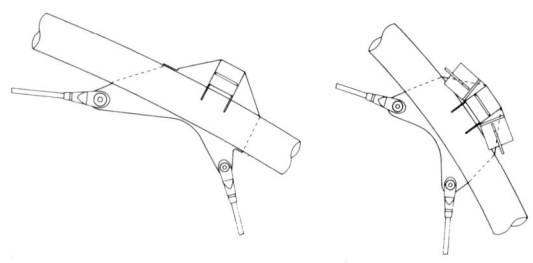

Detail of connection, Wing rib — tie bar
ウイングリブ・タイバー接合部詳細図
0　0.5　1　2 (m)

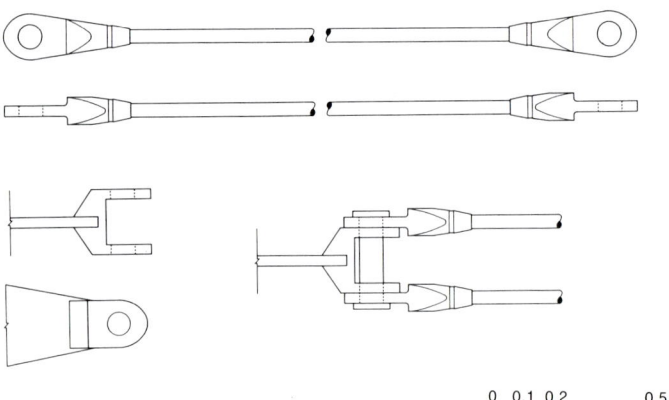

Detail of Tie bar　タイバー詳細図
0　0.1　0.2　0.5 (m)

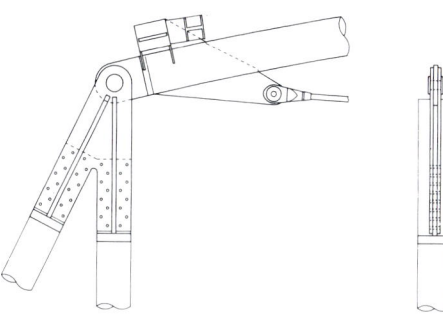
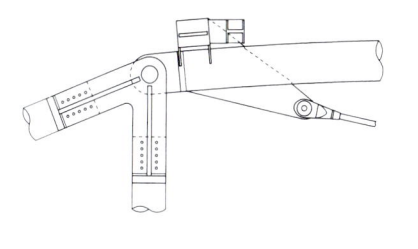

Detail drawing of steelworks at the joint part of landside of Wing top
ウイング・ランドサイド頂部接合部鉄骨詳細図

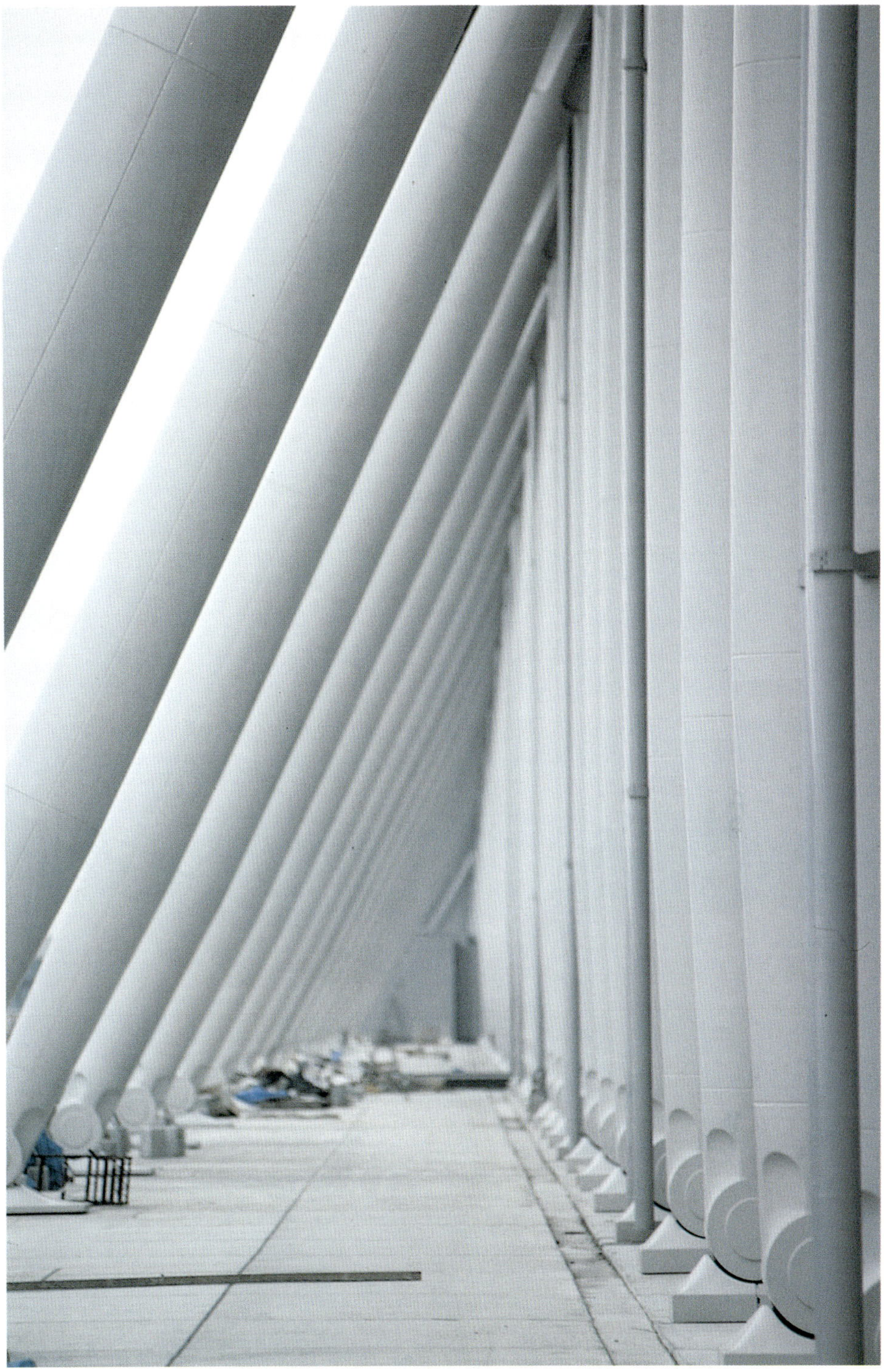

Boarding gate. 搭乗ゲート

Outside view of boarding bridges.
ボーディングブリッジ外側.

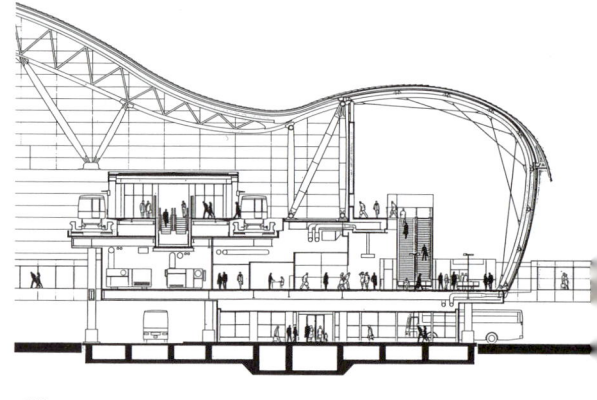

Wing section　ウイング断面図

Color of chairs are distinguishable by flight, but purple shows smoking area.
椅子の色分けは，ゲート別である．紫色は喫煙席．

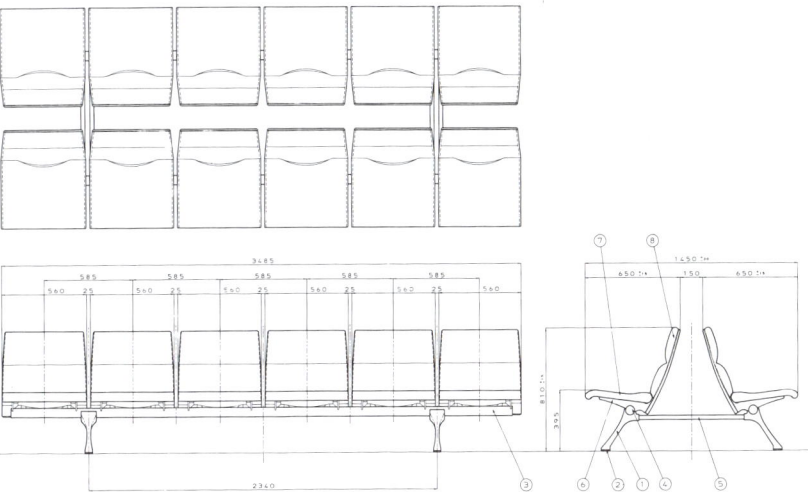

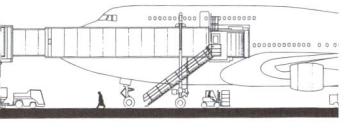

Lounge chair designed by RPBW.
レンゾ・ピアノ・ビルディング・ワークショップ設計のラウンジチェア．

159

Round-Shaped Nozzle System

Air diffusers suspended from the ceilings are used in locations such as the customs inspection area on the first floor of the MTB, the immigration inspection section on the second floor, the domestic departure lobby, and the baggage pick-up area for domestic passengers. They consist of round-shaped glass-wool ducts and line-shaped air diffusers, and are installed on colored aluminum racks. Through this arrangement, which reduces ceiling thickness, the ceilings are kept five meters above the floor.

円形吹出口システム

ＭＴＢ１階税関検査場，２階入国審査場，国内線出発ロビー，国内線手荷物引渡場などには，円形グラスウールとライン状吹出口を一体化し，カラーアルミでラッキングした天井吊り下げタイプの吹出口を採用し，天井内スペースの削減により高い天井高（５ｍ）を確保している。

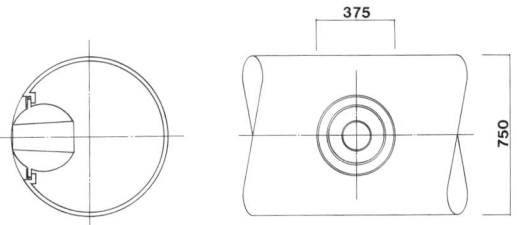

Round-shaped air supplying system, eyeball nozzle.
アイボールノズル(円形吹き出し口)

Air-conditioning of the gate lounge involves two methods. The first method is perimeter air-conditioning along the glass walls of the lounge. The second method is interior air-conditioning for the rest of the lounge.

Perimeter air-conditioning disposes of heat on the glass surface by jetting the air from fish tails (linear nozzles shaped like fish tails) located at floor level near the glass walls. Interior air-conditioning disposes of heat in the interior portions of the gate lounge by jetting air horizontally from linear nozzles installed near floor level on the walls of the third floor.

ゲートラウンジの空調は，ゲートラウンジのガラス面用のペリメーター空調とラウンジ居住域用のインテリア空調によって構成されている．

ペリメーター空調は，ガラス面足元の床面に設置されたフィッシュテイル（魚の尾の形をしたライン状吹出口）からガラス面に沿って吹き出し，ガラス面の熱負荷処理をする．インテリア空調は，3階床レベルの壁面からライン状吹出口によって横向きに空調空気を吹き出し，インテリア部の熱負荷を処理する．

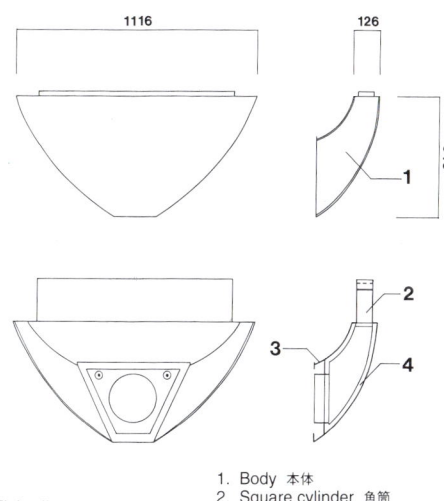

Fishtail
フィッシュテイル

1. Body　本体
2. Square cylinder　角筒
3. Dewatering　水切り
4. Thermal insulation　断熱材

On the wings, general artificial illumination through indirect lighting and direct lighting from poles known as technical trees are used in combination. Indirect lighting using open air ducts of the MTB and the indirect lighting of wing ceilings by brackets on the third floor are combined to create a 1.7-kilometer-long river of light. Lighting equipment designed for the space is installed at the bases of successive handrails to illuminate floor with soft lighting.

The passenger terminal building is divided into three main zones — the passenger and public zone, the shopping and dining zone, and the business and office zone. In the public zone, an automatic control system is adopted to switch the light on and off according to the operating hours. The use of this system is intended to reduce energy consumption and improve operational efficiency. Early in the morning and late at night, there are few landings and take-offs. Energy consumption during such periods could be reduced by selecting areas to be illuminated based on the gate lounges in use and the path of passenger circulation. For this reason, circuits for turning on and off the light in sections subject to this cost-reduction technique must be classified in an appropriate manner.

In the Canyon, natural light enters through the rooftop for the sake of growing foliage plants. In an additional step, an auxiliary illuminant is installed so that plants can receive sufficient light during winter when natural light tends to be scarce. A great deal of natural light also enters the gate lounge and concourse on the second and third floors. Lights are automatically switched on and off in these areas, as well as in the Canyon by optical sensors.

— *Nikken Sekkei*

ウイング部分においては間接照明による全体的な人工照明と，テクニカルツリーと呼ばれるポールからの直接照明が組み合わされている．ＭＴＢのオープンエアダクトをつかった間接照明とウイングの天井面への３階のブラケットからの間接照明が連続して1.7kmにおよぶ空間のつながりを醸しだす．連続する手すりの下部には，空間のデザインにあわせた照明器具が設置され，やわらかく人の進む場所を照らす．

旅客ターミナルビルは大きく旅客パブリックゾーン，物販飲食ゾーン，業務・事務室ゾーンにより構成されている．パブリックゾーンについては，これらの利用時間に合わせた照明の点滅が自動的にできるスケジュール運転制御を採用し，消費エネルギーの節減および業務の効率化を図っている．航空機の離発着が少ない早朝・深夜は，必要なゲートラウンジと旅客動線に沿ったスペースの照明を選定し，点灯することが消費エネルギーの節減となる．このため対象エリアの点滅回路を適切に分割してある．

キャニオンでは，植栽を育てるために，屋根のトップライトから自然光を取り入れている．加えて植栽用補光照明を設置し，冬期の自然光の少ない時期の補助として，充分な照度を得られるようにしている．２階や３階のゲートラウンジ，コンコースでも自然光をふんだんにとり入れ，キャニオンとともに光センサーによって照明が自動点滅するようになっている．　　　　（文責／日建設計）

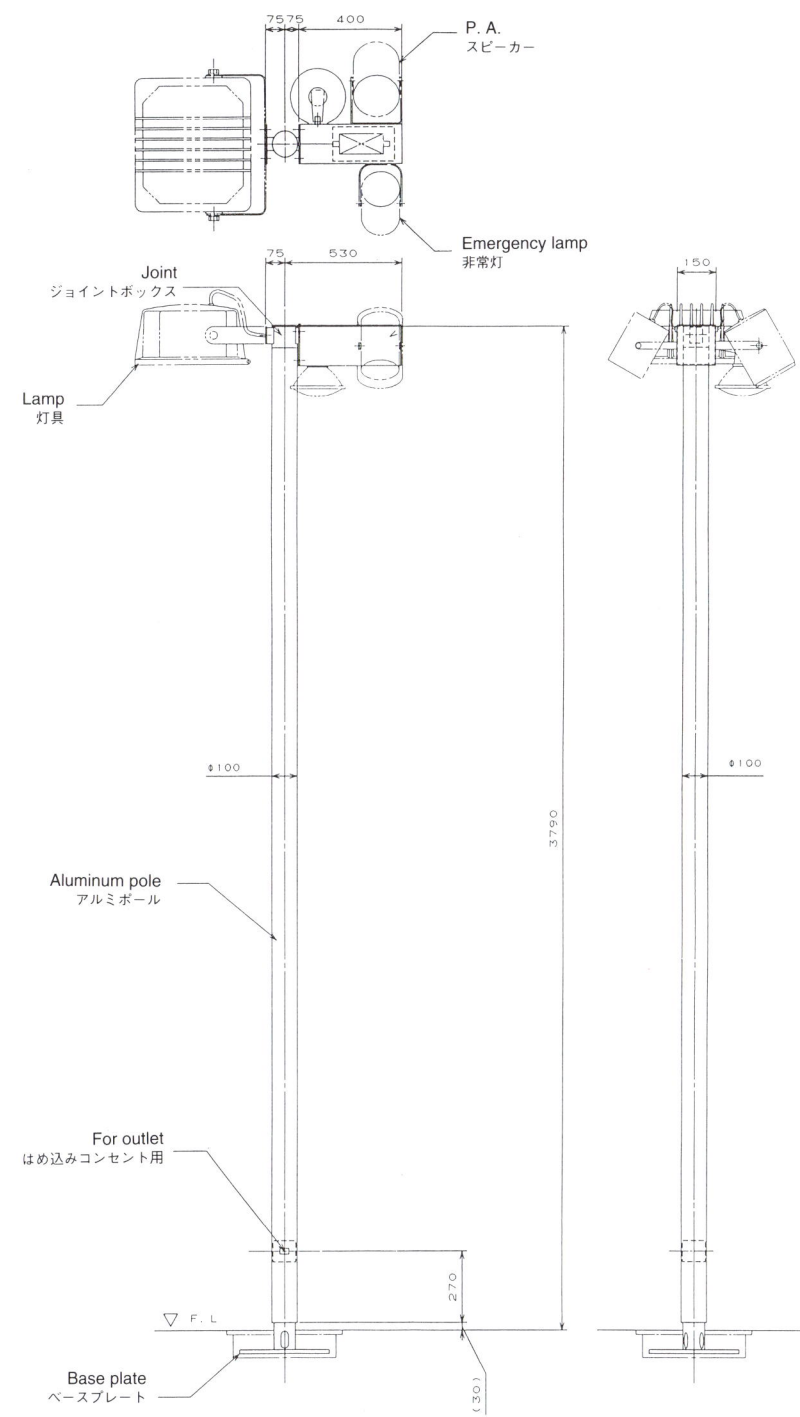

Technical tree lighting　テクニカルツリー照明　Ⓒ松下電工

Indirect lighting installed under handrails.
手摺の間接照明

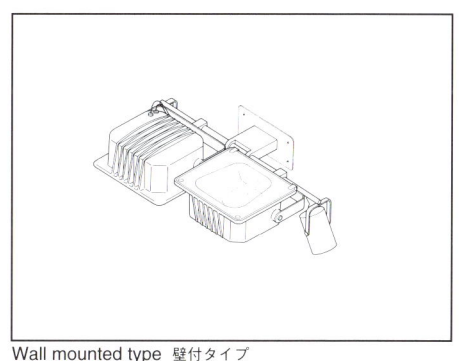

Wall mounted type　壁付タイプ

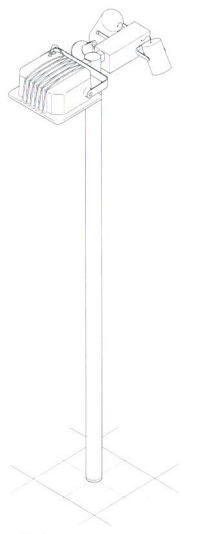

Pole type　ポールタイプ

ANTI—SUBSIDENCE MEASURES
不同沈下対策

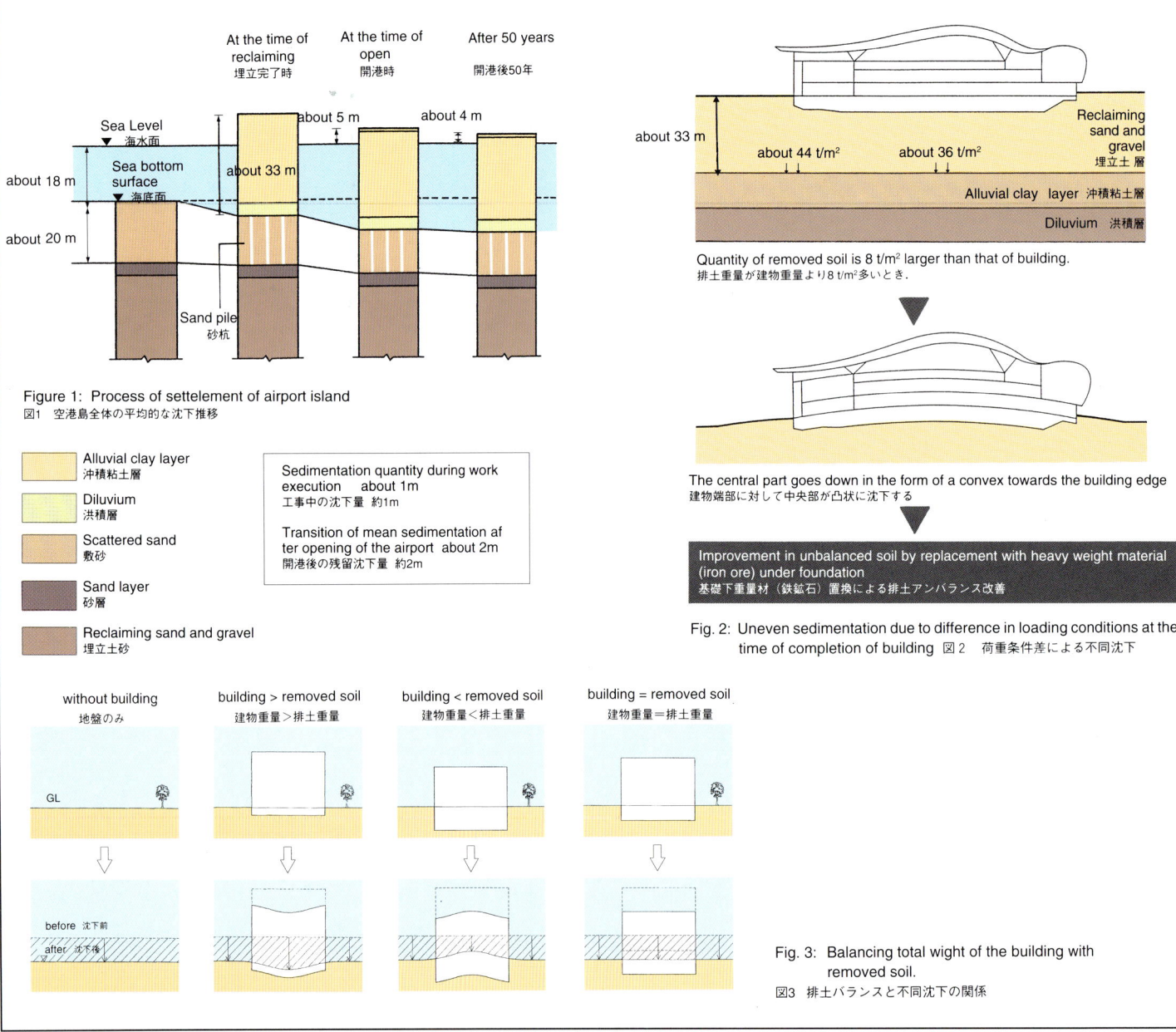

Figure 1: Process of settelement of airport island
図1 空港島全体の平均的な沈下推移

Fig. 2: Uneven sedimentation due to difference in loading conditions at the time of completion of building 図2 荷重条件差による不同沈下

Fig. 3: Balancing total wight of the building with removed soil.
図3 排土バランスと不同沈下の関係

The Kansai International Airport is the first full-fledged airport in the world built on a manmade island (called Kukoto), which is located five kilometers off the Southern Osaka coast of Senshu. This offshore location was picked mainly in order to solve noise-related problems. The effort to solve one problem, however, resulted in extraordinary technological difficulties stunning from geographical conditions, especially the estimated 11 meters of ground sinkage that was experienced. This section describes the particular measures for building facilities on artificial ground that is sinking.

Outline of Subsidence
The airport island was built in five short years in responds the urgency of the project. It is an artificial ground site formed by reclaiming the sea area (with the average depth of about 18 meters) with 180 million square meters of sand and soil. The sea bed of the area was originally covered with a 20-meter layer of new and soft clay called the alluvial clay bed. Underneath this layer lies an old stratum called the diluvium. Consisting of alternating layers of clay and sand, this stratum is 400 meters thick. The sand and soil used for reclamation measure 33 meters in thickness. Their load is estimated at 45 tons per cubic meter when buoyant force over underwater areas is taken into the account. Under this load, water carried in the clay layer gets squeezed out and the entire airport island sinks because of the volume compression. This process is known as "subsidence by consolidation." This is the basic mechanism behind land subsidence at the airport island.

The final volume of subsidence is determined for the most part by the nature of the sea-bed soil and the weight of the sand and soil used for reclamation. It is possible to control the speed of subsidence to a certain extent. At the Kansai International Airport, the sinking process was promoted by about 1 million sand piles known as "sand drains" driven into the alluvial clay bed underneath the entire airport island to facilitate drainage. The sand piles caused the island to sink at a pace that would take 100 years in a natural setting.

However, at this same site, the diluvium, the stratum beneath the alluvial clay bed that is generally believed to sustain the load and remain solid, is beginning to sink slowly under the heavy weight of sand and soil. This stratum lies at a depth that cannot be reached using current technology.

By the time the airport opens for business, the airport island is expected to have sunk by about 9.5 meters. About 5.5 meters of this subsidence was caused by sinking of the alluvial clay bed which virtually stopped upon completion of reclamation thanks to the effective appli-

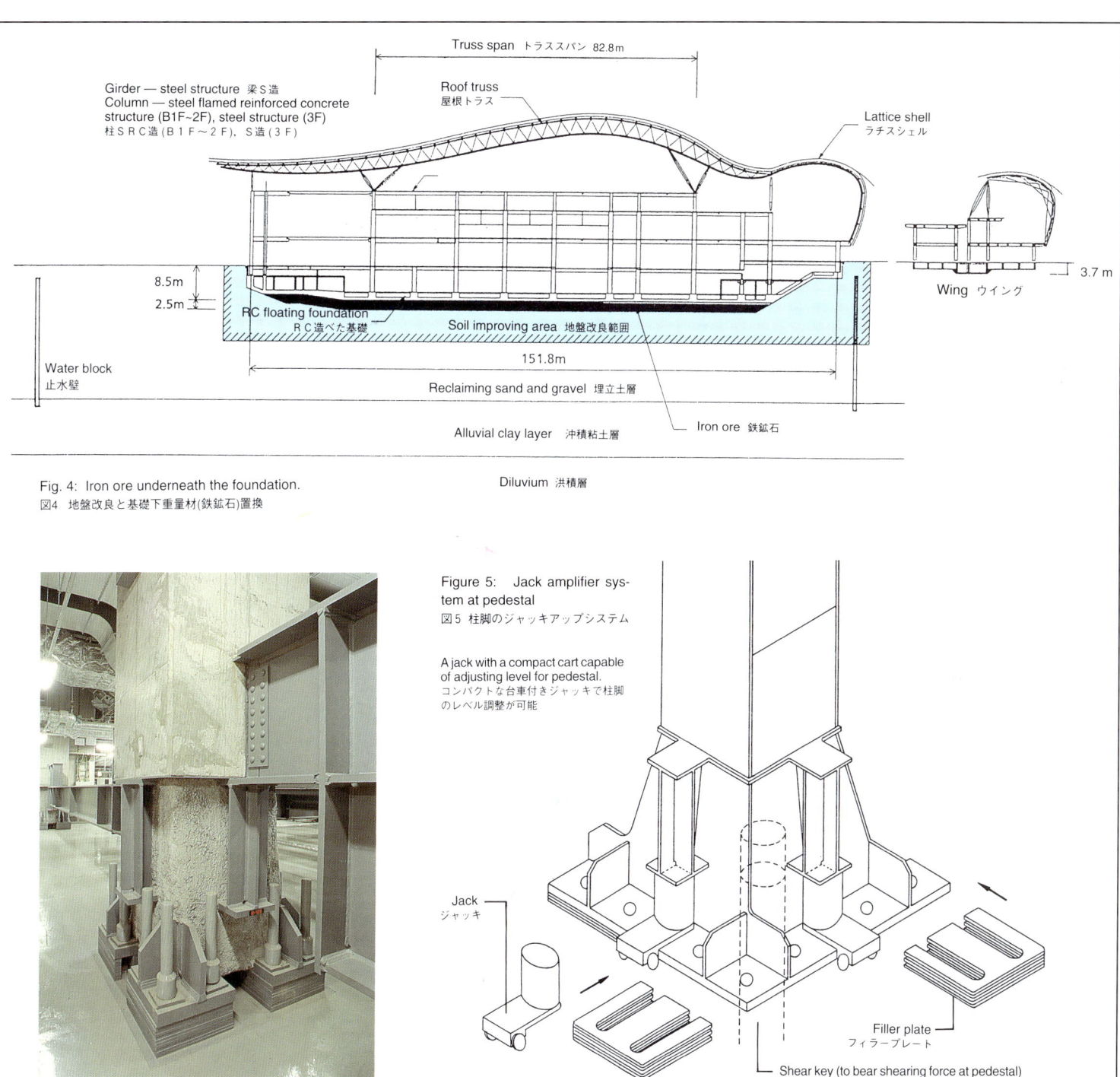

Fig. 4: Iron ore underneath the foundation.
図4 地盤改良と基礎下重量材(鉄鉱石)置換

Figure 5: Jack amplifier system at pedestal
図5 柱脚のジャッキアップシステム

A jack with a compact cart capable of adjusting level for pedestal.
コンパクトな台車付きジャッキで柱脚のレベル調整が可能

cation of the sand drainage method. The remaining 4 meters of subsidence has to do with the diluvium. It is predicted that this stratum will sink another 1.5 meters to 2 meters over a period of 30 or more years (Figure 1).

Differentials in Subsidence and Measures

As discussed above, land subsidence at the airport island is quite large in scale. Nevertheless, sinking of the ground is not a big problem as long as the land and the building subside to the same extent and at the same speed. In other words, the problem arises from differentials in subsidence levels. Therefore, the top priority in designing the 1,700-meter-long terminal building was to predict differentials in subsidence levels and prevent any unevenness.

As mentioned earlier, land subsidence that affects buildings takes place in a stratum deep under the ground that we have no control over because of the heavy load of sand and soil used for reclamation. In light of this, engineers decided to let the ground subside equally at all points. Under this basic policy, sand and soil commensurate in weight to the buildings was removed to adjust the depth of the foundation. In other words, the first principle was to keep the total weight of the buildings and that of removed soil in balance (Figure 2). As for foundation work, engineers adopted the method of first consolidating the reclaimed ground and then letting the foundation support the buildings with no external assistance. A popular method in past reclamation cases has been the use of pile foundations. In this project, however, balanced subsidence was attempted (Figure 3).

Because of its design, the MTB needed to house major machine rooms on its first underground level. Under this restriction, the building was bound to become 8 tons lighter than the removed soil per square meter. This meant that the central part of the building would become 40 centimeters higher than its edges. To reduce this differential and restore load balance, engineers graveled 360,000 tons of crashed iron ore underneath the foundation (Figure 4).

Besides these steps, engineers attempted to reduce the gap in sinking levels by raising the ground on the tip of the south wing — the area feared most susceptible to disproportionate subsidence due to the delay in reclamation compared to that of the north wing — using soil removed from the ground underneath the MTB.

Wiring Surpluses
Electrical and telecommunications wiring are done so as to leave surpluses at points at which sliding mechanisms for absorbing height changes are installed. In this arrangement, height changes are absorbed by talking advantage of the flexible nature of materials (photo shows the wiring surplus for a sliding mechanism on a wall for absorbing height changes).

ケーブル余長
電気・通信配線は，階高変化を吸収するスライド機構の設置してある部分に余長を持たせることによって，材料自体の柔軟性を生かした階高変位吸収をしている．(写真は壁の階高吸収スライド機構部分の配線余長)

Jack-Up Stands
Equipment such as air-conditioners and electric fans are installed on steel stands designed so that their heights can be adjusted to those of pillars subject to jacking up. Flexible joints are used to connect the piping of such equipment to the steel stands, while canvas joints are attached to the ducts to absorb the transitional gap in height between the pillars and the steel stands (the margin of height absorption is 50 millimeters).

ジャッキアップ架台
空調機・ファンなどは，柱のジャッキアップ・ダウンと同様に高さを調整することのできる鋼製架台上に設置し，柱の高さ調整に合わせる．これらの機器との接続部は，配管にはフレキシブルジョイントを，ダクトにはキャンバス継手を取り付け，柱と架台との高さ調整の時間的なずれを吸収している（吸収変位50mm）

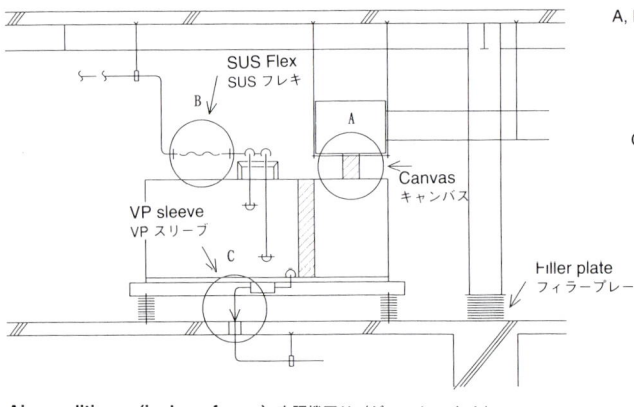

A, B: Absorb max. 50mm towards the work time lag at jacking up/down the pillars and the AC frame
柱ジャッキUP・DN時と，AC架台ジャッキUP・DN時の作業時間のずれに対し最大50mm を吸収する

C: Absorbs the same quantity and the pillar jack up/down quantity
柱ジャッキUP・DN量と同量を吸収する

Air conditioner (jack-up frame) 空調機回り（ジャッキUP架台）

Measures for Rectifying Differentials in Subsidence

As stated above, the basic rule is to take whatever actions are necessary to minimize differentials in subsidence. Still, it is impossible to avoid subsidence completely for many reasons, including the uneven ocean floor and the fact that reclamation work performed at different periods. To deal with this, a minute adjustment system using jacks is being adopted.

The terminal building has as many as 900 pillars. Each of them is designed in such a way to enable height adjustment through jack-up operations (Figure 5). The level measuring system that covers the whole terminal building is constantly monitored horizontality. Then pillar heights can be adjusted before differentials in subsidence can have a negative effect on the building.

The adoption of the jack-up system means that the building's lowest level rises and falls as needed. There is an enormous amount of interior furnishings, equipment, and piping on this floor, the details of which are all designed so as to be adjustable to all possible changes in height, however minute. The system is intended for the construction of a buffer zone that incorporates two different worlds: one in which the meter-scale is adopted to perform reclamation work in view of land subsidence, and another in which we adopt a millimeter scale for architectural concerns.

One of the biggest technological challenges faced by those who designed the passenger terminal building at the Kansai International Airport was a land subsidence of unprecedented proportion. It is no exaggeration to call the process of implementing actual desk plans — from subsidence monitoring during the construction phase to the realization of designs allowing jack-up operations to the actual process of jacking up — a series of experiments during which no mistake could be made. The passenger terminal building now stands elegantly and gracefully, but its tranquil appearance is deceiving: the building was only possible through the united and passionate efforts of those involved in the design and construction of this great project, as well as those who ordered it.

— *Nikken Sekkei*

Joints for Absorbing Changes in Floor Heights
Sliding joints are installed on piping that connects the floor to the upper levels so that they could absorb changes in height resulting from pillar jack-up operation. More precisely, sliding joints for water are used on pressure piping, sliding joints for steam are used on steam piping and sliding joints are also used on piping for drainage by gravity.

階高変化吸収継手
床面と上階を結ぶ配管には、スライド式の継手(圧力配管系は、クローザージョイント、蒸気系はガンパクトジョイント、重力排水系はやりとりソケット継手)を設置し、柱のジャッキアップ・ダウンに伴なう高さの変化をそのまま吸収できるようにしている。
(吸収変位最大400mm)

Floors for Installing Heat-Generating Equipment
Heat-generating equipment such as pumps, headers, and tanks, as well as piping that links them to one another are large in number and complex in terms of their connections. As such, they are not adjusted according to pillar height changes. Instead, they are all installed on steel floors bridged between pillars. They are in this way unaffected by height changes resulting from pillar jack-up operations.

熱源機器設置床
ポンプ、ヘッダ、タンクなどの熱源機器とそれらを結ぶ配管類は、各々の接続が複雑で多数となるため、個々の変位吸収対応とせず、柱と柱の間にかけ渡した鋼製床の上に一括して設置し、柱のジャッキアップ・ダウンによる階高の変化の影響を受けないようにしている。

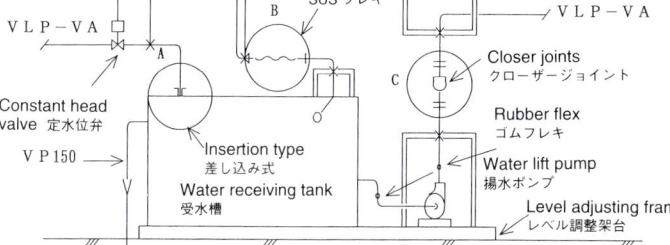

Water receiving tank and water lift pump 受水槽・揚水ポンプ回り
A, B, C: Absorb the same quantity and the pillar jack up/down quantity
柱ジャッキUP・DN量と同量を吸収する

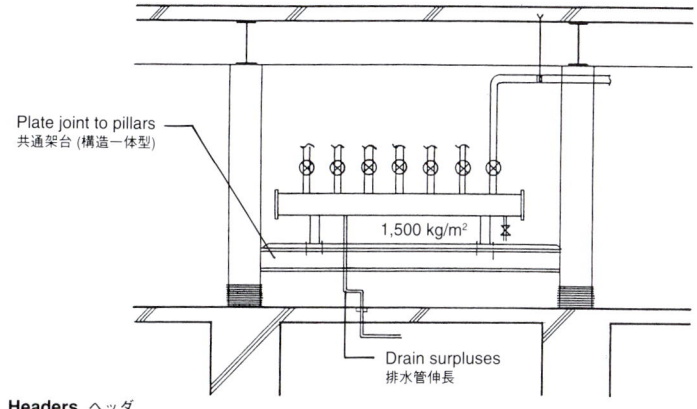

Headers ヘッダ
Headers should be fixed to upper siub.
Headers installed of floor plete which is settled between pillars.
ヘッダは配管の一部であるために上部より支持する。
柱間に柱と一体化した共通架台を設け、この上にヘッダ類を据え付ける。

　関西国際空港は、泉州沖5kmの海上の人工島(空港島)に建設された世界初の本格的な海上空港である。陸地から5km離れた場所が選ばれたのは、主として騒音問題の解決のためであったが、この人工島建設は、その地理的条件のためにとてつもない技術課題を抱えることになった。最終的に11mを越えるであろうという地盤沈下問題である。ここでは、このような人工地盤上施設の計画にあたって特に配慮された地盤沈下対策について述べる。

地盤沈下の概要

　空港島は、平均水深約18mの建設海域に、1億8,000万立方メートルもの土砂を投入して造成された人工地盤で、プロジェクトの緊急性により、5年という短い工期で建設された。空港島の海底には、厚さ20mもの「沖積粘土層」と呼ばれる、新しくて柔らかい粘土層が横たわっており、さらにその下には、「洪積層」と呼ばれる粘土層と砂層が互い違いにあらわれる古い地層が厚さ400mにもわたって続いている。その上に、層厚33m、水中にある部分の浮力を計算に入れても1㎥あたり45トンにも達する埋立土砂の荷重がかかる。この荷重によって粘土層に含まれる水分が押し出され、体積圧縮すなわち圧密沈下で空港島全体が沈下する。これが空港島の地盤沈下の基本的なメカニズムである。

　最終的な沈下量は、海底地盤の性質と、埋め立て土砂の重量によってほぼ決まるが、沈下のスピードをコントロールすることはある程度可能である。この場合、空港島全域の沖積粘土層に約100万本も打たれたサンドドレーンといわれる水抜き用の砂杭の効果により沈下が促進され、100年はかかろうという沈下を一気に引き起こさせている。

　ところが、沖積粘土層の下の、一般には沈下を起こさない、加重に対してしっかりした地盤として扱われていた洪積層が、ここでは、あまりの埋め立て土砂の重量のために、現在の技術ではコントロールできない深い地層までがゆっくりと沈下を起こしているのである。

　埋め立て開始から、開港までの沈下量はおよそ9.5m。このうち約5.5mは沖積粘土層の沈下で、サンドドレーン工法の成果により埋め立て完了の時点でほぼ沈下は収まっている。残り4mが洪積層の沈下で、しかもこの沈下はこの後30年以上かかっておよそ1.5~2mも沈下すると予測されている(図1)。

不同沈下とその低減対策

このように大きな地盤沈下であるが、地盤も建物も、まったく同じように沈むということであれば、極端な話いくら沈下しても建物にとってはあまり問題はない。それよりも、建物のいろいろな箇所で沈下量が少しずつ違う「不同沈下」が問題となる。1,700mもあるこのターミナルビルが、でこぼこになってしまわないように、不同沈下を予測し、それに対抗していかに水平を保つかということが構造設計上の最重要課題となったわけである。

前述のように、建物にかかわる沈下は、埋立土砂の重量が原因となって、現在ではコントロールの及ばない深い地層で起こるものであるから、沈下対策の基本方針を「地盤とともに沈下させる」こととした。そのために、建物重量に見合うだけの土を掘削するように基礎の深さを調整する、すなわち「排土バランス」をとることを第一の原則としている(図2)。また、基礎工法としては、建物直下の埋立地盤を充分に締め固めてから、直接支持させるという方法を採用している。これまでの埋立地では、杭基礎が一般的であったが、ここでは、むしろ積極的に周辺の地盤の沈下にうまく追随することをねらっているわけである(図3)。

主要な機械室を地下1階に納める必要があるターミナルビル本館の場合、取り除いた土の重量より、建物の方が1m²につき8トン軽いため、そのままでは建物の端部に対して中央部が、最終的に40cmほども高くなってしまう。これを低減するために、基礎下に36万トンもの鉄鉱石を敷き詰めて重量バランスを回復するという特殊な解決策もとっている(図4)。

このほか、埋立工程のずれによる不同沈下が特に懸念された南ウイング先端部には、本館の掘削土を利用して載荷盛土(プレロード)を行ない、ほかの部分との残留沈下量の差を低減させるように工夫している。

不同沈下修正対策

以上のように、できるだけ不同沈下が起こらないように対策をとることが基本である。それでも、埋立履歴差や海底地盤の不均一性などのさまざまな理由で、不同沈下は避けられない。それに対する対処法がジャッキアップによる微調整システムである。

ターミナルビルには約900本もの柱があるが、そのすべての柱脚でジャッキを使って高さ調整ができるようにしている(図5)。そしてターミナルビル全域に取りつけられているレベル計測システム

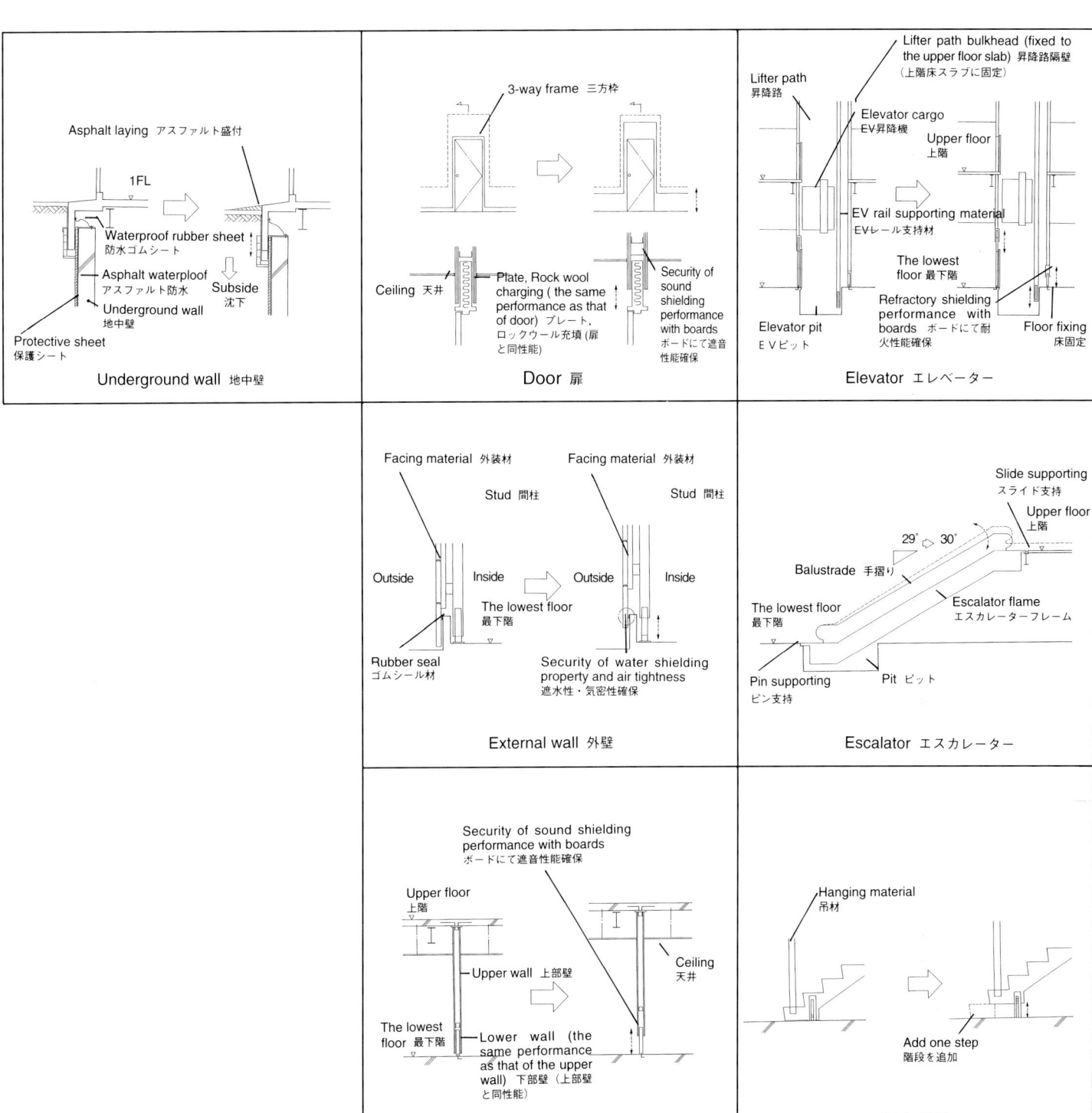

　によって水平状態を常に監視し，不同沈下の悪影響が出る前に柱の高さを調整してしまうのである．
　ジャッキアップシステムの採用は，最下階が伸び縮みするということであり，その階にある，膨大な数の内外装や設備機器配管などは，すべて階高の変化に追随できるディテールを備えている．それは，メートル単位の地盤沈下を対象とする埋立造成の世界と，ミリ単位でものをつくる建築の世界とを結び付ける，いわば緩衝ゾーンの構築であったともいえる．

　かつて経験のなかった大きな地盤沈下に対する挑戦，それが関西国際空港旅客ターミナルビルの構造設計上の最大の技術課題の1つであった．机上の予測・検討を現実のものとしていく過程，すなわち工事中の沈下計測管理・各種ジャッキアップ対応ディテールの具現化・ジャッキアップの実践等々，すべてが後戻りの許されない実験の連続であったといっても過言ではない．この壮大なテーマに対する，発注者・設計者・施工者の三位一体の真摯な取り組みを背景に，旅客ターミナルビルが何ごともなかったかのようにその流麗な姿をいま現わしたのである．
　　　　　　　　　　　　　（文責／日建設計）

FIRE PREVENTION
防災計画

Fire hydrant nearby Wing Shuttle (AGT) station on the 3rd level of wing. ウイング3階，ウイングシャトル (AGT) 乗り場脇の消火栓．

Fire Prevention

At the time of the competition, important proposals had already been made involving prevention of Fire in large, open spaces. Such proposals dealt with ways to assure safety in the connected large, open spaces measuring 90,000 square meters in total area, as well as ways to expand low-risk zones transparency in this enormous area. As a result of such proposals, shops and restaurants at a high risk of fire were restricted to the third floor. In addition, fire prevention equipment was installed in so-called protected zones such as check-in counters at which papers and computers create a certain risk of fire. Such an attempt to confine dangers to high-risk zones is known as the "cabin concept" in this project.

Large, open spaces inside the terminal building require special air-conditioning systems. In the same way, it is necessary for fire prevention planners to take advantage of their physical characteristics. Fire prevention plans that have been adopted at the airport take advantage of the characteristics of such large, open spaces. They include an unobstructed view that aids in fire detection and evacuation, a safety space that is large compared to the potential size of the fire, and a large roof that attracts and dilutes smoke.

From a structural and functional viewpoint, the terminal building is divided into the following three zones -the B zone that houses the airport, the A zone for passengers (this zone is covered by the large roof), and the C zone comprising successive large, open spaces. All three zones are designed to prevent fire and smoke from spreading out in the event of a disaster. (After assuring safety, they received the approval of the government ministers involved regarding points conflicted with existing laws in zones A and C.). Fire prevention plans for this enormous terminal building have the following seven additional characteristics:

— *Nikken Sekkei*

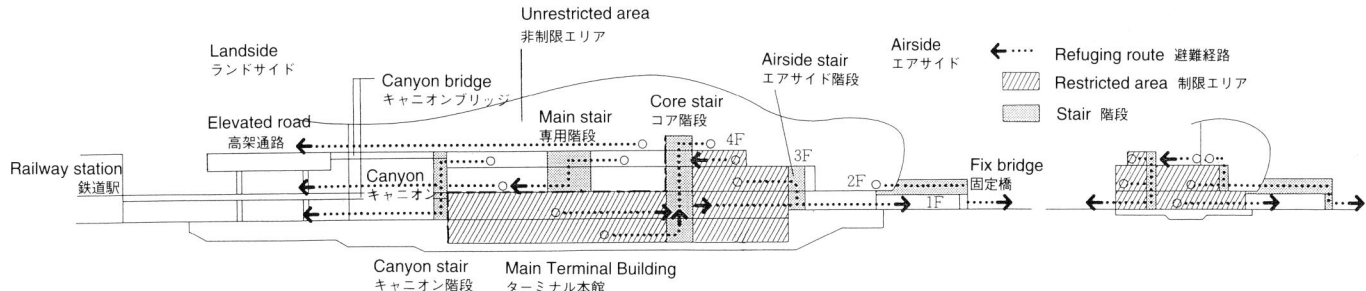

Evacuation Floors and Horizontal Evacuation
Horizontal evacuation constitutes the majority of the evacuation plan for the terminal building because of its structural characteristics such as the horizontal succession of spaces and the three floors available for evacuation.

避難階と水平避難
水平方向に空間が連続し，避難階を3つ持つ建物の構造的特徴を生かし，避難計画では水平避難を主体としている．

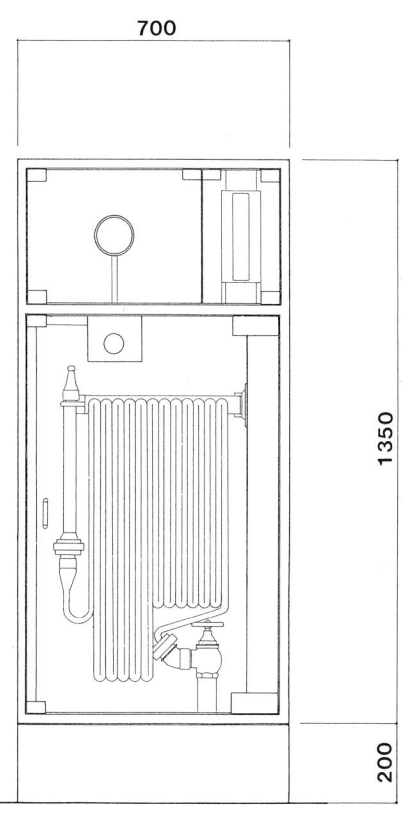

Fire hydrant with glass box, designed by RPBW.
ガラスボックスでできた消火栓（RPBW設計）．

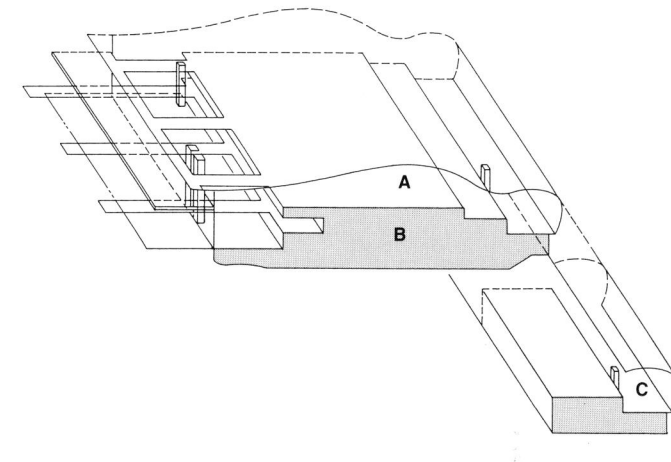

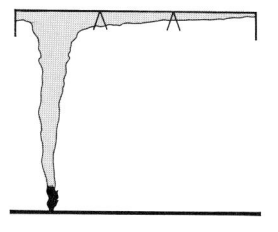

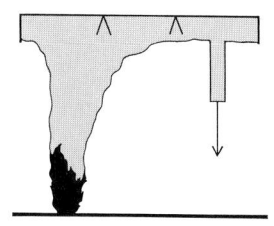

Cabin Concept
Lobbies and lounges in airports are the primary areas in which passengers spend time. As a result, lobby and lounge areas with a high danger of fire, such as shops, are covered by a canopy (cabin) equipped with sprinklers and high-powered smoke discharging devices. Through this arrangement, fire is prevented from spreading to outlying areas.

キャビンコンセプト
空港ロビー，ラウンジは，旅客の移動空間が大半を占めるため，店舗など火災荷重の高いエリアをスプリンクラー，大風量の排煙設備をもつ天蓋（キャビン）で覆い，周辺空間への火災拡大を防いでいる．

防災計画
コンペ時においてすでに大空間防災に対する重要提案がなされた．連続する9万m²の大空間の安全を確保し，同時に空間全体の透明性，透過性を獲得する提案である．それは3階部分に火災荷重の高いショップ，レストランを限定し，それ以外の，紙類やコンピューターなどを扱うある程度火災荷重の高いチェックインカウンターなども，防災機器を配慮したプロテクトゾーンとして取り扱った．これらの危険率の高いゾーンを区切ってとじこめる方法をキャビンコンセプトとよんだ．

ターミナルビルの大空間が，形態上特別な空調システムを求めているのと同様，防災計画でもその特色を生かした工夫が必要になる．大空間だからこそ見通しの良さが火災の発見と避難を助け，火災規模に比べて空間が充分大きく，さらに大屋根は煙を蓄煙し希釈させるのに適しているなど，大空間の特徴を生かした防災を計画している．

ターミナルビルは形態上および機能上，空港機能部としてのB部と，それを覆う大屋根によって形成された旅客ゾーンであるA部，C部（連続する大空間）に分けられる．火災と煙の拡大防止のために，A部，C部とB部を防火区画している．（A，C部の法に抵触する部分については，安全を確認の上，大臣認定を取得した．）（文責／日建設計）

Smoke Accumulation Plan

The smoke accumulation system is adopted for the international departure lobby on the fourth floor and most wing sections in an attempt to take advantage of the high ceilings and large, open spaces under the big roof. Smoke that accumulates in the large, open space is diluted and does not come down during evacuation periods. Fire prevention engineering studies have confirmed that evacuees will not be adversely affected by smoke when a fire breaks out at these locations.

蓄煙計画

天井が高く懐が深い大屋根の空間特性を生かし、4階国際線出発ロビー、キャニオンおよびウイングの大部分は蓄煙方式を採用する。大空間に溜った煙は希釈され避難時間内には降下しないので、火災時に避難者には煙の影響がないことが防災工学的検討で確認されている。

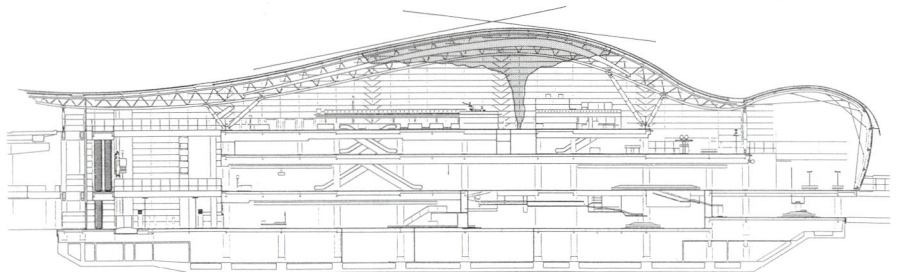

Smoke accumulation of fire caused on the 4th floor
ターミナルビル4階における火災からの蓄煙

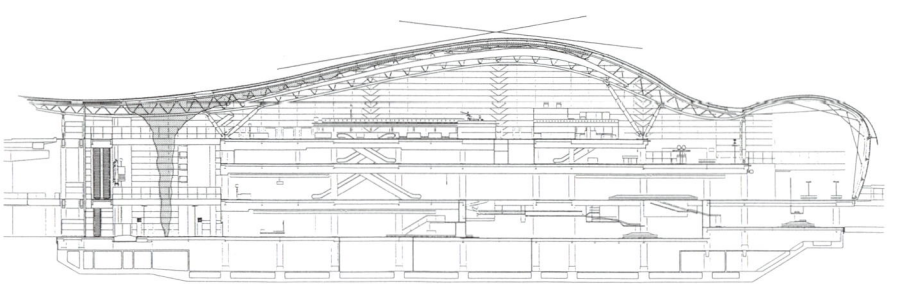

Smoke accumulation of fire caused in the Canyon
キャニオンにおける火災からの蓄煙

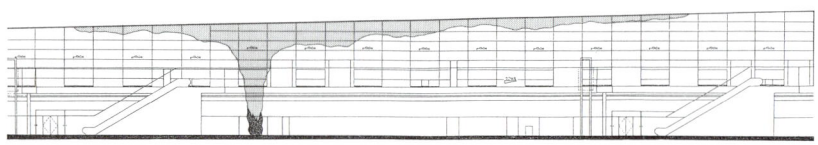

Smoke accumulation in Wing　ウイングでの蓄煙

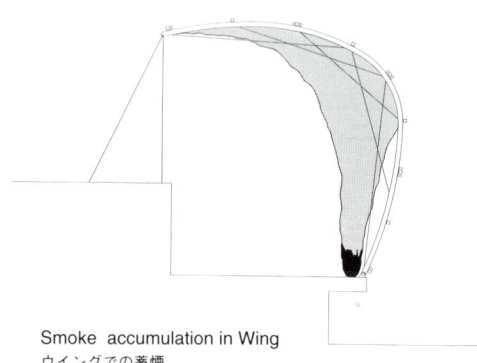

Smoke accumulation in Wing
ウイングでの蓄煙

Before cladding. 耐火被覆前

Fire cladding before finish. 仕上げ前の耐火被覆.

Fireproof Covers

Fire prevention engineering studies were conducted to determine whether steel trusses and rooves of a steel-shell structure could sustain their safety and structural beauty without fireproof covers. These studies revealed that sections of structures heated by fire during evacuation periods were not damaged beyond allowable stress levels. The study results also confirmed that outlying structures would not be adversely affected and that damage would be partly limited should a major fire engulf the gates of one wing. Intumescent paint (equivalent to one-hour resistance class by BS) is applied to all structural components of the terminal building less than four meters from the floor as an additional method for ensuring safety.

鉄骨部材の耐火構造(耐火被覆)

鉄骨造トラスおよび鉄骨シェル構造屋根は、その美しい構造美を活かすため、耐火被覆をせずに耐火安全性を確保できるかどうか防災工学的検討をした。その結果避難時間中に火災による加熱を受けた構造体に破損がなく(許容応力度以下)、万一大規模な火災がウイングのゲート部分を覆っても、構造体の破損は局部的に溜り、他のブロックの構造体に影響を及ぼさないことがわかった。さらに付加安全措置として、床から4m以下の構造材には耐火塗料(BS規格の1時間耐火)を施している。

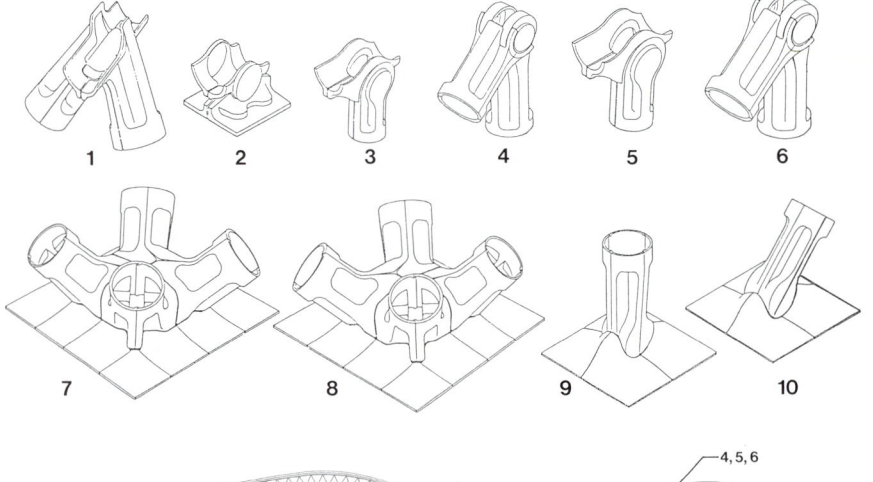

Special Fire-Fighting Arrangement

A special fire-fighting arrangement comprising water cannons and wall-installed open-type sprinklers is adopted in large, open spaces with high ceilings where conventional closed-type sprinklers have proven ineffective. The six water cannons installed in the MTB have a maximum water-shooting distance of 80 meters. They detect heat radiated from the location of the fire with fire-flame detectors and extinguish the fire by shooting water using automatic direction and distance mechanisms. Open-type sprinkler heads are installed on the walls of the Canyon, the gate lounge, and other large, open spaces. The system for shooting water and extinguishing fire used in these sections operates on the basis of alarms from highly sensitive photo-electric beam-type detectors (sensors that detect a fire by sensing decreased transmission between a light emitter and a light receiver).

特殊消火設備

大空間では天井が高いため通常の閉鎖型スプリンクラーでは消火が有効でないエリアに，放水銃設備，壁付き開放型スプリンクラー設備という特殊消火設備を採用している．ＭＴＢに6台設置している放水銃は放水距離が最大80ｍで，出火に伴う熱放射エネルギーを走査型火災検知器で感知し，放水方向，放水距離を自動設定して消火する．キャニオン，ゲートラウンジなどの大空間に面した壁には開放型スプリンクラーのヘッドを設置し，高感度光電式分離型感知器（送光部と受光部の間で，煙による減光を感知することによって火災を検出する感知器）で検出された火災報によって，放水・消火するシステムである．

Highly Sensitive Fire Alarm System

Fire detection by ordinary sensors take much time in the large, open space on the fourth floor because of the high ceilings. To cope with this, highly sensitive beam sensors that detect a fire when the smoke reaches a density of 20 percent are installed in this area. These sensors make early fire detection and evacuation possible. This is an intelligent emergency prevention system from which dust-related errors have been eliminated through repeated tests.

高感度自火報システム

4階大空間では，天井が高いので通常の感知器では火災の発見が遅れる．そこで火災による煙濃度20％の高感度で感知する高感度分離型感知器を使って，早期の火災発見と避難が可能になった．このシステムは埃などの影響についても充分フィールド試験をして誤報を避けることができるインテリジェント防災システムである．

Water cannon on the check-in counter. チェックインカウンターの上の放水銃．

Highly sensitive beam sensors of wing. ウイングの高感度分離型感知器．

CANYON
キャニオン

Canyon viewed from the 4th floor level.　4階から見るキャニオン.

For departing passengers who arrive at the airport from the city center on trains and in cars, the Canyon of the Passenger Terminal Building is the point at which they disperse by destination, including the international departure floor, the domestic departure floor and the concession area (consisting of shops and restaurants). This Canyon is also the passengers' gateway to the sky. In addition, for those arriving on flights, the Canyon is the point of entry into Japan (or into Osaka from other districts in Japan). As people pass through for various purposes, the Canyon can be thought of as a city within the terminal building. The trees in this canyon are evergreens, which are indigenous to the region and therefore suitable for Kansai's gateway to the sky as a representation of Japan and the Kansai region. The concept for the planting of these trees is "chinju-no mori," which refers to a shrine protecting an area. These indigenous evergreen trees are deep green in color, blending well with the colors of the Canyon's facilities. In addition, outside the end walls on both the southern and northern sides, 120 bamboo trees are planted, creating a sense of continuity with the bamboo trees within the Canyon. Natural light shines through the skylight into this four-lined city.

The glass surface of the skylight is equipped with punching metal to prevent glare within the control tower and soften the incoming natural light. Because of this arrangement, the luminous intensity near the Canyon's floor is expected to reach approximately 1,000 luxes to 1,500 luxes. A method, crushed rock cultivation has been adopted for growing plants found in the Canyon in view of such factors as temperature, humidity, wind, soil, and water. The relatively strict conditions on luminosity were also a factor.

For crushed rock cultivation, it is usually necessary to grow plants in water for six to twelve months and then acclimate them to the luminous intensity. In the case of the Canyon, it was six months before the plants were ready to be installed. To acclimate the plants, it is necessary to first wash the soil off the roots and relocate the plants into a sponge-like, permeable, water-storing soil known as ceramic calcined granules made of diatoms. The plants then need to be grown under cheesecloth (which blocks out 70 percent of sunlight) with the periodic spraying of vaporized water. No fertilizer is provided during the early stages of the acclimation process. When roots thicker than their normal counterparts called hydroponic roots sprout after

approximately 50 days, solid fertilizer that takes effect slowly is placed. This method is known as rekiko saibai, as opposed to the conventional method, soil cultivation. The method can ensure the permeability and water-conserving capacity of the roots, as well as prevent the roots from dying of infections.

Beginning in June 1994, it took approximately two months to install pots of trees and plants acclimated in this manner and transplanted into ceramic calcined granules in square-shaped holes dug out on the Canyon's floor. Including all the bamboo trees inside and outside the end walls, there are more than twenty varieties of trees in a wide array of heights, from arbors to cover trees.　— *Shinichi Okumura*

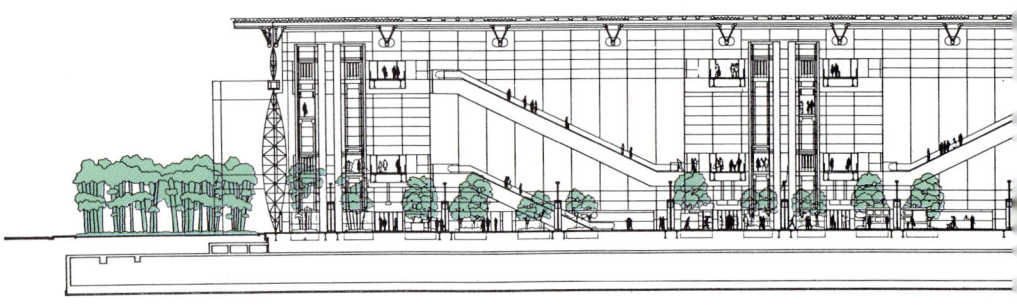

旅客ターミナルビルのキャニオンは，市内から車や列車でアクセスしてきた旅客にとって国際線，国内線，コンセッション（飲食・物販店）といった，それぞれの目的の場所へとわかれていく場であり，空への玄関である．また，国内外から航空機で到着した旅客にとっては，日本あるいは大阪への最初の入口となる．このように人々が多種多様な目的をもって接触し，行き交う場所であるキャニオンはターミナルビル内の都市的空間といってもよいスペースである．ここではトップライトから自然光がそそぎ，樹木がたち並び，壁面が街のファサードをつくっている．

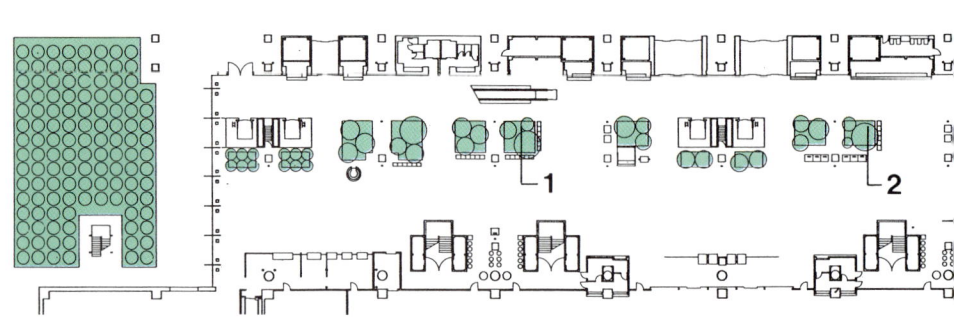

このようなキャニオンに植栽される樹木は，関西の空の玄関にふさわしい，日本あるいは関西を代表する常緑和木で構成される．一言でいうなら「鎮守の杜」が植栽のコンセプトである．これらの常緑和木は落ち着きのある濃緑色で，キャニオンの施設と色彩的にも調和する．また，南北両サイドのエンドウォール外部には，各々120本の竹林を配植し，キャニオン内部の竹林との連続的一体性を生み出している．

キャニオン上部のトップライトには管制塔への照り返しを防ぐため，また，自然光を柔らかな光とするために，ガラス面の上にパンチングメタルが設置されている．それによってキャニオン床面近くでの照度は1,000～1,500ルクスと予想される．このように比較的厳しい照度上の条件に加えて，植栽を導入するには温度，湿度，風，土壌，水などの条件を考慮し，キャニオンの植栽には礫耕栽培という工法を採用している．

礫耕栽培では，通常6～12か月の水耕と照度についての順化が必要であり，キャニオン植栽のためには6か月を要した．順化の過程では，あらかじめ根回ししてある樹木の根を洗って土を落とし，新たに多孔質焼成培土という珪藻土からできたスポンジ状の通気性・保水性に優れた土に植え換える．その後70％遮光寒冷紗という網で覆った中で定期的にミスト散水しながら養生する．順化のはじめの期間は肥料を与えず，50日前後たって水耕根という通常よりやや太い根が出てきたら遅効性の固形肥料を施肥する．従来の植栽工法である土耕栽培工法に対し，これを礫耕栽培工法といい，樹木の根の通気性，保水性が充分に確保され，根ぐされなどを防ぐことができる．

こうして順化された樹木は，多孔質焼成培土の入った鉢のまま，1994年6月から約2か月かかってキャニオンの床に設けられた植桝のなかに植えられ，エンドウォールの内外にある竹林を含めて中高木，地被あわせて30種類になる．（奥村信一）

植栽一覧

高　中　木		地　被	外部竹林
モウソウチク	ユズリハ	ユキノシタ	モウソウチク
マテバシイ	ヤブツバキ	フィリギボシ	シャガ
オガタマノキ	カクレミノ	フッキソウ	クサソテツ
タブノキ	サザンカ（白・赤）	ヤブコウジ	ヤブラン
ヒメユズリハ	カラタネオガタマ	フィリシャガ	
ホルトノキ		フィリヤブラン	
モチノキ		キチジョウソウ	
クロガネモチ		エビネ	
ナギ		シュンラン	
シラカシ		オモト	
モッコク		カンアオイ	

1．マテバシイ，モッコク

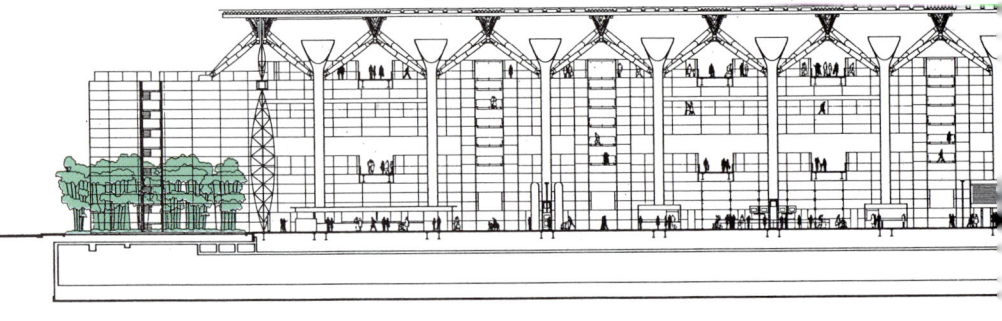

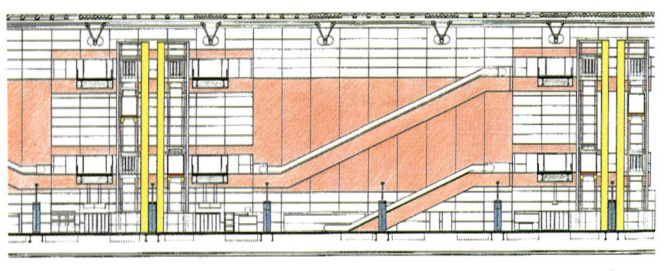

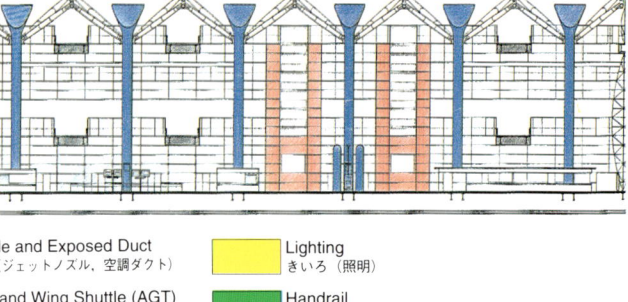

Color plan for Canyon.
キャニオンの色彩計画

Canyon Wall
かわらけ色（キャニオン壁面）

Return Shaft
くちなし色（還気シャフト）

Entrance Box
はいみどり（風除室外側）

Jet Nozzle and Exposed Duct
そらいろ（ジェットノズル，空調ダクト）

Elevator and Wing Shuttle (AGT)
赤（エレベーター，ウイングシャトル）

Lighting
きいろ（照明）

Handrail
若草色（手摺）

Landside wall plan of Canyon. キャニオン内部ランドサイド側.

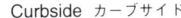
Curbside カーブサイド

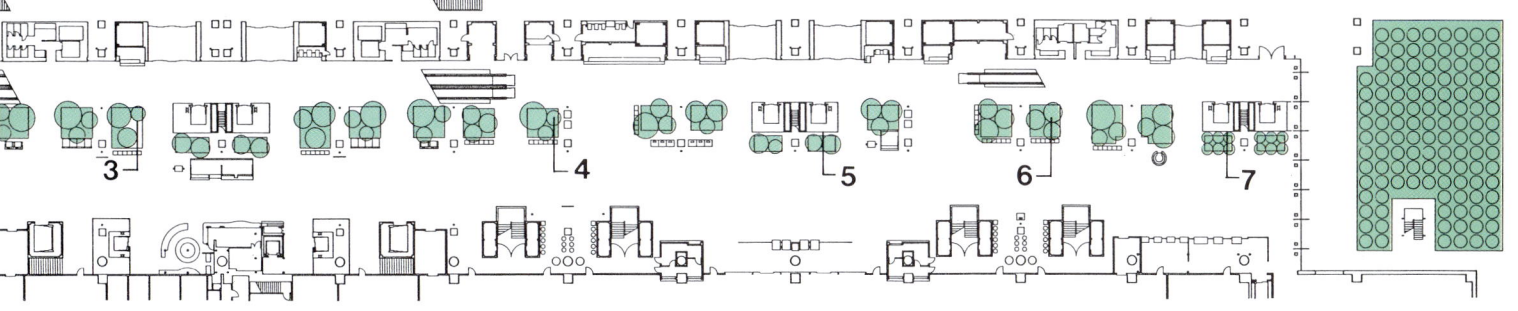

International arrival lobby 国際線到着ロビー

Plan of Canyon. キャニオン平面図

2．ヒメユズリハ，ユズリハ　　3．サザンカ，モチノキ　　4．カクレミノ，ホルトノキ　　5．ナギ　　6．ヤブツバキ　　7．モウソウチク

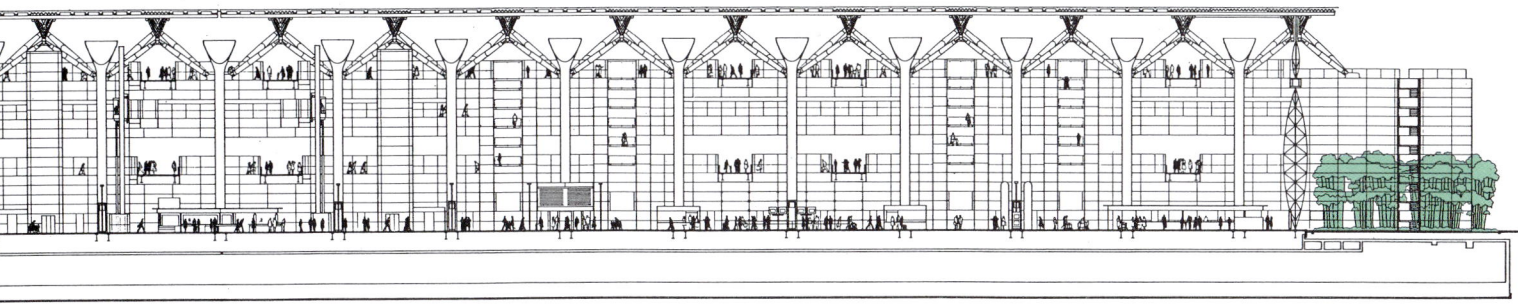

Lobby side wall plan of Canyon. キャニオン内部ロビー側

Adapting to poor sunlight.
木の順化（ヤブツバキ）

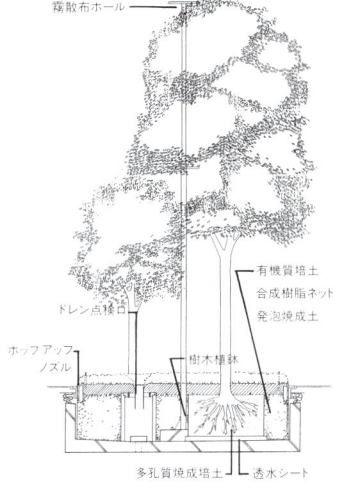

Air-supplying trees (vertical jetting boxes)　給気ツリー（箱型空調吹き出し口）

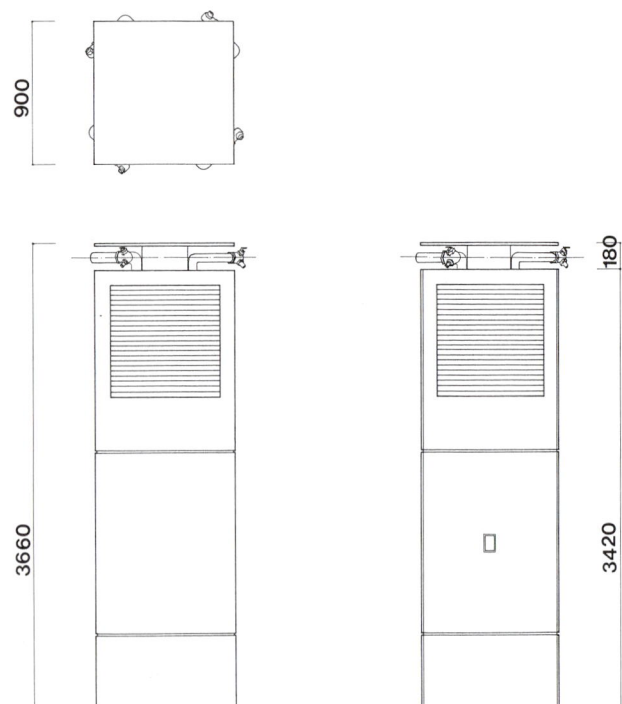

The Canyon is air-conditioned by the air jetted out of air-supplying trees and posts (vertical jetting boxes) located at its base. The air is circulated back from the ceilings area. This system effectively air-conditions heavily populated areas, as well as spaces such as bridges for horizontal movement on the second and fourth floors and escalators for vertical movement between all four floors from bottom to top. The system thus makes the best use of the supplied energy.

キャニオンの空調は，キャニオン底部の給気ツリー・給気ポスト（縦型吹き出しボックス）から空調空気を吹き出し，キャニオン天井付近からリターンをとる．これは，人の滞留域を効率よく空調するとともに，2階，4階レベル水平移動用ブリッジや1〜4階の垂直移動用エスカレーターなどの空間を順次下から上へ空調し，供給したエネルギーを使いきる方式である．

Air supplying trees (vertical jetting boxes)
給気ツリー

Canyon and curbside viewed from glass box stairwell. Color of all handrails of PTB is pale green. Peter Rice's DPG method is used for glazing clips.
ガラス張りの階段からキャニオンを見る．手摺はPTB内すべて若草色で統一されている．ガラス面を固定する金具はピーター・ライスが開発したDPG工法が使われている．

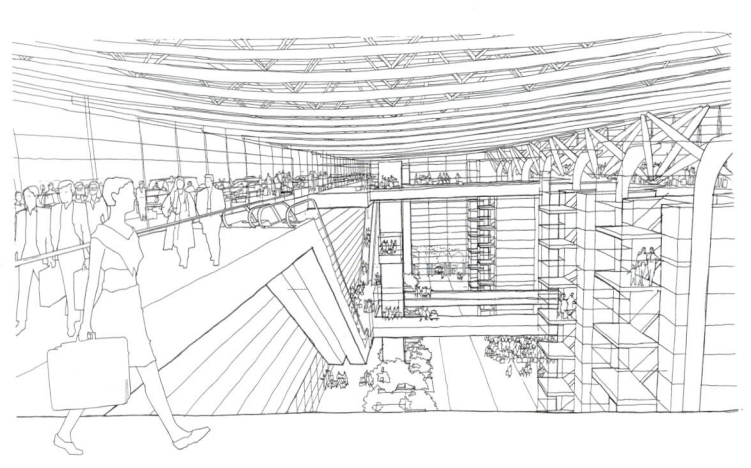
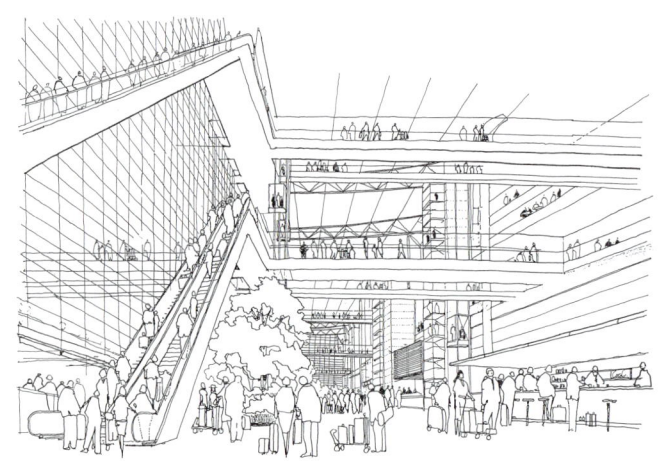

View of 4th floor lobby through Canyon from curbside, 4th floor entrance.
カーブサイド4階入口からキャニオンを通して4階ロビーを見る。

Skylight of Canyon.　キャニオンのトップライト

Bamboo trees outside and inside end wall.
エンドウォール内外の竹林.

Outside bamboo trees, canopy of MTB in right.
エンドウォール外側の竹林. 右にMTB屋根を見上げる.

Soft and Light: A Sense of Sight Verging on Touch

We wanted to make the theme of the KIA terminal building project "soft lightness," and tried our best to prevent aggressive impressions of structure as well as complex expressions of technology. We chose an approach quite different from that of the Pompidou Center in Paris, for example. In both the relationship and hierarchy of the structure and other elements, and the mutual relations among the elements, we searched for an expression that would not give a sense of weight or mass. The 150-meter-long main beams in the roof structure of the main building and the connecting wing shells reveal no unsightly joints, for instance, which might distract those gazing upward. The graceful tubes of the main trusses curve in a series of gentle waves linked at their extremity to the ribs of the wings. In the main building, in order to eliminate structural roughness, secondary members — which tend to become "visual noise" — were hidden in the ceiling, with only their undersides showing slightly as modules.

The roof itself consists of double corrugated steel panels, and the roof exterior is covered with 1.8 x 0.6-meter tiles of stainless-steel. At the point where the roof meets the glazing (the glass-curtain wall), the roof separates from the arched geometry and becomes an eaves overshadowing the glass surface. A sense of separation is also felt between the thin membrane of the open air ducts and the roof, creating an expansive effect of light and gently flowing air. This separation-oriented design method was conceived not only out of consideration for environmental control by preventing direct sunlight, but also with the intention of achieving a soft and light expression for the roof and building space.

The approximately 90.000 stainless steel tiles that cover the gentle undulation of the roof were given a dull finish (pear-skin surface finish) to prevent strong reflections that might obstruct the visibility and duties of the air traffic controllers. An array of features, including the unshined, soft texture of the stainless material, the precise geometric fit of the tiles, and the extremely thin, tileless edge detailing will bring into sharp relief the distinctive, delicate, and glowing form which has been created, and which is subtly transformed from season to season and hour to hour by the sunlight's changing angles and intensity. —*N. O.*

Torii, or shrine gate.

Shoji, or sliding paper doors

Bamboo trees in nature

Rice field as Japanese natural green.

ソフト・アンド・ライト ── 触覚にせまる視覚

ソフトな軽やかさをテーマにしたいと考えた関西国際空港旅客ターミナルビルでは、構造体のアグレッシブな印象とテクノロジカルでコンプレックスな表現を、極力排除していくことにした。パリのポンピドー・センターの方向とは異なるアプローチをとったわけである。

構造とその他のエレメントとのかかわりとヒエラルキー、さらにエレメント相互の関係に、重量感のない表現を探した。メインビルディングの屋根構造の150mのメインビームとそれにつづくウイングのシェルは、下から見上げる人々には、わずらわしいジョイント部分が見えない。なめらかなメイントラスのチューブが、ゆっくりと連続波を描きながらウイングのリブへとつながってゆく。メインターミナルビルでは構造の荒々しさを除くために、ビジュアル・ノイズとなる2次材は天井内に隠れ、2次材下部のみがかすかに現われてモジュールの規範となる。

屋根本体は二重折板で構成されるが、外装は1.8m×0.6mのステンレス・スチールのタイルでおおわれる。屋根とグレージング(ガラスカーテンウォール)の接続点では、屋根が円弧のジオメトリーから剥離して、ガラス面に影をつくるひさしとなる。薄い膜で構成されたオープンエアダクトとルーフの間にも剥離の距離感があり、広がりのある美しい光とやわらかく流れる気流圏を構成している。これらの剥離によるデザイン方法は、直射日光を防ぐ環境制御などの配慮と同時に、屋根とボリュームをかろやかに表現する意図からも構想された。

形態のなだらかな波形をおおう約9万枚のステンレス・タイルには、航空管制に障害をきたすきつい反射を避けたダル仕上げ(梨地状表面をもった仕上げ)が施されている。あたりのソフトなステンレスのマテリアルの生の質感、幾何学的に緻密に組み込まれたタイルの構図、タイルだけ剥離した極薄のエッジのディテールなどが、四季と時間で移り変わる太陽光線の強度を微妙に異なる角度で受けつつ、シャープでデリケートで壮麗な光の造形物を浮上させてくれることだろう。 (N.O.)

Outside bamboo trees.
エンドウォール外の竹林

Geometry as the Common Language

The geometry approach was developed in the process of creating the KIA terminal building design and moving into the construction phase. Now forming the common communication parameter at the construction site, this geometry is the basic criterion for finishing a mammoth project. Underlying this common language of geometry in both the processes of design and construction are the earlier-mentioned concept of fractals, as advanced by Benoit Mandelbrot; the valuable experience at Bercy II; and the great lessons learned from the difficulties encountered in the design and construction of the Sydney Opera House.[1]

The Sydney project produced a structure of rare beauty which is not only a landmark in architectural history, but which has also contributed greatly to advances in technology. The Opera House, too, is a story about geometry. Experiments were pursued in the rib and panel geometry paralleling the search for structural solutions, which led to the evolution from parabolic to spherical surfaces, and from shell to rib structures. Peter Rice, who has cooperated in the KIA project from the outset, took part in the Sydney Opera House project as a young OAP staff member who was already among the leading engineers engaged in structural analysis.

The Sydney experience is replete with valuable lessons to be learned. We cannot but continue to be impressed, for instance, with the beautiful correlation between the skin and the geometry so astutely foreseen in Utzon's initial design vision of a white-tiled surface.

The geometrical approach of the Sydney project was based on a combination of spheres. By contrast, the geometrical approach used at the terminal building of the Kansai International Airport was flexible. The shapes of cross sections could thereby be altered without compromising work tolerance. This can be referred to as a soft geometrical approach. —*N. O.*

1. Among valuable documents are a 1968 report by Yuzo Mikami, who joined the project as a collaborator of OAP, and Utzon, "Sidoni Opera Hausu no kiroku (1, 2)" (A Record of the Sydney Opera House [1 and 2]) (Kenchiku bunka, 1968) and a report by OAP's Ove Arup and J. Zunz, "Sydney Opera House" (Arup Journal, 1973).

共通言語としてのジオメトリー

ジオメトリーの方法は，KIAターミナルビルの設計デザインから製作施工へと至るプロセスの中で発展してきた．現在，現場における共通のコミュニケーション・パラメーターとなったジオメトリーは，巨大なプロジェクトを精緻に仕上げる規範なのだ．デザインと施工の両過程の共通言語となったジオメトリーの考え方の背景になったのは，先述したようにブノワ・マンデルブローのフラクタル思考と，ベルシー2の先行した貴重な経験と，そして多大な困難をこえて実現されたシドニー・オペラハウスの設計と建設の偉大なる教訓だった．＊

シドニーのプロジェクトは類いまれな美しい建築物を歴史に残しただけではなく，多大なる技術的な貢献を果たした．ここにもひとつのジオメトリーの物語がある．パラボリックから球面へ，シェルからリブへと展開した構造上の解決と並行して，リブとパネルのジオメトリーの関連にさまざまな実験がなされたからだ．KIAプロジェクトに最初から協力してくれている構造家のピーター・ライスは当時シドニー・オペラハウス・プロジェクトに若くしてOAPのスタッフとして参加し，構造解析にたずさわった主要なエンジニアのひとりであった．

シドニーの記録は，記憶されるべき豊富な示唆に富んでいる．白いタイルの表皮をデザインのはじめからイメージしていたウッツォンの先見的感性は，スキンとジオメトリーの美的な関係性を，今日でも私たちに力強く語りかけてくる．シドニーのジオメトリーの方法は球体の組み合わせをベースにしている．これに比して，関西空港ターミナルビルのジオメトリーは，施工のトレランスを内包した上で断面を移動する方法をとることで断面形を変化できるという，フレキシビリティを持っている．その点で，ソフトジオメトリーのアプローチと呼んでもいいかと思う．　　　(N.O.)

＊： OAPとウッツォンのコラボレーターとしてプロジェクトにたずさわった三上祐三氏の1968年の報告書（シドニー・オペラハウスの記録1，2，建築文化，1968年）や，OAPのサー・アロップ氏とジャック・ズーンズ氏によるレポート（The Arap Journal "Sydney Opera House" by Ove Arup and J. Zunz, October 1973）が貴重な記録として残されている．

The Balance against Chaos

In retrospect, our adventure into unknown realms of expression for the KIA terminal building through the study of geometry and expression of flow was an endeavor to overcome volume-oriented expressionism. The conditions and standards for creating an airport terminal building were very strict, but they presented us with an architectural challenge enabling us to achieve a truly novel kind of expression. In that sense, we were much inspired and encouraged by such pioneering works as Eero Saarinen's TWA building and Jorn Utzon's Sydney Opera House.

The KIA project differed from these two now-classic landmarks in architectural history in the extremely tight restrictions of budget and time involved. Because of these constraints, the theme of the design became the challenge of constructing a totally new kind of architecture on a giant scale within a short time span.

I would also like to add here that, in striving to transcend Western methods and expressions oriented to massive structures and in our quest to form of a light and soft expression for the terminal building, we occasionally drew inspiration from traditional Japanese architecture and treatment of space. The rhythmical beauty of a series of segments of a roof, the detailed elaboration at the eaves based on geometric composition, and the expression of light in a separated space — such as that created by the double layers of a *shoji* screen and sliding door *(hikido)* — are part of the vocabulary we derived from Japanese architecture. We sought to live up to the standards of spacial quality expressed in Japanese architecture.

If we can afford to take expressionism as volume out of the main context of architecture and make it parenthetical, we might release a liberated and lyrical wellspring of refreshing chaos and finely balanced conformism—imbued with the affinity for fractals.

—*N. O.*, August 1992, Paris

October, 1988.

カオスとバランス

流れの表現やジオメトリーの研究を通して，未知の表現をめざしたターミナルビルの探究は，今日ふりかえってみれば，ボリュームとしての表現主義をのりこえる試みでもあったように思える．空港ターミナルビルの厳しい条件と規範は，逆に斬新な表現と建築的挑戦の機会となった．こうした意味でも，エーロ・サーリネンのTWAとウッツォンのシドニー・オペラハウスは挑戦の意志を鼓舞してくれる勇気ある先達となった．

KIAプロジェクトには，この2つのプロジェクトのような充分な予算と時間が与えられていたわけではなかった．こうした限られた条件のためにかえって，短期間の設計建設の時間の中で巨大さをどうのりこえるか，そして新たな建築にどのようにして到達するかがデザインのテーマとなったのだ．

かろやかなターミナルビルの表現を求めて，重厚な西欧の構築物の方法と表現を超克しようとしたとき，日本の伝統建築と空間表現が折りにつけ私たちにさまざまな示唆を与えてくれたことも記しておきたい．分節化しつつ連続する屋根のリズムの美，繊細な幾何学で構成されたひさしの絶妙なディテール，障子や引戸の膜面の重層によって構成される剥離空間の光の表情などは，すぐれて日本建築が生み出した建築のボキャブラリーである．私たちはこうした日本の空間の質と水準に到達することをめざしたともいえる．

ボリュームとしての表現主義を一度カッコに入れてみれば，解放された詩的な気流の中でフラクタルへの憧れとともに，さわやかなカオスと精妙な整合のバランスが生み出されてくるかもしれない．

(N.O.)

APPENDICIES

Winning Design of the Competition
New Departures — Background to the PTB
PTB Designers' Credits
Afterword
Authors' Profiles
Credits

付記

設計競技優勝案
新たなる試み──設計共同体
設計共同体クレジット
あとがき
執筆者経歴
クレジット

Winning Design of the Competition
設計競技優勝案

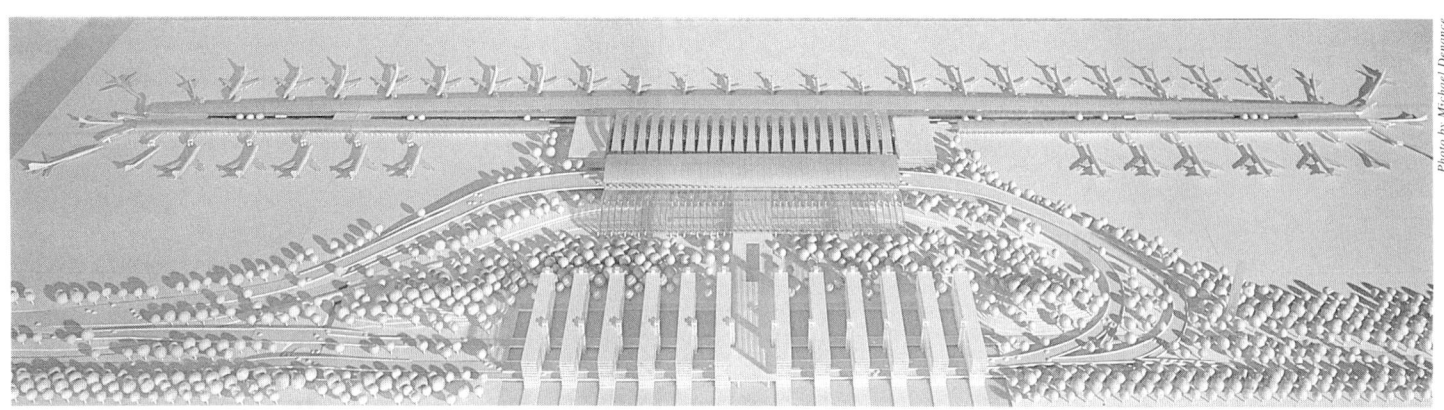
Model photo including Aeroplaza space　現在のエアロプラザの敷地まで含む計画の全体模型

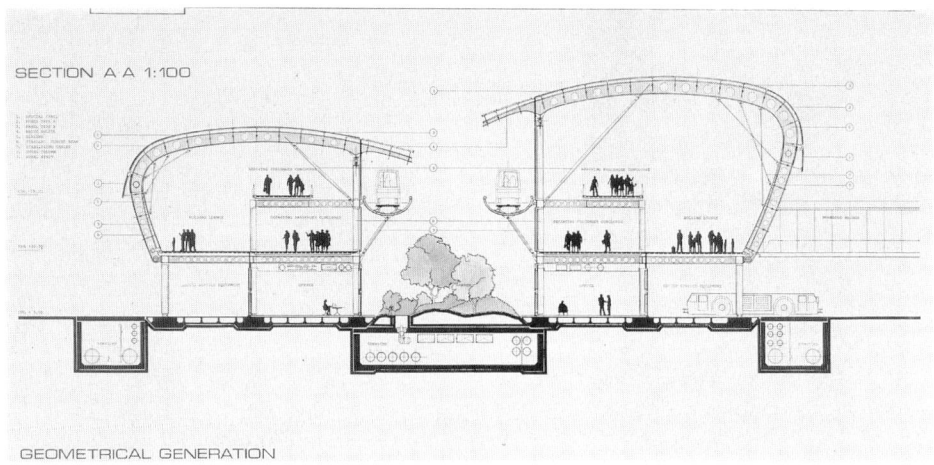
Wing section　ウイング断面図

Macro air conditioning plan　マクロ空調計画

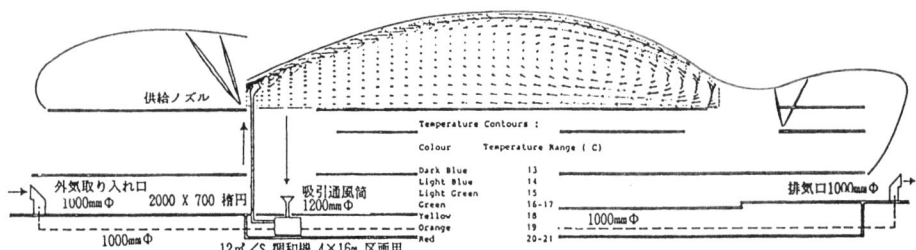

Micro air conditioning plan　ミクロ空調計画

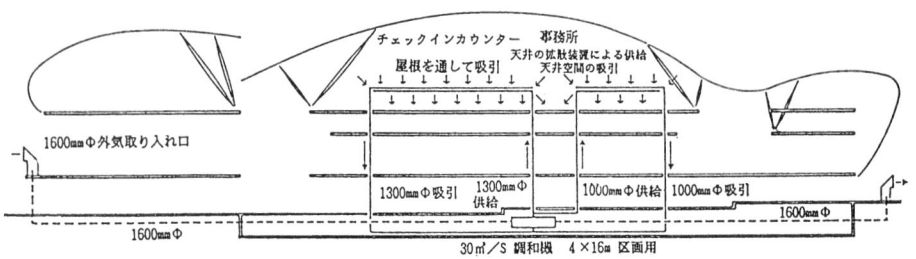

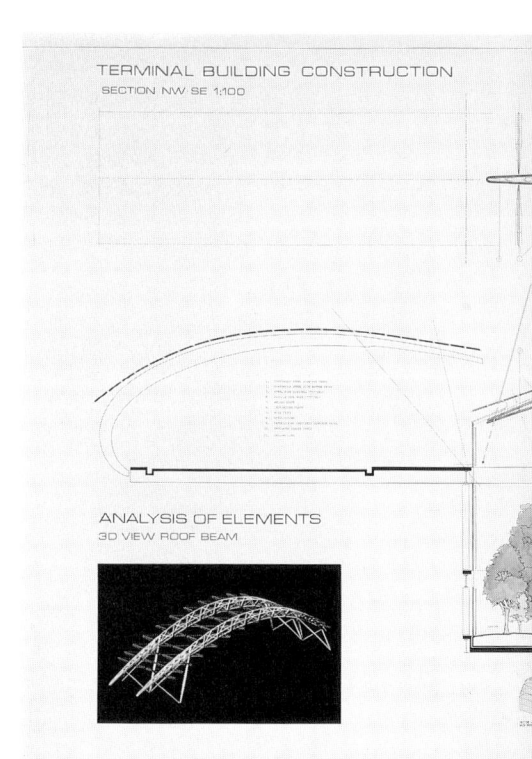

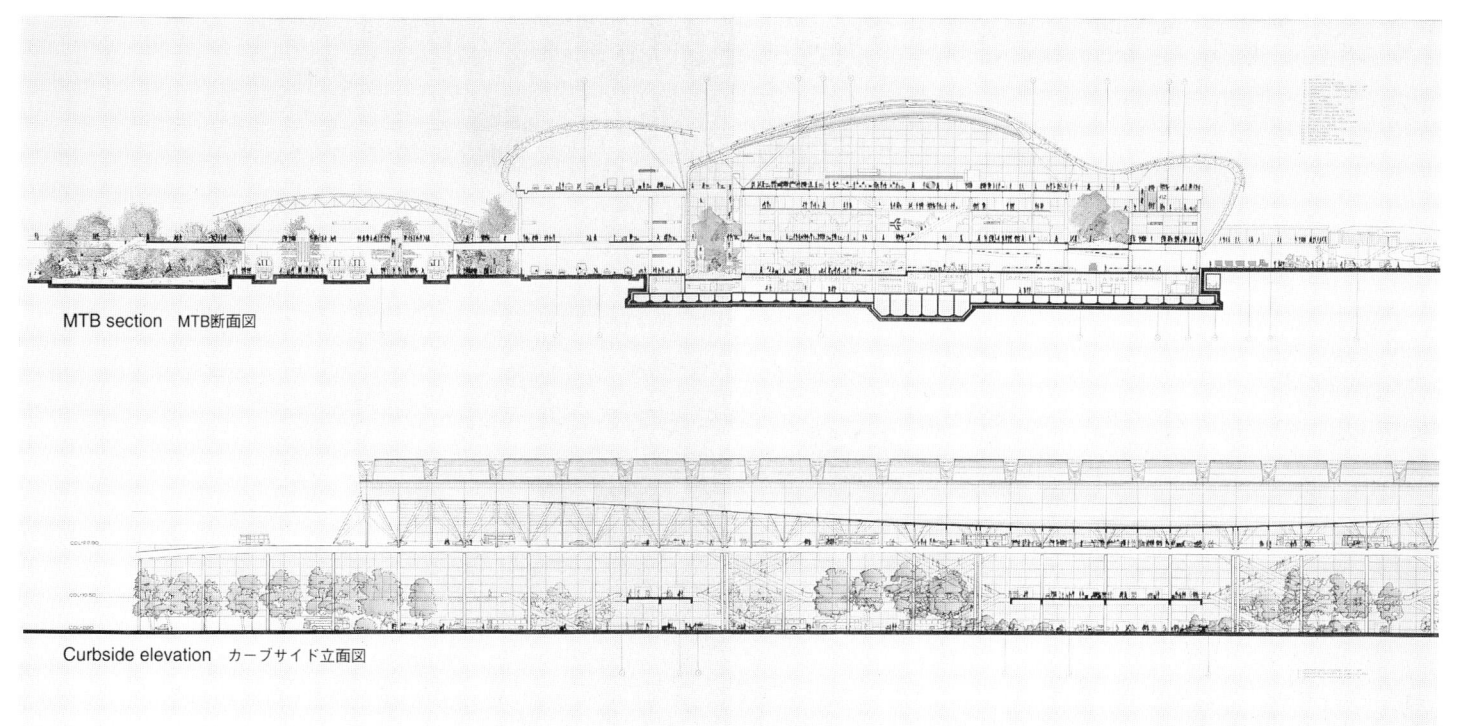

MTB section　MTB断面図

Curbside elevation　カーブサイド立面図

Model photo of MTB　MTBの模型

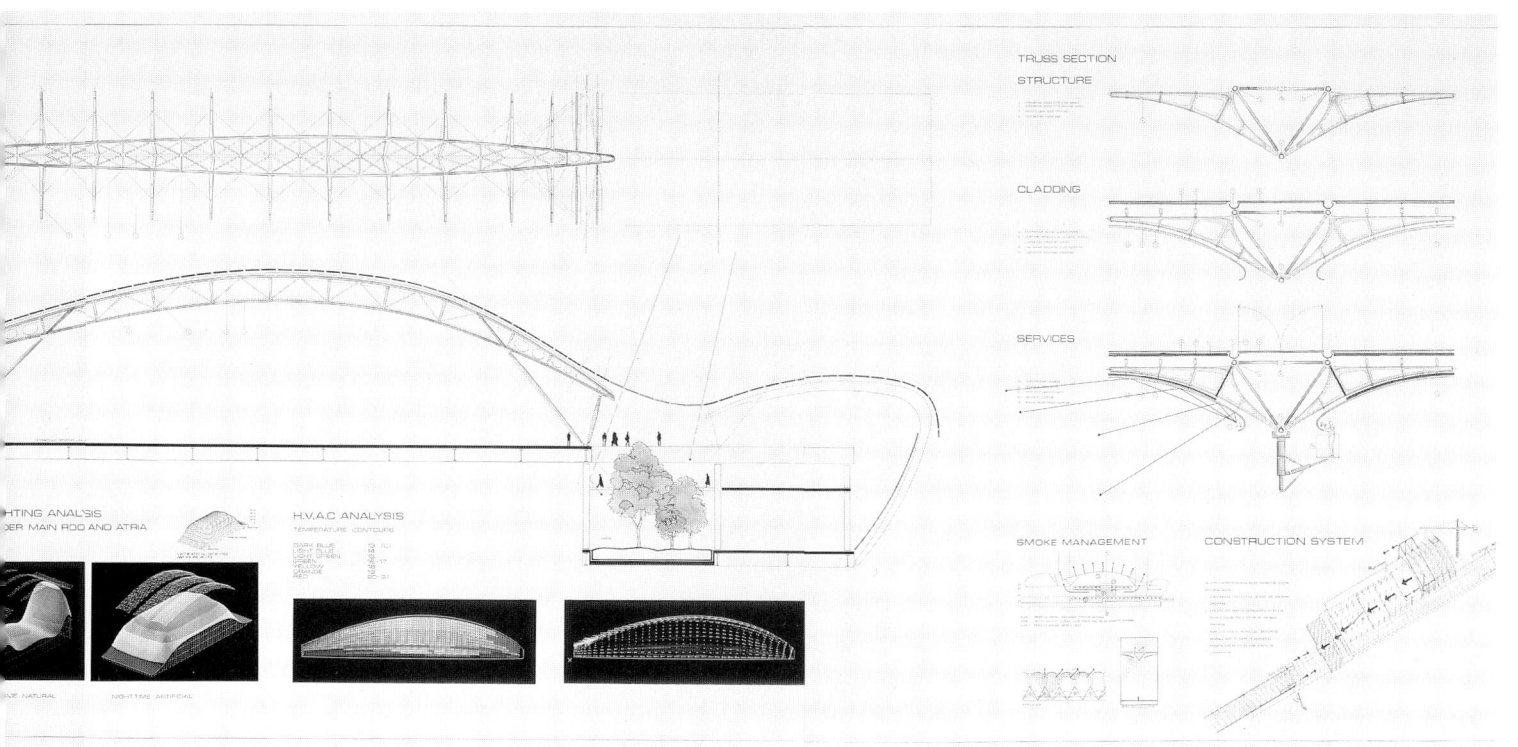

New Departures—Background to the PTB
新たなる試み—設計共同体

In May 1988, an agreement was reached between the United States and Japan on opening of the construction market in Japan. Since then, it has become possible for foreign firms to take part directly in construction work on large scale public projects in Japan, in accordance with Japanese government policy favoring neither foreign nor domestic firms.

However, problems between the United States and Japan over entry into the construction market first arose, in May 1986, when the possible inclusion of American firms in the Kansai International Airport project was muted. Subsequently, however, after negotiations started in March 1988, it was finally agreed in May the same year that foreign firms would be able to take part in 17 projects, including the one for Kansai International Airport, and others such as Minato Mirai in Yokohama, and the building of a new passenger terminal for Tokyo's main domestic airport at Haneda.

The agreement, which was signed by Ambassador Matsusaki for Japan and by Secretary of Commerce Verity on behalf of the United States, became known as the "construction agreement" and included special measures related to public projects. As a result of the signing of this agreement, it became possible for foreign architects to be involved directly in design work in Japan. In fact, conditions of the agreement cover such things as design and consultancy, as well as provisions for various commodities and construction work, too. The number of specially recognized projects has now risen to 34. Therefore, apart from the design arguments, it is also important to recognize exactly under what circumstances the project for Kansai International Airport was undertaken. It is important because a comprehensive synthesis of everything that happened is sure to prove useful in the future, especially as it was the most talked about project ever to be undertaken in Japan up until that time, and because of the many opinions which were voiced by all those concerned with the construction of the airport at various times.

The Kansai International Airport Company (KIAC) took the decision to hold an open international design competition in April, 1988. However, even before the competition got underway, KIAC had already taken steps to draw up a preliminary scheme for terminal facilities.

A group of six companies was commissioned to work on the first phase of this initial scheme at the end of January, 1986. In autumn the same year, the same "group of six" were entrusted with work to draw up the second stage of the scheme. This work lasted until the end of June, 1987. The six companies involved were, Japan Airport Consultant, Nikken Sekkei, Yasui Architects and Engineers, Azusa Sekkei, Matsuda, Hirata and Sakamoto Architects (now MHS Architects), and Airport Engineering.

However, as pressures from abroad mounted, KIAC sponsored a seminar on the project, specifically to satisfy factions in the United States, immediately before contracts were signed with the group of six to do work on the second phase of the preliminary scheme. As a result, KIAC decided that an American consulting firm should also take part in the project, working in collaboration with the previously established group of six. A proposal as to what facilities should be installed in the terminal as a whole was made by KIAC. Then in January, 1987, Bechtel Inc. was chosen out of the six American consulting companies nominated by KIAC, two of the others being Leo A. Daly and TR International. However, quite contrary to general opinion, Bechtel Inc. did not submit a scheme for the design competition.

Then in June 1987, the second stage of the preliminary scheme which had been entrusted to the group of six was completed. Out of the three schemes submitted outlining basic concepts, Plan B was chosen. It had been drawn up jointly by Nikken Sekkei and Japan Airport Consultants. What, in fact, had happen was that pairs of companies had work jointly on schemes, each pair producing one scheme each.

With the preliminary scheme complete, the next stage was to draw up a basic plan. However, at this stage KIAC decided to have the three schemes submitted by the group of six assessed independently, and showed them to six airport authorities in five countries. These were Aéroports de Paris, the British Airports Authority, and the airport authority responsible for Schiphol Airport in Holland. The schemes were also assessed by the Dallas Fort Worth Interna-

1988年(昭和63年)5月に、日米建設協議が合意した。これにより、日本での大型公共事業は内外無差別という日本政府の方針により、外国企業の日本市場への参入が可能となった。

しかし日米建設問題が起こったのは、その2年前の1986年5月からである。当初は、関西国際空港プロジェクトへの米国企業の参入という形だったが、その後、両国は1988年3月に日米建設協議を開催し、5月には関西国際空港や横浜みなとみらい、羽田空港新旅客ターミナルビルなど、17プロジェクトで外国企業の参入を可能とすることで合意した。

これが、当時、日本の松崎大使と米国のヴェリティ商務長官によって、公共事業に関する特例措置を記して署名された協定、つまり建設合意といわれるものである。この合意によって、欧米の建築家が設計分野に参入が可能となったのである。合意事項も、物品調達や建設工事の調達、デザイン及びコンサルティング業務の調達にまで及んだ。その結果、特例措置プロジェクトは、現在まで34件にもなった。関西国際空港の位置づけは、デザイン論議のほかに、そうした背景の中にあったということを確認しておかなくてはならない。なぜなら、空港建設をめぐって、さまざまな時点で、それぞれの関係者の思惑が入り乱れ、かつてないほどの議論がなされたからであり、そのことを充分に総括することが、今後にも役立つからである。

関西国際空港会社は、1988年4月、同空港旅客ターミナルビルを国際公開コンペにすることを決めた。しかし関空会社は、国際コンペを実施する前からターミナルビル施設の基本構想作業にとりかかっていた。

1986年1月末にステップ1として、6社企業連合に委託。続いて同年秋に、同じ6社にステップ2を委託した。業務期間は、1987年6月末までである。6社とは、日本空港コンサルタンツ、日建設計、安井建築設計事務所、梓設計、松田平田坂本設計事務所(現、松田平田)、空港エンジニアリングである。

しかし日増しに強まってくる外圧に対して、関空会社はステップ2の契約直前に米国向けに「関西国際空港プロジェクトに関するセミナー」を開催する。その結果、関空会社は6社企業連合に協力する形で、米国コンサルタント会社の参画を決定する。ターミナル施設に導入する諸施設をプロポーザルで実施した。その結果、1987年1月、レオ・A・デイリーやTRインターナショナルなど指名された6社の中からベクテル社が選ばれた。ちなみにベクテル社は、大方の予想と違って関空国際コンペには応募しなかった。

その後、1987年6月に6社企業連合に委託していたステップ2がまとまる。A、B、Cの3タイプのコンセプト案のうち、最終的に残ったのが日建設計と日本空港コンサルタンツJVによるB案である。つまり6社は2社ずつJVを組んで、1案ずつ作ったのである。

基本構想が決まったのだから、次は基本計画である。ところが関空会社は、その3案を5か国6当局の空港関係者に示し、意見を求めたのである。パリ空港公団(フランス)、スキポール空港公団(オランダ)、ブリティッシュ・エアポートサービス(イギリス)、ダラス空港公団(アメリカ)、ニューヨーク・ニュージャージー空港公団(アメリカ)、フランクフルト空港公団(ドイツ)である。検討は2か月、3案に対するアドバイスのほかに提案も求めた。なぜ、そうしたのか、理由はわからない。

その結果、1988年3月、関空会社は記者会見をし、関空会社としての基本構想を発表した。意外にも、関空会社が採ったのはパリ空港公団が提案したコンセプトだった。同公団案をまとめたのが、ポール・アンドリューである。関空会社は、日建設計と日本空港コンサルタンツJVのB案でなく、パリ空港公団案をよしとしたのである。なぜ、そうなったのかも関空会社からの説明はなかった。

発表されたパリ空港公団案は、ターミナルビル延床面積30万m²、長手方向が1,743m、短手方向

tional Airport Board, the Port Authority of New York and New Jersey, and the authority overseeing Frankfurt Airport, *Flughafen Frankfurt Main AG*. The plans were assessed over a two month period and, apart from seeking advise, proposals were also sought. However, the reason for doing this is not known.

Subsequently, a press conference was held in March 1988, at which KIAC publicly announced what it had adopted as its preliminary scheme. Quite unexpectedly, KIAC actually adopted a scheme put forward by Aéroports de Paris. This scheme had in fact been drawn up by Paul Andreu. This new proposal was therefore adopted in preference to the scheme drawn up jointly by Nikken Sekkei and Japan Airport Consultants, a decision which was never explained by KIAC.

The scheme drawn up by Aéroports de Paris proposed a large terminal building with a total floor area of 300,000 sqm, measuring 1,743 meters by 102 meters. It also proposed that movement of passengers between international and domestic flights should only be in a vertical direction, and that a "people mover" be used to move both international and domestic passengers.

Having adopted the Aéroports de Paris proposal as the preliminary scheme in March 1988, the terminal building then became the subject of a international design competition. It should also be mentioned that Nikken Sekkei and Japan Airport Consultants subsequently worked in collaboration with Aéroports de Paris on the drawing up of a basic plan. However, out of the other companies in the group of six, Yasui Architects and Engineers were the only organization to enter a design for the terminal building competition, and their scheme was among the 15 chosen by KIAC for final selection. Azusa Sekkei, Matsuda, Hirata and Sakamoto Architects, and Airport Engineering, on the other hand, made no submission.

In a sense, there were two stages to the competition, the first comprising publication of the brief outlining actual facilities, the open submission of designs and judging, followed by a nominated design competition.

Before going into the details of how the competition progressed, it must be mentioned that the internationally famous architect, Kisho Kurokawa played no small part in making this momentous competition a reality. Kurokawa let it be known after the airport was opened that he had told the president of KIAC, Yoshio Takeuchi, that the holding of an international design competition would be advisable, and that it should be in two stages. Furthermore, it seems that the selection of fifteen entries from all those submitted was also made jointly by Kurokawa and KIAC. The thinking at the time was that "an ideal solution would be to have a highly creative architect working in collaboration with a support team." Conversely, what this also meant was that "a construction company working together with a consultancy doing all the organizational work did not seem so ideal," a fact which becomes plain if we look at the list of fifteen nominated organizations.

The fifteen nominees at the competition	コンペで指名された15社
Naco/Taller de Arquitecture Ricardo Bofill	ナコ/タレル・デ・アルキテクトゥーラ, リカルド・ボフィール(オランダ・スペイン)
Renzo Piano Building Workshop Paris	レンゾ・ピアノ・ビルディング・ワークショップ・パリ(フランス)
Planning Association Prof. Ungers-Airconsult	プランニング・アソシエイション, プロフェッサー・ウンガース/エア・コンサルト(西ドイツ)
AXS Satow Inc.	佐藤総合計画(日本)
Foster Associates/Ohbayashi Corporation	フォスター・アソシエイツ/オオバヤシ・コーポレイション(英国・日本)
Design System & JD Architekten BDA	デザイン・システム/ヨットデー・アルヒテクテン・ベーデーアー(日本・西ドイツ)
Kikutake Architects and Associates	菊竹清訓建築設計事務所(日本)
Ellerbe Becket/Parsons/Shimizu, a Joint Body	エラブ・ベケット/パーソンズ/シミズ 共同体(米国・日本)
Cesar Pelli & Associates, Inc./Takenaka Corporation	シーザー・ペリ・アンド・アソシエイツ/竹中工務店(米国・日本)
Kajima Corporation/Hellmuth, Obata & Kassabaum Inc.	鹿島建設/ヘルムース・オバタ・アンド・カッサバウム(米国・日本)
Yasui Architects and Engineers Inc.	安井建築設計事務所(日本)
I.M. Pei & Partners/Kumagai-Gumi Corporation	I.M.ペイ・アンド・パートナーズ/熊谷組共同体(米国・日本)
Kazuhiro Ishii Architect and Associates	石井和紘建築研究所(日本)
Bernard Tschumi	バーナード・チュミ(米国)
Jean Nouvel et Associes, SARL	ジャン・ヌーヴェル・エ・アソシエ(フランス)

Judges of the Competition
Yoshio Takeuchi (President of KIAC), Ryu Akiyama, Souichi Nishimura, Arata Isozaki, Kiyoshi Kawasaki, Kisho Kurokawa, Helmut Jahn, Richard Rogers.

審査会委員(役職は当時のもの)
竹内良夫(関西国際空港株式会社社長, 審査会長), 秋山龍(航空審議会委員長代理, 運輸政策審議会特別委員), 西村壮一(大阪府副知事), 磯崎新(磯崎新アトリエ代表), 川崎清(京都大学教授), 黒川紀章(黒川紀章建築都市設計事務所代表取締役社長), ヘルムート・ヤーン(エール大学客員教授), リチャード・ロジャース(ロジャース&パートナーズ代表)

Out of the forty-eight submissions made, KIAC selected fifteen in June, 1988 and made the schemes public. Selection was made on the basis of five criteria: what kind of work the entrant had done previously; their past experience; basic design ability and whether or not the entrant had the ability to complete a job smoothly; if the entrant was well known or not both at home and abroad; and finally whether they could be expected to produce something novel. The fifteen nominees and the names of the judges appear on the previous page.

There were a number of things which made this competition special. There is no denying, for example, that it was one of the first significant spin-offs to came from the agreement which had been reached between Japan and the United States on construction market entry. The fact that entries were submitted by all the world's top-class architects, added to fact that they teamed up with big Japanese general contractors was also noteworthy. Furthermore, the panel of judges was one of the very best, and all the selected entrants were architects with a design flair. Besides which the amount of discussion over the way the project was actually administered also made this competition special.

Out of a total of forty-eight entries, twenty-two were from Japan and twenty-six were from overseas, making it a truly "international competition" because of the good response there was from overseas. Furthermore, out of the twenty-six entries from abroad, twelve were from the United States. Seven of these were submitted jointly by Japanese and American firms. Clearly, the amount of interest there was from the United States was directly connected with the fact that the project itself had been one of the bones of contention of the construction agreement between Japan and the United States.

The final outcome of the competition was that the proposal put forward by the Renzo Piano Building Workshop Paris in collaboration with Ove Arup and Partners was chosen. Piano became the design architect and the Renzo Piano Building Workshop Japan, again working in collaboration with Ove Arup and Partners, was established. This partnership teamed up with Aéroports de Paris, Nikken Sekkei and Japan Airport Consultants, the three companies which had been responsible for drawing up the basic plan, to form a new, four party partnership. Forming just such a partnership, in fact, was what had been clearly stated in the competition brief.

Under normal circumstances, the architect would have be responsible for everything from outlining the original scheme, doing the basic plan and for doing the basic design. However, in the case of this particular project there were those who were of the opinion that because the whole process had been broken up into a number of individual stages, the independence of the designer as well as their copyright on the design were none existent as were their rights and responsibilities. But that was not the only opinion to be voiced. Despite the fact that among the nominated entrants they were general contractors working in collaboration with an architect, there were also those who considered that the adopted system in actual fact completely ignored the generally accepted way in which design and construction are separated in the case of public sector work in Japan. Various architectural bodies including the Japan Institute of Architects as well as architects associated with them also had a great deal to say about the way the job was run.

In all events, the design for Kansai International Airport was ultimately realized jointly by the Renzo Piano Building Workshop, Nikken Sekkei, Aéroports de Paris, and Japan Airport Consultants. Inevitably, therefore, the structuring of such a new design partnership and any future developments in the same vain are now the topic of much discussion, especially as the number of actual examples of such partnerships is increasing.

The total project costs were 1.5 trillion yen, or approximately $15,000,000,000. So, although projects of this scale are few and far between, at least it can be said that much has been learnt from the design consortium which for the building of Kansai International Airport was an entirely new departure.

— *Editors' Section, Process Architecture*

Examples of foreign firms of PTB project

Flour daniel Japan Incorpolated (USA, building construction of the north area), Overseas Bechtel Incorpolated (USA, building construction of the south area), Robert Watson & Co., Ltd. (England, roof steel of wing), Eiffel Construction Matellique (France, endwall), Nullifire Limited (England, fire cladding of the north area), Focchi Giuseppe s.p.a. (Italy, glass fence of the sough area), YKK Architectural Products (USA, airside glazing), Repla Italia s.r.l. (Italy, artificial marble, Square D. (Electric Services Cordination, high voltage), and so on.

Kansai International Airport Passenger Terminal Building

Client
Kansai International Airport Co., Ltd.

Competition-Winning Design
Renzo Piano Building Workshop Paris
(Architects: Renzo Piano + Noriaki Okabe)
with a collaboration of :
Ove Arup & Partners International Ltd.
(Engineers: Peter Rice + Tom Barker)
<The International Design Competition was held on the basis of the basic scheme proposed by ADP>

Basic Design & Detail Design Consortium for Knasai International Airport Passenger Terminal Building
● Design Leader / Representative:
Renzo Piano Building Workshop Japan K.K.
● Design — architecture, structure, buiding services:
Renzo Piano Building Workshop Japan K.K.
(Renzo Piano + Noriaki Okabe)
with a collaboration of:
Ove Arup & Partners International Ltd. (Peter Rice)
Nikken Sekkei Ltd. (Kimiaki Minai)
● Basic Concept, Functional Aspect and Design of the Moving Elements
Aéroports de Paris (Paul Andreu)
● Negotiation w/ CIQ + CAB, Design of the CIQ Facilities and Airside Planning
Japan Airport Consultants, Inc. (Misao Matsumoto)
<CIQ= Custum / Immigration / Quarantine, CAB=Civil Aviation Bureau, Airside Planning=Cordination on PBB (Passenger boarding bridges), etc.>

Site Supervision
Kansai International Airport Co., Ltd.

Site Supervision Services for Construction (Supervision Work)
Nikken Sekkei Ltd.

The Consortium for Supervision Services for Construction (Design Work) of Kansai International Airport Passenger Terminal Building
Renzo Piano Building Workshop Japan K.K.
Nikken Sekkei Ltd.
Aéroports de Paris
Japan Airport Consultants, Inc.

Building Constructors:
North Passenger Terminal Building Joint Venture
Obayashi Corporation, Shimizu Corporation, Flour Daniel Japan Incorpolated, Toda Corporation, Okumura Corporation, Konoike Construction Co., Ltd., Nishimatsu Construction Co., Ltd., Hazama Corporation, Sato Kogyo Co., Ltd., Fudo Construction Co., Ltd.
South Passenger Terminal Building Joint Venture
Takenaka Corporation, Kajima Corporation, Taisei Corporation, Overseas Bechtel Incorpolated, Fujita Corporation, The Zenitaka Corporation, Asanuma-Gumi Co., Ltd., Matsumura-Gumi Corporation, Tokyu Construction Co., Ltd., Tobishima Corporation.

Electric Services Cordinators:
● Super High-voltage; Hitachi Plant Engineering & Construction Co., Ltd., ● High-voltage 1; Kinden Corporation, Square D Company, Churitsu Electric Corporation, ● High-voltage 2, 3; Daihen Corporation, ● Emergency Eletric Generator; Niigata Engineering Co., Ltd.

Electric Services:
● Part 1; Kinden Corporation, Toko Electrical Construction Co., Ltd., Kandenko Corporation, ● Part 2; Sumitomo Densetsu Co., Asami Electric Co., Sanpo Electrical & Mechanical

Machinery Services:
● Part 1 & 5; Shinryo Corporation, Saikyu Kogyo Corporation, Kawasaki Setsubi Industries Co., Ltd., ● Part 2; Takasago Thermal Engineering, Shin Nippon Air Technologies Co., Ltd., Sanken Environmental Engineering, Daiichi Kogyo, Hibiya Engineering Ltd., ● Part 3; Dai-Dan Co., Ltd., Suga Co., Ltd., Sanko Air Conditioning Co., Ltd., To-yoko Riken Co., Ltd., Namirei Co., Ltd., ● Part 4 & 6; Sanki Engineering Co., Ltd., Asahi Kogyo-sha Co., Ltd., Toyo Netsu Kogyo Co., Ltd.

Communication Engineering Service:
Kurihara Kogyo Co., Ltd., Yachiyo Densetsu Electrical Construction, Kinki Kogyo Co., Ltd.

Elevatior Service:
● Part 1; Marubeni Machinery & Engineering Corporation, Schindler Elevator Co., Ltd., Schindler Management Ltd., ● Part 2; Toshiba, ● Part 3 & 8; Mitsubishi Electric Corporation, ● Part 4; Fujitec Co., Ltd., ● Part 5 & 7; Hitachi Plant Engineering & Construction Co., Ltd. , ● Part 6; Nippon Otis Elevator Company

Outline of Building data

Building Name
Kansai International Airport Passenger Terminal Building

Location
About 5km offshore of the Senshu region in the southeast of Osaka Bay. Izumisano city, Osaka, Japan

Area
Island: 511 ha
Site: 453,193.96 sqm
Building: 113,878.94 sqm
Floor: 291,269.58 sqm

Number of stories
Main Terminal Building:
4 floors above ground, and 1 below.
Wing: 3 floors above ground

Structure
Steel Rigid Frame. Partly, Steel Reinforced Concrete.
(Floating foundation and jack-up system have been introduced to offset any subsidence in soft soil)

Roof Structure
Main Terminal Building: Steel Truss
Wing: Steel Lattice Shell

Runway
One. 3,500 meters long by 60 meters wide.

Capacity
Approx. 160,000 flights a year

Island Connecting Bridge
Two levels, road above and railway line below;
3.75 km long.

関西国際空港旅客ターミナルビルプロジェクト・クレジット

施主:
関西国際空港株式会社

国際設計競技優勝案:
レンゾ・ピアノ・ビルディング・ワークショップ・パリ
(建築設計:レンゾ・ピアノ、岡部憲明)
協力事務所:オーヴ・アラップ&パートナーズ・インターナショナル・リミテッド
(構造+設備:ピーター・ライス、トム・バーカー)
<国際設計競技は、パリ空港公団の作成した基本構想をプログラム・ベースとしている。>

関西国際空港旅客ターミナルビル
基本設計・実施設計作成共同体:

● デザイン・リーダーおよび代表者業務:
レンゾ・ピアノ・ビルディング・ワークショップ・ジャパン

● 設計(建築+構造+設備):
レンゾ・ピアノ・ビルディング・ワークショップ・ジャパン
(レンゾ・ピアノ+岡部憲明)
協力事務所:オーヴ・アラップ&パートナーズ・インターナショナル・リミテッド(ピーター・ライス)
株式会社日建設計(蓑袋公明)

● 基本コンセプト、機能計画および動的エレメントの設計:
パリ空港公団(ポール・アンドリュー)

● CIQ, CABとの調整およびCIQ施設設計、エアサイド計画:
株式会社日本空港コンサルタンツ(松本 操)
<CIQ=税関・出入国管理・検疫、CAB=運輸省航空局、エアサイド計画=旅客搭乗橋の調整など>

施工監理:
関西国際空港株式会社

施工監理業務(委託):
株式会社日建設計

関西国際空港旅客ターミナルビル施工監理業務(設計)共同体:
レンゾ・ピアノ・ビルディング・ワークショップ・ジャパン
株式会社日建設計
パリ空港公団
株式会社日本空港コンサルタンツ

建築工事共同企業体:
関西国際空港旅客ターミナルビル北工区建築共同企業体
(株)大林組、清水建設(株)、フルーア・ダニエル・ジャパン(株)、戸田建設(株)、奥村組、西松建設(株)、(株)間組、佐藤工業(株)、不動建設(株)
関西国際空港旅客ターミナルビル南工区建築共同企業体
(株)竹中工務店、鹿島建設(株)、大成建設(株)、オーバーシーズ・ベクテル・インコーポレーテッド、(株)フジタ、(株)錢高組、(株)浅沼組、(株)松村組、(株)東急建設、飛島建設(株)

電気調達:
● 特別高圧/(株)日立製作所、● 高圧その1/(株)きんでん、スクエアディ・カンパニー、中立電機(株)、● 高圧その2,3/(株)ダイヘン、● 非常発電機/(株)新潟鉄工所

電気設備:
● その1/(株)きんでん、東光電気工事(株)、(株)関電工
● その2/(株)住友電設、浅海電気(株)、三宝電機(株)

機械設備:
● その1、5/新菱冷熱工業(株)、斎久工業(株)、川崎設備工業(株)、● その2/高砂熱学工業(株)、新日本空調(株)、三建設備工業(株)、第一工業(株)、日比谷総合設備(株)、● その3/ダイダン(株)、須賀工業(株)、(株)三晃空調、(株)トーヨコ理研、ナミレイ(株)、● その4、6/三機工業(株)、(株)朝日工業社、東洋熱工業(株)

通信設備:
栗原工業(株)、八千代電設工業(株)、近畿工業(株)

昇降機設備:
● その1/(株)丸紅、Schindler Management Ltd.、シンドラーエレベータ(株)、● その2/(株)東芝、● その3、8/三菱電機(株)、● その4/フジテック(株)、● その5、7/(株)日立製作所、● その6/日本オーチス・エレベータ(株)

建物概要

建物名称
関西国際空港旅客ターミナルビル

建築場所
大阪湾南東部の泉州沖約5kmの海上。大阪府泉佐野市泉州空港北、泉南郡田尻町泉州空港中

地域・地区
市街化調整区域

面積
空港島全体　　511 ha
敷地面積　　453,193.96 m²
建築面積　　113,878.94 m²
延べ床面積　291,269.58 m²

階数
メインターミナルビル:地上4階、地下1階
ウイング:地上3階

構造
鉄骨ラーメン構造
一部鉄骨鉄筋コンクリート造
(軟弱地盤対策として、浮き基礎およびジャッキアップシステムを導入)

屋根構造
メインターミナルビル:鉄骨トラス構造
ウイング:鉄骨ラチスシェル構造

滑走路
1本、3,500m、幅60m

離着陸可能回数
年間約16万回

空港島連絡橋
道路・鉄道併用橋、長さ3.75km

PTB Designers' Credits
設計共同体クレジット

Renzo Piano Building Workshop

Competition Team

Name of the office:
Renzo Piano Buidling Workshop
Paris

Partners in charge:
Renzo Piano - Architect; Noriaki Okabe - Associate Architect, Project Leader

Architecural team (in alphabetical order):
Jean-Francois Blassel, Ross Brennan, Antoine Chaaya, Loïc Couton, Robert Keiser, Laurent Koenig, Ken McBryde, Noriaki Okabe, Renzo Piano, Sandra Planchez, Renaud Rolland, Graciela Torre, Olivier Touraine

With the collaboration of (in alphabetical order):
Catherine Ardilley, Gaëlle Breton, Pierre Henneguier, Marie Henry, Frank Hughes, Tobias Jaklin, Jean Lelay, Anna O'Carrol, Maria Salerno, Patrick Senne, Anne Hélène Temenides, Nicolas Westphal

Consultant:
Structure and Services: Ove Arup & Partners International Ltd. (see seperate staff credit for OAP)
Landscape: Michel Desvigne

Project Team (Basic Design + Detail Design Phases)

Name of the office:
Renzo Piano Building Workshop
Japan

Partners in charge:
Renzo Piano - Architect; Noriaki Okabe - Associate Architect, Project Leader

Architectural team (in alphabetical order) :
Jean-Francois Blassel, Ariel Chavela, Ivan Corte, Kenneth Fraser, Robert S. Garlipp, Marion Goerdt, Greg Hall, Kohji Hirano, Akira Ikegami, Shunji Ishida, Amanda Johnson, Christopher Kelly, Tetsuya Kimura, Stig Larsen, Jean Lelay, Ken McBryde, Takeshi Miyazaki, Shin'ichi Nakaya, Noriaki Okabe, Renzo Piano, Norio Takata, Taichi Tomuro, Olivier Touraine, Mark Turpin, Masami Yamada, Hiroshi Yamaguchi, Tatsuya Yamaguchi

With the collaboration of (in alphabetical order):
Alexandre Autin, Geoffrey Cohen, Anahita Golzari, Barnaby Gunning, Gunther Hastrich, Masahiro Horie, Ikuko Kubo, Simone Medio, Keisuke Miyake, Sandro Montaldo, Shin'ichiro Mukai, Kamran Afshar Naderi, Koung Nyunt(landscape), Stefan Oehler, Tim O'Sullivan, Patrizia Persia, Milly Rossato, Randy Shields, Takehiro Takagawa, Takuo Ueno, Kiyomi Uezono, Jean-Marc Weill, Tetsuo Yamakoshi

Consultants:
Structure and Services: Ove Arup & Partners International Ltd. (see seperate staff credit for OAP)
Accoustic Consultant: PEUTZ et Associés - Yves Dekeyrel
Endwall Glazing Study: Robert-Jan van Santen
Quantity Survey: Davis Langdon & Everest, Futaba Quantity Surveying Co., Ltd.

Publicist:
Noriko Takiguchi, Emi Yoshimura

Secretary:
Tomoko Komatsubara, Hiroko Nishikawa, Madoka Shimizu

Project Team (Site Supervision Phase)

Name of the office:
Renzo Piano Building Workshop
Japan

Partners in charge:
Renzo Piano - Architect; Noriaki Okabe - Associate Architect, Project Leader

Architectural team (in alphabetical order):
Akira Ikegami, Tetsuya Kimura, Noriaki Okabe, Renzo Piano, Taichi Tomuro, Yoshiko Ueno

With the collaboration of (in alphabetical order):
Shin Kano, Aki Shimizu

Consultants:
Endwall Glazing Development: RFR - Jean-Francois Blassel
Canyon Plantation: Toshi Keikan Sekkei Inc. - Shin'ichi Okumura

Publicist:
Noriko Takiguchi

Secretary:
Hiroko Nishikawa

Ove Arup & Partners

Competition Team

Project Leaders:
Peter Rice, Tom Barker

Engineering Team:
Alistair Hughes, Andrew Sedgwick, Mahadev Raman, Raymond Yau

Project Team (Basic Design + Detail Design Phases)

Project Leaders:
Peter Rice, Tony Stevens, Philip Dilley, Alistair Guthrie, Paula Beever

Engineering Team (in alphabetical order):
Rod Buchanan, Mark Chown, Martin Cooper, Rob Davis, Nick Dibben, Giovanni Festa, Andrew Gardiner, Jeppe Hundevad, Margaret Law, Rory McGowan, Alain Michaelis, Paul Murphy, Roberto Muzzetto, Catherine O'Brien, Heraclis Passades, Tony Philiastides, Andrew Sedgwick, William Stevenson, Chris Taylor, Tom Tomaszczyk, Mike Wilford, Raymond Yau

Cost Consultants:
ES Associates (Eiji Sato)
Futaba Quantity Surveying
Setsubi Giken

Project Team (Site Supervision Phase)
John Batchelor

Nikken Sekkei Ltd.

Project Team (Basic + Detail Design Phases)

Principal in Charge:
Kimiaki Minai

Architectural Team:
Takayuki Inokura, Hiroshi Sasaki, Nobuhiro Tomatsu, Toshiaki Nakatsu, Takehide Watanabe, Yasuji Sugimoto, Kazuhiro Muramoto, Hiroshi Miyakawa, Susumu Hada, Hiromi Morimoto, Takashi Daito, Shinji Shitamukai, Kazuo Nakamoto, Kenji Kurita, Kouya Sugawara, Masato Goto, Ryohei Iwasaki, Minoru Asahi, Akira Oyama

Structural Team:
NaokiUchida, Minoru Fukui, Akira Hanajima, Keizo Fukai, Hidemitsu Tanahashi, Kenzo Taga, Yuji Kobayashi, Hitoshi Ozaki, Minoru Kondo

Mechanical Team:
Ken Fujimoto, Hirokazu Ikezawa, Kazuhiro Otaka, Takashi Sugiyama, Ken'ichi Kajino, Hiroshi Ninomiya

Electrical Team:
Yoshihiro Murakami, Toshiaki Miyoshi, Koji Kawanishi, Satofumi Miyano, Tadashi Yoshimura

Planning Team:
Naoki Hayashi, Yoshihiko Masuda, Kazunori Wachi

Fire-engineering Team:
Nobuyoshi Hamada, Yoshio Makita, Mamiko Kujime

Quantity Surveyor:
Shogo Yamaguchi, Kazuo Furusawa, Shinya Toyota, Tadahiko Kobayashi, Kenji Arikawa

Civil-engineering Team:
Susumu Sunami, Tsukasa Yoshifuku

Supervision Team:
Tomonori Hirano, Shogo Kaiwa

CAD Team:
Shigehito Sugiyama, Hideshi Okada

Project Team (Site Supervision Phase)

Principal in Charge:
Kimiaki Minai

Architectural Team:
Hiroshi Sasaki, Toshiaki Nakatsu, Yasuji Sugimoto, Kazuhiro Muramoto, Won-ki Yoon, Takayoshi Sei, Shinji Nishiike, Susumu Hada, Ichiro Ogata, Takashi Daito, Kazuo Nakamoto, Ryohei Iwasaki, Mitsuhiro Iwahori

Structural Team:
Kenzo Taga, Yuji Kobayashi, Minoru Kondo

Mechanical Team:
Keijiro Inoue, Takashi Sugiyama, Hiroshi Ninomiya, Kunihiko Takebe, Yoshio Nakamura

Electrical Team:
Toshiaki Miyoshi, Koji Kawanishi, Tatsuo Imai, Kazuo Takaai, Takeji Shinagawa

Planning Team:
Kazunori Wachi

Aéroports de Paris

Project Team (Basic Design + Detail Design Phases)

Project Leaders:
Paul Andreu, Jean-Marie Chevallier

Architectural Team (in alphabetical order):
Paul Andreu - Architect, Geoffroy Belmont, Nicolas Descamps, Jean-Michel Fourcade - Associate Architect, Maurice Kruk, Graciela Torre, Yannis Valugeorgis, Marie-Laure Vincent-Genod, Ryohei Yamada (Osaka)

Engineering Team (in alphabetical order):
Claude Bonnet, Jean-Marie Chevallier, Xavier Dubrac, Pierre Kopff (Osaka), André Lamoureux, Alain Lévvy, Pierre Rochereuil

Project Team (Site Supervision Phase)

Project Leaders:
Paul Andreu, Jean-Marie Chevallier

Architectural Team (in alphabetical order):
Paul Andreu - Architect, Jean-Michel Fourcade - Associate Architect

Engineering Team (in alphabetical order):
Claude Bonnet, Jean-Marie Chevallier, Xavier Dubrac, Pierre Kopff (Osaka), Alain Lévvy, Pierre Rochereuil

Japan Airport Consultants Inc.

Project Team (Basic Design + Detail Design Phases)

Project Leaders:
Takeshi Kido, Yoshiaki Niina

Architectural Team (in alphabetical order):
Tadao Kanazashi, Kunio Kato, Yoshiaki Niina, Genri Nozaki, Shigeo Sasaki, Eiji Sera, Yoshihiro Takeuchi

Engineering Team (in alphabetical order):
Kunihiro Kanaya, Akio Yamamoto

Documentation (in alphabetical order):
Mikako Inui, Kumiko Kishimoto

Project Team (Site Supervision Phase)

Project Leaders:
Takeshi Kido, Yoshiaki Niina

Architectural Team (in alphabetical order):
Kunio Kato, Yoshiaki Niina, Genri Nozaki, Masahiro Onoue, Eiji Sera, Yoshihiro Takeuchi

Engineering Team (in alphabetical order):
Kunihiro Kanaya, Akio Yamamoto

Documentation (in alphabetical order):
Saori Chiba, Izumi Iwai

Afterword
by Noriaki Okabe

あとがき　岡部憲明

The construction of a vast artificial island and the building of an immense 1.7 km long structure on it, is now all complete and this project of such dynamic proportions has now come to an end, a degree of concentration of effort and determination on a scale never seen before having been committed by so many people in the building of Kansai International Airport.

One of the aims of compiling of this special issue featuring this momentous project was to produce a publication which would serve to help users of the airport and the general public at large to gain a better understanding of the entire project. Furthermore, it also presented the chance to share once again with all those involved, the process by which both the island and the buildings on it came into being, while also relating something of what went on behind the scenes.

I was, of course, very happy to have been involved in the project. However, being able to share that sense of great happiness at having complete something with a large number of people rather than just sharing those feelings of deep emotion with those involved, is very important, especially in the case of a public building.

The amount of time and energy it was possible to devote to the job of editing this publication was limited, because I was having to do it while work on the construction of the airport was still in progress. Nevertheless, I was greatly assisted not only by the client—Kansai International Airport Company, but also by those from the consortium of companies involved in the design including those at Nikken Sekkei, various persons employed by the consortium of construction companies concerned with the north and south block, as well as others from numerous manufactures, all of whom have willingly provided much data and some valuable articles. To them all I extend my most grateful thanks.

Last but by no means least, I must also express my heartfelt thanks, firstly to Murotani Bunji, the publisher of Process Architecture, for providing the opportunity of producing what I hope will be seen as a most valuable record of the project, and secondly to Yumiko Fujimaki who, with great patience, worked tirelessly on the many jobs I myself could not cover.

—*Noriaki Okabe, September, 1994*

巨大な人工島の建設に並行して1.7kmの長大な建設プロジェクトが進められ，今，このダイナミックで壮大な計画が実現された．多くの人々の意志と努力が，かつてないほどの集中度で，関西国際空港計画に投入されてきた．本特集は現実となった建築とその空間の生成のプロセスを，その背後にある建設のドラマの記録を含めて，プロジェクトにたずさわった方々と再びわかちあい，同時にこの空港の使用者となる一般の人たちに理解していただくことを目的としてまとめられた．

こうしたプロジェクトに参加できたことを，本当に幸せだったと思う．実現できたことのこの大きな幸せを，関係者の間だけの感慨にせずに，多くの人々とわかち合えることは，公共建築であるがゆえにより大切なことだと思える．

編集作業は建設が進行中に行なわれたために，それに費やすことのできる時間もエネルギーもきわめて限られていた．施主である関西国際空港株式会社，設計JV，とりわけ日建設計，建設JV（北工区，南工区），多数の製作メーカーの方々には，資料や論文の面で援助していただいた．この場を借りてお礼を申し上げたい．

最後にこうした貴重な記録を作成する機会を与えてくださり，はかどらない編集作業にもかかわらず，忍耐強く全体をカヴァーしてくださったプロセスアーキテクチュア発行人の室谷文治氏，編集にたずさわった藤巻由美子さんに，心から感謝を申しあげる．

Renzo Piano

- 1937: Born in Genova, Italy
- 1962-64: Worked under the design guidance of Granco Albini.
- 1964: Graduated from the school of Architecture, Milan Polytechnic, and subsequently worked with his father.
- 1965-70: Worked with Louis I. Kahn, in Philadelphia, and Z.S. Makowsky in London.
- 1971: Won the first prize in the international design competition for Georges Pompidou Cultural Centre in Paris, (codesigned with Richard Rogers)
- 1971-77: Engaged in the projects of Georges Pompidou Cultural Centre and IRCAM; Institute for Acoustic/Musical Coordination and Research., Collaboration with Richard Rogers (Piano & Rogers)
- 1977-82: Collaboration with Peter Rice in projects as FIAT's VSS experimental prototype car for the 90s.
- 1982-88: Established "Building Workshop"s in Paris and Genova. Menil Collection Museum (Houston), IBM Travelling Pavilion (major cities in Europe), Renovation of the Schlumberger Facility (Paris) are as his main projects.
- 1988: Won the first prize in the international design competition for Kansai International Airport Passenger Terminal Building (codesigned with Noriaki Okabe, associate architect)
- 1989: His "Building Workshop"s are established in Paris, Genova, and Osaka, and has become bases on his worldwide design activities.
- 1992: Won the first prize in the international design competition for the urban renual project of Potsdamer Plats in Berlin.

He has been visiting professor at the Columbia University, New York; University of Pennsylvania, Philadelphia: the Oslo School of Architecture etc., and has lectured in major cities in Europe, USA and Japan.

He was awarded prizes such as the Commandeur des Arts et des Lettres ('84) and the Legion d'Honneur ('85) in France; the Union Internationale des Architects ('78) in Mexico City; the Compasso d'Oro ('81) and the Cavaliere di Gran Croce ('89) in Italy; the RIBA Gold Medal ('89) in UK; the Kyoto Prize ('90) in Japan; the Neutra Prize in Pomona, California ('91); the honorary doctorship at Delft University ('92); the American Academy of Arts and letters, the Arnold W., Brunner Memorial Prize ('94). He is also an Honorary Fellowship of the AIA in USA, of the RIBA in UK and of the University of Stuttgard in Germany.

レンゾ・ピアノ

- 1937: ジェノヴァ(イタリア)生まれ．
- 1962-64: フランコ・アルビーニの下でデザインの手ほどきを受ける．
- 1964: ミラノ工科大学建築学部卒業，同時に父の下で修業．
- 1965-70: ルイス・カーン(フィラデルフィア)、Z.S.マコウスキー(ロンドン)の下で設計活動．
- 1971: ポンピドーセンター国際競技設計に優勝．(リチャード・ロジャースと共同設計)
- 1971-77: ポンピドーセンター、およびIRCAM音響研究所の設計・建設を指揮．(リチャード・ロジャースと協働(ピアノ＋ロジャース))
- 1977-82: ピーター・ライスと協働．主要プロジェクトとして、FIATサブシステムカー等．
- 1982-88: パリ、ジェノヴァにビルディング・ワークショップを設立して活動．主要プロジェクトとして、メニルコレクション美術館(ヒューストン)、IBM巡回パビリオン(ヨーロッパ各都市)、シュルンベルジェ社本社ビル(パリ)等．
- 1988: 関西国際空港旅客ターミナルビル国際設計競技で優勝．(アソシエイト・アーキテクト岡部憲明との共同設計)
- 1989-: ビルディング・ワークショップをパリ、ジェノヴァ、大阪に設置．3拠点を中心として世界的な活動を行なう．1992年には、ベルリン・ポツダム広場再開発競技設計に優勝．

また、コロンビア大学(ニューヨーク)、ペンシルヴァニア大学(フィラデルフィア)、オスロ建築学校などで客員教授を務めた経験を持つ．ヨーロッパ、アメリカ、日本等の主要都市で講演も行なっている．

レジョン・ド・ヌール勲章(1985、仏)、メキシコ・シティー国際建築家連盟賞(1978)、「金のコンパス」賞(1981、伊)、カヴァリエレ・ディ・グラン・クロシェ勲章(1989、伊)、RIBAゴールド・メダル(1989、英)、京都賞(1990、日)を受賞．
また、AIA(米)、RIBA(英)の名誉会員、シュツットガルト大学(独)の名誉教授でもある．

Noriaki Okabe

- 1947: Born in Shizuoka, Japan
- 1971: Graduated from Waseda University, Tokyo
- 1973: Studied in France as Franch Government's Scholarship student
- 1974-77: Joined Piano & Rogers
  Participated in projects as Centre George Pompidou and IRCAM
- 1977-81: Participated in the establishment of Piano & Rice Associati together with Renzo Piano, Peter Rice (engineer) and Shunji Ishida
  Took charge in projects as FIAT's VSS, experimental prototype car for the 90s with a new concept in styling and manufacturing
- 1984-88: Worked as Chief Architect for Renzo Piano's office in Paris.
  Headed as Chief Architect the Renovation project of the Schlumberger Facility.
  In 1988, continued the collaboration with Renzo Piano as Associate Architect and Chief Architect for Renzo Piano Building Workshop Paris.
  Took charge in projects as Bercy II Shopping Centre and IRCAM extention.
  Headed the competition-winning Kansai International Airport Passenger Terminal Building as Project Leader (co-holder of the copyright of the project with Renzo Piano).
- 1989: Participated as Associate Architect in the establishment of the Renzo Piano Building Workshop Japan, for which he is now the Representative.
  Started the basic and detail design of Kansai International Airport Passenger Terminal Building.
- Present: Project Leader for the Kansai International Airport PTB in its site-supervision and shop-drawing orientation phaze, as well as for Ushibuka Port Connecting Bridge, Kumamoto.

岡部憲明

- 1947: 静岡生まれ．
- 1971: 早稲田大学理工学部建築学科卒業．
- 1973: フランス政府給費留学生として渡欧．
- 1974-77: ピアノ＋ロジャーズの一員としてポンピドー・センターおよびIRCAM音響研究所の設計、さらに建設に携わる．
- 1977-81: レンゾ・ピアノ、ピーター・ライス(構造家)、石田俊二と組んで、ピアノ&ライス&アソシアーティを設立．イタリア・ジェノヴァで設計活動に従事．新たなコンセプトによる自動車、FIATサブシステムカープロジェクト等を担当．
- 1981-88: パリのレンゾ・ピアノ・オフィスでチーフ・アーキテクトとして活動．パリ郊外にあるシュルンベルジェ・モンルージュ社の本社ビル設計・建設の主任建築家を務める．
  1988年からは、レンゾ・ピアノ・ビルディング・ワークショップ・パリのチーフ・アーキテクト、ピアノのアソシエート・アーキテクトを務め、ベルシーIIショッピングセンター、IRCAM音響研究所増築計画等を主任建築家として担当する．さらに、関西国際空港競技設計画等をプロジェクトリーダーとして担当し、優勝．(ピアノと共に同作品の著作権共同所有者)

1989年、大阪にレンゾ・ピアノ・ビルディング・ワークショップ・ジャパンを設立、レンゾ・ピアノのアソシエート・アーキテクトとして代表取締役に就任、現在にいたる．関西国際空港プロジェクト、および牛深漁港連絡橋を、レンゾ・ピアノ・ビルディング・ワークショップのプロジェクト・リーダーとして遂行．

フランス建築家協会会員、フランス政府公認建築家

BWJ STAFF
(Site Supervision Phase)

Akira Ikegami
Tetsuya Kimura
Taichi Tomuro
Yoshiko Ueno
Koji Hirano
Tatsuya Yamaguchi

BWJスタッフ
(現場監理段階)

池上　明
上野美子
木村哲矢
戸室太一
平野耕治
山口達也

Authors' Profiles
執筆者経歴

Hiroyuki Suzuki
Born in Tokyo in 1945, he graduated from the Architectural Course in the Department of Engineering at Tokyo University in 1968. After being a part-time lecturer at both the Science University of Tokyo and at Hosei University from 1971, he then completed a doctorate at Tokyo University. Between 1974-75 he was a research fellow the Courtauld Institute of Art at London University. Having been a part-time lecturer at Tokyo University of Art and Design, a full-time lecturer in the Department of Engineering at Tokyo University, and an assistant professor there, he is now a Professor of Architecture at Tokyo University. A prolific writer and translator, he is also a very active member of a number of societies and groups concerned with architectural history and research.

鈴木博之
1945年東京生まれ．1968年東京大学工学部建築学科卒業．1971年から東京理科大学，法政大学の非常勤講師を経て，1974年東京大学工学系大学院博士課程修了．1974〜1975年，英国政府給費留学生としてロンドン大学コートゥールド美術史研究所に留学．東京造形大学非常勤講師，東京大学工学部専任講師，助教授を経て，現在同大学同学部建築学科教授．著書，共著書，監修書，訳書など多数．日本建築学会正会員，イコモス国内委員会委員，建築史学会常任委員，明治美術研究学会常任委員．

主な著書
「建築の世紀末」(1977年，昌文社)，「建築は兵士ではない」(1980年，日本文化デザイン賞受賞)「建築の七つの力」(1984年，芸術選奨文部大臣新人賞，以上鹿島出版会)，「都市の文化」(共著，1984年，丸善)，「夢のすむ家」(1989年，平凡社)，「東京の地霊(ゲニウス・ロキ)」(1990年，サントリー学芸賞受賞)，「建築家たちのヴィクトリア朝」(1991年，平凡社)，「明治の洋館100選」(1992年，講談社カルチャーブックス)

John Thackara
John Thackara, 43, is the first Director of the Netherlands design Institute in Amsterdam, a "think-and-do" tank which was established in May 1993. Mr Thackara has worked in book publishing in London and New York, and was editor of Design Magazine. He has lectured in 23 countries, and has produced exhibitions at the Centre Pompidou, the National Museum of Modern Art in Kyoto and other venues. T-Zone, co-produced with Riichi Miyake, was voted best design event of the year in the UK in 1992. He is the former managing director of Design Analysis International, and was director of Research of the Royal College of Art.

John Thackara's books are: New British Design (Thames and Hudson 1987) and Design After Modernism (Thames and Hudson 1988; Kajima 1992).

ジョン・サッカラ
1951生まれ．「シンク＆ドゥ」タンクとして1993年5月にアムステルダムに設立された，オランダデザインセンターの初代館長．以前はロンドンとニューヨークで出版に従事し，「デザインマガジン」の編集長をつとめた．他にも23か国での講演をこなし，ポンピドーセンターや京都の国立近代美術館などでの展覧会のプロデュースもした．三宅理一氏と共同プロデュースした「Tゾーン」は，イギリスで1992年度のベストデザインイベントに選ばれた．デザイン・アナライシス・インターナショナルの専務取締役，英国王立美術学校大学院教授を歴任．著書に，「モダニズム以降のデザイン」(訳書：鹿島出版会刊，1992年)などがある．

Teiji Matsumasa
Born in 1955, he studied at Kyoto Institute of Technology and completed a course in Architecture and Engineering in the post-graduate school in 1981, after which he became a research fellow at Kyoto University. He then went to study in France on a French Government Scholarship. He complete a course of study at the former Ecole d'Architecture de Paris-Conflans (UPA4), and then went on to gain an official French Government Architects Qualification (DPLG). Having complete a special course (CEAA: Architecture Urbaine) at the Ecole d'Architecture de Paris-Belleville (UPA8), he returned to Japan in 1987. After being a part-time lecturer in the Faculty of Engineering at Kansai University, he is now an assistant in the Section of Environmental Engineering in the Faculty of Technology at Osaka University. He is also a part-time lecturer at Ritsumeikan University. His speciality is urban architectural design and planning, and he has also been involved in the co-authorship and translation of a number of publications.

松政貞治
1955年生まれ．81年京都工芸繊維大学大学院修士課程建築工芸学専攻修了後，京都大学研究生を経て，フランス政府給費留学生として渡仏．旧エコール・デ・ボザール(UPA4)修了，フランス政府公認建築家資格取得．UPA8で都市建築専門課程修了後，87年帰国．関西大学工学部非常勤講師等を経て，現在大阪大学工学部環境工学科助手．立命館大学非常勤講師．仏国第3課程博士．専門は都市建築設計計画．

共著書に「都市ストックを創る」(学芸出版)，訳書に「ル・コルビュジエ建築設計資料集成」(同朋舎出版)「ル・コルビュジエの六手帖―東方への旅」(共訳，同朋舎出版)などがある．

Thomas Fisher
Thomas Fisher has been the Editorial Director of Progressive Architecture since 1987. Prior to joining the magazine in 1982, he worked in architectural offices in Hartford, Connecticut, and Cleveland, Ohio, and served as the Historical Architect for the state of Connecticut. He has an undergraduate degree in architecture from Cornell University and a graduate degree in interdisciplinary studies from Case Western Reserve University. He is a frequent juror and lecturer at architectural schools around the United States.

トーマス・フィッシャー
1987年以来，プログレッシブ・アーキテクチュア誌の編集ディレクター．1982年に同誌に参加する以前は，コネチカット州やオハイオ州の設計事務所で設計活動に従事し，また，コネチカット州の歴史建築家として活躍．コーネル大学建築学科卒業，ケース・ウエスタン・リザーブ大学学際研究の大学院修了．全米の多くの建築学校で教鞭をとる．

Shin'ichi Okumura
Born in Nara in 1948, he studied on the Forestry Course in the Department of Agriculture at Shinshu University, graduating in 1972. Having worked for the Environmental Planning Institute, he then established Toshi Keikan Sekkei Inc. in 1984. He has always been attracted to streetscapes landscaping which is in some way concerned with nature, people and culture and this is the driving force behind his work. For Kansai International Airport, he worked in collaboration with the Renzo Piano Building Workshop on the planning of the planting scheme for the Canyon. Since 1992, he has been a part-time lecturer in the Department of Environmental Design at Kyoto University of Art and Design.

Some of his major work has been for the IBM Japan Makuhari Building, a job which he supervised and did in collaboration with Peter Walker; Rokko Island River Mall in Kobe (design for second phase); and the Kamo-cho Planetarium, in Kyoto (design and supervision).

奥村信一
1948年奈良県生まれ．1972年信州大学農学部林学科卒業．(株)環境事業計画研究所を経て1984年(株)都市・景観設計設立．現在に至る．自然と人，そして文化にかかわる景観に魅力を感じて現在の仕事を続ける．関西国際空港ではキャニオンの植栽計画をビルディング・ワークショップと協同．

1992年より京都造形芸術大学環境デザイン学科非常勤講師．代表作は，IBM幕張(千葉県．造園工事監理．ピーター・ウォーカーと協同)，六甲アイランドリバーモール(神戸市．2期工事設計)，加茂町プラネタリウム館(京都府．設計・監理)．

Photographer
Kazuaki Hosokawa
Born in Osaka in 1940, he took up free-lance photograph in 1975. Since then he has been recording the changes through which Osaka and the city around him is going through, while engaged in public work, and has exhibited much.

細川　和昭（写真家）

1940年大阪市生まれ．1975年からフリーとなり写真を始める．公共の仕事をしながら、変わりゆく大阪の身近な姿をフィルムに記録し続ける．作品展多数出品．写真の立体的展開も行なう．

1980年写真展「淀川」／阪神百貨店
1982年写真展「淀川パート2」／大阪駅前第四ビル公開空地で野外展
1985年写真展「川からのメッセージ」／服部緑地公園など数ヵ所で野外巡回展
1986年写真展「水は大地の旅人（トラベラー）」／大阪・淀屋橋〜北浜の地下道などで巡回展
1988年写真展「なぎさのコレクション」／コダックフォトサロン
1988年「細川和昭」展／大伸社DCギャラリー
1993年写真展「へたっぴんの美学」／大阪府立文化情報センター，佛教大学四条センター，大伸社DCギャラリー，コダックフォトサロン
1993年「夢の軌跡」展―詩と写真の近代建築―／INAXギャラリー（詩：倉橋健一氏）

■グループ展
1985年「動詞都市」展／ノースフォート
1986年「イメージ・プレゼンテーション―都市伝説」展／コダックフォトサロン
1988年都市伝説'88 アットリューム展／大阪ビジネスパーク・ツイン21ビルアトリューム

■工事塀アート
1991〜2年「みる・きく・ウォール」／もと大阪市立南中学校あと再開発の工事塀で写真と音（藤本由紀夫氏）による共同制作．また同作品で大阪市都市環境アメニティ表彰を受ける．

■著書
「へたっぴんの美学」今井祝雄氏と共著（ブレーンセンター刊）．

■写真撮影・提供
スカイフロント株式会社　p.40-41
樋渡寛治（撮影）　p.42, 43, 44, 46, 47, 48-49上（航空写真）, 188
Michael Denance（撮影）　p.56下
Building Workshop Paris　p.57下
Ove Arup & Partners　p.63, 143下（CG）, 147（CG）, 150
港　千尋（撮影）　p.87
田中昌彦（撮影）　p.104上
Building Workshop Genova　p.104下（6点）
日建設計　p.168左, 右上
田中ひろ美（撮影）　p.168右下
都市・景観設計　p.177（木の順化）
細川和昭（上記以外すべて撮影）

■図面トレース・製図
三宅啓介　p.84, 86, 95, 103, 106, 107上2点, 133, 134, 135, 153-157

■図面資料提供・協力
Ove Arup & Partners　p.138-139, 142中, 143
関西国際空港株式会社　p.47
淀川製鋼所＋ヤマキ工業＋日本ステンレス　p.69（ウイングエンド・メタルタイル側面図）, 74
三晃金属工業　p.82-83
YKKアーキテクチュラルプロダクツ　p.94下, 98
川崎重工業　p.129
松下電工　p.163
日建設計　p.164-167, 169, 171上・右
都市・景観設計　p.177（植鉢断面図）

■取材協力・資料提供
戸室太一（レンゾ・ピアノ・ビルディング・ワークショップ・ジャパン），薬袋公明，佐々木洋，和地一則，多賀謙蔵，杉本寧治，中本和夫，杉山隆，村本和博（以上，日建設計），奥村信一（都市・景観設計），関西国際空港株式会社

本誌取材・編集にあたり，左記はじめ，多くの方々にご協力いただきました．
また，p.120-178の技術的な解説部分は日建設計の方々にご協力いただきました．
キャニオンの植栽に関する資料では，都市・景観設計の奥村信一氏にご協力いただきました．
そして，長い期間に及ぶ編集作業の最後まで，監修・確認にご協力下さった戸室太一氏，和地一則氏にお礼申し上げます．

ありがとうございます．

（プロセスアーキテクチュア編集部）

竣工を迎えて

太田進一（大林組）
関西国際空港旅客ターミナルビル北工区共同企業体所長
関西国際空港建設協力会会長

旅客ターミナルビルをはじめ空港島内の諸施設建設工事に於いては，そのスケールの大きさとほとんどの施設を実質3年余りという急速施工で行われた点で，他に類を見ないものであったと思います．

またこのプロジェクトは，従来の一般工事には見られない特異点をあげることができます．

以下，旅客ターミナルビル工事を中心にこの特異点について振り返ってみました．

1．海上輸送
このプロジェクトの特徴の第一にあげられるのは，全ての人員，資機材は海上輸送によったことです．ピーク時1万人に及ぶ作業員のほとんどと，資機材輸送トラックはフェリーによって毎日対岸との間を往復致しました．工事担当者は，工事計画よりまず如何に輸送をスムーズに進めるかに頭を悩ます毎日でした．海上気象によっては，船の進行に支障をきたし，稼働率低下の事態も多く発生しました．また海上輸送は，朝夕の時間帯に集中し，限られた船隻と接岸施設のため，時差調整が常時行なわれました．

人員，資機材の他飲料水，工事用水も内陸からの直結水道がないため，工事前半は陸側取水施設から船による輸送に頼る毎日でした．

2．建物地下工法
空港島地盤は，対岸阪南丘陵と淡路島からの採取土砂で埋め立てられましたが，砕石部分が多く，極めて透水係数の大きい地盤です．建物地下部分には海面レベル以下の掘削を必要とし，そのドライワークのために地下部分を囲う大規模な止水壁を施工致しました．

北工区では，止水壁に大林組のOWS-SOLETANCHE工法による自硬性止水壁が採用されました．

また基礎構造体鉄筋には，塩害防止のためエポキシ樹脂塗布防錆鉄筋が採用されました．

3．不同沈下対策
空港島地盤の圧密沈下は，ターミナルビル着工時点で平均8cm/月間，現在では2～3cm/月間程度で進行中です．建物には杭はなく，地盤と共に沈下してゆく構造になっていますが，全長約1,700mの長大な建物のため場所による不同沈下対策が最重要課題です．

不同沈下低減対策として，ターミナルビル本館地下マットベース下全面に鉄鉱石が敷設されました(厚さ2.5m)．これは，本館地下部分掘削によって圧密荷重が減少し，ウイング部分との間にできる沈下速度の差を修正するための沈下促進荷重の役目となります．

不同沈下修正対策としては，全ての柱脚部にジャッキによるレベル修正機構が設けられています．さらに，水盛管方式によるレベル計測機器が各柱頭に設置され，計測された不同沈下量は中央の集中管理装置に送られ，各柱位置のレベル修正最適値が常時把握できるシステムが導入されています．

工事中もしばしば(屋根鉄骨建方開始前など重要な時点で)レベル修正が行なわれました．

建物柱脚部のみならず，各種設備機器のベースにもレベル修正機構が設けられ，配管，配線には通常より大きな変位に追随できる工夫がなされております．

4．海外開放
最近の海外開放圧力が強まるなか，空港施設建設には海外調達を積極的に行なう方針が打ち出されました．

ターミナルビルに於いても，従来に比べ大幅に海外調達を致しました．従来からもタイル，石材の様な仕上材については海外製品が多く入っていますが，本工事ではウイングシェル鉄骨，エアーサイドガラスカーテンウォール，本館エンドウォールの様な現地組立構造材をイギリス，アメリカ，フランスから調達しました．従来ごく少量の韓国製鉄骨が輸入された例はありますが，今回の様な大規模にまた欧米から輸入されたのは初めてのことです．

イギリスROBERT WATSON社が新日本製鐵の傘下で担当したウイングシェル鉄骨は，複雑な構造で柱脚はピン構造ですが全社をあげて努力された結果，製品精度，納期とも正確で全くトラブルはありませんでした．

エンドウォールを担当したフランスEIFFEL社は，エッフェル塔を設計した伝統あるメーカーですが，設計者レンゾ・ピアノ氏の設計概念を忠実に実現した製品を提供してくれました．

ターミナルビル北工区共同企業体には，米国フルーア・ダニエル社が参加し，米国人社員がJV事務所に勤務しました．日本人社員，協力会社との間に言語，ビジネス習慣の壁はありますが，海外調達業務を中心に現場管理業務に於いても努力してくれました．

国際化が進むなか建設工事に於いても今後海外調達が増加すると思いますが，そのためには様々な規制の緩和が前提になることを痛感致しました．

5．関西国際空港建設協力会
空港島諸施設工事着手に際して，関西国際空港会社により島内施設工事に参加する全企業のコーディネーター役を大林組に御下命があり，これに伴い関西国際空港建設協力会が設立されました．

前述の海上輸送に伴う工事参加企業間，フェリー運行会社との輸送計画調整，航行安全確保のため海上保安庁への窓口業務，地元漁業関係者との調整などの他，空港島内，対岸陸地に設置された作業員宿舎の管理，運営，日常の生活環境づくりのための物心両面の活動，建設工事に伴う一般・産業廃棄物処理について，各企業間の連絡調整など多岐にわたる業務には専任職員を配置し組織的に行なわれました．

6．まとめ
着工当初はバブルが残存している時期で，協力会社は多忙を極め，資材，作業員の確保について前途多難なスタートでしたが，工事半ば以降のバブル消滅は，このプロジェクトにとっては幸しました．バブルが存続したなら，この未曾有の悪条件下の現場に人を集めるのは不可能だったと思います．

海上輸送，沈下進行中地盤上での工事，海上調達と初めての事ばかりで暗中模索の毎日でしたが，無事完成を迎えることができました．これも偏に関西国際空港株式会社，レンゾ・ピアノ・ビルディング・ワークショップ・ジャパン，日建設計の皆様方の絶大な御指導，御鞭撻の賜物と厚く御礼申し上げます．

大西三博（竹中工務店）
PTB・S-10（旅客ターミナルビル南工区）建設共同企業体総括所長

関西国際空港．大深度，急速埋立て施工で造成された人工島へ，これまた，3年余りの短工期で空港諸施設を建築するという世界でも例を見ない一大土木，建設プロジェクト．その中核施設となる旅客ターミナルビルの建設工事を平成6年6月に無事竣工させることができた．

この度の工事においては，不同沈下対策をはじめ，技術上の様々な課題の克服と共に，着工当初の段階においては，島内には水，電気，道路といったインフラ設備が完成されてなく，またバブルの影響下での人手不足，さらに海上輸送という大きな制約条件を背負って如何に工事の工程を確保していくかに社内外の英知を集め，工事の合理化，省力化に務めこの国際的プロジェクトに対応した．

以下に主な工法，提案の実施について振り返ってみた．

1．止水壁工法
空港島の埋立て土は，30cmアンダーの岩砕が主体で，しかも層厚は33cm．透水性が高く，水位は潮位と連動している．地下躯体工事のドライワークを行なうために，南北工区合わせて1.7kmにも及ぶ止水壁が必要だった．遮水の不具合は他工区にも被害を及ぼすということで完璧な止水壁が要求され，工法を絞り込み，臆病とも思える程慎重に検討を重ね，当工区では，先行真砂土置換ソイル柱列工法を開発実施した．結果は良好で，開発した工法は，島内エアロプラザ新築工事へも水平展開された．

2．不同沈下対策
埋立て履歴差，荷重差，土質定数のばらつき等が主要因となる不同沈下に対し，土工事段階の対策である南ウイングのプレロード，本館基礎下の鉄鉱石置換そして鉄骨建方以降のジャッキアップによる不同沈下対策が盛り込まれていた．

不同沈下対策は，工事工程の観点からはマイナス要素．特にウイングのプレロードによる着工の手待ちは，工程の面からも，作業員の全体山積みからも問題であった．これに対し，設計時点の埋立て工程，計画工程と実施工程のずれに着目し，沈下解析を竹中工務店技術研究所で実施し，プレロード期間を2か月短縮できることを提案し，実施した．

計測結果もほぼ計画値どおりで推移し，後工程の確保を図ることができた．

ジャッキアップによる不同沈下対策は，六甲アイランド等でも既に当社で実施してきたが，施工中から修正が必要となる条件下での施工は初めてであった．竣工までに，ほぼ予測どおりの2～3回の修正を各建屋で実施し，そこでの経験は，メンテナンスマニュアルに活かされ，今後とも続く不同沈下から建屋を健全に維持させていくことと思う．

3．屋根鉄骨建方方法
流麗な外観を形造る屋根鉄骨．それ自体が重要なデザイン要素であるとともに，屋根仕上げの精度の基準ともなる．曲線を組み合わせた複雑な形状であるが，その繰り返しによって全体を形成するという工業化の思想が込められている．

おりからの人手不足の懸念と，品質，精度，安全性の確保のために，現場工数の低減と高所作業，危険作業の低減をめざした合理化工法を開発実施した．建方ブロックの大型化，現地塗装ヤードでの行先仕上げ塗装，移動式足場を多用した移動工法，独特のジオメトリーで設計されたウイングシェル鉄骨の構造特性を十分に考慮したワイヤーサポート工法等アイデアを随所に取り入れた省力化工法が工程短縮にも大いに寄与し，仕上げ工程の確保へと弾みを付けていった．

合理化により山積ピークは当初計画の25％減となり，総労務も18％減で工事を終えることができた．

4．海外調達
建設の海外開放ビッグプロジェクトとして国際入札が実施されたターミナルビル．ターミナルビル建設にあたってもメリットのある部材については積極的に海外調達を行なった．原材料では不同沈下対策に用いられた鉄鉱石．これは，南ア，チリ，オーストラリアから．ウイングシェル鉄骨はイギリス．本館エンドウォールグレージングはフランス．エアサイドカーテンウォールはアメリカ．ガラスフェンス，人造大理石はイタリア，ゴムタイルはドイツ．契約上あるいは，施工上での問題が全く無かったとは言えないが，世界の技術を結集させてより良い品質を創り上げていく貴重な体験ができた．

国際コンペで選ばれたイタリアの建築家レンゾ・ピアノ氏案での実施設計による関西国際空港旅客ターミナルビル．数多くの問題を抱えながらも，工事を無事竣工させることができたのは，関西国際空港株式会社，レンゾ・ピアノ・ビルディング・ワークショップ・ジャパン，株式会社日建設計の皆様方の工事に対する情熱と作業員一人一人にまで浸透した工事に対する誇りが大きな推進力となったものであると感謝している．

関西国際空港テクニカルデータ

旅客ターミナルビル キャニオン植栽工法

- 礫耕栽培工法
- 礫耕順化
- 自動灌水設備
- けいそう土焼成粒　イソライトCG

1.「ようこそ日本へ＝Welcome to Japan」

これは，関西国際空港旅客ターミナルビルキャニオン植栽のコンセプトである．このキャニオン植栽は，国際空港の玄関として，日本あるいは大阪を訪れる人々を迎え入れる空間を構成する重要な要素である．そこで，基盤の高中木植栽樹種としては，日本の自然・風景を表現するために常緑和木より選択した．また林床の地被類は，常緑高中木の緑と組み合わせて，明るい斑入り種を中心に選定し，全体として華やかで落着きのある空間を演出する植栽構成とした．

植栽樹木の配植は，キャニオン内の人の動きに合わせて植栽の強弱・高低を作り，人の集まる場所に重点的に高木を配植することとした．また，南北のガラスエンドウォールの内と外に竹林を配植することで，キャニオンの開放感を演出した．

2. キャニオンの環境圧

多くの人々が行き来するキャニオンにおいては，人々にとって快適な屋内環境が求められる．また，空港という特殊機能を果たすために，管制塔への照り返しを防ぐ目的で，キャニオントップのガラス面にはパンチングメタルが施されている．このような環境は，光条件，温・湿度条件，風条件，土壌条件，水条件など，植物にとっては環境圧を生じさせる．その中で特に光条件については，通常の屋内植栽の場合，3,000～5,000Lxの照度を確保することが目安となっているが，キャニオン内の照度は，1,000～1,500Lxとなることが予想された．

3. 礫耕栽培工法

屋内緑化の事例調査，および緑化工事の施工関連各社へのヒアリングの結果，前述のような条件下においては，従来の植栽工法である土壌への植栽（土耕植栽）では，樹木の健全な生育が困難であることが予想された．そこで，このような低照度下植栽に対応するために，「礫耕（れきこう）栽培工法」を採用することとした．この工法の特徴として，特に①樹木の低照度・礫耕順化，②自動灌水設備，③焼成培土の使用の3点が挙げられる．

4. 樹木の順化

礫耕栽培工法は，低照度下における，植物の光合成低下による根系の根腐れを防ぎ，透水性・通気性を良好に保ち，健全な生育を促すものである．この工法では，予め根廻し済みの樹木を散水しながら根鉢の土を落とし，パンチング加工したステンレス製樹木植鉢（径0.8～1.8m）の中へ多孔質焼成培土を詰めながら植え込んだ後，70％遮光の寒冷紗で覆った網室内で，葉面および根鉢にスプリンクラー・ドリップ散水を定期的（1回5分/時，1回1分/時）に行いながら，約3ヶ月から6ヶ月間，礫耕順化を行った．順化が進行しているかの判断は，葉の陰陽化（葉が低照度に対応し，大きく，薄く，葉色が薄くなる）および発根した根が，礫耕順化（疎で太い根になる）しているかによる．なお，樹木順化については，㈱グリーンテックの技術協力をもとに検討したものである．

植栽樹木一覧表

キャニオン植栽		外部竹林植栽
高中木	地被類	高中木
モウソウチク	ユキノシタ	モウソウチク
マテバシイ	フイリギボウシ	
オガタマノキ	フッキソウ	
タブノキ	ヤブコウジ	
ヒメユズリハ(株立)	フイリシャガ	
ホルトノキ	フイリヤブラン	地被類
モチノキ	キチジョウソウ	
ナギ	エビネ	シャガ
シラカシ	シュンラン	クサソテツ
モッコク	オモト	ヤブラン
ユズリハ	カンアオイ	
ヤブツバキ		
カクレミノ		
サザンカ(白・赤)		
カラタネオガタマ		
クロガネモチ		

完成植栽写真

地被類アップ写真

住友林業緑化株式会社

〒542 大阪府大阪市中央区南船場3丁目4番2号
TEL (06) 241-6983　FAX (06) 241-0640
SUMITOMO FORESTRY LANDSCAPING CO.,LTD
8F Idemitsu Nagahori Bldg, 3-4-26 Minamisenba, Chuo-Ku, Osaka, 542

松下興産株式会社　緑化事業部

〒525 滋賀県草津市野路町1922-499
TEL (0775) 64-7411　FAX (0775) 65-3460
MATSUSHITA INVESTMENT AND
DEVELOPMENT CO., LTD. HORTICULTURAL DEPT.
1922-499 Nojicho, Kusatsu, Shiga 525

5．植栽工事

　キャニオン内の植栽地は，約2～4m角・深さ1mの植桝が，長さ約275mのキャニオンの床の間に列状に大小34ヶ所配置されている．その植桝の内には，排水ドレンの点検のためのドレン点検口，樹木への葉水散水のための霧散布ポール，樹木植鉢に入った順化樹木が設置されている．植桝の隙間は，多孔質焼成培土によって埋め込み，透水性・通気性を良好に保った．植鉢の上部には，合成樹脂ネット，有機質培土を敷きつめ，地被類を配植した．なお，地被類は予め土壌を洗い落とし，有機質培土に植え替え養生したものを使用した．

　散水設備は，霧散布ポールによる樹木への葉水散水，ドリップチューブによる地中灌水，ポップアップスプリンクラーによる地被類への葉水散水の3系統を設け，それぞれの散水時間をタイマーで制御している．

　外部竹林植栽は，植栽範囲に，土壌改良土を深さ1m埋め込み，暗渠排水を施し，周囲を竹地下茎遮断シートによって囲んだ．散水はドリップ散水とし，キャニオン内と同様タイマー制限している．

6．植栽維持管理

　植栽維持管理については，屋内環境条件である低照度，病虫害，ホコリ，乾燥等，屋外とは環境が異なることから，よりきめ細やかな管理が要求される．特にキャニオン植栽は，人と植物との関係が身近になっていることから，病虫害，葉のよごれ，枯れ等により生じる不快感を与えないよう，日々の樹木チェックと速やかな対応が求められる．

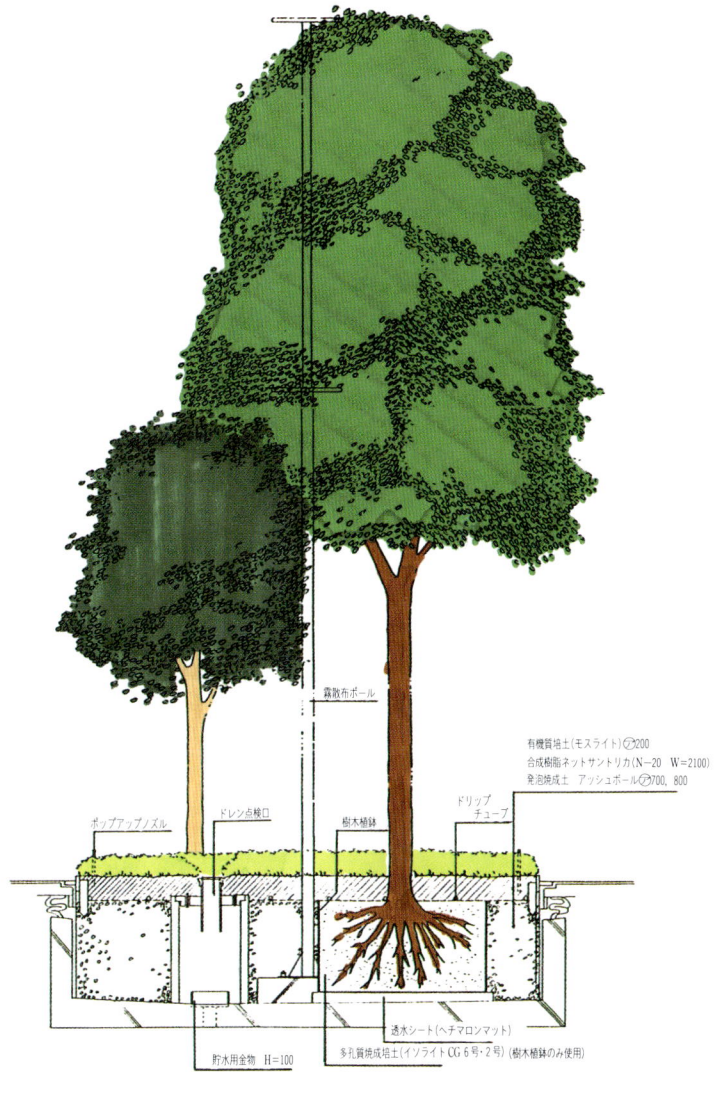

関西国際空港テクニカルデータ

株式会社 三水社
〒536　大阪府大阪市城東区今福東3丁目8番2号
TEL(06)932-1293　FAX(06)932-8420
SANSUI CORPORATION
3-8-2 Imafuku-Higashi, Joto-Ku, Osaka 536 Japan

トロカンパニージャパン
〒141　東京都品川区西五反田8-3-9 KHビル4F
TEL(03)5434-2931　FAX(03)5434-2910
The Toro Company
KH Bldg. 4F 8-3-9 Nishigotanda Shinagawa-Ku, Tokyo 141 Japan

7．自動灌水設備

礫耕栽培工法における水の条件は，樹木の育生を左右する最大の条件のひとつである．キャニオン植栽の灌水は目的により，次の3種類に分けられる．それぞれの灌水時刻や運転時間が複雑に設定され，最適の灌水状態に管理されている．運転制御は，電磁弁の開閉でおこなっており，制御盤から自動運転信号が送られている．

①霧散布ポール

主として，木々の幹や葉に水分を与えると共に，ほこりを流して瑞々しさをもたせるものである．構造は，木の高さに応じたステンレスの柱に，リング状にスプレーノズルを配置し，木に向けて100μ(ミクロン)程度の霧を噴霧している．この霧は，木にやさしく，葉の間に吸い込まれていくのが理想的だが，空調の風などの影響を受けやすいので，場所により，スプレーノズルの種類を使い分けた．

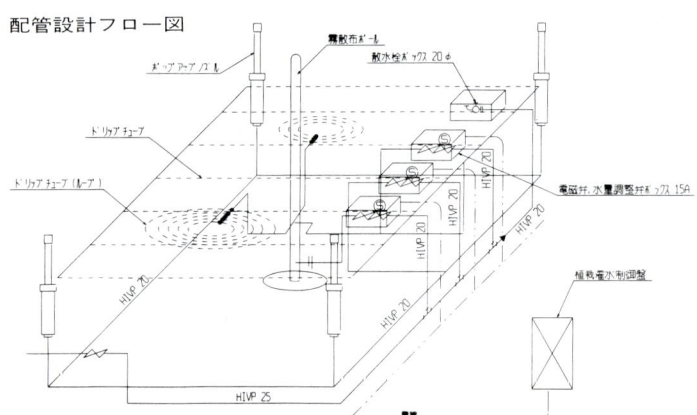
配管設計フロー図

②灌水パイプ

木への灌水量の大部分を，樹木根鉢へ年輪状に巻いた灌水パイプが受け持っている．このパイプは，多孔質の材料でできており，全表面からにじみでる水は，確実に木の根全体を潤している．同時に別系統の灌水パイプで，地被類への灌水も受け持っている．

③ポップアップノズル

地被類の葉を潤し，ほこりを流すために，ポップアップノズルを多数配置した．通常は地中にあり，灌水するときだけノズルが30cm上がる．設置場所により，ノズルの種類(90°)等を使い分けた．

霧散布ポールから漂う霧は，人の心をなごませるひとつの水景であるが，時々しか目にすることができない．特に幸運な人には，木漏れ日に映る虹が出迎えてくれるだろう．

イソライト工業株式会社

〒530　大阪府大阪市北区堂島浜1丁目2番6号（新ダイビル）
TEL(06)345-7231　FAX(06)345-6698
ISOLITE INSULATION PRODUCTS CO.,LTD.
Shin-Daibiru Bldg. 1-2-6 Dojimahama, Kita-Ku, Osaka, 530, Japan

旅客ターミナルビルキャニオン植栽工法

文責
株式会社　都市・景観設計
代表取締役　奥村信一
〒540　大阪府大阪市中央区大手通1丁目2番1号
TEL(06)949-3750　FAX(06)949-0647

8．けいそう土焼成粒　イソライトＣＧ（多孔質焼成培土）

「けいそう」とは単細胞藻類(植物性プランクトンの一種)の一つで，淡水中，海水中に生息する生物である．この生物は体の周囲に珪酸(SiO_2)質の殻をつくるのでこの名がつけられている．形状は通常弁当箱状の構造でフタとソコの2部よりなるザルのような形をしており，表面および内部に0.1～数μmの多数の細かい孔があいている多孔質構造を有している．内部には「生きた部分」つまり原形質(有機物)が存在し「けいそう」が死ねば内部の原形質は分解し腐蝕消失するが，珪酸質の殻はそのまま，海底や湖底に沈み堆積し地層を形成する．こうしてできた土が「けいそう土」である．

この「けいそう土」は世界各地に分布しており，我が国でも北海道から九州にかけて各地に存在する．けいそう土焼成粒「イソライトＣＧ」は和倉温泉で有名な能登半島に産する「和倉けいそう土」を原料としている．

この和倉けいそう土を均一な粒径に造粒し，1000℃の高温で焼き固めセラミック化した土壌改良資材，これが「イソライトＣＧ」である．イソライトＣＧは前述したように微細な多孔質構造を持つけいそう土を原料としているため，粒の内部には0.1～数μmの連続した気孔を無数に有している．これを粘土質焼成粒と比較すると，細孔容積はイソライトＣＧが0.66cm³/g，粘土質焼成粒は0.26cm³/gであり，それら細孔の占める割合(気孔率)はイソライトＣＧで60～70%，粘土質焼成粒で20～30%である．またイソライトＣＧの細孔は毛管孔隙として働く孔径1μm付近のものがほとんどを占める一方，粘土質焼成粒は保水効果のない0.1μm以下の細孔が全細孔容積の50%以上を占めている．

土壌改良資材として土壌の透水性(排水性)，通気性，保水性を改善・向上させる効果はもちろんのこと，セラミック化されているため水を含んで膨潤したり破壊したり分解することもなく，無菌でpHも中性を示し化学的に安定していることから，礫耕栽培の培地としての利用も各地で行われている．

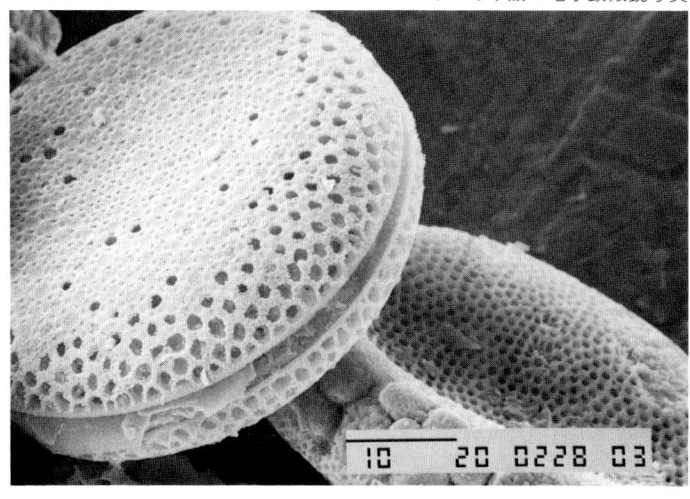

けいそう殻の電子顕微鏡写真

粘土質焼成粒(ハイドロボール等)の
細孔径分布グラフと顕微鏡写真

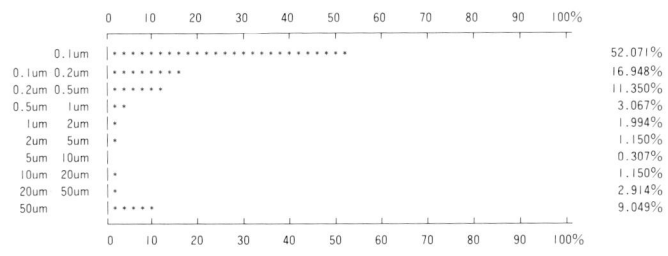

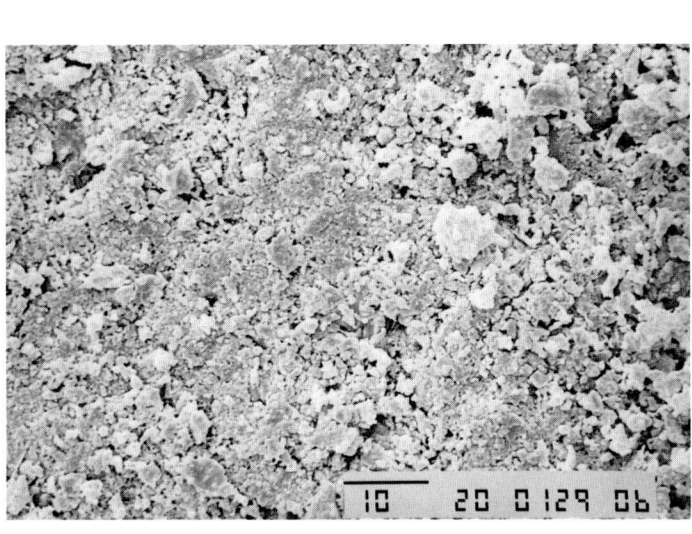

イソライトＣＧの細孔径分布グラフ
と顕微鏡写真

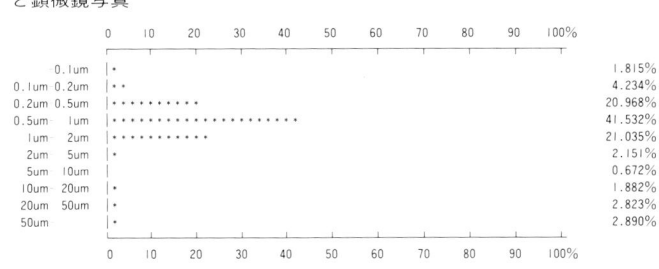

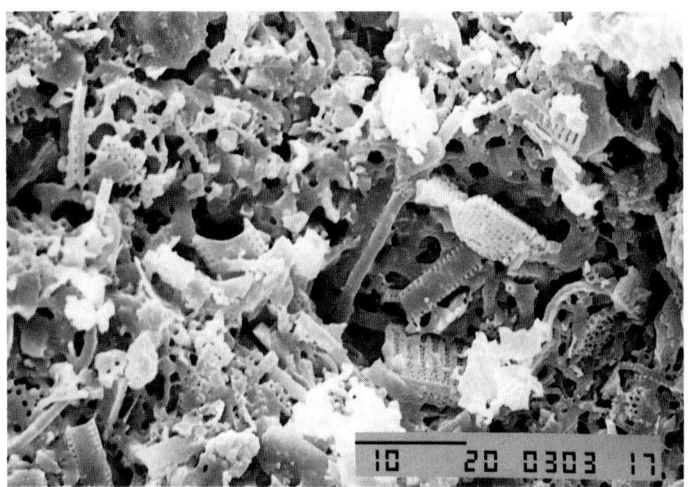

関西国際空港テクニカルデータ

オープンエアダクト

太陽工業株式会社
〒532 大阪府大阪市淀川区木川東4-8-4　〒153 東京都目黒区東山3-22-1
TEL (06) 306-3033 FAX (06) 306-3154 TEL (03) 3714-3470 FAX (03) 3791-7725
TAIYO KOGYO CORPORATION
4-8-4 Kigawa-Higasi, Yodogawa-Ku, Osaka, 532 Japan

1．オープンエアダクトの役割

旅客ターミナルビル4階の国際線出発ロビーの天井面に設置された19基のオープンエアダクト。その最大幅は9.8m、長さ76.6mで、膜構造物としては稀な凹面形状を構成した張力膜です。フロアの端に並んだ巨大ジェットノズルから吹き出される空気を膜下面に沿って流し、旅客ターミナルビル内の空気を循環させる役割を果たしています。また光の反射板としての機能も兼ね備え、その間接光が出発ロビーの空間を快適に演出しています。

2．素材

このオープンエアダクトの素材は、ガラス繊維に四フッ化エチレン樹脂をコーティングしたものですが、より軽く、光の反射機能を満足させるために、オリジナル生地を約2年をかけて開発しました。空気循環装置という役割のため、空気が抜けないよう繊維織り目をスキ間コーティングで防ぎ、さらに反射板の役割を強化するために、コーティング材料にチタンフレークを混入させ白色度を上げました。これにより、エアタイトで反射率70％以上、厚さ0.8mm、重さ800g/㎡の生地が誕生したのです。

3．構造

オープンエアダクトの構造は大屋根の2次材鉄骨から吊り下げられた構造物で、形状を構成する膜とそれを形成させるアルミニウムのフレームによって成り立っています。膜はフレームの下面に張力を入れた状態で凹面形状を出さなければならない為、張力導入システムとして桁サイドは膜を上方へ巻き込み、膜端のエッジロープをアルミファスナーで掴む方法を取りました。①フレームストリンガーアングル材を中間部に4列配し、②テンションボルトにて上方へ膜を引き上げて張力が入れられるよう、③先端部分はアルミの平板で膜をサンドイッチし、固定しました。

4．ディテールの設計

ディテールを設計するにあたり、軽量化を考慮し、フレームの構成と膜の張力導入システムをムダの無いように組合せをする必要がありました。レンゾ・ピアノ氏の望まれている薄く、シャープなイメージを実現させるべく、ケーススタディを1年半にわたり行ったほか、実物大の試作を2度製作し、先端部についてもデザイン上の美しさに配慮しながら試作張りを行うという地道な作業により、実現に向けての自信を深めていきました。

5．施工

一方施工においても難題がありました。凹面形状をしたオープンエアダクトは引力に逆らって下から張らなければならないということです。軽減したとはいえ、1枚の膜の重量は1トン。流線形をした屋根に沿わせるため、微妙な形状をしています。しかもシワひとつなく張らなければ美しくありません。80の施工方法を考案、その結果、真下にエアダクトと同じ形をした台をテントで作り、そこに膜を広げて空中から骨組みを下ろし、膜を取りつけ、最後に引き上げて仕上げを行うという方法を採用しました。

関西国際空港テクニカルデータ

Floor System ニューファンクション フロアシステム

UNION 建設環境金属製品の 株式会社ユニオン

- コンコースやアトリウムなどの大空間では，落ち着くことのできる"安らぎの場"が必要です．
- ロビーフロアでのアメニティづくりをサポートするユニオンでは，"ヒューマン スケールの憩いの場"を設営できるニューファンクション フロアシステムを開発しました．
- 自立式で移設ができるパーティション システムでポールとスクリーンの組み合わせが自在にできます．動線に合わせ直線型，L字，U字，屏風型をはじめ，レストブースをつくりだすT字，クロス型，ウェイティング コーナーとしてのS字，コの字型などの間仕切り展開ができます．
- スクリーンにはパンチングメタルを採用し，透過性があるので圧迫感がありません．
- 団体の集合場所やバゲージエリアのご案内，受付カウンターでの誘導，喫煙場所のご指示などを行うサインボードをポール上部に取り付けることができます．

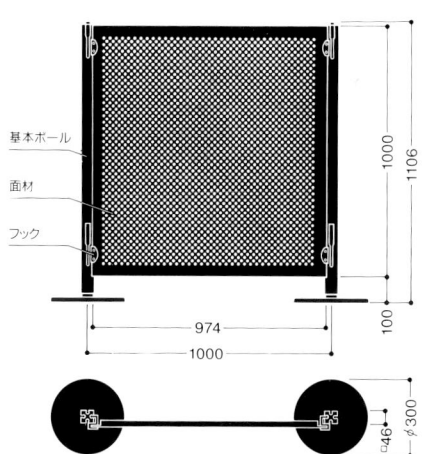

■基本ポール
NF-UP-940
- 素材／アルミ＋ステンレス
- 仕上／グレー塗装（2色）
- サイズ／φ300×H1106

■面材
NF-PA-941
- 素材／スチール
- 仕上／グレー塗装
- サイズ／φ974×H1000

■フック
NF-PA-942
- 素材／アルミ
- 仕上／グレー塗装
- サイズ／W35×H72×D51

1m当たりの
　　参考価格　￥57,000
1mに含まれているもの：
　基本ポール(1本)＋
　　面材(1枚)＋フック(4ケ)

■本社・ショールーム
大阪市西区南堀江2-13-22 〒550
☎06(532)3731代 FAX06(533)3747

■東京支店
東京都江東区白河2-9-5 〒135
☎03(3630)2811代 FAX03(3630)2816

■東京ショールーム
東京都港区虎ノ門2-3-22 〒105
☎03(3506)1717代 FAX03(3506)1718

■名古屋営業所・ショールーム
名古屋市中川区舟戸町3-20 〒454
☎052(363)5221代 FAX052(363)5255

関西国際空港テクニカルデータ

旅客手荷物処理システム

カワサキ-オースチン-ボイマー共同体
The Kawasaki -Austin- Beumer Consortium
川崎重工業株式会社
〒105　東京都港区浜松町2丁目4番1号（世界貿易センタービルディング）
TEL(03)3435-2111　FAX(03)3436-3037
KAWASAKI HEAVY INDUSTRIES, LTD.
World Trade Center Bldg., 4-1, Hamamatsu-Cho 2-Chome,
Minato-Ku, Tokyo 105, Japan

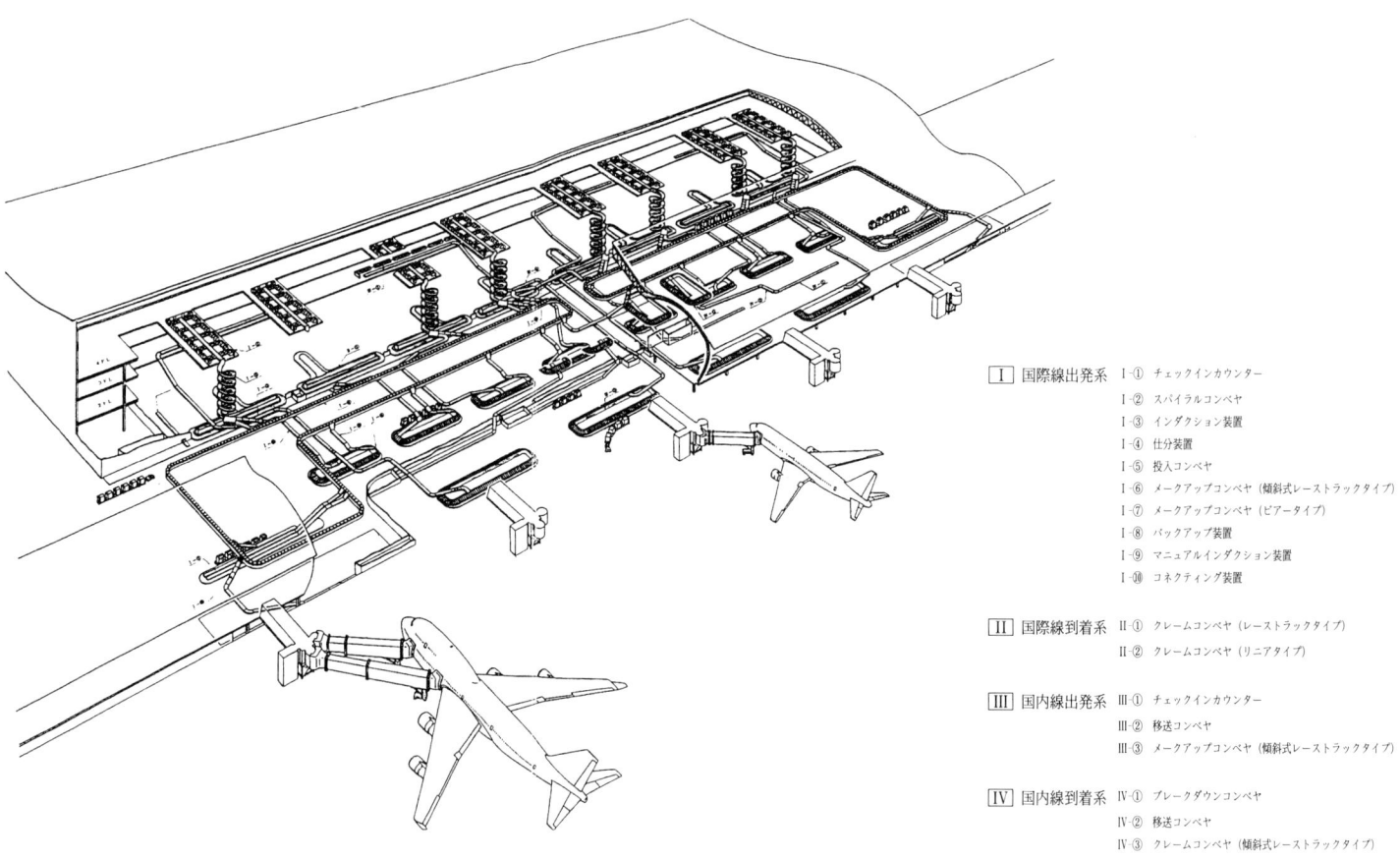

Ⅰ 国際線出発系
- Ⅰ-① チェックインカウンター
- Ⅰ-② スパイラルコンベヤ
- Ⅰ-③ インダクション装置
- Ⅰ-④ 仕分装置
- Ⅰ-⑤ 投入コンベヤ
- Ⅰ-⑥ メークアップコンベヤ（傾斜式レーストラックタイプ）
- Ⅰ-⑦ メークアップコンベヤ（ピアータイプ）
- Ⅰ-⑧ バックアップ装置
- Ⅰ-⑨ マニュアルインダクション装置
- Ⅰ-⑩ コネクティング装置

Ⅱ 国際線到着系
- Ⅱ-① クレームコンベヤ（レーストラックタイプ）
- Ⅱ-② クレームコンベヤ（リニアタイプ）

Ⅲ 国内線出発系
- Ⅲ-① チェックインカウンター
- Ⅲ-② 移送コンベヤ
- Ⅲ-③ メークアップコンベヤ（傾斜式レーストラックタイプ）

Ⅳ 国内線到着系
- Ⅳ-① ブレークダウンコンベヤ
- Ⅳ-② 移送コンベヤ
- Ⅳ-③ クレームコンベヤ（傾斜式レーストラックタイプ）

Of the whole Kansai International Airport Passengers' Baggage Handling System (BHS), the system for international departure is the one which is characterized by its function of carrying baggage, which is deposited at check-in counters on the 4th floor, down to the baggage sorting area on the 1st floor by means of vertical transportation, and which is further characterized by its function of sorting the baggage correctly for each flight No.

Some of its characteristics are described as follows;

1．Automatic sorting by tracking system

Tracking system is the system for automatically tracking data of each baggage, which is given as an input at the start of transportation, while ensuring the baggage being forward to make up conveyer through vertical conveyer, tilt-tray sorter. This is the BHS system implemented for the first time in the world.

This tracking system is a highly reliable system which comprises a window control system, sequence monitor system and tray transportation system.

2．Spiral conveyor has realized vertical transportation.

A vertical transportation along the height of 14m from the 4-th to 1-st floor has been achieved by connecting vertically 10 units of 180° spiral conveyors.

This is the first BHS in the world to carry baggage along this height, and has resulted in reduced space for installation and a larger quantity of baggage to transport.

3．3D tilt tray sorter has been employed for sorting device.

Unlike an ordinary tilt tray sorter, 3D tilt tray sorter discharges baggage 3-dimengionally (parabolically), thus softtouching the baggage in ejection.

4．Golf bags can be transported.

Golf bag is a non-standard baggage, because it exceeds 1m in length. As it is carried in a transit container of less than 1m in length, the sensor, the BHS's eye, cannot detect actual length what is inside.

The transit containers are also used for carrying those items that roll easily or items with sharp projections.

All the information necessary for the overall operation and maintenance of these systems is collectively monitored by a control center. Additionally, LCD terminals and LED displays are provided at the baggage sorting area to support the operators in their sorting.

写真1　国際線出発チェックインカウンター

写真2　国際線出発チェックインカウンター及び搬送コンベヤ

写真3　スパイラルコンベヤ

写真4　仕分装置(ソータ)

写真5　メークアップコンベヤ

写真6　国際線到着クレームコンベヤ

　関西国際空港旅客手荷物処理システム(BHS)のうち，国際線出発系のシステムは，ターミナルビル4階にあるチェックインカウンターで預かった手荷物を，1階の荷捌場まで垂直搬送し，便別に正確に仕分ける特徴あるシステムである．以下に特徴の幾つかについて述べる．

1. トラッキング方式による自動仕分け

　トラッキング方式とは，搬送開始時に入力された手荷物1個1個の情報を，手荷物の移動を確認しながら自動追跡する方式で，4階から1階まで垂直搬送を含めた搬送設備での実施は，世界のBHSとしては初めてである．

　本トラッキング方式は，ウインドウ制御方式，順序監視方式及びトレー搬送方式の3方式により構成され，信頼性の高いシステムとなっている．

2. 垂直搬送をスパイラルコンベヤで実現

　4階から1階まで落差14mの垂直搬送に，180度の螺旋式コンベヤを10台垂直に組み合わせたスパイラルコンベヤで実現している．

BHSでこの落差は世界で初めてであり，これにより設置スペースの削減及び大容量搬送が可能となった．

3. 仕分け装置(ソータ)に3Dティルト・トレイ・ソータを採用

　3Dティルト・トレイ・ソータは，一般のティルト・トレイ・ソータと異なり，手荷物の排出を三次元的(放物線状)に行うもので，これにより手荷物に与える衝撃を和らげている．

4. ゴルフバッグの搬送が可能

　ゴルフバッグは，その長さが1mを越えるため，本BHSでは規定外手荷物ではあるが，通い箱に収納して搬送することにより，BHSで目の働きをしているセンサーを騙している．

　この通い箱は転がり易い手荷物，鋭利な突起がある手荷物を収納する通い箱としても使用している．

　これらシステム全体の運転・保守に必要な情報はすべて中央から監視している．又，荷捌場の作業者用にLCD端末やLED表示装置を設け，荷捌作業のサポートを行っている．

関西国際空港テクニカルデータ

エアサイド・カーテンウォール

⊙ 日本板硝子株式会社
〒105 東京都港区海岸2丁目1番7号　日本板硝子東京ビル
Tel 03-5443-9570　Fax 03-5443-9559
NIPPON SHEET CLASS CO.,LTD.
NSG Tokyo Bldg. 1-7, 2-Chome, Kaigan Minato-ku
Tokyo 105 Japan

エア・サイド・カーテンウォールのガラスユニットの製作のために仮設工場を大阪府泉南市に設置し，約1年6ヶ月の間に，完全な品質管理のもと4400枚のガラスユニットが製作されました．

空港島内の建設現場では，イラストのような形ですべて乾式の施工を行い，17000㎡におよぶカーテンウォールを短期間で均質な施工とすることができました．

高い可視光線透過率と熱エネルギー・コントロール機能により、熱線吸収ガラス「グレーペーン」が関西国際空港の顔を飾る

関西国際空港の旅客ターミナルビルのエアサイド・カーテンウォールは，日本板硝子の熱線吸収ガラス「グレーペーン」が使用されています．

ジオメトリーという構成原理に基づく建築形態は，これまでに出会った，どのカーテンウォールにもあてはまらない，新しい発想のカーテンウォールです．幅1.7kmにおよび，滑らかな多角形を描く巨大な皮膜は，幅3600mm×高1100mm×厚12mmのガラス・パネル4400枚により構成されました．

ステンレスの屋根とグレーのガラスが，滑らかな形態をシャープなモノトーンに仕上げています．また，「グレーペーン」の高い可視光線透過率が，海上に浮かぶ空港を難なく見渡せるよう演出しています．

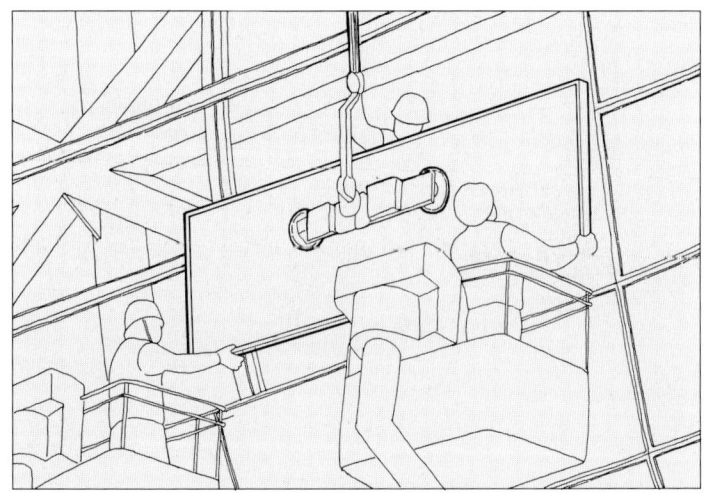

4400枚のガラス・パネルが世界を結ぶ顔となる

昇降機設備

三菱電機株式会社 関西支社
〒530 大阪府大阪市北区堂島2丁目2番2号
TEL(06)347-2306　FAX(06)347-2794
MITSUBISHI ELECTRIC CORPORATION KANSAI BRANCH
2-2-2 Dojima, Kita-Ku, Osaka, 530 Japan

1. 昇降機設備

旅客ターミナルビルでの垂直方向の移動手段である昇降機設備として，本館とウイングを合わせて，エレベーター91台，エスカレーター76台の総台数167台(メーカーは6社)が納入されている．三菱電機はこの内，メインターミナルビルに，屋内オープンタイプの展望用を初めとする油圧エレベーター15台と，手荷物を運搬するための空港用カートを輸送できるエスカレーター14台を納入した(表1参照).

旅客ターミナルビルの本館には，キャニオン(峡谷)と呼ばれる1階から4階までの吹き抜け大空間がある．自然の光と緑が調和したこのキャニオンは，すべてのフロアがつながっており，エレベーターやエスカレーターで各階にスムーズに移動できるようになっている．また，ビル全体の透明感を出すために，壁面にガラスが多く用いられ，ロビーとロビーとを結ぶブリッジの両サイドや，階段部分の壁にもガラスが使用されて，各階の導線が一目でわかるようになっている．

2. エレベーターの特徴

①昇降路の特徴——エレベーターの出入口側の面は，かごからの万一の転落を防止するガラス製保護板(フェッシャープレート)が設けられているが，これ以外は各階の高さ2.32mのガラスフェンスのみで，油圧ジャッキ側の建築柱以外は，昇降路の囲いがない構造となっている．
②かごの特徴——かご室は，壁・天井及びかごの戸の約65%をガラスで構成した特殊形状である．天井にガラスを使用したり，法規より大きなガラスを使用するため，建築基準法第38条に基づき大臣認定を取得した(写真参照)．また，かご室のイメージを軽快にするため，窓ガラスの固定は，金属枠なしのシーリング材による方法とした．

3. 地盤沈下対策

①油圧ジャッキ——油圧ジャッキは，シリンダ表面を上下2ヶ所部分的に機械加工を施し，ふっ素樹脂材をシューとするガイドを設け，固定支持用のUボルトを緩めることにより，油圧ジャッキ全体が上下に摺動できるようにした．
②ガイドレール——かご側のガイドレールは，レール下端をスライディングシューでガイドする構造とし，建物の伸縮に追従できるようにした．
③油圧配管——油圧配管は，金属製管継手とエルボ管を組み合わせることにより，建物の伸縮に追従できるようにした．

4. 空港用カート搭載エスカレーター

①カート利用者の傾斜部での不安感を和らげるため，傾斜角度を30°～25°とし，緩やかにした(写真参照)．
②昇降部の水平ステップの長さを長くした．
③カートの乗り降りがよりスムーズにできるよう，昇降口の床板の傾斜を緩やかにした．
④エスカレーターは欄干パネルに通常より板厚を厚くした透明ガラスを採用し，キャニオン部の建築デザインコンセプトに沿うものとした．

表1　昇降機設置台数　()内は，大臣認定取得数．

	メインターミナル		ウイング		
	エレベーター	エスカレーター	エレベーター	エスカレーター	
自社	15(14)	14	—	—	
他社	32(2)	20	44(19)	42(8)	総台数
小計	47(16)	34	44(19)	42(8)	167(43)

ステンレスタイル

川崎製鉄株式会社

〒530 大阪市北区芝田1-1-4　　〒100 東京都千代田区内幸町2-2-3
TEL(06)315-4562(阪急ターミナルビル)　TEL(03)3597-4030(日比谷国際ビル)

KAWASAKI STEEL CORPORATION
1-1-4 Shibata, Kita-Ku, Osaka, 530 Japan

　関西国際空港は，海上空港であるため，旅客ターミナルビルの屋根に使用されるステンレスは，耐候性に優れていること，また，管制官やパイロットが眩しくないように防眩性をもつことが要求された．これら条件に加えて，ステンレス鋼の表面の色感も重視された．

1．鋼種の選択

　建築分野では汎用ステンレス鋼としてSUS304が，少し厳しい腐食環境では，SUS316が使用されている．しかし，海塩粒子が多く飛来する沿岸地域においては，SUS316では耐食性が不十分であるため，旅客ターミナルビルのステンレスタイルとして，より優れた耐食性のステンレス鋼が求められ，SUS447J1が採用された．

　SUS447J1の耐食性は，潮岬における暴露試験や実験室における電気化学的実験により評価された．一例を写真1に示す．チタン及びSUS447J1は，潮岬で1.5年間暴露しても高い耐食性を維持している．

　川崎製鉄のSUS447J1は，川崎製鉄独自の特殊精錬技術により，表1に示すように，（C＋N）量を0.01％まで低減している．このC，Nの低減により高い加工性と溶接性が得られ，建築部材への加工が可能になっている．

2．防眩性

　SUS447J1のステンレスタイル用素材は，表面を放電ダル加工した圧延ロールを用いて冷間圧延され，写真2に示す凹凸のある表面に仕上げられた．

　このSUS447J1ダル仕上げ材の防眩性は，光沢度で評価した場合，通常の建材用ステンレス鋼の約1/3に低下している．

3．耐食性

　防眩性を得るためのダル加工は，SUS447J1の耐食性を低下させる．しかし，川崎製鉄のSUS447J1ダル仕上げ材は新しく開発された製造プロセスにより，ステンレス鋼の色感を損うことなく通常の仕上げ材（2B）と同等の耐食性が賦与されている．

4．出荷

　SUS447J1ダル仕上げ材は色調に方向性があるため，圧延方向を明示した保護フィルムが貼付されて出荷された．

　加工メーカーで600×1750mmの大きさに成形されたステンレスタイル82,400枚は，圧延方向が同じになるように旅客ターミナルビルの90,000m²の屋根に取り付けられた（写真3）．

写真1　潮岬で1.5年間暴露したステンレス鋼の表面

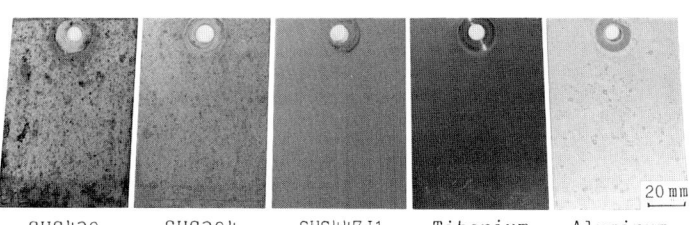

SUS430　　SUS304　　SUS447J1　　Titanium　　Aluminum

表1　SUS447J1の化学組成（％）

	C	Si	Mn	P	S	Cr	Mo	N
JIS規格	<0.01	<0.40	<0.04	<0.030	<0.020	28.50〜32.00	1.50〜2.50	<0.015
川鉄の製造例	0.003	0.09	0.10	0.022	0.006	30.0	2.00	0.007

写真2　SUS447J1ダル仕上げ材の表面

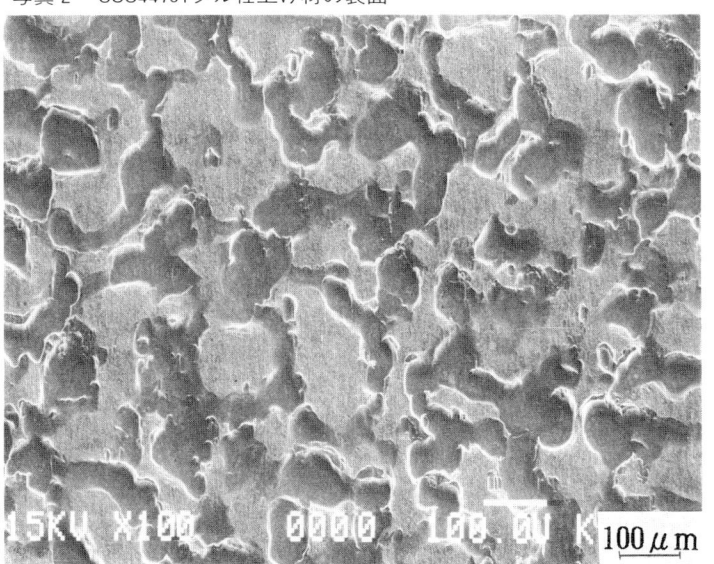

写真3　旅客ターミナルビルの屋根のステンレスタイル

AQUASCAPES II

アクアスケープII 水の造景

世界中のランドスケープアーキテクト，建築家，デザイナーの間で大変な好評を得た，「アクアスケープ」発行から3年が経過した．この間に日本の各地でアクアスケープの重要性が増し，また見直されてきている．

「アクアスケープII」は多くの読者の要望に応えてこのたび発行されることとなった．

● 事例／しながわ水族館，エコール鹿の子台，庄和町役場庁舎，長野県信濃美術館・東山魁夷館，日本城郭研究センター，ハウス・テンボス，他

発行日／1994年6月
総頁／224頁（カラー218頁）
文章／日本語，英語
サイズ／A4ワイド版
装幀／ハードカバー，ジャケット付き

定価9,800円（本体9,515円）

アクアスケープ：水の造景

かつては庭園や公園で脇役をつとめてきた水．最近では水に対する意識の高まりを受けて，重要なスタンスを持つようになった．水がその場のコンセプトであったり，水の遊び場であったり…．私たちはこのようなデザインされた水をアクアスケープと呼ぶことにした．この本では最近の日本のアクアスケープ，そして様々な水の演出の好例を多数紹介する．

お待たせしました．アクアスケープ：水の造景を再版いたしました．この機会に是非お買い求め下さい．

定価9,800円（本体9,515円）

ハードカバー，ジャケット付き
A4変形版
208頁（カラー190頁）
日本語，英語

女性たちの庭

女性の庭,それは珠玉のように育まれ,いつくしまれてできあがった美しい庭である。キッチンのまわり,バスルーム前,周囲の景色を借りた庭,廃品利用でつくった庭,生活の場としての手づくりの庭。美しい自然に満ちたニュージーランドの庭27,センシティブな日本の庭17を,美しい写真でめぐる。この本ではニュージーランドと日本というライフスタイルの全く対照的な2国の女性たちの庭を紹介する。

●責任編集者／杉尾邦江,総頁／200頁(オールカラー),サイズ／A4変形版,定価／5,600円

世界のランドスケープデザイン

本書は,世界18か国,97点の作品を収録し,そのジャンルも庭園や都市空間のデザインから,自然環境や歴史的環境の保全・再生に至るまで,極めて多岐にわたっている。21世紀に向けて環境文化の創造と地球規模での環境保全が最も重要な社会的要請となっている今日,ランドスケープアーキテクトたちの活動は,そうした課題に取り組むための確かな手掛かりを与えてくれる。

●責任編集者／小林治人・奥水 肇・宮城俊作・横張 真,総頁／256頁(カラー244頁),サイズ／A4変形版,定価／12,500円

都市環境のデザイン
空間創造の実践

本書はINAXが発行する機関誌「ESPLANADE」の創刊号から16号までを再構成し,集大成したものである。対談は建築家,アーバンデザイナー高橋志保彦氏を聞き手に,アーバンデザインの専門家,研究者,行政者など,その道の第一人者をゲストに迎え,計画報告書などでは読み取れない"街づくりのソフトとハードの両面のノウハウが実感として伝わってくる対談"として,連載中から大変話題を呼んだ。

●著者／高橋志保彦,総頁／196頁(オールカラー),サイズ／A4変形版,定価／3,800円

現代日本のランドスケープⅡ

自然との共生,都市空間の中でのうるおいの創造等,さまざまな環境の中での建築外構,公園,広場,庭園など,建築及びランドスケープデザインの第一線で活躍する作家の代表的作品をオールカラー写真と資料を加えて編集したものである。1988年11月発行の「現代日本のランドスケープ」に収録されなかった作品やその後の新作品を加えた最近10年間の38作品,さらに「花博EXPO'90」も併せて紹介する。

●総頁／219頁(カラー173頁),サイズ／A4変形版,定価／9,800円

SEKINE 関根伸夫

包含する環境美術を開拓目指してきたパイオニア,関根伸夫。常に人間の生の始原的感動に視線を注いで活動する彼の力強い空間演出を,その代表作のみを選りすぐって浮き彫りにする。高密度分解の高級美術印刷による美しい作品集である。

●責任編集者／林 芳史,総頁／116頁(カラー60頁),サイズ／A4変形版,定価／3,000円

ビルディング イリュージョン
カルロス・ディニーズに描かれた建築

カルロス・ディニーズは世界中にプロジェクトを持つアメリカの建築画家である。彼の仕事は,レンダラー,イラストレーター,などといった分類には当てはまらないほど広い領域を持つ。この本では,2,500もの仕事の中から44作品を選び,建築をこよなく愛する彼によって「描かれた建築」をテーマにカルロス・ディニーズのイリュージョンを集大成する。

●責任編集者／カルロス・ディニーズ,総頁／220頁(カラー204頁),サイズ／A4変形版,定価／9,800円

イタリアの水辺風景

大規模な開発に取り込まれた人工的な水辺ではなく,「生活」や「文化」に入り込んだ自然のものを真のウォーターフロントと呼びたい。陣内秀信のさがし求める水辺が各地に存在するイタリアを北から南までたずね歩いて知られざる素敵な水辺風景を紹介する。

●責任編集者／陣内秀信,総頁／224頁(カラー215頁),サイズ／A4変形版,定価／12,500円

日本的広場のある街
ミドリ・ミズ・ツチ

日本の街には広場がないとよく言われる。しかし人々が集まり,憩うといった,広場的な場所を探すことはできる。その背景には,そこに住む人々や,地区の特色が浮かび上がってくる。これらの日本的広場を4つの成熟度合をタテ軸に,3つの主な素材(ミドリ・ミズ・ツチ)をヨコ軸にして構成。著者が長年調査してまとめあげた31の場所的広場を紹介する。

●著者／加藤晃規,総頁／160頁(カラー148頁),サイズ／A4変形版,定価／3,800円

建築のなかの都市
上田 篤作品集

上田 篤の活動は,広場の追求,日本の聖性空間の研究,ウォーターフロントの重要性など,日本の建築界にいくつかの問題を投じてきた。これらの「日本的な生活空間の現代化」というテーマを一貫して追い続け,実践するユニークなプロフェッサー・アーキテクトの作品集である。

●著者／上田 篤,総頁／160頁(カラー152頁),サイズ／A4変形版,定価／3,800円

珠玉のホテル[環太平洋]編

ホテルには仕事・生活・出会い,などの「街」そのものの事柄が凝縮されている。しかし,ここでも均一化が進んでいる。この本で集められた18のホテルはその地域の文化やその「しつらい」や「もてなし」のオリジナリティを肌で感じることのできる「スモール&ラグジュアリー」タイプである。今回は環太平洋を巡り,東洋と西洋の個性の差異を見る。

●著者／秋山寿郎,総頁／232頁(カラー224頁),サイズ／A4変形版,定価／8,800円

JAPAN LANDSCAPE 季刊ジャパンランドスケープ

●定価2,580円（本体2,505円）

No.1～11, No.13, 14は品切れ, No.12は在庫僅少, No.15「海の景」, No.16「時空の景」（定価各2,580円）は好評発売中．

No.17●特集 テーマパークの景
- ●対談／「テーマパークとランドスケープデザイン」
- ●PEOPLE SCAPE／「ディズニーランドにおけるランドスケープ計画」

No.18●特集 森の景
- ●序論／「人と森のランドスケープ」樋渡達也
- ●人と森のニューライフ／森にあそぶ，森をつくる，森と生きる

No.19●特集 色彩の景
- ●LANDSCAPE NEW WAVE／西宮市大谷記念美術館庭園，カナダ大使館庭園，他
- ●LANDSCAPE WORKS／上野 泰

No.20●特集 駅の景
- ●座談会／「駅のランドスケープ」
- ●序文／「ステーションフロントの時代」樋渡達也
- ●PEOPLE SCAPE／佐藤 昌

No.21●特集 エコ・シティの景
- ●日本のケーススタディ／野川の川霧，横浜・本牧市民公園，西京桂坂，見沼田圃
- ●LANDSCAPE WORKS／近藤典生

No.22●特集 石の景
- ●座談会／「石を知る手技」
- ●現代作家にみる石心，石使い
- ●特別企画／ヨーロッパのスカルプチュアガーデン

No.23●特集 都の景
- ●LANDSCAPE NEW WAVE／宮の森カントリー倶楽部，保土ヶ谷公園—シンフォニー広場，他
- ●特別企画／「らんの里・堂ヶ島」の実験

No.24●特集 キャンパスの景
- ●LANDSCAPE NEW WAVE／マオイ・オートランド，千葉県立房総のむら，紫川十橋
- ●特別企画／屋上緑化のビジョンと新技術

No.25●特集 田園の景
- ●LANDSCAPE NEW WAVE／高野文彰のランドスケープ
- ●特別企画／「ミルフォード・トラック」体験から学ぶ

No.26●特集 緑と建築の景
- ●座談会／環境に生きる建築
- ●LANDSCAPE NEW WAVE／ウィーン市ドゥブリング区「世田谷公園」／生活工房サッポロファクトリー，他

No.27●特集 海遊都市の景
- ●対談／アーバンリゾート都市をつくる
- ●PEOPLE SCAPE／陣内秀信
- ●特別企画／遊具─遊び環境を再構築する

No.28●特集 木の景
- ●論文／ランドスケープデザインの近代史
- ●LANDSCAPE NEW WAVE／播磨科学公園都市「先端科学技術支援センター」，霧の彫刻，他

JAPAN LANDSCAPE No.29 ●特集● 島の景
定価2,580円 好評発売中

いま、島から学ぶとき

島のイメージが変わった—同化する東南アジアの島々／島のランドスケープエナジー／島々の過去と未来／島からの声／島の空間と時間が教えるもの／島はパラダイスか／世界遺産に登録された屋久島の今日的意味／島の護岸景観を守る

■座談会
島に観光は必要か？
大矢内生気／古賀 学／森本 孝／長嶋俊介／斉藤 潤

■LANDSCAPE NEW WAVE
ベルギー国ハッセルト市における日本庭園作庭にあたって（井上卓之）／寝覚の床美術公園（坪山幸王）／美浦ゴルフ倶楽部クラブハウス周り造景（内藤恒方）／サザンドームのしろ（志田憲一・望月 昭）／阿波之里（マーク・ピーター・キーン）／風のメッセージ（新宮 晋）

■OVERSEAS REPORT
開発前夜のベトナム

■People Scape
丸田 祥三

■論文
ランドスケープデザインの近代史
佐々木葉二／登坂 誠／三谷 徹／宮城俊作

■連載
都市風景塾／テクニカルノート／JLひろば

JAPAN LANDSCAPE No.30 ●特集● 園の景
定価2,580円 好評発売中

造園は現代の楽園をつくれるか

園をつくる
「『作庭』への求道」とは

現代庭園考
次代を担う造園家7人

映画に見る現代の楽園
黒沢明監督の原風景が昇華した夢の楽園

イサム・ノグチの楽園
"宇宙の庭"を標榜する
札幌「モエレ沼公園」の造園設計思想

■LANDSCAPE NEW WAVE
三景園
新潟県立近代美術館
YKK R&Dセンター中庭および外構
宮部緑地
天城ベコニアガーデン「プランティオ」
児玉慎憲のアート

■OVERSEAS REPORT
イタリアのランドスケーププランニング

■コンペ報告
「川のある風景」コンペ

■People Scape
増田俊彦

■シンポジウム報告
「閉鎖室内空間における植物栽培」第2回

■連載 視点／Photo Scape／都市風景塾／テクニカルノート／JLひろば

JAPAN LANDSCAPE

人・都市・自然のコミュニケーションマガジン 季刊 ジャパン・ランドスケープ

No.31 ●特集● **街並の景**

定価2,580円
好評発売中

風土に根ざしたまちづくり

どうしたら街は美しくなるか
まちづくり20年のながれ
「古都保存法」の見直しと世界遺産登録を目指して

佐賀県・有田町／長野県・小布施町／愛媛県・内子町
和歌山県・白浜町／京都府・舞鶴市／山形県・金山町
新潟県・津川町／神奈川県・真鶴町

■People Scape
鈴木博之

■OVERSEAS REPORT
イタリアのランドスケープ・プランニング
第2回 丘の上の都市の遠景保護

■論文
ランドスケープデザインの近代史
第5回 ランドスケープの地と図
佐々木葉二 登坂誠 三谷徹 宮城俊作

■連載 視点／Photo Scape／都市風景塾／テクニカルノート

■LANDSCAPE NEW WAVE
アンドレ・シトロエン公園
小松製作所 中央研究所
GUAM REEF HOTEL
コリア庭園
足立区生物園
救世神教本部のランドスケープファニチュア

■特別企画
ランドスケープフラワーの新展開

発行／㈱プロセスアーキテクチュア 〒151東京都渋谷区笹塚1-47-2-418 ☎03(3468)0131　編集／㈱マルモ・プランニング 〒150東京都渋谷区道玄坂1-20-1大沢ビル ☎03(3496)7046

PROCESS Architecture 108

ダン・カイリーのランドスケープデザインII：
語りかける自然

アメリカのランドスケープデザインをリードしてきたダン・カイリーの作品集，第二弾．最近10年の作品を中心にまとめ，初期の秀作の一部を加える．さらに1930年代から今日に至る主要作品を年表にして巻末に収録．

責任編集者	山田美智子
発 行 日	1993年2月
総 頁	160頁（カラー130頁）
文 章	日本語，英語
定 価	2,990円（本体2,903円）

PROCESS Architecture 109

ヴェネト：
イタリア人のライフスタイル

何世紀にもわたる伝統を今に残しつつ生活を営むかたわら，洗練されたデザインや精巧な技術で世界をリードしてゆくイタリア．特に第3次産業によって社会・経済的にも，文化的にも豊かさを増してきている北イタリア・ヴェネト州の4都市，22の家庭を訪ねて，住宅類型や彼らの生活こだわり学をさまざまな角度から深く掘り下げてゆく．

責任編集者	陣内秀信
発 行 日	1993年3月
総 頁	208頁（カラー138頁）
文 章	日本語，英語
定 価	3,600円（本体3,495円）

PROCESS Architecture 110

坂倉建築研究所：
半世紀の記録―日本の戦後近代建築の伏線

第2次大戦中から現在まで，日本の建築を代表する役目を果たして来た建築家集団，坂倉事務所の活動の軌跡を見ることは，そのまま日本の近代建築の系譜を見ることに通じる．日本の近代建築は大いなる変革を遂げたのだろうか．坂倉事務所の歴史のみならず，日本の近代建築の本質的一端を垣間見る一冊．

責任編集者	小宮山昭
発 行 日	1993年5月
総 頁	152頁（カラー54頁）
文 章	日本語，英語
定 価	2,990円（本体2,903円）

PROCESS Architecture 111

RTKL
米国大手組織の展開

RTKLは世界中にプロジェクトを持つアメリカの大設計事務所である．巨大な組織を統一し，方向づける基本的理念は「経営すること(manage)」と「すぐれたデザイン(design excellence)」という2つ．この号では，商業複合空間を中心にインテリア，プランニング，ランドスケープなど多岐にわたるRTKLの活躍を紹介する．

責任編集者	ローリン・マックラッケン
発 行 日	1993年7月
総 頁	148頁（カラー117頁）
文 章	日本語，英語
定 価	2,990円（本体2,903円）

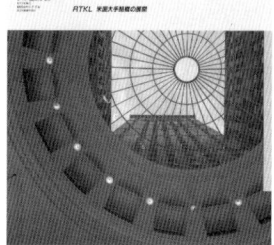

PROCESS Architecture 112

オランダの集合住宅

オランダ，特にアムステルダムの集合住宅の歴史は古い．19世紀半ばから住宅数を増やす動きが始まり，今世紀初頭には早くも法的整備によって質の改善が進められたのである．集合住宅先進国としてのオランダ，この伝統と最近の動きを紹介する．

責任編集者	八木幸二，矢代真己
発 行 日	1993年9月
総 頁	152頁（カラー108頁）
文 章	日本語，英語
定 価	2,990円（本体2,903円）

PROCESS Architecture 113

人の集まるデザイン：
プランニングプロセス7章

商空間，住空間，働空間いずれにしてもその中心になる軸は人間をとりまく世界である．人間生活の満足度をより正確に捉えるために，建物内部から都市計画まで，プランニングプロセスに必要な7つの分野とインテリアの関わり方を，各章に分けて述べていく．

責任編集者	RDD Inc.
発 行 日	1993年10月
総 頁	152頁（カラー116頁）
文 章	日本語，英語
定 価	2,990円（本体2,903円）

PROCESS Architecture 114

魅力ある街づくり：
住宅・都市整備公団の都市再開発事業

総合的な都市環境づくりのパイオニアをめざす住宅・都市整備公団は都市の再開発をその重要な業務の1つとしており，四大都市圏を中心にさまざまな都市整備事業に取り組んでいる．本特集では事業実施中の地区を中心に，各々のテーマに対し，どのようなイメージの街をつくろうとしてきたか，何を提案したかったのかという視点にたち，できる限りビジュアルにまとめ上げ紹介する．

責任編集者	大和 稔
発 行 日	1993年12月
総 頁	148頁（カラー124頁）
文 章	日本語，英語
定 価	2,990円（本体2,903円）

PROCESS Architecture 115

プラハ：
建築博物館の街

「北のローマ」「百塔の街」などと呼ばれるプラハは，千年の歴史のなかで築かれてきた．ロマネスク，ゴシック，ルネッサンス，バロック，アール・ヌーボー，キュビズムとヨーロッパのおよそあらゆる建築様式がある．本書では，このようなプラハの建築散歩をこころみる．

責任編集者	田中充子
発 行 日	1994年2月
総 頁	152頁（カラー146頁）
文 章	日本語，英語
定 価	2,990円（本体2,903円）

PROCESS :Architecture 116

好評発売中　定価2,990円

Kyoto Its Cityscape Traditions and Heritage

京の都市意匠──景観形成の伝統

山崎正史・編

建都1200年を迎える京都，その歴史的景観がどのような伝統を持ち，継承されてきたのか，歴史的経緯と景観の特質を，絵図と写真を多用して視覚的に概観する．また，京都の歴史の中から日本的な都市の造形言語を読み取り，その文脈の上で今後の都市のデザインを考えていこうとする一冊．

- ●論文／山崎正史
- ●テーマ／洛外の意匠，モニュメントの都市意匠，町家と町並み景観の発展，伝統的町並みの意匠，河川の都市意匠，京の眺望景観，現代の課題

ハードカバー（上製本）同時発売

定価5,000円（本体4,854円）

PROCESS :Architecture 117

好評発売中　定価2,990円

The Art and Mechanics of Landscape
Aspects of the Road

ランドスケープの手法：道のディテール

人間の行くところ，どこにでもある「道」．「道」は人間の行動の媒体として，集いの場として，生活の上で不可欠である．

本誌では，万国共通してランドスケープのデザインに主要な「道」に焦点を当て，その構成要素を3つの章に分けてランドスケープ・デザインの役割を説明するとともに，それぞれの参考例，失敗例，プロのコツを満載した．

- ●内容
- 1章：道路，水路，階段，橋／道路，水路，階段，橋
- 2章：ヒューマン・ランドスケープにおける樹木／木の基本形態，人間と樹木，都市の植物，根，家との関係
- 3章：ストリート・ファニチュア／車止め，ベンチ，ごみ箱・鉢・水のみ場，照明，郵便受け・消火栓・電話ボックス・その他

PROCESS :Architecture 118

好評発売中　定価2,990円

Peter Walker William Johnson and Partners
Art and Nature

ピーター・ウォーカー・ウィリアム・ジョンソン&パートナーズ：アートと自然の調和

1989年のPA85号，ピーター・ウォーカー作品集以来，彼はウィリアム・ジョンソンとパートナーシップをとり，プランニングとデザインの両分野で新しいランドスケープの展開を試み始めた．本誌では国内の建築界の巨匠と組んだ，最近の作品を中心に取り上げた．彼らの目指すアートと自然の調和された世界が充分に堪能できる．

●主な作品
ソラナ計画，IBMプラザタワーとタウンセンターパーク，プリンシパル生命保険会社ビル；日本IBM幕張ビルディング，ソニー幕張技術研究所・豊砂公園，カリフォルニア大学サンディエゴ校，播磨科学公園都市マスタープラン，丸亀ステーションプラザ

PROCESS :Architecture 119

好評発売中　定価2,990円

CAMBRIDGE SEVEN ASSOCIATES

ケンブリッジ・セブン・アソシエイツ

今年で創立32年目を迎えた，米国のケンブリッジ・セブンは，事務所の創立時点から異分野のデザイナーとの協働体制を明確に打ち出してきた．彼らのデザインの特徴は，設計活動の中心部を成してきた公共水族館に表われている．外部空間だけではなく，展示デザインの効果を充分に意図した豊かな内部空間をつくり出している．

本号では初期の作品から最近のプロジェクトまで，各種建物タイプを年代順に扱った総数47題の作品部分の他に，論文3題を掲載し，ケンブリッジ・セブンの設計手法を見る．

●作品／ニューイングランド水族館，サンアントニオ美術館，ボルチモア水族館，Innova，NBCプラザ，大阪海遊館，オーランド・アリーナ，他

PROCESS :Architecture 120

好評発売中　定価2,990円

EDAW: The Integrated World
Landscape Design and Sustaining Environments

EDAW：エコロジカル・ランドスケープ

1942年，エクボとウィリアムが始めた事務所が変遷を遂げ，約半世紀を経た今，EDAWとしてアメリカ全土と世界各国にわたり，環境という広範囲の問題に対処している．

ランドスケープの世界では，今やエコロジカルなアプローチが前提であり，このEDAW特集ではこれらの環境問題への具体的事例を多数紹介する．

● 主な作品
エコシティ計画，アジア・太平洋トレードセンター，神戸アーバンデザイン，ディズニー・ポート・オリーンズ・リゾート，ユーロディズニーのリゾート地区，他

PROCESS :Architecture 121

好評発売中　定価2,990円

Environment Architecture
Design and Concept　Mitsuru Man Senda and Environment Design Institute

環築の設計―仙田 満＋環境デザイン研究所―

本誌79号で好評のうちに品切れとなった仙田満の特集号，第2弾．

仙田満はこどもの遊び方を観察することで，遊び空間の法則性を見いだし，〈遊環構造〉と名づけた．その理論は遊具や建築ばかりでなく，仙田満のすべての作品に反映されている．

今回の特集では，これらの作品をスポーツ，こども，住まい，文化の4つのテーマに分け，その生き生きとした再新作を紹介する．

● 主な作品
東京辰已国際水泳場，常滑体育館，富山こどもみらい館，姫路御立公園たつまきロード，松庵の家，Stars Art 23，多摩六都科学館，伊勢原図書館・こども科学館，他

PROCESS : Architecture 123

12月発売予定　予価2,990円

"Toryo Spirit in Architecture"
Works by Takenaka Corporation
棟梁の精神　竹中工務店作品集

急激な社会環境の変化の中で，常に建築界の最先端を歩み続けている竹中工務店．最新技術に取り組みながらも，日本に昔から伝わる「棟梁の精神」を持ち続け，超高層ビルから小規模建築に至るまで，良質な建築活動を各地に展開している．今号では「プロセスアーキテクチュア」45号で大好評を得た竹中工務店特集号に続き，近作を中心に40作品を再びまとめあげた．「棟梁の精神」というテーマに焦点をあて，「技の探究」，「型の継承」，「素材への執心」，「街の興隆」，「作庭への感応」，「数寄の発揚」，「芸術の統合」の7つの章に分けて紹介する．

- ●論文／「棟梁の精神を心の定規に」
- ●作品／福岡ドーム，武者小路千家・起風軒，播磨屋本店円山店，睦学園神戸国際中学校舎，アプローズタワー，竹中技術研究所，松陰大山セミナーハウス，アシックスラボプラント，他

No.103
Landscape Design and Planning at The SWA at The SWA Group
SWAグループ：ランドスケープとプランニング

好評につき再版いたしました．
この機会に是非
お買い求め下さい．

建築・土木書フェア
東京秋葉原・書泉ブックタワー

東京・秋葉原に，この5月オープンした「書泉ブックタワー」3階理工書コーナーでは，11月1日から12月25日までの2ヵ月間，「建築・土木書フェア」が開催されています．
「プロセスアーキテクチュア」「ジャパンランドスケープ」のバックナンバーはもちろんのこと，建築雑誌のバックナンバーが多数展示されるので，買い忘れてしまった人にとっては，揃えるチャンスとなるでしょう．もちろん，雑誌だけではなく，単行本も併せて展示されているので，ぜひ一度，実物をご覧の上，お買い求め下さい．

- ●書泉ブックタワー「建築・土木書フェア」
住所／東京都千代田区神田佐久間町1-11-1
電話／03(5296)0051　担当／重野・熊木
営業時間／午前11時～午後7時30分
（日曜・祭日は午後7時まで）
JR秋葉原駅　昭和通り口（東口）下車1分
都営新宿線　岩本町駅下車2分
営団地下鉄日比谷線　秋葉原駅下車すぐ横

予約購読・既刊のご案内

当社では「プロセスアーキテクチュア」「ジャパンランドスケープ」の予約購読およびバックナンバーのお申し込みを受け付けております．予約購読お申し込みの方には，発行の都度ご指定の送付先に郵送します．また，ご希望の方にはカタログを進呈いたします．送料250円分の切手を同封の上，係までお申し込み下さい．

- ●プロセスアーキテクチュア

予約購読：1年間（ 8冊）23,900円（平均単価：2,988円　税・送料込み）
　　　　　2年間（16冊）45,000円（平均単価：2,812円　〃　）
　　　　　3年間（24冊）64,500円（平均単価：2,688円　〃　）
お申し込み時に発行されている号は予約購読対象外となります．

単冊購読：定価は号により異なりますが，2,990円（税込，送料別）からとなっています．
送料380円，2冊目より1冊につきプラス100円．

- ●ジャパンランドスケープ

予約購読：1年間（ 4冊）10,300円（前払，税・送料込，国内限）
　　　　　2年間（ 8冊）19,600円（　　〃　　）
　　　　　3年間（12冊）27,800円（　　〃　　）
お申し込み時に発行されている号は予約購読対象外となります．

単冊購読：1冊 2,580円（税込，送料別）．
送料380円，2冊目より1冊につきプラス100円．

- ●バックナンバー

定価は号によって異なります．右のバックナンバー表またはカタログでお確かめ下さい．

詳しくは係まで．TEL.(03)3468-0131 FAX.(03)3468-0133